How To
Design & Deliver
A Speech

SIXTH EDITION

LEON FLETCHER

Emeritus Professor of Speech, Monterey Peninsula College

 LONGMAN

An imprint of Addison Wesley Longman, Inc.

New York • Reading, Massachusetts • Menlo Park, California • Harlow, England
Don Mills, Ontario • Sydney • Mexico City • Madrid • Amsterdam

To my wife, Vivian

Acquisitions Editor: Deirdre Cavanaugh
Project Editor: Bill Mahaffey, Gama Book
Text Design: Interactive Composition Corporation
Cover Design: Lili Schwartz
Art Studio: Interactive Composition Corporation
Photo Researcher: Mira Schachne, Schachne Assoc.
Full Service Production Manager: Eric Jorgensen
Manufacturing Manager: Hilda Koparanian
Electronic Page Makeup: Interactive Composition Corporation
Printer and Binder: Courier/Kendallville, Inc.
Cover Printer: Coral Graphic Services

For permission to use copyrighted material, grateful acknowledgment is made to the copyright holders on pp. 424, which are hereby made part of this copyright page.

Library of Congress Cataloging-in-Publication Data

Fletcher, Leon.
    How to design & deliver a speech / Leon Fletcher. — 6th ed.
      p.   cm.
    Includes index.
    ISBN 0-321-01544-4
    1. Public speaking.   I. Title.
  PN4121.F526 1995
  808.5'1—dc21   97-34465
                                            CIP

ISBN 0-321-01544-4

12345678910—CRK—00999897

CONTENTS

PREFACE

This textbook continues to be truly distinctive—probably unique.

Foremost is the purpose of this book: to actually *teach,* rather than merely present, the skills of how to design and deliver speeches.

If you have not used this book before:

You'll quickly see that purpose is *fulfilled*—not merely promised—through the innovative combination of three well-established teaching techniques:

Measurable Objectives

Interaction

Independent Study

Those techniques are effective in this book because they utilize a variety of potent instructional tools, including

Diagnosis Folder

Programmed Learning

Self-Evaluations

Self-Tests

Immediate Follow-Up

Check-off Tip Sheets

Speech Evaluation Forms

And more.

Those tools, through step-by-step instructions, guide students to present effective speeches. What makes speeches effective is detailed precisely in this book through 68 specific criteria.

Those criteria cover every essential of the three elements of productive speeches:

Content

Organization

Delivery

The criteria focus on platform-tested, real-world specifics about speaking. Students completing the study of this textbook are successful speakers.

Because this book actually teaches, the instructor is released from routine presentation of material. He or she can then concentrate on the much more productive and challenging tasks of:

Evaluating students' speeches

Identifying the strengths and weaknesses of those speeches

Prescribing ways the student speakers can further improve their skills.

Thus the instructor has the time to guide students individually.

Such personalized teaching is made possibly by another feature of this book—*flexibility.* Both the instructor and the students benefit from that. Although the total instructional design of this textbook is structured, individual lessons or even parts of lessons can be studied separately, profitably.

If you have used this book before:

There are five changes in this edition to which you should be alerted.

- **Multicultural speaking and speakers** have been included more prominently and extensively.

  Reason for this change: obviously our students and the audiences to which they can be expected to speak are growing in diversity.

- **Diagnosis Folder** is now presented as a separate section between Lesson 1, on how to control nervousness, and Lesson 2, on how to design speeches.

  Reason for this change: to further increase the flexibility of both learning by students and teaching by instructors. For the instructor, the options are clear:

  1. You can use the **Diagnosis Folder** in its entirety as a productive teaching aid as recommended and detailed in the **Instructor's Manual.**
  2. You can assign only those parts of the **Diagnosis Folder** that you decide are beneficial for your particular students.
  3. You do not have to use the **Diagnosis Folder** at all.

  Whichever option the instructor chooses, this textbook still provides accountability, validity, continuity, and productive learning.

- **Evaluation Forms** for speeches have been made easier to use.

  Now there is a briefer, clearer system to indicate strengths ("+'s") of speeches and weaknesses ("−'s"). This simplified procedure replaces the previous cumbersome "grids" which provided grading on five levels. Note that it is recommended you evaluate only five or so strengths and about the same number of weaknesses of each speech. That is, all the criteria need not be rated on every speech. Rather, it is suggested you appraise only a few of those criteria each individual student needs to be concerned about at the particular level of her or his development as a speaker.

  Reason for this change: to facilitate concentrating on listening to the speeches, rather than focusing on the **Evaluation Form,** and to make assessing speeches easier and faster.

- **Computer use in designing speeches** has been expanded to include introductions to some of the great many current online resources that are helpful to speakers. Further, students are alerted to watch for and take advantage of the ever-increasing wealth of online information and assistance.

  Reason for this change: computers of course continue to grow in use, expand in resources, and provide greater aid to speakers.

- **Sources of information** which many students do not think of using have been added in a brief but specific listing.

  Reason for this change: While students enrolling in speech classes are typically expected, as a prerequisite, to have mastered basic library skills, they often overlook other sources of information.—for example, local organizations, area experts, public relations departments, trade associations, and such.

Additional changes have been made in this edition in response to recommendations submitted by reviewers and users of the book at various colleges and universities.

Finally, of course, this edition includes the usual—the expected—updating, including quotes and examples from currently prominent speakers.

Before national publication of the first edition of this textbook, its teaching effectiveness was documented through extensive testing. More than 1500 student comments were received and most were incorporated.

Now, experience using this book shows that 90 percent of students qualified to study college-level English learn 80 percent or more of all assignments the first time they study them. Indeed, when I teach with this book I give my students—in the first few minutes of the first meeting of the course—a written "guarantee" that they'll become effective speakers. Details—brief, easy—on how to do that are presented in the **Instructor's Manual.**

The result: Here is a textbook that truly responds to the plea that persistently comes from so many in our society today—the appeal for **accountability in education.**

Leon Fletcher

ACKNOWLEDGMENTS

Thanks to:

- Instructors and students who have used previous editions of this textbook and have sent to me their valuable suggestions. Sorry I can't name you, but, there were more of you than I was able to note.

- Students in speech classes taught by *Willis Warner,* Instructor of communication, Shasta College, Redding, California, for nominating speakers whose photographs and quotations they recommended to appear in this book; six of their nominees are included in this edition.

- *Dorcas Abbott,* Manager of the Felton Library, Felton, California, for very valuable assistance in research.

- *Gary Decker,* Reference Coordinator, Santa Cruz County Libraries, and his fine staff of skilled researchers, for help in finding elusive data.

- *Dr. Jon Lindsay,* author of 2 books about computers; *Pat* and *Warren Edwards, Art Lee,* and *Wayne Thalls,* all experienced users of various word-processing programs, for their suggestions concerning Lesson 13, "Using a Computer to Design Speeches."

- *Vivian,* my wife; her proofreading is my first line of defense against bloopers and blunders, faults and fallacies, and all the many other ways a writer can go astray. Still, of course, all the goofs that may remain are my responsibility—alone. But I do wish I could figure out somehow to blame someone else.

Leon Fletcher is the most-published author writing about speech since Dale Carnegie.

This is his 16th published book. They include *How to Speak Like a Pro,* published by Ballantine Books as a trade edition in 1996, and, previously, as a massmarket paperback..

He has also written more than 600 articles, mostly on speech, education, travel, and amateur radio, published in such diverse magazines as *TV Guide, Writer's Digest, Education Digest, Monitoring Times, Sail, 73 Amateur Radio, Honolulu, Weekend, Sea Classics,* and others. For TOASTMASTERS, the international organization in which members help each other improve their speaking, he has written 30 articles and two training programs.

As a mentor and columnist for America Online *(AOL),* he has guided hundreds of beginning writers. His column of tips for writing nonfiction is posted in the *AOL Writers Club.* He also writes a column for the newsletter *Writing for Money.*

When not writing, his activities include talking to people worldwide via his amateur radio station; his call: AA6ZG.

He and his wife, an accomplished organist and quilter, live near a mountain village close to the California coast.

Students and Instructors . . .

. . . using this textbook are invited to send to the author any questions they may have about designing or delivering a speech. You are also requested to send to the author any suggestions you may have for improving this book—changes, corrections, additions, deletions, or such.

> E-mail: LeonFlet@AOL.com
> Conventional Mail: 274 Webster Drive
>   Ben Lomond, CA 95005

L E S S O N 1

Controlling Nervousness

OBJECTIVES After completing this lesson, you will:

1. Be able to name the 11 techniques for controlling nervousness.
2. Use all of those techniques to control your nervousness to the extent that fewer than 10 percent of the students in your speech class will be able to name any significant indications that you are nervous while giving a speech.
3. Feel more comfortable about speaking in public.

RELEVANCE Nervousness. Stage fright. Jitters.

Some speech specialists call it "communication apprehension," "speech reticence," "speech anxiety," "performance anxiety," or other such terms.

NERVOUSNESS:

"I'm always nervous doing this show!"
David Letterman, on his ***The Late Show.***

Actors call it "flop sweat." Psychologists call it "topophobia."

"Don't soften it with those gentle words!" one student told me. "Panic! That's what it is—PANIC!"

Whatever you call it, nervousness is certainly the biggest, most frequent, most persistent concern of almost all speakers—from highly acclaimed professionals to first-time speakers. Many speech instructors will confirm that in public speaking classes, more questions are usually asked about stage fright than about any other topic.

Because of such widespread concern, nervousness is the very first topic in this textbook.

HOW TO CONTROL NERVOUSNESS

Very few of us ever shake off all our nervousness about public speaking, but most people can learn to control it, reduce it, accept it, live with it. Here are 11 practical, platform-tested techniques that will help you reduce your suffering from stage fright.

A l e r t !   Study the following techniques carefully. Later in this lesson you'll be asked to take a written self-test to check that you remember them.

1. Nearly Everyone Suffers Nervousness About Giving a Speech

In a special high-tech booth overlooking the San Francisco Giants' baseball field in Candlestick Park, legal secretary Sherry Davis settled into her chair before a microphone to become the first female public-address baseball announcer in the major leagues. "I was nervous," she said. "I just have to get the jitters out."

A few days earlier Bill Walsh, the perfect model of cool as he coached the San Francisco 49ers football team to three Super Bowl titles, was inducted into the Pro Football Hall of Fame; before the ceremonies he said, "I've been haunted for the last month, losing sleep as to how I'm going to be able to get up and receive this award."

He was not alone in his stage fright.

Eddie DeBartolo, Jr., super-millionaire owner of the 49ers, was so nervous during his speech presenting the award to Walsh that he accidently skipped over a full page of his prepared talk.

Or consider these recent statements by or about people who speak and perform in public frequently:

- *Rosie Perez:* "I was successful (at auditions) when I'd say, 'Can you wait a minute? I'm really nervous.'"
- *Luciano Pavarotti, world-famous opera singer:* "I am now as nervous as the first day I was on stage."
- *Frank Sinatra:* "I tremble every time I walk on stage."
- *Gloria Steinem* is a "natural speaker who's paralyzed by audiences," according to a news reporter.
- *Holly Hunter:* "I'm almost petrified [being on this talk show]," she said, during an interview on a TV show.
- *Barbra Streisand:* "She has battled stage fright throughout her career," reported a news service.
- *Jane Robelot:* "I was scared to death," she said about working as a CBS morning news anchor.
- *Brian Boitano:* "He's been really nervous" serving as an ABC sports commentator, despite winning more than 50 skating titles, according to a magazine writer.

- *Kenny Rogers:* "He's so nervous his feet grab the stage," said the narrator of a TV profile.
- *Grant Tinker:* "I was terrified to get up and talk to more than three people at a time. Meetings were fine, but more formal events could induce something close to a panic attack. Colleagues would breeze through sales pitches or presentations to clients; I would change jobs to avoid them." So wrote the former chairman of NBC in his book *Tinker in Television*.
- *Hugh Downs:* "Nervousness is an essential element to truly great success."

And dozens of other well-known, greatly experienced speakers have said they get nervous when speaking in public, including the following:

Jeff Bridges	Joe Montana
Katie Couric	Mary Tyler Moore
Phil Donahue	Paul Newman
Geraldine Ferraro	Mike Nichols
Henry Ford	Conan O'Brien
Franklin Graham	Rhea Perlman
Dustin Hoffman	Michelle Pfeiffer
Erica Jong	Sidney Poitier
Jay Leno	Christoper Reeve
Elaine May	Maureen Stapleton
Matthew McConaughey	James Taylor
Liza Minelli	Oprah Winfrey

ARE NEW STARS NERVOUS?

You may have noticed that few newcomers to TV, video, film, or the stage, contemporary comedians, current musicians, or such, have been named as being concerned about nervousness.

Reason: It takes considerable self-confidence, acceptance of one's self, openness, and maturity to talk candidly about one's own apparent shortcomings such as nervousness when in the spotlight.

Indeed, in all my teaching of speech classes—mostly community college classes but also classes ranging from seminars for upper-level executives to instruction for junior high school youngsters—I have had only one student who claimed to be "completely free of stage fright." That student was a young woman blessed with an outstandingly beautiful singing voice. She had been singing in public since she was six years old. When I met her, she was a student in a college speech course, and her years of singing for audiences had apparently led her to believe that butterflies in her stomach, sweaty palms, and trembling knees were such routine feelings that she did not consider them unusual.

On the other hand, probably the most nervous speaker I've ever worked with was a highly honored fighter pilot. A navy commander with extensive combat experience, he'd been decorated repeatedly for his bravery during duel-to-the-death dogfights high in the skies over enemy territories. I met him when he tried to give just a six-minute speech before only four fellow officers. His speech was to determine if he should enroll in a speech seminar so that he'd be better prepared for advancement to higher commands, in which he would be giving speeches to other officers, presentations to congressional committees, and briefings to influential business leaders. But he simply could not bring himself to give that short diagnostic speech. He started, stalled, started again, and then strode out of the room.

But the extent of nervousness is documented not only by personal stories and quotes by the famous. Look at some statistics.

About 3000 Americans were asked, "What are you most afraid of?" Their most frequent reply: "Speaking before a group." More people said they were afraid of speaking in public than said they feared snakes, heights, illness, or even death.

One researcher found that "about 85 percent of us feel uncomfortably anxious speaking in public." Clearly you are not alone in your nervousness about giving speeches. But you won't suffer the same stage fright about every speech you give, because . . .

2. Experience Reduces Nervousness

After you've given even just one speech, you'll realize that your greatest fear—your fear of fear!—is not really as serious as you'd thought. You'll feel better for your first speech than you probably thought you would—and, usually, much better for your following speeches.

"But what if my mind goes blank?" beginning speakers often ask. "Suppose I fumble a word and it comes out funny? Or insulting? Or dirty? Or . . ." "Suppose I open my mouth and nothing comes out?"

The fact is, such problems are rare—very rare. Have you ever heard a speaker who had such problems? Not likely. And don't point to such goofs on TV shows; often those errors have been written into the script, planted just to make the programs seem spontaneous.

What about all those horrible fumbles on the blooper TV shows and the blooper records? Some of those are real, but not all; again, many are scripted.

Perhaps the most famous fumble of all time occurred more than 50 years ago when the then well-known radio announcer Harry Von Zell introduced President Herbert Hoover by saying, "President Hoobert Hever."

Think of all the speakers you've heard over the years—TV newscasters, politicians, religious leaders, teachers, salespersons, lecturers, and such. You'll be hard-pressed to remember a single example of a serious, significant goof that you've heard yourself. Sure, such errors happen. But they are rare, hard to catch, and most important, very seldom are they serious.

But on the slight chance you do fumble a word or two, you may be able to easily switch it to your advantage by delivering one of the many old cover-up gags that continue to get laughs:

"Now I'll try that in English."

"Guess I need to untie my tongue."

"They told me not to buy teeth at a flea market."

After you've given just one or a few speeches, you'll feel much more confident. You'll discover that you can live with your nervousness—and survive! You'll find that your mind won't really go blank. Words and ideas will come out of you. You can indeed be an effective speaker!

3. Realize You Appear More Confident Than You Feel

There are two readily available ways for you to check that out.

First, you can ask a few of your friends in this speech class if you look nervous when you give a speech. Class discussions after student speeches verify that signs of nervousness do not show nearly as much as speakers think they do.

Second, you can find out for yourself just how nervous you appear to your listeners by having a videotape recording made of yourself as you give a speech—a practice speech or an actual one, in class or out, privately or before an audience.

The videotaping of speeches sounds quite threatening to many people. But if you look with even a bit of objectively at a recording of yourself giving a speech, you're almost certain to agree that you look much more confident than you may feel. Try to identify on the tape any specific indications that you were nervous; chances are you'll be hard-pressed to find any. While you may not appear ready to replace Barbara Walters or Peter Jennings, your poise and polish are probably not really very different from theirs.

Or, rather than looking at yourself to verify that speakers appear much more confident than they may appear, take a careful look at the speeches given by the presidents of our nation. Certainly most of us would agree that they appear about as confident as anyone can. But look a little closer:

- President Clinton, when standing at a lectern, giving a speech, can be seen in TV shots from behind him to have his legs crossed; according to some researches of body language, that indicates nervousness. He also reveals his nervousness, some observers claim, by biting his lips—but he didn't seem to do that during his 1996 television debates. At least one reporter claimed Clinton had "behavior modification" to eliminate that sign of his weakness.
- Former President Bush "stood nervous and uneasy with a controlled smile trying to assert calmness" just before a debate with his opponent Michael Dukakis, one reporter wrote.
- Reagan, while serving as president, said, "I still get puckered up just before I go in to give a speech."
- Carter, while giving a speech, usually clasped his hands together, fingers intertwined so tightly his knuckles turned white.
- Ford twisted his lips, gestured gracelessly, fumbled one-syllable words.
- Nixon, starting with his early speeches as a college debater and continuing throughout his career, suffered such stage fright that sweat poured down his face in rivers of misery.
- Johnson repeatedly said "ah," struggled for words, sprinkled his speeches with long pauses.
- Kennedy clawed the air with his index finger, nervously searching for a word or idea.
- Eisenhower's nervousness produced sentences so complex many English teachers could neither diagram nor understand them.
- Truman showed his anxiety while speaking by repeating one gesture almost continually—moving both hands up and down in unison.

In sum, every one of our last ten presidents has shown signs of stage fright—and their service as leaders of our nation add up to well over fifty years of experience in public speaking.

You, like them, very probably look much more confident than you may feel.

4. Visualize Yourself Succeeding

Look upon yourself as a poor speaker—an ineffective speaker—and you'll greatly increase your chances of being less effective than you can be.

On the other hand, visualize yourself as succeeding in your speaking, and you'll raise your speaking effectiveness considerably. There's significant evidence and logic to support that.

Back in the 1950s, Dr. Norman Vincent Peale began popularizing "positive thinking"—a process of telling yourself that you can indeed attain a desired goal.

The goal could be virtually any reasonable quality or achievement—earning higher grades, becoming more knowledgeable, developing more effective leadership, obtaining a better job, winning more games, and so on.

To apply positive thinking to improving your success in public speaking, you should tell yourself the *truth*—that

- you *will* be effective in expressing your ideas.
- many of your listeners *will* receive, understand, learn from, be convinced of, and enjoy much of what you say.
- your nervousness *will NOT* interfere with your speaking.

Such mental self-enhancement has helped the careers of many speakers, actors, actresses, and other performers. When *Baywatch* television actor David Hasselhoff was filming *Knight Rider,* he said, "At first they were going to let me go from the show because of my nerves. But I turned myself around through positive thinking."

But as effective as positive thinking is, about thirty years after Dr. Peale originated it, he took it a step further. In 1982 he developed what he calls *imaging.* He wrote:

Imaging consists of picturing vividly in your conscious mind a desired goal or objective and holding that image until it sinks into your unconscious mind, where it releases great untapped energies. . . . When the imaging concept is applied steadily and systematically, it solves problems, strengthens personalities, improves health and greatly enhances the chances for success in any kind of endeavor.

Visualizing yourself succeeding, positive thinking, imaging, whatever comparable technique you call it or you use, will indeed work—*if you utilize them for* **realistic goals.**

If you're a shy, quiet person about to give your first speech, you can't simply picture yourself as a dramatic, golden-voiced spellbinder and suddenly, magically be turned into a crowd-moving orator. But you certainly can convince yourself that you will not be as shy as you have been, that you will speak up with greater assurance, that you will be able to express your ideas with greater fluency. And once you convince yourself that you can achieve such goals, your chances are indeed much greater that you will.

Or consider another aspect of visualizing yourself succeeding. When you go to hear a speaker—a lecturer at your college, a preacher at your church, a politician at a community meeting, whomever—do you think, "I sure hope this speaker does a poor job"?

Of course not. As you go to hear a speaker, you carry the hope that the speaker will be stimulating, informative, motivating, and all those other good characteristics you expect from an effective speaker.

Extend that hopeful attitude to the audience you are to speak to—they, too, are anticipating your speech with a positive attitude.

5. Occupy Your Mind with What You Want to Say

One of the traps that many speakers, especially beginners, fall into is thinking about concerns other than those they should focus on—the content of their speeches.

Many speakers detract from their effectiveness by thinking about such things as:

What are my listeners thinking about me?

Can they hear me O.K.?

Does my hair look all right?

Is my blouse or shirt tucked in properly?

Does my voice sound squeaky?

Was that the right word I just used?

Should I be gesturing more?

Instead of thinking about such details, concentrate your thoughts on the *content* of your speech. Think, *More than anything else at this moment, I want these people to get what I have to say to them.*

6. Understand that Nervousness Can be Controlled

You have two options: You can convince yourself that you can't control your nervousness, or you can persuade yourself that you are indeed master of your own feelings.

Select that first option—that you can't overcome your nervousness—and your apprehension will likely increase still more. Dr. Jeff Sorg, who operates a clinic in Los Angeles to help professionals control their anxieties, said:

> If you make a negative statement to yourself often enough, you can come to believe it: "I'm going to embarrass myself (or fall, hiccup, vomit)." The fact is, even if these things do happen, they needn't be catastrophic. So what if you stumble. You won't die from hiccups. And even vomiting isn't so bad; it's a release. You can conquer all of these miseries. For performers and nonperformers, the show *can* go on.

So turn to your second option—telling yourself that you are master of your feelings. First, admit to yourself that you are—or will be—nervous. But also remind yourself of this fact: *You can indeed live with your nervousness.*

You may become uncomfortable, but you won't let yourself be overcome by that uncomfortableness. You may perspire, but you won't drown. You may gasp for air, but you certainly won't suffocate. You may tremble, but few, perhaps no one, in the audience will notice; if they do, so what? Your listeners are there to hear what you have to say; they didn't come to see if your hands are shaking.

The important point here is to remember that you can certainly control your nervousness, although very few of us eliminate nervousness entirely. Carroll O'Conner, one of TV's long-time actors, star of *Heat of the Night, All in the Family, Archie's Place,* and other shows, said, "A professional actor has a kind of tension. The amateur is thrown by it, but the professional needs it."

7. Settle into a Routine for Relaxing

Sammy Davis, Jr., legendary performer used to ease his severe stage fright before a show by methodically selecting the jewelry he'd wear. Some speakers pace. Others stretch, do push-ups or other exercises. I catnap.

The point is to shift your attention before you speak to some easy routine you can repeat with little or no thought. That will help clear your mind so you can concentrate on the task you are about to undertake—your speech.

In his book *The Body Language of Sex, Power & Aggression,* Julius Fast wrote: "Many people use elaborate routines with pencils, notebooks, and eyeglasses—little rituals of movement—to absorb their nervousness."

Author Stephen Phillip Policoff, in an article entitled "Coping with Stage Fright," published in *Cosmopolitan,* recommended that you "get someone to massage your shoulders, or [you massage] someone else's. Releasing tension in others often eases our own anxiety."

Other routines to relax before speaking that are used by speakers I know include:

▶ Taking a hot bath.
▶ Swimming.
▶ Before the audience arrives, wandering around the room in which the speaker is to talk.
▶ Reading a book about a complex subject—a scientific report, for example.
▶ Reading a book about a very light topic—a summer romance novel, for instance.
▶ Doing crossword puzzles.
▶ Sitting in your car, parked near the speaking location, admiring the scenery.
▶ Listening to music.

You can, of course, select one of those routines to use as your own method for relaxing, or you can find some other outlet on your own. Either way, the important point is that you do develop a routine.

8. Nervousness Needs an Outlet

There's no valid reason to try to hold back your nervousness. Why bother to try to avoid stage fright? As we've established, for almost all of us, it's going to be there, whatever we do. So let it have whatever outlet feels best for you.

"If your body trembles, let it tremble. Don't feel obliged to try to stop it. Don't even strive for relaxation. Don't be too concerned because you are tense and cannot relax." Those are the recommendations of a leading medical expert on nerves, Dr. Claire Weekes, writing in *Reader's Digest*.

9. Enjoy Speaking

"The first duty of man is to speak; that is his chief business in this world."

That was the view of 19th-century Scottish author Robert Louis Stevenson. Even if he was partly right, it seems that since we all do so much talking, we might as well enjoy it.

But the point is more critical than that. If you don't enjoy speaking, many of your listeners will quickly, somehow, sense your lack of concern.

"But I can fake my interest!" some students reply.

That can be true in some situations—if you're skilled, if your audience is not alert, if the situation is sufficiently casual.

But you're taking chances. If the speech is important, any reluctance you may have in wanting to communicate may well jeopardize your success.

In your public speaking, you'll be less nervous—and more effective—if you'll just let yourself enjoy speaking.

10. Stop Fighting Your Nervousness

Just let your nervousness be. Don't try to fight it. Look on nervousness as "nature's way" of helping you to be ready to do your best.

Stage fright before a speech is a lot like the pregame tension most athletes experience. Many football players, even professionals with years in the major leagues, will tell you that they're extremely nervous before a game. After one especially dramatic game, San Francisco 49er cornerback Troy Nixon said:

"Was I scared? That's the understatement of the year. It's funny though—I wasn't really as nervous as I thought I might be. I kept telling myself, 'It's just like practice, it's just like practice. Just relax, challenge them, and you have nothing to lose.'"

Such self-encouragement can also help speakers reduce their nervousness. Think of your actual speech as "just like practice." Besides, you, too, "have nothing to lose," but you can gain experience, assurance, polish.

Athletes also point out that once they make their first contact with an opposing player, they feel far more at ease, far more confident. Similarly, once you as a speaker make your first contact with your audience—give them that first direct, straight-in-the-eye look—you, too, will feel more assured.

11. Simple Key: Prepare!

Preparation is—by far!—the most effective step toward controlling nervousness about giving a speech. And how to prepare speeches—effectively, efficiently—is, of course, the purpose of this book, the purpose of this course.

But now it's time to remember that "Alert" presented back on page 2—the alert that said you'd be tested on your remembering those 11 techniques for controlling nervousness. Well, here comes that test.

To be sure you're ready for the test, take a moment right now to look over the list again—*and note in particular the first letter of each of the techniques.*

You've noticed, of course, that the first letters to those techniques spell—what? You're right!

N-E-R-V-O-U-S-N-E-S-S!

That mnemonic certainly makes it easier for you to remember those techniques. So now is the time to take your self-test.

Importance of Speech

"The first duty of man is to speak; that is his chief business in the world."

So said Scottish writer *Robert Louis Stevenson.*

ASSIGNMENT 1: CONTROLLING NERVOUSNESS: SELF-TEST

ACTION: Write, below, a list of the techniques for controlling nervousness.

1. N _____

2. E _____

3. R _____

4. V _____

5. O _____

6. U _____

7. S _____

8. N _____

9. E _____

10. S _____

11. S _____

Compare your list of techniques for controlling nervousness with the list on the next page.

Remember that back on page 1, the first objective of this lesson was "Be able to name the 11 techniques." Therefore:

▶ If the list you wrote on your self-test includes all of the 11 techniques stated essentially as on the next page, you're ready to move on to the next lesson. (Check with your instructor: If you are going to be using the Diagnostic Folder system, make sure you give yourself credit on the Grade Record Form, which is coming up on page 23.)

▶ If your list does not include all 11 of the techniques—stated pretty much as on the next page—please review the text until you are able to list them correctly.

You Too?

"The human brain is a wonderful thing. It operates from the moment you're born until the moment you get up to make a speech."

Anonymous

CONTROLLING NERVOUSNESS: CHECK-OFF TIP SHEET

INSTRUCTIONS: If you need help in controlling your nervousness before giving a speech, check off each item below, and think about how each one can help you. If you need additional help, review the tips presented in the text. For more help, confer with your speech instructor.

N   1. Nearly everyone suffers nervousness about giving a speech.

E   2. Experience reduces nervousness.

R   3. Realize that you appear more confident than you feel.

V   4. Visualize yourself succeeding.

O   5. Occupy your mind with what you want to say.

U   6. Understand that nervousness can be controlled.

S   7. Settle into a routine for relaxing.

N   8. Nervousness needs an outlet.

E   9. Enjoy speaking.

S 10. Stop fighting your nervousness.

S 11. Simple key: Prepare!

Now it's time for you to take a brief break from learning techniques of speaking, to find out how this book will guide you to becoming an effective speaker.

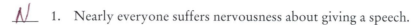

Alert! "But I Don't Hear Many Speakers Using These Techniques!"

Many students in speech classes, after they've learned even just a few of the techniques of effective speaking, suddenly realize that a great many speakers they hear do not use many of the tips taught in courses such as this.

For example:

- Politicians plead for your vote, but you rarely remember any specific reasons they present.
- Ministers exhort their congregations, but their examples are often unrelated to the experiences of their parishioners.
- Visiting authorities speak to college and university students, but many use stilted language and present forgettable generalities.

Why do so many professional speakers ignore so many basic techniques of effective speaking? There are several reasons, including:

- Many speakers never learn the basic techniques of public speaking; they attain their reputations on their expertise, not their speaking skills.

- Some speakers learned the essentials of public speaking, then drift away from using them as they rise in prominence.
- Other speakers rely on their past reputations as effective speakers, now no longer take time to prepare as carefully as they did early in their careers.
- Some speakers think they are above using time-tested techniques.

But you know the result of many such speakers—soon after hearing them, it is difficult, often impossible, to remember more than just a tiny bit of what they said.

Effective Speeches Follow Guides, Not Rigid Rules

It is important for you to recognize that public speaking is an art, much like music, drama, painting, and other creative endeavors. Every art has its own basic principles and techniques. But those practices are guides, not absolute laws. Often the most successful painter, musician, or speaker is the person who first masters the essentials of his or her art, then goes on to adapt, adjust, modify, elaborate, and expand the application of those basics.

As you start your development as a speaker, you should learn thoroughly the guides presented in this course. But always remember that the principles and techniques of public speaking are flexible. Later, as you gain experience in speaking and as you get further into this course, you'll learn how to adapt the basic practices to your own personality, skills, and interests, so you'll be even more successful as a speaker.

A Possible Icebreaker Speech

Many speech instructors have their students give some type of brief introductory speeches at the very start of their courses. If your instructor has you give one of these speeches, keep in mind that the general purpose is to ease you into speaking in public. The idea is to try to free you from at least some of the threats some students may feel in having their speeches graded, and to try to eliminate much of the intimidation some students experience when presented with comments on their speeches and what might be improved.

Such speeches are usually informal and often they are not graded; typically, students are simply given credit for having presented these talks. Actually, these speeches are generally more of a casual exercise than an assignment.

Objectives

After giving this speech, you should:

1. Begin to reduce your stage fright.
2. Begin to recognize the pleasures you can get from speaking to a group.
3. Have a good idea of how you feel when you give a speech.
4. Be better acquainted with the other students in your class and thus feel somewhat more at ease in speaking to them.

You may be asked to present a brief talk—say, two to perhaps five minutes long—about something such as:

- An introduction of yourself:
You might cover such points as your name; where you live; where you were born; other schools you've attended; your major; whether you work, live at home, are married, or such; your major interest; your plans for the future.

▶ An introduction of someone else in your speech class:

Your instructor may pair you with another student in your speech class, or have you select someone else in the class, then give you both time to meet to learn something about each other. Then you'd each give a short speech introducing the other student to your classmates.

▶ A descriptive speech:

You might describe one of your favorite possessions, an animal you like, a place you enjoy visiting, a trip you've taken, or such.

▶ Your pet peeve:

You'd tell about a situation you feel strongly about—some law or rule you feel is silly, an event you think is poorly run, something you consider grossly unfair, etc.

Of course, your speech instructor may give you—as for other exercises and assignments in this book—additional instructions.

The main thing at the beginning of this course is to relax. Believe me, when these speeches are over, most students, if asked how they felt, say something like, "Good!" "Wasn't at all as scary as I expected." "I was a lot better than I thought I'd be!!"

Summary

In this first lesson in this book, you have:

1. Learned 11 techniques to help your control you nervousness.
2. Been introduced to the purpose of this textbook—that is, to teach you to be an effective speaker—and to the content, structure, and procedures this book will provide to help you attain that purpose.
3. Prepared a Diagnosis Folder, if your instructor has asked you to do so, in which to record your progress in this course.
4. Completed an evaluation of yourself as a speaker now—before you take this course.
5. Learned a little about why so many experienced speakers fail to follow basic guides to effective speaking.
6. Learned that speech is an art and consequently follows general guides rather than strict rules.
7. Obtained a better idea of how you feel when you give a speech, if you gave a self-introduction—an icebreaker—speech.

You are now ready for Lesson 2, Designing Speeches.

DIAGNOSIS FOLDER

OBJECTIVES After you've completed this section of this textbook, you'll:

1. Have prepared the **Diagnosis Folder** in which you can keep track of your progress in this course.
2. Have a specific basis—your completed *Precourse Self-Evaluation*—on which to improve your speaking skills.

Alert! Your instructor may give you other instructions about preparing your **Diagnosis Folder** or about using other forms presented in this book; your instructor may change the subject, emphasis, or such of speech assignments and may make other changes in the course. You should of course follow the instructions of your instructor rather than those in this book.

INTRODUCTION TO THIS TEXTBOOK

Now that you've got at least some relief from what is probably your biggest concern, controlling your nervousness about public speaking, it's time for you to learn a little about this truly distinctive—perhaps unique—textbook.

IMPORTANCE OF PUBLIC SPEAKING:

Early in his career, *General Colin Powell* was selected to be an instructor—"a coveted assignment, much sought after and an impressive career credential," as he wrote in his best selling book **My American Journey.** "Before I could go near a classroom, I had to complete an instructors course. For three intense weeks, we learned how to move before a class, use our hands, adopt an authoritative tone, hold center stage, project ourselves, and transmit what was inside our heads into someone else's . . . . If I had to put my finger on *the* pivotal learning experience of my life, it could well be the instructors course. . . . Years later, when I appeared before millions of Americans on television . . . I was doing nothing more than using communicating techniques I had learned a quarter of a century before in the instructors course."

Purpose of This Textbook

The purpose of this book is to teach you how to be an effective speaker. Such a speaker is able to get all, or most, listeners to accept his or her ideas, to remember at least the main points of what's said, and to respond as desired.

To put it another way, after completing this course, you'll be prepared for such speaking situations as:

- Talking to a group of fellow students, informing them about your views of the need for them to become involved in a community program, suggesting a new club activity, urging a change in requirements for graduation, and other such subjects.
- Giving the oral reports that are assigned in other classes—book reviews, discussions, historical summaries, and the like.
- Presenting your ideas about the needs of your community to local groups, such as the League of Women Voters, Rotary, Kiwanis, or Lions.
- Presenting your views about establishing, abolishing, or changing a law, in a speech to a city council, a county administration, a school or college board, or a similar official body.
- Speaking to a meeting of specialists in your current or future profession— perhaps college majors or executives in your field—suggesting, for example, changes you believe should be made in entrance requirements, college preparation, employment practices, or similar subjects.
- Delivering the business and professional talks required in your chosen occupation—such as reports to management, briefings for employees, public information presentations, company communications, proposals.
- Any speaking situation you might face—informing people, persuading them, even entertaining them with, perhaps, stories of your encounters abroad, your unusual experiences on a job, whatever.

To prepare yourself for these situations, your goal must be to develop the ability to plan and present effective speeches. Effective speeches:

1. Present ideas and data that are new, relevant, or significant to the listeners.
2. Are organized clearly and logically.
3. Are delivered with appropriate style, confidence, enthusiasm, and sincerity.

These general features of effective speech can be summarized in one word each:

1. Content
2. Organization
3. Delivery

How to be skilled in each of those is the point of this course.

Learning Techniques

To prepare you to design and deliver effective speeches, this book will use three educational techniques:

1. **Measurable Objectives:** statements that tell you clearly and precisely what you are to learn from studying each lesson and assignment.
2. **Independent Study:** instruction that allows you learn just as fast as you want to. Your instructor may schedule your speeches and perhaps other assignments according to the needs of your entire class, but this book is organized so you can still continue to learn at your own rate.

3. **Interaction:** opportunities for you to express your ideas, review what you've studied, test what you've learned, and design original presentations. In effect, you will be "talking with this book." If you'll take the time to write out your answers to the questions in this book—*interact* with the book—you'll reinforce your learning of public speaking techniques, you'll master in the long run more material at a faster pace, and you'll remember it longer.

The distinctive features of this text include

Diagnosis Folder: a 10-page system in which you and your instructor can keep track of what has been learned. It includes forms on which to record grades, comments on speeches, consultations, etc.

Check-off Tip Sheets: step-by-step guides for the essentials in speaking—outlining, data, introductions, and more.

Self-Tests: quizzes on techniques and ideas through which you can evaluate your own progress.

Evaluation Forms: lists of the guides to designing and delivering effective speeches so you receive specific, immediate feedback on your strengths and weaknesses from your instructor and peers.

Samples: examples of note cards, outlines, and other aids.

The teaching in this book is organized into:

18 lessons, with
25 assignments:
10 speeches
8 self-tests
7 outlines, analyses, etc.

Some assignments take but a few minutes to complete. Other assignments—speeches, for example—need more detailed preparation.

Your task is to learn 80 percent or more of each assignment and each lesson. What it takes to get that 80 percent is explained to you at the start of each lesson and assignment. At the end of each, there's either a self-test so you can grade yourself on how well you met the objectives or some other way for you to document your learning.

PREREQUISITES

To learn effectively and efficiently from this book, you should be qualified to study college-level courses in English. In general terms, that means it is expected that you are already able to:

▶ Read quickly and understand what you've read.
▶ Use correct grammar habitually.
▶ Take useful notes.
▶ Write effectively.
▶ Use a library efficiently.
▶ Speak distinctly and correctly.

And what if you can't? Well, of course you should still be able to improve your speaking skills by studying this book. But you may have to take more time on some of the assignments.

If you are concerned about your preparation for this course, you may want to meet with your instructor and, perhaps, ask for a copy of the self-test in the *Instructor's*

Manual that accompanies this book. That self-test will take you less than a half-hour to complete, and you can grade it yourself.

However, if you are eligible to enroll in a college-level English course offered by your college or university, you should have no difficulty in learning from this text.

In any event, you are encouraged to take a moment right now to make either one of two decisions. You might consciously acknowledge to yourself that you do indeed have the prerequisite skills listed above as basic to more than likely insuring your success in studying this text. Or, if you may not have those skills, you might make a serious commitment to yourself to give the course a real—an intense, sincere, dedicated—try anyway.

The "Basic Key" to Effective Speaking

All of the instruction, guidance, recommendations, coaching, and such about how to speak effectively—advice that has been poured out to so many people for so many centuries—can be summarized in just two steps, expressed in a "basic key" of just three words:

"BASIC KEY" TO EFFECTIVE SPEAKING

1. Be yourself.
2. Prepare.

Be yourself means following the counsel that Shakespeare had Polonius give his son Laertes in Act I scene iii of *Hamlet:* "To thine own self be true." Don't try to imitate that network newscaster you admire. Don't try to talk like that professor who lectures with such power that students wait in line to enroll in his or her classes. Don't dream of speaking like that guy who is a gift-of-gab salesman or that gal who is a polished TV reporter. Rather, heed the advice given to the sportscaster pictured below.

That second step of the basic key to effective speaking—*prepare*—is, of course, the subject of this book.

BE YOURSELF:

"Should I be funny? Be serious? Be long? Be technical?"

Those questions were asked by *John Madden,* former head coach of the Oakland Raiders and former professional football player, just after he signed his first contract with CBS television to be a sportscaster. In his book *Hey Wait a Minute,* he wrote that television executives told him, "Don't worry. Just be yourself."

ASSIGNMENT 2: DIAGNOSIS FOLDER

 ACTION: Prepare a folder as instructed below.

OBJECTIVE:

After preparing this **Diagnosis Folder,** you will have a system for you and your instructor to keep a record of your progress in this course.

VALUE:

As you maintain your **Diagnosis Folder,** your progress toward becoming an effective speaker will be clear to you and your instructor at every step of the course.

INSTRUCTIONS:

As you complete each of the following steps, check it off below so you'll have a record verifying you've done each one.

_____ 1.   Obtain a standard, letter-sized (8½ × 11-inch) manila file folder.

_____ 2.   Since you'll be using your **Diagnosis Folder** a lot, please fill in the following information by typing or by writing in ink.

_____ 3.   Write your name in large letters on the tab of the folder.

_____ 4.   Remove from this book the five pages of forms that follow these instructions. The pages are perforated so they will come out easily.

_____ 5.   Fill in the information asked for on the PERSONAL DATA FORM.

_____ 6.   Staple that PERSONAL DATA FORM on the left inside of the file folder. Staple just at the top of the form so it can be raised to write additional information under it.

_____ 7.   On the right side of the manila folder, staple the GRADE RECORD FORM, the PROGRESS SUMMARY FORM (two pages), and the CONSULTATION RECORD FORM. (Keep them in the order listed, with the GRADE RECORD FORM on top.) Again, staple these forms at the top only so each one can be raised to write on the forms below. (Thus you'll have a one-page form stapled inside the manila folder on the left and four pages stapled on the right.)

_____ 8.   As you complete each assignment, fill in the information on the GRADE RECORD FORM.

_____ 9.   Before you present a speech in class, place the appropriate SPEECH EVALUATION FORM inside the folder. A form for each speech is included later in this book.

_____ 10. At the start of a class meeting during which you are to give a speech, give this **Diagnosis Folder,** with all the information up-to-date as far as you've gone in the instruction, to your instructor.

_____ 11. At the end of a class meeting during which you deliver a speech, pick up your **Diagnosis Folder** from your instructor.

_____ 12. After you have delivered a speech, write on your PROGRESS SUMMARY FORM a few words summarizing the major strengths and weaknesses of your speech. You'll get those from:
   (1) Your instructor's notes on your SPEECH EVALUATION FORM.
   (2) Comments your instructor may have made after your speech.
   (3) Suggestions your classmates may have offered.

(4)   Your own opinion of your strengths and weaknesses on that particular speech.

____ 13.   Bring your **Diagnosis Folder** to any conferences you have with your instructor.

____ 14.   Following each conference with your instructor, summarize on the CON-SULTATION RECORD FORM what you both said.

Inaugural Speeches

The longest: two hours, by *William Henry Harrison.* The shortest: 90 seconds, by *George Washington.*

Source: *The Guinness Book of Records.*

Just one more preliminary and you'll start studying public speaking. Back off and take a serious look at yourself. Just exactly where are you in public speaking now, before you start your studies to become an effective speaker?

ASSIGNMENT 3: PRECOURSE SELF-EVALUATION

 ACTION: Submit the following self-evaluation.

OBJECTIVE:

On completion of this assignment, you will have the start of a specific basis on which to build your own plan for improving your speaking skills.

RELEVANCE:

In order to improve your skills in public speaking, you need to establish a basis from which you are to grow. In other words, where are you now as a speaker? Then, at the end of the course, you can measure how far you have progressed.

You'll establish that basis for determining your growth through two means: first, the following Precourse Self-Evaluation Form and, second, your first speech. That speech will be the major benchmark against which your improvement can be measured.

The nine questions you are about to answer on the following pages have been selected to get you to start thinking about public speaking, to start considering your own attitudes and feelings about where you are in public speaking.

Some are intended to get you started thinking about the qualities that make for effectiveness as a speaker. The next step, of course, is for you to start incorporating some of those good speaking techniques in your own speeches.

INSTRUCTIONS:

Answer the questions on the following pages with specific responses. Don't generalize. For example, don't answer the first one with a vague reply such as "Not as good as I'd like." Rather, name particular features or characteristics you really feel describe yourself.

Quick, top-of-the-head answers won't give you a real basis on which to build a self-improvement plan. Give these questions some thought. Prepare a serious analysis of yourself, with some depth and introspection.

On completion, turn in your replies to these questions to your instructor for comment and reaction.

PRECOURSE SELF-EVALUATION FORM

Name: _____

1. What image do you think you now project as a speaker?

2. What image would you like to project as a speaker?

3. What do you expect will be your best skill in public speaking?

4. What do you expect to be hardest for you in this course?

5. Who is the best speaker you have ever heard? _____

Why do you rate that speaker "best"?

6. Why are you about to study public speaking?

7. What is your commitment to the study of public speaking?

8. Right now, before this course starts, what's one quick thing you'd like to know about public speaking?

9. For you to give this course a grade of *A* after you have completed it, what would it have to do for you? *Very specifically,* what do you want to learn in this course? Don't respond with a generalization such as "be a better speaker"; rather, name the specific qualities you want to develop.

_____

(Please save the space below until the end of the course, to evaluate the course on whether or not it did for you what you wanted it to do.)

L E S S O N 2

Designing Speeches

OBJECTIVES ▶ After you have finished this lesson, you will be able to:

1. Name the types of speeches.
2. State the type of speech most appropriate for typical speaking situations.
3. Write out the basic format for a speech.

RELEVANCE ▶ Whatever kind of speech you give first in class, you need to start by learning the basic design of a speech, as presented in this lesson.

Here, at the beginning of this course, you'll get only the essentials you need for that first speech. But these basic principles can be used to design almost any speech, for

DESIGNING SPEECHES:

Considered one of our nation's most effective speakers ever, former President *John F. Kennedy* followed these guides for designing his speeches:

1. short speeches, short clauses, and short words, wherever possible;
2. a series of points or propositions in numbered or logical sequence, wherever appropriate; and
3. the construction of sentences, phrases, and paragraphs in such a manner as to simplify, clarify, and emphasize.

That was Kennedy's plan as described by one of his speech writers, *Theodore C. Sorenson,* in Sorenson's book ***Kennedy.***

almost any speaking situation. Later lessons will build on these principles, going into greater detail and adding more sophisticated and specialized techniques.

TYPES OF SPEECHES

There are four types of speeches. They are classified on the basis of the SITUATIONS in which they are given, the STYLE or mode of delivery, and the PREPARATION required.

The four types of speeches are:

1. Impromptu
2. Extemporaneous
3. Manuscript
4. Memorized

Each is appropriate for different speaking situations. Here are the definitions, situations in which each one is typically used, preparation required, and advantages and disadvantages of each.

1. Impromptu Speech

You would give an impromptu speech when you are called on to speak on the spur of the moment and did not know ahead of time that you'd be asked to talk.

For example, you are at a meeting of your college's student government as they consider sending a representative to a national conference on political action. You recently attended a local seminar on the same subject. The chairman might well ask you to "say a few words" about your ideas on the value of such seminars. Since you did not know before the meeting that you'd be asked to speak, you'd have to give an impromptu speech.

But that does not mean you'd speak without preparation. Your preparation for an impromptu speech comes mainly from your existing knowledge, experience, feelings, and opinions. In our example, just by attending the seminar you probably developed some opinions about the value of political action, and so you'd of course base your remarks on those views.

Other ways to prepare for impromptu speeches are detailed later in this book in Lesson 17. You'll learn there are many techniques, tips, and tricks you can use to give a good impromptu speech.

There are two advantages of the impromptu speech. The main advantage is that by giving an impromptu speech, you can present your ideas, make an appeal, or disseminate information at a time when it may be most appropriate or most needed by your listeners. Consequently, what you say may have greater value and impact. Another advantage is that a good impromptu speech can often "raise your stock"—improve your image—in the minds of your audience.

But there are two important disadvantages to the impromptu speech. First, it's easy to do poorly. When asked to talk on the spur of the moment, many speakers feel they must get up and speak even though they have nothing to say. So they often ramble, wander, and hem and haw, wasting their time and the audience's. The second disadvantage is that many of us worry about having to give an impromptu speech. We realize the situation may not come up often, but we're still concerned we might not do a good job if called on. Both of these disadvantages can be eliminated if you'll use the techniques presented in Lesson 17 of this book.

2. Extemporaneous Speech

An extemporaneous speech is given when you have had an opportunity to prepare. You deliver this speech either by referring occasionally to brief notes or by recalling from memory the points, ideas, and specifics, but you do not write your speech out or memorize it.

This is the type of speech appropriate for most speaking situations. It is the type of delivery most speakers use most frequently.

This is the speech you usually hear as the typical college lecture; presentations by visiting authorities ("Tonight: Connie Chung Speaks out About Network TV News— Auditorium, 8:00 P.M."); reports to governmental agencies; informational speeches to civic organizations and clubs; talks about a trip, a study, a hobby, an event, etc.; fund-raising and informal (in general, the non-TV) campaign speeches. In brief, most of the speeches you hear are extemporaneous speeches.

Preparation, this course will teach you, follows an easy 4-step process:

1. Establish a purpose.
2. Gather data.
3. Organize.
4. Practice.

The advantage of the extemporaneous speech is that through preparation you become confident that you know what you're going to say, so you are more relaxed and self-assured. This type of delivery conveys the impression that you are really sincere, concerned, and informed, that you indeed want your audience to receive and to remember what you say.

The disadvantage of the extemporaneous speech is that it depends on the speaker's skill in speaking fluently without word-by-word preparation. As with the impromptu speech, beginning speakers are concerned that they may hesitate and stumble, even though they have prepared the material to be delivered. If worried speakers try to get around the problem by writing speeches out completely, they run into the disadvantages of the manuscript and memorized speeches described next.

This is the type of speech that is emphasized in this course. This is the speech you will find, just as most other speakers have found, is most practical, useful, productive, convenient, and effective.

3. Manuscript Speech

A manuscript speech is presented when very exact wording is required, such as presenting policies, contracts, and scientific reports. The speech is written out word for word and delivered by reading the script to the audience.

Preparation for the manuscript speech follows a 5-step process—the same 4 steps used for the extemporaneous speech, plus an additional step:

1. Establish a purpose.
2. Gather data.
3. Organize the data.
4. Practice.
5. Write a full script.

The advantage of the manuscript speech is obvious: It provides you assurance that you'll be able to deliver the precise words you want to present.

But the manuscript speech has the serious disadvantage of being difficult to deliver effectively. It's hard to present a manuscript speech with feeling and emphasis and also to maintain contact with your audience.

The manuscript speech has another disadvantage. It is difficult to adapt quickly the content or the style of the speech to the speaking situation. When there are conditions the speaker did not envision when writing a speech, the speech may miss entirely.

Therefore the manuscript speech is not recommended for any but the most exacting, structured speaking situation.

Besides, if a written document seems most appropriate, why bother to read it to the audience? Delivery is usually stilted and artificial, and communication is impaired. Why not just distribute copies of the speech and let the audience read it? That would be a time-saver; your typical listener can read three or more times faster than you can speak.

Manuscript and memorized speeches are not recommended for most speaking situations in the real world. Manuscript and memorized speeches probably will not be assigned in this course, and students are urged not to try to use them to get through the extemporaneous speeches that are assigned.

4. Memorized Speech

The memorized speech is used when exact wording is required but reading from a script is inappropriate; therefore the speech is committed to memory.

There are few speaking situations today in which this speech is appropriate. It may be used at presentations of high-level awards, welcomes to very important visiting dignitaries, and such. It is often used in contest speaking and oratorical competitions such as those sponsored by various civic and fraternal organizations.

Preparation: Again, follow the 4-step process used for an extemporaneous speech plus the additional step for a manuscript speech (write a full script), then add one more step. So there are 6 steps in preparing a memorized speech:

1. Establish a purpose.
2. Gather data.
3. Organize the data.
4. Practice.
5. Write a full script.
6. Memorize.

There's just one advantage to the memorized speech. As with the manuscript speech, you can plot out ahead of time the best wording throughout the speech.

There are three major disadvantages. The manuscript speech is difficult to deliver with feeling, sincerity, and spontaneity. There's also the hazard that you might forget what you were going to say. And there's the obvious disadvantage of having to take the time to memorize the speech.

Recommendation: Don't use a memorized speech in this course or in the real world except in very specialized situations.

Review

You have no doubt noticed that the *type of speech you should give depends on the speaking situation.*

Now let's see how well you have learned that principle and how well you can apply it.

Following this is the first of many opportunities for you and this book to INTER-ACT—to reinforce your learning—one of those distinctive teaching techniques used in this book that you read about in the first few pages. Remember the purpose of interacting: to reinforce your learning so you'll learn faster and remember the material longer.

Please be sure you answer all the questions; respond to all the situations *in writing*. By actually writing rather than merely thinking of your answers, you will greatly—GREATLY—increase your learning.

After you've written your answers, please check them with the book's answers, which follow. Even if you are quite confident that you answered each question correctly, you should compare each of your answers one by one with the book's responses—by doing that, you'll further reinforce your learning of the material, thereby helping you to implant the information in your memory still more strongly. That, in turn, will help you recall the material faster and easier whenever you need it as you design and deliver your speeches.

> You should follow the same routine of *writing out each answer, then checking each response immediately* for every review, reaction, and self-test in this book. Make that routine automatic and you'll help yourself greatly in remembering the material longer, more completely, and more accurately.

INSTRUCTIONS: Write the type of speech each of the following is, in the blanks to the right.

1. You've been asked to speak at next week's luncheon meeting of a local business association to tell how stores could attract more college students as customers. _____

2. You're a member of a group of college students asked to appear before the students at a nearby junior high school to answer questions the youngsters will ask about your ideas on how students of different multicultural backgrounds can improve their success in school. _____

3. You've entered a national speech contest for college students of environment. The theme for the speeches: "What America Should Be in the Year 2000." _____

4. You're giving a speech to the board of directors of the local recreation department to present your ideas on the need for more activities. _____

5. You're president of a group and you're announcing the terms of settlement of a strike. _____

6. You were chairman of last year's "Get-out-the-Vote" Committee, and now you're sitting in on a meeting of a similar group at a neighboring college. They get into a hassle over whether the group should include high school students or be exclusively for college students. They ask you for a summary of how your committee handled this question. _____

7. You're one of a team of amateur scientists who have dug up bones which seem to be of white men, and they've been dated as 100 years older than any previous record of non-natives in the area. You've been asked to speak to the college anthropology class to inform them about the findings. _____

ANSWERS

1. Extemporaneous
2. Impromptu
3. Memorized
4. Extemporaneous
5. Manuscript
6. Impromptu
7. Extemporaneous

Now try a blockbuster of a question—a question emphasizing the very essence of selecting the type of speech to use, but a question many students miss on first thought. Think through your answer carefully before writing it down.

Which is the **one** best type of speech? _____

OK, you're committed; you've written down your answer. And it is hoped that the answer you gave was "None." Reason: It depends on the speaking situation. You can't determine which is the best type of speech until you have identified the situation in which the speech is to be presented.

It is true that extemporaneous is the most frequently used, the one used by most speakers in most speaking situations. But that's distinctly different from awarding it the title of "best."

If at this very moment I ask you to give—right now—a speech about your reactions to this book so far, the extemporaneous speech could not be "best" because you'd *have* to give an impromptu speech. You'd not have time to do the preparation for an extemporaneous speech or for a manuscript or a memorized speech.

Again, the type of speech you give depends on the speaking situation. Until you know what the speaking situation is, you cannot determine which would be the best type of speech to use.

Format for a Speech

Webster's defines *format* as a "general plan of organization or arrangement."

A speech—any speech—has a general plan.

Of course, there are different speech formats, but almost all successful, effective speeches include certain common elements. (Later we'll define the term *effective speech* quite specifically; now we can work with the definition that an effective speech is one that achieves its purpose. If you gave a speech because you wanted the audience to know about the advantages of contact lenses, and after your speech most in the audience did know what you'd told them, you gave an effective speech.)

So a speech has a *format*—a basic form, pattern, structure, design. And, as we just said, certain basic features are included in just about every speech.

The speech format you're about to learn is one that experienced speakers have found most effective for a variety of speaking situations. You should know this speech format perfectly, completely, and be able to recall it without a moment's hesitation.

Two techniques for learning the format are presented in this book. First, memorize the following:

BASIC FORMAT FOR A SPEECH

I. Introduction
   A. Attention
   B. Preview
II. Discussion
   A. Main points
   B. Arrange logically
   C. Support with data
III. Conclusion
   A. Review
   B. Memorable statement

Got it? Fine.
But just to be sure, check yourself on the next page.

Most Overworked Word

The word "set" has more definitions than any other English word. It has 194 meanings—126 as a verb, 58 as a noun, and 10 as a participial adjective, according to *The Guinness Book of Records.*

Below, write out the complete format for a speech—without referring to the previous page.

Finished? Now check your version with the one on the previous page.

Are they both the same? *Exactly* the same? Including every number and letter (I., B., etc.)?

Knowing this format is so basic to the rest of this speech course that you are now asked to reinforce your memory of it by using a second technique of learning—the following programmed unit. It has two advantages:

1. You'll gain considerable additional insight into the meaning and value of each part of the speech format.
2. You'll have a stronger imprint of the format for a speech in your mental file cabinet.

FORMAT FOR A SPEECH—PROGRAMMED

You may already have had some experience in studying programmed material. It presents information in small, step-by-step statements.

But Two Warnings

1. Programmed learning starts out in such small, easy steps that some students get the idea that it's too simple and not worth doing. But the fact is that research shows that this kind of instruction is very effective for learning certain kinds of material, especially for learning details such as you are about to study. So do go through this program carefully, seriously.

2. This program includes many more specifics—examples, applications, details—than just the speech format itself. Thus there are many new, additional points for you to learn in the following program.

INSTRUCTIONS:

1. Use a piece of paper to hide from yourself all information below each of the broken lines.

2. Read each statement carefully and thoughtfully. It is easy to slip into quick skimming, but then learning is greatly reduced.

3. After reading each statement, react—write out the answer asked for. It is easy to take a shortcut and just think of the answer, but the physical act of actually writing it out further increases and strengthens your learning.

4. Then slide the paper hiding subsequent material down the page a bit to reveal the answer. Check it with your answer. If you missed, take the time to figure out quite clearly *why* your answer is different. The error, you see, might be by the author, because he is supposed to write the program so clearly that you will not be misled. (Thousands of students have already checked out this program; it works.)

---

1. Most of us can look at a number of different buildings and identify those structures that are homes. Even though there are a great many differences in the many homes we see, we have come to recognize something that might be called a "basic format" for a home. Speeches, too, have a great many variations, but in general most speeches can be identified as having a_____.

- -

Basic format

---

2. The basic format that virtually all effective speeches follow is composed of these *main parts:*

    I. Introduction
   II. Discussion
  III. Conclusion

So a speech includes how many main parts? _____*three*_____

- -

Three

---

3. The three *main parts* of a speech are:

I. _Introduction_

II. _Discussion_

III. _Conclusion_

(If you need to, take another look at the previous frame.)

Introduction, Discussion, Conclusion

4. In the basic format of a speech, the INTRODUCTION, DISCUSSION, and CONCLUSION are known as the _Main Parts_ of a speech.

Main parts

5. It is important, for uniformity in planning a speech, always to use the same *symbols* to indicate the various parts of a speech. For identifying the three main parts of a speech we have used the symbols _/_, _//_, and _///_.

I., II., III.

6. These, of course, are Roman numerals. Roman numeral I identifies the main part of a speech known as the _Introduction_.

Introduction

7. Roman numeral II is used to identify the second part of a speech, called the _Discussion_ part of a speech.

Discussion

8. The final main part of a speech, the _Conclusion_, is identified by the symbol III.

Conclusion

9. Since members of an audience often make up their minds about how good speakers are soon after they begin a talk, it is important to prepare carefully the opening part of a speech, which is called the _Introduction_.

I. Introduction

10. Some speech textbooks and some speech instructors call the second main part of a speech the "body," the "main part," or something else. We prefer to call it the Discussion because it is the part of your speech in which you go into detail about your subject and really talk about—or "discuss"—your topic. Thus, the main part of a speech, which follows the Introduction, is called the _Discussion_.

II. Discussion

---

11. The last part of a speech is called the Conclusion. It is, of course, the part in which you draw your speech to a close. The three main parts of a speech, then, are

    I. _Introduction_

    II. _Discussion_

    III. _Conclusion_

  I. Introduction
 II. Discussion
III. Conclusion

---

12. The Introduction, Discussion, and Conclusion are known as the _Main Parts_ of a speech.

Main parts

---

13. The longest part of a speech is that in which you go into the details of your topic. This main part of a speech is called the _Discussion_.

II. Discussion

---

14. Most speakers plan very carefully what they are going to say in the first few sentences of a speech because the opening remarks of a speech have such a great impact in establishing a speaker's impression on an audience. Thus, many speakers spend considerable time preparing the first part of a speech, the _Introduction_.

I. Introduction

---

15. The final remarks of a speaker also are important in establishing the effectiveness of a speech; the last part of a speech, the _Conclusion_, requires very careful planning, too.

III. Conclusion

16. What are the main parts of a speech? (Be sure to include the symbols used to identify each part.)

    I. Introduction
    II. Discussion
    III. Conclusion

I. Introduction
II. Discussion
III. Conclusion

17. The first statement presented in a speech—the first part of the Introduction—should be designed to capture the interest of the audience. We call it an "Attention-getter." What would be the main basis for selecting what you might say as an Attention-getter? *get the audience interested.*

(In your own words) Must be interesting to the audience.

18. A speaker who begins his speech with a statement that is designed to get the audience interested in his subject is using an *Attention getter*.

Attention-getter

19. There are many different kinds of Attention-getters. Some speakers start a speech with a joke, a story, a startling statistic, a fascinating fact, or a stimulating question. Whichever one of these or other kinds of openings a speaker may use, the purpose of the Attention-getter is *To get the audience interested.*

(In your own words) To get the audience interested in the subject of the speech.

20. For example, suppose a speaker starts a speech on the impact of television with this statement:

    > Each evening more Americans view the typical dramatic television show than have viewed all of the stage performances of all of Shakespeare's plays in all the years since they were written.

    This, most people in an audience would agree, is an interesting and startling statistic. Such an opening statement in a speech is called an *Attention getter*.

Attention-getter

21. We are now beginning to expand the basic format for a speech from the three main parts with which we started. At this point our basic format for a speech consists of these items:

    I. Introduction
       A. Attention-getter
    II. Discussion
    III. Conclusion

    What, in your opinion, should a speech present after the Attention-getter?
    Discussion

    Your opinion was asked for, so your answer is, well, your answer. Our answer would be that after the Attention-getter a speech should then preview the subject of the speech.

22. Thus, how many things should be presented in the Introduction of a speech?
    Two

    Two

23. The opening part of our basic speech format now looks like this:

    I. Introduction
       A. Attention-getter
       B. Preview

    What is the purpose of that second part of the Introduction? _to let the audience know what you are going to talk about._

    (In your own words) To let the audience know exactly what you are going to talk about.

24. Many speakers find it effective to be specific and precise in wording the Preview of a speech. After opening with a short dramatic story about a blind teacher, for example, a speaker might preview the subject with these words:

    That story emphasizes the importance of what I want to talk about with you today—the need for more medical research to prevent blindness.

    The two parts of the Introduction of a speech are:

    A. _Attention getter_
    B. _Preview_

    A. Attention-getter
    B. Preview

25. While the three main parts of a speech are identified by Roman numerals, the sections of the Introduction are identified by symbols, which are _____.

Capital letters

Capital letters

26. Thus, the symbols to identify the two sections to be presented in the Introduction are ___*A*___ and ___*B*___.

A. and B.

27. The first statement to be presented in the Introduction, *along with the symbol used to identify that section,* is ___*A: Attention getter*___.

A. Attention-getter

28. The second part of the Introduction, along with the symbol used to identify it, is ___*B. Preview*___.

B. Preview

29. After the Introduction, the next *main part* of the basic format of a speech is the ___*II. Discussion*___.

II. Discussion

30. In the Discussion, you should present the *Main Points,* or aspects or ideas, of the subject of your speech. Main Points are divisions of the general subject you are talking about. If, for example, the general topic of your speech is electronic communications and among the things you talk about in the Discussion are:

   A. Telegraph
   B. Telephone
   C. Radio
   D. Television

   Those four things would be considered the ___*Main Points*___ of your speech.

Main Points

31. Now our basic form for a speech looks like this:

    I. Introduction
        A. Attention-getter
        B. Preview
   II. Discussion
        A. Main points
  III. Conclusion

The last items we added to this basic format are the *A. Main Points*.

- -

Main points

32. If these were the main points in the Discussion part of a speech:

    A. Monitor
    B. Word Processor
    C. Keyboard
    D. Surge Protector
    E. Modem

then the subject of a speech would most likely be *Computers*.

- -

Computers

33. If you were to give a talk about show business, what main points might be presented in the Discussion part of your speech? (Please fill in the blanks with your suggested points.)

    A. *Actors*
    B. *Television*
    C. *Entertainment*
    D. *Background Music*
                   (Etc.)

- -

There are, of course, many possibilities, including these:

A. Television	OR	A. Actors	OR	A. Cost
B. Movies		B. Actresses		B. Availability
C. Theater		C. Directors		(Etc.)
(Etc.)		D. Writers		
		(Etc.)		

34. Such subtopics, or parts of the subject of your speech, are called

    _____.

Main Points

---

35. Now our basic format for a speech looks like this in "skeleton," or outline form
    (Please fill in all the blanks.)

         I. _____

            A. _____

            B. _____

        II. _____

            A. _____

       III. _____

  I. Introduction
     A. Attention-getter
     B. Preview
 II. Discussion
     A. Main Points
III. Conclusion

---

36. The next guide for our speech is that those Main Points of the Discussion should
    be arranged logically. That means that the main points should be in a clear or
    expected order or sequence. For example, a logical order of the main points in a
    speech on migration:

    A. Migration before 1925
    B. Migration 1925–1950
    C. Migration 1950–1975
    D. Migration 1975–present
    These main points are arranged logically on what basis?_____

In your own words: A time sequence, or chronologically, or in the order in which
migration took place.

---

37. A time sequence is only one of several different types of sequences that might be
    used to arrange the Main Points of a speech. But whichever order is used, the
    Main Points of a speech, presented in the Discussion, should be arranged in a
    sequence, or order, which is _____.

Logical

38. Presenting the main points of a speech in a logical order helps the audience remember what you talk about in the main part of your speech, known as the

_____.

II. Discussion

39. Now we have two guides to what should be presented in the Discussion part of your speech, and so the "skeleton" of the basic format for a speech as we have developed it so far looks like this. (Please fill in all the blanks.)

I. _____

   A. _____

   B. _____

II. _____

   A. _____

   B. _____

III. _____

I. Introduction
   A. Attention-getter
   B. Preview
II. Discussion
   A. Main Points
   B. Arrange logically
III. Conclusion

40. You will notice that just as we did in the Introduction, we are using _____ as symbols to identify the subsections of the Discussion part of a speech.

Capital letters

41. There is one additional guide to the basic format of a speech that applies to the Discussion. That means there is a total of how many guides for the Discussion part of a speech? _____

Three

42. Not only should the Discussion present the Main Points of a speech, arranged logically, but each Main Point should be *supported with data.* Example: A speaker presents as a Main Point that educational television is expanding rapidly. She then states that in 1954 there were about 45 stations and today there are more than 260 stations. The speaker has supported her Main Point with _____.

Data. The particular type of data in this case is a statistic.

43. If you were to give a speech about the importance of the music program at your school, one Main Point in the Discussion part of your speech might be that the music program helps to build a student's ability to work with others. Following that statement you should _____ _____.

Present data that will support that Main Point

44. Not only should the Main Points in the Discussion part of a speech be arranged in a logical order, but each point should be _____ _____.

Supported with data

45. Suppose a speaker says this in a speech:

There are three reasons why you should vote for my candidate. First, he is experienced. He was president of the statewide association last year, and he has held other elected positions, too. Second, he is a hard worker. And third, he is informed about the needs of this organization. He attended the planning meeting last month when the needs of our group were discussed in detail.

1.   Is the first point supported with data? _____

2.   Is the second point supported with data? _____

3.   Is the third point supported with data? _____

(1) Yes. (2) No. (3) Yes.

46. In the Discussion part of a speech, each _____ should be supported with data.

Main Point

47. The outline of the basic format of a speech as we have developed it so far looks like this. (Please fill in the blanks.)

   I. _____

      A. _____

      B. _____

   II. _____

      A. _____

      B. _____

      C. _____

   III. _____

- -

   I. Introduction
      A. Attention-getter
      B. Preview
   II. Discussion
      A. Main Points
      B. Arrange logically
      C. Support with data
   III. Conclusion

48. We now have only the Conclusion to plan. What, in your opinion, is the first point to present in the Conclusion? _____

- -

The question asked for your opinion, so your answer is, of course, accepted. Our reply would be a Review of the speech.

49. Often a speaker will say something like this toward the end of a speech:

   And so those are the reasons that led me to believe that educational television is a valuable teaching tool. Let me go over those points once again, very briefly.

   When a speaker says something like that, it is apparent that she is starting the Conclusion of her speech and is presenting a _____.

- -

Review (or summary)

50. A Review is the first thing that should be presented in the Main Part of a speech that is known as the _____.

- -

Conclusion

51. When a speaker briefly goes over the general subject or the Main Points of his speech, he is presenting the section of the Conclusion called the _____ (include the symbol, too).

A. Review

---

52. The last point to be presented in the Conclusion—and thus in the speech—is called a Memorable Statement. We therefore have how many items which should be included in the Conclusion? _____

Two

---

53. After the review in the Conclusion of a speech, the Memorable Statement should be presented. The Memorable Statement should be designed to emphasize the main idea or general subject of your speech. The Memorable Statement should help your audience remember what you have said. The last thing presented in a speech should be a _____.

Memorable Statement

---

54. The Memorable Statement should be presented in the Conclusion of a speech, right after the _____.

Review

---

55. To emphasize to your audience the general subject, or main idea, of your speech as you conclude, the speech should end with a Review and a _____.

Memorable Statement

---

56. A Review and a Memorable Statement are the two sections that should be presented in the Main Part of a speech called the _____.

Conclusion

---

57. Suppose a speaker concludes a speech with a statement such as this:

And so those are my reasons for wanting our schools to use more of the new techniques and technology of teaching. Our knowledge has doubled since today's college seniors entered the first grade, and our knowledge will double again before the toddlers of today finish high school.

She is ending her speech with a technique designed to emphasize to her audience the basic idea of her speech. That technique is called a _____ (include the symbol, too).

B. Memorable Statement

58. The same symbols that were used to identify the sections of the Introduction and the Discussion are used to identify the sections of the Conclusion; those symbols are _____.

Capital letters

---

59. Can you now write out the basic format for a speech? Let's go through a brief review as a final checkup. A speech, you will remember, includes three main parts. They are:

    I. _____

    II. _____

    III. _____

Introduction
Discussion
Conclusion

---

60. What should be presented in the first main part of a speech?

    I. _____

        A. _____

        B. _____

  I. Introduction
    A. Attention-getter
    B. Preview

---

61. What should be included in the second Main Part of a speech?

    II. _____

        A. _____

        B. _____

        C. _____

  II. Discussion
    A. Main Point
    B. Arrange logically
    C. Support with data

62. What should be included in the last Main Part of a speech?

    III. _____

        A. _____

        B. _____

- -

III. Conclusion
   A. Review
   B. Memorable Statement

63. Putting this all together, you now know the _____ of a speech.

- -

Basic format

64. As a final check, let's see you write out the complete basic format of a speech.

- -

  I. Introduction
    A. Attention-getter
    B. Preview
 II. Discussion
    A. Main Points
    B. Arrange logically
    C. Support with data
III. Conclusion
    A. Review
    B. Memorable Statement

You now have a model—the basic format for a speech—to use as a pattern as you design your own speeches.

Students often ask, "How long should each of the main parts of a speech be?"

The answer is that, in general, the lengths should be:

I.   Introduction   10%
II.   Discussion   85%
III.   Conclusion   5%

But those percentages are *general* guides only. They will vary depending on the speaking situation, as you will learn in later lessons in this book.

Now you are urged to take a break from studying this material. Do something else for, say, at least 15 minutes. Even better, wait until tomorrow and then check yourself on the following self-test. Taking a break before you test yourself will help you be sure you have indeed learned the basic format for a speech.

Maya Angelou . . .

. . . is an intense, powerful, commanding speaker.

She is an actress, African American activist, conductor, dancer, film director, historian, playwright, singer, songwriter, writer, and the first African American woman to have a book—*I Know Why the Caged Bird Sings*—on the best seller lists.

She says she has led a "roller-coaster life."

Born Marguerite Johnson in a segregated rural area of St. Louis, Arkansas, in 1928, she brought herself up from a broken home, being raped when 8 years old, an unwed mother at 16, to become one of our nation's foremost cultural and intellectual leaders.

In 1971 she became the first Black woman to have an original screenplay produced—*Georgia, Georgia.* She was nominated for Emmy Awards for her acting in *Georgia* and *Roots.* She is fluent in French, Spanish, Italian, West African Fanti, as well as English, of course. And she has composed music recorded by B.B. King.

She married a South African freedom fighter and lived in Cairo, Egypt. During five years in Africa she was editor of *The Arab Observer,* the only English-language weekly newspaper in the Middle East. She taught in Ghana and was feature editor of *The African Review.*

President Ford appointed her to the Bicentennial Commission, and President Carter selected her to be on the National Commission on the Observance of International Women's Year. In 1993 she wrote and delivered the presidential inauguration poem for President Clinton.

One of Ms. Angelou's many significant quotes: "The honorary duty of a human being is to love."

ASSIGNMENT 4: ESSENTIALS OF SPEECH DESIGN: SELF-TEST

🛈 **ACTION:**
1. Take the following self-test.
2. Grade your answers. See instructions on next page.
3. Enter your grade on the Grade Record if you are using your **Diagnosis Folder.**

INSTRUCTIONS: Write out the answers to the following questions without referring to any source other than your memory.

1. Name the types of speeches.

2. Write out the basic format for a speech.

3. What is the main basis on which you should decide which type of speech to use?

   _____

4. The types of speeches are classified on the basis of three features: (1) the style, or mode, of delivery, (2) the situation in which they are given, and (3) _____

   _____

5. The best type of speech is the _____

6. Which type of speech would be best for each of the following situations?

   (1) Reporting to a church group about your work at a summer camp sponsored by the church: _____

   (2) Accepting an award you did not know ahead of time you were to receive:

   _____

   (3) Announcing at a press conference the demands your committee will make at the evening's meeting about contract details: _____

   _____

Now check your answers on the next page.

ANSWERS:

1. Impromptu, extemporaneous, manuscript, memorized
2.   I. Introduction
       A. Attention-getter
       B. Preview
    II. Discussion
       A. Main points
       B. Arrange logically
       C. Support with data
   III. Conclusion
       A. Review
       B. Memorable statement
3. The speaking situation
4. The preparation required
5. None; it depends on the speaking situation
6. (1) Extemporaneous
   (2) Impromptu
   (3) Manuscript

HOW TO GRADE YOUR SELF-TEST:

You earn one point for each correct answer. To be considered correct, an answer must be complete as well as accurate. That means that in writing out the format for a speech, you should include the symbol (I., A., etc.) for your answer to be considered correct. And your version of the format for a speech should be in the right sequence too. Give yourself points on the following basis:

Question 1:	4 points, 1 for each correct type of speech
Question 2:	10 points, 1 for each correct line of format
Question 3–5:	3 points, 1 for each correct answer
Question 6:	3 points, 1 for each correct answer

A perfect—complete—answer would earn you 20 points. Remember that your goal is to learn 80 percent or more of the concepts in each lesson. That means that if you earned 16 points or more on that self-test:

1. Give yourself "credit."
2. Enter that on your **Grade Evaluation Form,** if you are maintaining your **Diagnosis Folder.**

If you earned fewer than 16 points,

1. Please return to the first page of this lesson.
2. Study the lesson again.
3. Take the self-test again.
   a. If you now get 16 or more points, give yourself "credit." (Don't forget to enter that on your **Grade Evaluation form,** if you are using the **Diagnostic Folder.**)
   b. If on your second try you don't pass the quiz, you should confer with your instructor.

CONTENT FORMAT

Once you've got that format for speeches firmly in mind, consider the following variation that some students and speech instructors find more helpful.

I. Introduction
    A. Attention-getter
    B. Preview
II. Discussion
    A. Main Point #1
       1. Data
       2. Data
    (Additional data as may be needed)
    B. Main Point #2
       1. Data
       2. Data
    (Additional data as may be needed)
    C. (Additional points and data as appropriate)
III. Conclusion
    A. Review
    B. Memorable Statement

You of course notice that the differences between the two formats are in the ways the guides in the discussion part are stated. The first format for a speech is a "structural version," and the second is a "content version."

You're urged to remember—and use—the version you find most helpful. Or do as many speech students say is even more beneficial—remember and use both versions.

Now take a rest from your studying—go for a walk, watch TV, play a game of tennis, whatever. If you've been studying this last lesson seriously, refresh yourself before you go on to the next lesson. You've earned it!

DESIGNING SPEECHES: CHECK-OFF TIP SHEET

INSTRUCTIONS: If you need help in remembering these steps in designing your speeches, check off each item on the list below as you prepare your speeches.

TYPES OF SPEECHES:

____ 1. Impromptu

____ 2. Extemporaneous

____ 3. Manuscript

____ 4. Memorized

BASIC *STRUCTURAL* FORMAT FOR A SPEECH:

____ I. Introduction

    ____ A. Attention-getter

    ____ B. Preview

____ II. Discussion

    ____ A. Main Points

    ____ B. Arrange logically

    ____ C. Support with data

____ III. Conclusion

    ____ A. Review

    ____ B. Memorable Statement

BASIC *CONTENT* FORMAT FOR A SPEECH:

____ I. Introduction

    ____ A. Attention-getter

    ____ B. Preview

____ II. Discussion

    ____ A. Main Point #1

        ____ 1. Data

        ____ 2. Data

    (Additional data as may be needed)

    ____ B. Main Point #2

        ____ 1. Data

        ____ 2. Data

        (Additional data as may be needed)

    ____ C. (Additional points and data as appropriate)

____ III. Conclusion

    ____ A. Review

    ____ B. Memorable Statement

L E S S O N 3

Delivering Speeches

OBJECTIVES ▶ After you have completed this lesson and participated in the subsequent in-class practice sessions, 80 percent or more of the members of your class will agree that you're able to:

1. Step up to speak with a stride and bearing that express to your audience your enthusiasm and confidence.
2. Establish and maintain a contact with your audience that communicates your interest in and concern for your listeners as individuals.
3. Maintain a posture, delivery, and appearance while speaking that enhance your speech.

RELEVANCE ▶ To help you get ready for your first speech, you should now learn the basic techniques of how to deliver a speech—how to move up to a position before your audience, how to appear poised and prepared, how to give your speech. These are what some call the "mechanics" of delivering a speech.

DELIVERING SPEECHES:

How *President Clinton* delivers his speeches varies. "Speaking on TV from the Oval Office, he reads from a monitor. On formal occasions he relies on index cards. For less formal talks, such as on the campaign trail, the President follows a core message but wings some too."

That's according to a report by *Lorrie Lynch* in the magazine **Parade**.

From the following pages you'll get many specific and practical tips. But you'll learn much more much faster when you move from reading about these techniques to actually using them. The value of the following pages, then, is primarily to alert you to these essential techniques for delivering a speech. Practicing them later as you give your speeches will help you become skilled as well as comfortable in using them.

It is important for you to note at this point that this lesson introduces you to only some of the many techniques for delivering a speech. Now you'll get tips on 14 basic techniques; later, in Lesson 9, you'll acquire skill in 19 more advanced techniques—for a total of 33 techniques for delivering a speech effectively.

But you certainly do not need to remember all those techniques—you'll not be asked to write out a list of the techniques for delivering a speech. Rather, the goal is to get you to *use* those techniques. Besides, you already know many of them— you know you should maintain a good posture, speak loudly enough to be heard easily, and such.

JUDGING SPEAKERS

That old line "Don't judge a book by its cover!" is every bit as applicable to judging speakers. Most of us would agree that we should not evaluate a speaker's ideas or make decisions about what he or she says or anticipate our response on the basis of appearance. If a speaker wears torn jeans and sandals and has unkempt hair, those things shouldn't influence us, we'd agree.

And yet most of us do make such invalid and hasty judgments, don't we? For example, didn't you start to evaluate your instructor for this course from the moment you first saw her or him come into the classroom?

We recognize that such snap judgments are tentative and have little validity. Yet until a speaker speaks, we have no other basis for responding. Sure, we should hold off on evaluating the speaker until we've heard the speech. But we don't. At least most of us don't.

Now, assume you accept—at least for a moment—that you, too, start to make up your mind about speakers on the basis of your first view of them.

What are two things many speakers do, right at the start of their presentations, that help you tend to think they are good speakers?

1. _____

_____

2. _____

_____

On the other hand, what are two things many speakers do that start you questioning, doubting, even rejecting them?

1. _____

_____

2. _____

_____

Delivering Speeches

Guides to Effective Speech Delivery

The point of asking those questions was to get you to start analyzing the delivery techniques speakers use. You might compare your answers with those of a couple of your classmates. And what would this author and your speech instructor give as answers? Well, you'll probably be able to figure them out from points soon to come up in this text and in your class. Let's see.

Before You Speak

1. Dress to Help, Not Hinder, Your Speech

It's not hard to imagine what effect a speaker's dress would have on at least some city council members, for example, if a speaker were to present an appeal for control of pollution and appeared dressed in torn jeans and dirty T-shirt. Many council members might well think that the speaker's appearance is a kind of pollution itself. Whether they are right or wrong in that opinion is another question. I would agree, and most council members would probably agree, that ideas should be evaluated on their own merits, not on the basis of the package in which they are presented.

But if your purpose, as a speaker, is to influence your audience in a specific way, then I suggest *every* aspect of your presentation, including your dress, be evaluated by you to determine in your own mind if it contributes to or hinders what you want to achieve. Whether you do or you don't make such an evaluation, you can be sure that your audience will be judging your ideas, at least in part, on the basis of your appearance. Arguments that they shouldn't are valid, but they are beside the point.

If you can't bring yourself to change your style of dress to help support your speeches, then you have only two choices: Change your speeches, their ideas, content, and points, which I don't recommend, or select subjects and audiences that will be receptive to your appearance.

2. Limit the Number of Note Cards You Use

When I teach this course, I ask my students to use only one 3 × 5-inch note card for each speech. Reason: It's simply a teacher's technique to help student speakers concentrate on *ideas* rather than on overly detailed notes.

Must—should—you use but one note card? Students will discover what works best for them, but they should consult their instructors.

(Tips on how to prepare a useful note card will be presented in the next lesson.)

3. Step up to Speak with Confidence and Authority

Ever see a television or film star walking in a crowd? Or ever see a top stage performer in an everyday situation, such as shopping in a market or eating in a restaurant? Often your eyes come to rest on that one person. Somehow you notice that individual standing out. You focus your attention on him or her. In show business it's called "star quality"—the ability to get other people to concentrate their attention on you while you are doing conventional, commonplace things.

How is that done?

By creating and maintaining a powerful positive mental attitude of your own confidence, authority, and importance. If you think of yourself as weak, inferior, unattractive, hesitant, and unsure, other people will tend to think of you the same way. If you think of yourself, sincerely and deeply, as powerful, important, assured, and attractive, then you tend to project those qualities and other people tend to accept you as having those positive characteristics.

Some individuals tell themselves, "OK, I'll really think of myself as confident and authoritative. I don't really believe I am, but I'm really trying to think of myself that way." That bit of mental doubt, that reservation about yourself, will negate your attempt to think positively.

Most of us can tell much about a speaker's mental value of himself and what he considers the significance of what he says by the image we see and feel him project. Of course, we can identify the doubter who looks at his feet, picks at his fingernails, tugs at his clothes, smiles with shyness and embarassment as he steps up to speak. We can also usually identify the overconfident, swaggering, coming-on-too-strong individual—the one who gives us a feeling he's not really that confident and strong at all.

Audiences also get cues about speakers as they move up to the lectern. Even their style of rising from their chairs to speak can tell audiences about their confidence. Some bound out of their chairs with obvious eagerness to speak. Others rise slowly, reluctantly, their movements telling their listeners they really don't want to speak.

4. Get Set

If there's a lectern and you are not comfortable with its location, move it or have it moved before you begin your speech. If you need a table position on which to display some visual aids, get it where you want it, then start to speak. If there's a microphone that needs adjusting, a projector to position, visual aids from previous speakers to be removed, a spotlight to turn on or off, a glass of water or a pitcher that's in your way—get all such details taken care of before you begin your speech.

It is a major distraction to many in the audience if the speaker starts talking while adjusting the height of the microphone, fiddling with the release button, pulling the cord into place, and repeating all of that a few times. All such a speaker is doing is providing a diversion for the audience; few are concentrating on the words and ideas being spoken.

Once you have all the objects and props set, get yourself placed physically before your audience. Decide just exactly where and, more important, why you're taking the position you are.

Do you want to be behind the lectern? The lectern may be a bit of a block to personalized communication, but many speakers, especially as they start a speech, find that a lectern helps build their confidence. Also, staying behind it seems to convey an image of authority or reserve.

Do you want to come out to one side of the lectern, to express friendliness as well as confidence? Do you want to take a step or so in front of the lectern, so you'll be closer to your listeners and appear to talk with them as individuals, as people about whom you are concerned?

In other words, choose your spot in front of your audience consciously, with reason, and for a purpose.

5. Establish Contact with Your Audience Before Speaking

Contact—some speech professors call it *focus*—is a kind of bond or relationship a speaker makes with the audience. While contact is a bit hard to define, we all recognize a speaker who achieves it; he or she makes listeners feel they are being spoken to as individuals.

Effective contact is projecting a feeling—"vibrations," some people call it. It's communicating to your listeners that you are interested in them, in your subject, and in wanting to bring them and your subject together. Listeners like that. Good speakers can establish effective contact even when there are hundreds of people in the audience.

On a basic level, contact is made by looking into the eyes of individuals. Look from person to person as you speak. Don't just look toward them, but at them.

Studies conducted at the College of Charleston, in South Carolina, show that people who gaze steadily at an individual while they speak are considered to be more sincere. Another study, made at North East London Polytechnic, found that when people ask for money for charity, they'll get more donations if they look in the eye of a possible contributor.

While You're Speaking:

1. Maintain Contact with Your Audience

Once you've started to look at your audience, once you've established contact with them, you should continue to maintain that contact. Of course, you can look away, for example, to look at your notes when you need to refresh your memory about the next point. But after a brief look at your notes—just long enough to get the next point in mind—quickly reestablish contact with your listeners. Look at them intently, with interest, as you start to speak again. People prefer being talked *with,* not *at.*

If there are many people in your audience, you will not have time to look at each one, especially if you're giving a brief talk. But try to contact as many as you can. Don't move your eyes about the audience in a regular pattern. For example, don't look at each person in sequence in the first row and then move your eyes to the people in the second row. Rather, look around your audience at random.

If you look out the window frequently or at your notes, your feet, or the back wall, listeners get a sense that you are not talking with them personally. Your contact is poor or nonexistent.

But looking into the eyes of your listeners is just the basic step in establishing contact. The next level is still more difficult to pinpoint.

Effective contact comes largely through your mental attitude toward your listeners. Care about them. Want them to listen to your words, to remember your ideas, to believe your views, to respond as you desire. Tell yourself—BELIEVE!—that you are interested in your listeners as individuals, and you will project better contact.

2. Begin Without Referring to Your Notes

The classic example of a poor speaker is the one who looks at a note card to remember to say, "Good evening, it is a pleasure to talk with you."

You should have your opening words well in mind so you won't have to look at your notes before you speak. When you're called upon to speak, step up to the rostrum, get your notes in place—set them on the lectern or keep them in your hand or whatever you prefer—look directly at someone in your audience, take a good long pause, and then begin to speak.

As you get up to speak, carry your notes in your hand inconspicuously. Don't keep them in your pocket. I've seen many speakers, in their anxiousness to start speaking, try to take notes from their pocket, only to find the notes caught in the lining or jammed in a corner of the pocket. Other speakers fumble by reaching into one pocket for their notes and then remember they put their notes in another pocket. You'll avoid such embarrassments by keeping your notes in your hand as you step up to the lectern.

3. *Refer to Your Note Card only Occasionally*

The reason should be apparent. Refer to your card only occasionally so you'll maintain contact with your audience.

Many beginning speakers, when told that they have been looking at their notes, often reply, "Oh, no, I hardly looked at them at all. I remember. I didn't see them more than just a couple of times!"

Of course, "seeing" and "looking" are different. Many speakers, in their nervousness, look at their notes but do not register what's on the card and so must look again. Many look frequently at their card in a kind of nervous reassurance ritual, not really needing to see their notes at all. However, if you are well prepared, just an occasional, brief glance will usually recall your point.

One of the best techniques to keep from looking at your notes too much is to place them on the lectern, then step away from the lectern—to the side or toward the audience in front of the lectern—so the temptation and the opportunity to look are somewhat removed. This has another significant advantage—it moves you about before the audience, gets a bit of variety in your visual presentation, and, once you've tried it, usually helps you relax considerably.

4. *Sound Conversational, Not as if Reading or Delivering a Memorized Speech*

Your speech should be delivered with spontaneity, enthusiasm, and sincerity. It is very difficult for the beginning speaker to communicate these qualities if he or she has memorized the speech or tries to read it from a script.

The techniques for delivering a speech from a script or from memory are the subjects of unending hours of practice for the professional. Those techniques are taught in course in radio and television speaking. They usually are not the subject of this course in public speaking.

Disc jockeys, for example, take considerable pride in their ability to move in and out of a prepared script, mixing the written material with their own on-the-spot comments, remarks, and quips. Their goal is to try to make it appear that everything they say is off the cuff, off the top of the head. This adds informality, authority, and sincerity to their commercials. But it is difficult to do.

Other examples of applications of the techniques of reading a script are by newscasters and commentators. Again, moving from their own comments to those written out for them, making both sound like their own fresh words and thoughts, is a skill for which high sums, up in the hundreds of thousands of dollars a year, are paid. And the fact is that while some of our nationally prominent television news people are just as effective and at ease in person as they are on the air, there are others who do not communicate effectively at all before a live audience.

In the next lesson, on preparation, we will give you details on how to prepare your speech and how to practice it without writing it all out, without memorizing it.

5. *Avoid Ah, So, Ya Know, Well, 'Kay, Etc.*

It is difficult, probably unnecessary, for a speaker to try to eliminate all such interjections. They are bad, however, when they become so frequent that the audience starts to listen to them or, worse, *for* them.

But why does a speaker use such—well, grunts is what they really are? At least they communicate little more than a grunt. Why use them?

Because many of us feel that we must keep saying something in our speeches. We feel that anytime we have to pause to think of a word or an idea the audience will get restless. Often we may feel this only at a subconscious level.

But the fact is that an audience likes pauses in a speech. Pauses give listeners time to think through what the speaker has said, to work toward agreement, rejection, understanding, or enjoyment of the speaker's points.

Notice two or three people in an energetic conversation. Their pace varies greatly. Often one will talk quickly, then slow down, pause, think through an idea, consider a word, maybe utter it and then reject it, seeking still another way of expressing the concept. And the listeners do not become bored; they do not disengage from the conversation. Rather, they use such pauses to do their own thinking.

Speech audiences, too, need pauses in which to think. So eliminate most, if not all, of your grunts—your "ahs," "sos," and such.

Heed the words of Oliver Wendell Holmes:

> And when you stick on conversation's burs,
> Don't strew your pathway with those dreadful *urs*.

How do you get rid of them?

Like so many habits, the first step toward controlling them is to become aware of them. Your fellow speech students will no doubt let you know if you use grunts too often. The next step is surprisingly simple yet effective.

Take a 3 × 5 card and bend it in half lengthwise, so it will stand up like an inverted "V." Write your own particular grunt on it in big, bold, colorful letters. The next time you give a speech in class, place this card on the lectern just before you speak.

You see, that's one of the big advantages of a speech class: You can try different techniques without endangering your effectiveness in real speaking situations. Your classmates, you'll soon find, will also be trying different ways of becoming better speakers. And that little card up there in front of you will not distract them, but will remind you to avoid your grunts.

What seems to happen is that while you're speaking, you'll actually rarely look at the warning card, if at all. Apparently, just preparing it seems to be enough, very often, for most speakers to get almost immediate control over their unwanted, undesirable grunts.

"UH...UM..."

College science professors use an average of 1.39 "uhs" per minute, and college humanities professors use "uhs" nearly 3.5 times more frequently—4.85 "uhs" per minute, according to a *Harper's Index* report.

But they have some tough competition from speakers who—claims psychologist *Nicholas Christenfeld* of the University of California at San Diego—typically run up the following numbers of "ums" per minute:

9.8—Pat Sajak
8.1—David Letterman
2.4—Arsenio Hall
1.7—Former President Bush
1.5—Johnny Carson
.79—President Clinton
.64—Vice President Gore
.1—Former Vice President Quayle

6. Stop at the End of an Idea: Don't Hook Sentences Together with And, And Ah, Etc.

This point is, of course, closely related to the previous one. Tying many thoughts together into one rambling, seemingly never-ending sentence is another subconscious technique many speakers resort to because they seem to feel that they have to keep going, keep saying something to that audience.

We have a very simple directive on this: *STOP at the end of an idea.*

If using hooked-together sentences is one of your speaking problems, it is often quickly overcome when the instructor assigns someone in the audience—unknown to you as the speaker—to count the "and ahs." The record for a five-minute speech in my classes was nearly 100, or more than 20 "ahs" a minute, an average of 1 every 3 seconds.

The "ah" habit is like so many such habits: difficult to eliminate entirely. An occasional "and ah" is not harmful. The key question is: Are your "and ahs" so frequent that they detract from your speaking effectiveness?

7. Maintain Good Posture: Don't Lean, Cross Legs, Etc.

One technique I've found for making the seriousness of such sloppiness apparent to student speakers is to videotape one of their speeches. When they view the playback, showing them as the audience sees them, they will often straighten their posture during future speeches.

But again, there are exceptions. A casual but not sloppy posture is indeed effective in communicating to your audience that your want to take a relaxed, informal approach to your subject. But poor posture is more often an unconscious habit than a planned technique.

The key question is then: Is your posture helping or hindering your attainment of the effect you want from your speech?

8. Don't Play with Notes, Pencil, Clothes, Etc.

And all those other little nervous, unconscious fidgetings—brushing hair out of the eyes, hoisting skirt or trousers, scratching an elbow, or rubbing an ear—are bad speaking techniques when they detract from the effectiveness of your speech. Avoid the repetitious, distracting, unnecessary little habits that add up to a rather large distraction from what you're trying to say.

9. Speak Loudly Enough to Be Heard Easily

If you're in doubt before your first speech, try yourself in an empty classroom someday, with a friend along to tell you if you meet this criterion.

Often a beginning speaker who has difficulty being heard feels that he or she is really almost yelling at the audience. Before even a small group it does take more energy, does require speaking up with more force and volume. But obviously if the audience can't hear you, they can't be expected to react to your speech as you want them to.

Now let's find out just how effective you think you are in these 14 techniques of speech delivery at this moment, as you begin your program to become an effective speaker. The purpose of the following self-evaluation is to help you become more aware of these techniques.

ASSIGNMENT 5. DELIVERY: SELF-EVALUATION

🛈 **ACTION**

1. Check below to show how you rate yourself on each of these basic delivery tips before you give your first speech.
2. Grade yourself. See instructions on next page.
3. If you're keeping your **Diagnosis Folder** up-to-date, enter your grade on your **Grade Record.**

Technique	I'm already Effective on this	I need to improve this
BEFORE YOU SPEAK:		
1. Dress to help, not hinder, your speech.	_____	_____
2. Limit the number of note cards you use.	_____	_____
3. Step up to speak with confidence and authority.	_____	_____
4. Get set.	_____	_____
5. Establish contact with your audience.	_____	_____
WHILE YOU'RE SPEAKING:		
1. Maintain contact with your audience.	_____	_____
2. Begin without referring to your notes.	_____	_____
3. Refer to your note card only occasionally.	_____	_____
4. Sound conversational, not as if reading or delivering a memorized speech.	_____	_____
5. Avoid *ah, so, ya know, well, 'kay,* etc.	_____	_____
6. Stop at the end of an idea: don't hook sentences together with *and, and ah,* etc.	_____	_____
7. Maintain good posture: don't lean, cross legs, etc.	_____	_____
8. Don't play with notes, pencil, clothes, etc.	_____	_____
9. Speak loudly enough to be heard easily.	_____	_____

And two more questions: As you look at yourself right now, before you start getting feedback on your speeches from your fellow speech students and from your speech instructor, write out your version of these:

My *strengths* in delivery are _____

_____

_____

My *weaknesses* in delivery are _____

_____

_____

HOW TO GRADE YOURSELF

You can give yourself "credit" for having completed this self-evaluation of your delivery techniques. Later in this course you'll be getting oral comments and written evaluations on how successful you've been in using, improving, and extending your strengths in delivering a speech, as well as tips on how to overcome, control, reduce, or eliminate your weaknesses.

Now that you've got an introduction to both the design and the delivery of a speech, you're ready for Lesson 4, Preparing to Speak.

"A lot of managers aren't bad at public speaking. But 'not bad' ain't good enough."

Tom Peters, management consultant, business expert, lecturer, and author of several books, including *In Search of Excellence.*

DELIVERING SPEECHES: CHECK-OFF TIP SHEET

INSTRUCTIONS: If, as you prepare to present speeches, you need to refresh your memory of the basic techniques for delivery, check off each point below.

BEFORE YOU SPEAK:

_____ 1. Dress to help, not hinder, your speech.

_____ 2. Limit the number of note cards you use.

_____ 3. Step up to speak with confidence and authority.

_____ 4. Get set.

_____ 5. Establish contact with your audience.

WHILE YOU'RE SPEAKING:

_____ 1. Maintain contact with your audience.

_____ 2. Begin without referring to your notes.

_____ 3. Refer to your note card only occasionally.

_____ 4. Sound conversational, not as if reading or delivering a memorized speech.

_____ 5. Avoid *ah, so, ya know, well, 'kay,* etc.

_____ 6. Stop at the end of an idea: don't hook sentences together with *and, and ah,* etc.

_____ 7. Maintain good posture: don't lean, cross legs, etc.

_____ 8. Don't play with notes, pencil, clothes, etc.

_____ 9. Speak loudly enough to be heard easily.

Senator Ben Nighthorse Campbell . . .

. . . speaks with sincerity and interest emphasized by his eccentricities.

Elected in Colorado, he wears his hair in a pony tail, sports bolo ties, rides his motorcycle around Washington, D.C., and resists mandatory helmet laws. At ceremonies, he often rides his horse while wearing full Indian headdress. Often he carries a ceremonial eagle feather tuft.

Senator Campbell is a Native American of the Northern Cheyenne tribe. Every year he attends tribal ceremonies in Montana. Only eight men of his heritage have ever been members of Congress.

In Congress, he battles with his colleagues about ethics that allow them to collect unlimited royalties on the books they write, but he is restricted with limits on his income from the jewelry he makes as a recognized designer.

He is married, has two children. He has a bachelor's degree from San Jose State University, and attended Meiji University in Tokyo as a special research student for four years.

He was captain of the U.S. Olympic Judo Team in 1964 and served in the U.S. Air Force for four years. He is a member of the Council of 44 Chiefs, Northern Cheyenne Indian Tribe; the American Quarter Horse Association; American Paint Horse Association; American Indian Education Association; and other groups.

In addition to his legislative responsibilities, he's a rancher and horse trainer.

All that means he has come a long way, indeed, from the small town in which he was born and still lives, Ignacio, Colorado, near the New Mexican border, south of Durango. In 1995 he switched from the Democratic to the Republican Party, leading many people in his state to believe he was positioning himself to win the governorship of his state in 1998.

A lot more public speaking certainly seems to be in the future of Senator Campbell.

LESSON 4

Preparing to Speak

OBJECTIVES After you've completed this lesson, you will be able to:

1. Prepare useful notes to refer to while speaking.
2. Practice your speeches in a manner that will help you improve delivery of your speeches.
3. Present an effective demonstration speech—a speech that gets at least 80 percent of your audience to do something they could not do before, the subject being relevant, important, and of value to them.
4. List at least three of your strengths and three of your weaknesses as a speaker.
5. Describe your feelings and the actions you display that reveal your confidence and concerns about speaking in public.
6. Be more comfortable about your potential as a speaker.

IMPORTANCE OF PREPARATION:

"The fundamental rule is preparation. Test pilots bullet into space with scarcely a heart flutter because they know their business; good public speakers, cheerily and effortlessly rambling on without a glance at their notes, have also done their homework—they've gone over and over the points they want to make, the structure of the speech, even the flourishes of humor."

Television interviewer *Barbara Walters* gave that advice in her book ***How to Talk with Practically Anybody About Practically Anything.***

RELEVANCE ▶ Students often ask many questions about the first two points of this lesson—how to prepare notes to use while speaking and how to practice a speech. In the overall job of designing and delivering a speech, these two procedures are relatively minor steps, but completing them effectively can help you considerably in being a better speaker.

To give you practical experience in handling these details, you'll probably be presenting a demonstration as your first speech in this class. It's a type of speech you'll likely give in the real world outside this classroom. Employees give demonstration speeches to new workers, showing them how to do their jobs. Managers demonstrate new equipment. Executives, professionals, virtually everyone gives demonstration speeches.

In addition, your first speech will give you insights to your capabilities as a speaker. You'll get a basis on which to build your further development as a speaker.

Finally, your first speech will get you familiar with the "feel" of speaking in public. You'll get a taste of audience reaction. And believe me, you'll like it!

"*Like* it??" yells the doubter.

Yes! Once you've experienced the pride, the thrill, and, yes, even the power of having an audience listening to you, following your words, enjoying your stories, learning from your explanations, eager for you to tell them more, chances are that you will indeed like to speak in public.

OK—perhaps that scenario is a bit overdone for you. Still, although no one keeps score, it does seem that many people, once they give a speech or two—enough so they become a bit more comfortable in the speaking situation—do find that they really do enjoy giving speeches. Speakers are the center of attention. They can help people learn. They can let people know what they think. They can guide listeners to new ideas. They can . . .well, you get the idea. But don't make up your mind right now on how well you like to speak in public. Give a few speeches first and then see if it's not true that you, too, just might get hooked on speaking.

How to Prepare Note Cards

1. Recognize the TWO Purposes of a Note Card: Aid Recall and Add Confidence

One purpose of a note card is obvious—to help you as a speaker recall what you want to say.

The second purpose is sometimes overlooked, but it is just as important—to give you a greater sense of security. Just having notes available can give you considerable added assurance and confidence. You know that should you get a mental block or have difficulty remembering the next point you want to state, you have something to refer to, to help recall your ideas.

So you are urged to prepare notes and have them available should you need them. It is somewhat more effective to present a speech without referring to notes, but most audiences do not find it distracting when a speaker takes brief, occasional glances at cards. You will probably find yourself giving a better speech—talking with greater confidence and fluency—if you do have notes ready, even if you don't have to refer to them.

2. Limit the Number of Your Note Cards

Students ask, "How many cards should I use?"

You might want to consult your instructor, but because novice speakers often bring stacks of cards, even sheaves of papers, I find it an effective teaching technique to limit student speakers to only one card for a speech.

Of course, there is no guarantee that using just one card makes a successful speech or that using more than one card makes a speech automatically ineffective. But it is true that those speakers who step up to speak with a big supply of references often end up playing with their cards or just reading their speeches *at* the audience rather than talking *with* individuals in the audience. Hence, as a learning tool, you are urged to use only one note card.

PREPARING TO SPEAK

3. Study an Example of a Good Note Card

Below is a copy of a note card (one card, two sides of it) a student prepared for his first speech in this course, the demonstration speech. It is an effective, useful note card; it uses tips to be presented in this lesson.

```
                                          1
  I.   Introduction
       A. Hawaii's gold is found                                    2
          on its beaches
       B. How to find shells            2.  Check high tide line
 II.   Discussion                           a. Story of valuable
       A. Start early—be on beach              shell found under
          at sunrise                           flotsam (SHOW
          1. The need to be first              COWRIE)
          2. Story of women who             b. Use of walking
             camp there                        stick
       B. Make fast survey of          C.  Concentrate on promising area
          large area (SHOW MAP)             1. Judging the beach
          1. Check water's edge             2. Using screen (SHOW)
             a. Large shells                   a. In dry sand
                roll in (SHOW                  b. In damp sand
                CONE)                          c. In water
             b. Kick up new          III. Conclusion
                sand                        A. Be early, be fast, then
                                               concentrate
                                            B. Rewards of shell
                                               collecting (SHOW DISPLAYS)
```

4. Use a Card Rather than a Slip of Paper

Playing with your notes will distract your audience from what you are saying. You'll find that your tendency to play with your notes will be reduced if you use a card. A piece of paper is easy to roll, bend, crunch, crumple, fold, unfold, and refold, but the very stiffness of the card helps remind you not to play with your notes.

5. Use a Standard 3 × 5-Inch Note Card

A 3 × 5-inch card is large enough to hold enough to remind most speakers of what they're going to say, yet is not so large that it becomes cumbersome.

There are other benefits of the 3 × 5-inch size. It will fit in the palm of your hand easily, while a large card has to be held between your fingers. Since the large card sticks out beyond your hand, you're presenting to your audience a potential tip-off to whatever nervousness you might have. That larger note card will often seem to wave in a breeze when propelled by even minor shaking of your hand. And of course a full-sized piece of binder paper will, when held in the hand of a nervous speaker, flutter as if in a gale.

6. Write Your Material Across the Narrow Dimension of the Card

More information will fit on your card if you write your notes across the narrow dimension. Reason: The outline form for a speech is usually longer than it is wide.

7. Use an Outline Form

If you have used an outline form to design your speech, as you've been urged, you've already started to implant that structure in your own mind. Hence, using the same form on your note card will help reduce your need to refer to your card as you speak.

Further, if you have your notes arranged in an organized, set pattern, you'll be able to find points on your card more easily when you need them. You won't have to read through relatively disconnected, unstructured material to remind yourself of what's next in your speech.

Finally, using an outline form on your note card will help you keep and present your ideas in a logical, structured form. Remember that your audience is much more likely to react as you wish if the structure of your speech is definite and clear to them.

8. Number Your Cards

If you're giving a longer speech, say, 15 minutes or so, you'll need more than just one card. When using more than one card, you'll find it simpler to write on only one side of each card. Then you won't have to be flipping cards over and back again to find your next point. And with more than one card, be sure to number them prominently.

9. Write out the First Sentence of the Introduction and Conclusion

Before I get up to speak, I worry about such things as being embarrassed by what the chair says in introducing me. Or if I'm giving an after-dinner speech, I worry about spilling the dessert on myself just before I get up to speak. Or I find some other potential calamity to worry about.

Such things almost never happen. But even if they do, I'm still prepared at least to begin my speech effectively: I write out word for word the first sentence of the introduction to every speech I give. With that on my note card, my confidence is increased; my nervousness is decreased.

I also write the first sentence of the conclusion on my note card. That's helpful because occasionally I adjust my speech to the interests of my audience as I speak. For example, if my audience seems doubtful or confused about a point I present, I may restructure my speech as I deliver it, trying to add proof or clarity. But then, when it's time for me to conclude, I may have some trouble trying to bring the entire speech to a nice, neat, effective ending. With that first sentence of the conclusion written out on my notes, however, I can easily work into a conclusion that brings the entire speech together—my planned points and my additions as well.

10. Be Specific

You certainly should not have on your cards mere titles or headings such as "attention-getter" or "Joke." Those words will not help you remember exactly what you had planned to say to get the attention of the audience or just which joke you were to tell.

PREPARING TO SPEAK:

William F. Buckley, Jr., frequent public speaker, author, and syndicated columnist, told in his book ***Overdrive*** how he prepared for one of his speeches: "I had the whole morning clear, which is good, because there is a speech right after lunch at the Waldorf, which has to be thought through, as the occasion doesn't permit a regular lecture. I am to speak for only twenty minutes. I looked at the assignment and calculated the time it would take to prepare for it—say a half hour, leaning on familiar material. . . .

"I would make several points, beginning with the failure of the press to live up to its own critical criteria. This I'd illustrate primarily by examples taken from television. . . . I completed my notes, and ate the perfect chicken sandwich."

Similarly, merely writing "statistic" under a point will not help you remember the exact figures you were to present.

11. Note Where You Plan to Use Visual Aids

A surprising number of speakers—beginners and experienced—will go to considerable work to prepare visual aids, then forget to present them during their speech. I find it valuable to note on my card when and where I'm going to use an aid. I simply put a large asterisk (*), often in bright red, just in front of a point that will be supported with a visual. (Details on selecting aids are presented in Lesson 7, and specifics about using them are presented in Lesson 9.)

HOW TO PRACTICE

1. Go over Your Speech Three to Six Times

Most speakers usually find that number of practices to be about right for the short 5-minute talk as well as for the longer, say, 20-minute or more, speech.

Your goal in practicing your speech is to go over it often enough so that you deliver it with spontaneity, fluency, and enthusiasm, recalling to mind the various points and data with confidence and ease. But you should not practice your speech so much that it sounds memorized, stilted, artificial, canned.

If you practice fewer than three times, you may be failing to implant your ideas strongly enough in your mind for them to be recalled quickly and easily when you face the other concerns of speaking—concerns about how well you're doing, how good or poor the other speakers were or will be, how you appear, how receptive your audience is to your ideas, and such.

If you practice more than perhaps six times, your speech is becoming almost memorized. By then you may be remembering specific words rather than ideas.

2. Practice from Your Actual Note Card

Your note card, remember, should be made up from your outline. The reason for practicing from the card and not from your outline, and certainly not from a script, is so you'll get used to the same reference material you'll use when giving your speech. You'll get a mental image of your notes.

3. Work to Remember Ideas, Not Words

The point of the practicing should be so you'll have fixed in your mind two things: first, the specific ideas, points, concepts, and data you want to present and, second, the sequence and order of those points and data. You want to remember the points of your speech and their sequence. You're not—we urge—trying to remember exact, specific words to express each point.

4. Try Going over Your Speech Mentally Before Practicing Aloud

Many speakers find this method helpful, especially in the early stages of practicing speeches. When rehearsing my speeches, for example, I lie on my bed, close my eyes except to take an occasional glance at my notes, and "give" my speech in my mind only.

I have not found it helpful to practice speeches aloud. That seems artificial and useless to me. When I try practicing aloud, I soon start thinking of how I sound or what I should wear when giving the speech or a dozen things other than the content of the speech itself.

However, some speakers do prefer to practice aloud. Best tip: Try both techniques. Then settle on the one that is most comfortable for you.

5. Push Yourself Through the Entire Speech for Each Practice

Some beginning speakers practice the opening sentences of their speeches many times but don't get around to enough practice on the rest of their talks. They start to practice a speech, come upon a rough spot—an idea they can't express smoothly—and stop. They figure out how that point should be stated, practice it a couple of times, then return to the beginning of the speech. They end up practicing the introduction many more times than they practice the conclusion. Often the result is that the early parts of their speeches are much more polished than the endings.

It is far more productive to push yourself through your entire speech every time you practice. When you come to a point you have trouble wording, just express it as best you can and go right on. Don't linger on the problem; don't try to solve it right then. Don't worry because you can't find the right word. Don't fret because you end up with a sentence your sixth-grade English teacher would have rejected. Just continue on through your complete speech.

Later, after you've completed a practice of the entire speech, think back to that problem spot. Work on it. Perhaps the point needs to be placed in a different location in the speech. Maybe it needs another example or a different one. Do whatever repairs are needed. Then practice the speech again, in its entirety, from the opening words right through to the last.

Each time you go through your speech, you'll probably find yourself saying most points in somewhat different wordings. That's good. That's one of the major benefits of this technique of practicing.

By going all the way through your speeches, in every practice, you're storing in your mind not just one way, not just one set of words, but several versions of your ideas.

Then, when you get up to deliver your speech, you have in your mind a variety of ways of expressing the same ideas. You won't be stuck if one particular word does not come to your mind. Rather, the best version of your practices will usually pop into your mind.

Try it; it works. Speaker after speaker, beginner and old hand, will verify that practicing your speeches as complete units is most productive.

PREPARING TO SPEAK

6. Practice Gestures ONLY If You're Sure It Will Help YOU

Most speakers do not find it helpful to practice making particular gestures at specific points in a speech. It is usually not productive to practice, for example, a dramatic pointing of your finger as you proclaim. "Listen to what the opposition says!" Such practice usually produces gestures that are artificial, obviously staged.

But you can practice to improve your gestures and to increase your frequency of using gestures.

A good method is to apply the same principles of practice that many baseball players use just before they come up to bat. They'll slide onto their bat a "doughnut"—a chunk of heavy metal that fits on the swinging end of the bat—or they'll pick up three or four extra bats. Then they'll take several swings. When they step up to the plate, having set aside the extra weight of the doughnut or the extra bats, their own (single) bat feels much lighter, easier to swing.

Here's how to apply that principle of practice to improving your gestures. Practice in the privacy of your own room or some other place where the "crazy" drills you are about to do will not be observed. Say aloud something simple, such as the alphabet or numbers. On each letter or number, make a very exaggerated gesture. For example, say "A" and point threateningly toward the sky; say "B" and slam your hands together; say "C" and extend your arms as if appealing to an audience. Try to use a variety of gestures, and exaggerate them greatly.

The point is not that you should use such extreme gestures when you speak in public. Rather this is a drill to help you loosen up. It will help you to be more at ease when gesturing. It will also help give your gestures greater variety and force.

Some students ask, "Why do you say most speakers shouldn't practice specific gestures for particular points in their speeches, when everyone knows actors practice gestures for exact spots in plays?"

The answer: There's an important difference in the material that's spoken by actors and that which is spoken by speakers. Actors speak words written by someone else; actors play a role, usually characters at least somewhat different from their own personalities. Speakers, on the other hand, are delivering their own ideas, their own words. This difference, my teaching experience has shown, makes it difficult for most speakers to practice particular gestures.

7. Practice in Front of a Mirror ONLY If You're Sure It Will Help YOU

Such practice is helpful to very few students. Most claim it is distracting, artificial, and ineffective. I agree with them: I've never found I could learn anything from trying to watch myself in a mirror as I also tried to remember my ideas and figure out effective expression for those ideas. But you might want to try a practice or two in front of a mirror; you might be one of those who does profit from it.

8. Make an Audiotape or Videotape of Perhaps Two Practices

When you feel you're ready to move from practicing your speech mentally to saying it aloud, you may find it helpful to tape-record your practices. Some speakers find their most effective practice recordings are made informally—while they sit at their desks, for example. Others find it more productive to stand up and record their practices as if they were in the actual setting in which they'll be giving the speech.

The best tip: Try a variety of ways of practicing, including especially tape recordings—both audio and video recordings. Then settle into using whichever seems best for you. But DO practice!

9. Listen Objectively to Your Recordings

Don't be overly critical of yourself. Don't focus on slips of the tongue, an occasional slang word that might creep into a formal speech you're practicing, or similar concerns. Rather, listen to weaknesses in organization, logic, use of data, and other substantive features of your speech.

10. Practice Using Your Aids

There is a famous story from the days of live television about the legendary salesman who was showing an audience of millions how easy it is to operate a new can opener and, of course, the thing didn't work. More likely, the salesman didn't know how to operate the gadget. While this rarely happens on television today because nearly all commercials are videotaped or filmed, it could happen during one of your speeches.

To prevent such a calamity, practice using your aids. Practice repeatedly. Be sure you know not only how they work, but also everything that can go wrong with them!

If there are a few little switches or gizmos on your aid that you don't plan to use during your speech, learn how to operate them anyway—just in case you need them or in case some listener asks about them or, worse, in case you run into trouble and they might solve your problem.

Practice putting up your charts and practice taking them down.

Later in this book, in Lesson 9, you'll get detailed instructions on selecting and using aids. The emphasis here is on making sure you do indeed practice using them.

11. Time Your Speech

Most of us speak faster in front of an actual audience than in a practice session. We tend to express an idea more directly, more briefly, when in a real speaking situation than in practicing. But there are some, perhaps 15 percent of speakers, who do just the opposite; they become much more verbose when they get up before a live audience.

In your early speeches, timing is not very critical. But you should develop the ability to be within, say, 5 percent of the time assigned for your speech.

12. Don't Write out Your Speech Word for Word

We're studying extemporaneous speaking, not manuscript. Very rarely can students effectively deliver a speech for which they have prepared a full script. But the major point is that we're studying speech techniques that are practical and useful in the regular day-to-day speaking obligations of teachers, salespersons, executives, engineers, lawyers, administrators—all types of government, business, and industrial people. They just don't have time to write a speech out word for word, even if they could deliver it effectively.

13. Don't Memorize Your Speech

Delivering a memorized speech with sincerity, polish, and fluency is difficult. A memorized speech tends to sound . . . well, memorized. Flat. Dull. Uninspired, uninteresting. And you're adding the possibility that you may well forget what you're to say and find your mind blocked completely. Further, it takes much more time to prepare—memorize—such a speech than almost anyone can devote to the task in real-life speaking situations.

Those, then, are the major tips for preparing to speak, that is, the preparation that follows the designing of your speech.

Your success in meeting the first two objectives of this lesson—preparing useful notes and practicing speeches effectively—will best be determined by your own experiences as you deliver speeches. Use the Check-off Tip Sheet on the following page as a guide to helping you prepare productive speeches.

Were You On Schedule?

If you were an average kid, here's when you took various steps in learning to speak:

1–2 weeks:	cried intensely.
2–3 months:	cried to communicate a need—hunger, etc.
3 months:	babbled.
4 months:	shouted.
6 months:	mimicked simple sounds, pronounced most vowels and some consonants, but no words.
9–12 months:	imitated simple words.
12–14 months:	spoke five or six words, mostly "Mommy" and "Daddy."
18 months:	said simple phrases.
2 years:	said simple sentences.
2–3 years:	learned new words rapidly.
4–5 years:	talked in whole sentences.

Those facts came out of a study by *Dorothea McCarthy* and *Elizabeth B. Jurlock,* reported in the book ***American Averages,*** by *Mike Feinsilber* and *William B. Mead.*

NOTE CARDS AND PRACTICING: CHECK-OFF TIP SHEET

INSTRUCTIONS: As you prepare your speeches, check off each item below.

NOTE CARDS

_____ 1. Recognize the two purposes of a note card: aid recall and add confidence.

_____ 2. Limit the number of your note cards.

_____ 3. Study an example of a good note card.

_____ 4. Use a card rather than a slip of paper.

_____ 5   Use a standard 3 × 5-inch card.

_____ 6. Write your material across the narrow dimension of the card.

_____ 7. Use an outline form.

_____ 8. Number your cards.

_____ 9. Write out the first sentence of the Introduction and Conclusion.

_____ 10. Be specific.

_____ 11. Note where you plan to use visual aids.

PRACTICING

_____ 1. Go over your speech three to six times.

_____ 2. Practice from your actual note card.

_____ 3. Work to remember ideas, not words.

_____ 4. Try going over your speech mentally before practicing aloud.

_____ 5. Push yourself through the entire speech for each practice.

_____ 6. Practice gestures ONLY if you're sure it will help YOU.

_____ 7. Practice in front of a mirror ONLY if you're sure it will help YOU.

_____ 8. Make an audiotape or videotape of perhaps two practices.

_____ 9. Listen objectively to your recordings.

_____ 10. Practice using your aids.

_____ 11. Time your speech.

_____ 12. Don't write out your speech word for word.

_____ 13. Don't memorize your speech.

Now it's time for you to put to use all the principles, techniques, and tips you've learned in this course so far—it's time for you to give a speech.

Think back and you'll realize that you've indeed learned a lot already, including:

- The format for a speech
- Techniques for delivering a speech
- Tips on preparing a speech

Put them to work now as you prepare and present your first speech in this course:

ASSIGNMENT 6: DEMONSTRATION SPEECH: SPEECH 1

 ACTION: Design and deliver a 4- to 5-minute demonstration speech.

Note: The length (time) of this speech and of the other speeches in this textbook may be changed by your instructor.

OBJECTIVES:

After completing this assignment, including study of the material in this book, you will be able to:

1. Present a demonstration speech that is effective, that is, a speech that gets at leas 80 percent of your listeners able to do something they could not do before, with the subject of your speech being relevant, important, and of value to them.
2. Be more comfortable about your potential as a speaker.

(These objectives, you may note, are actually two of the six objectives specified for this lesson. You're making progress!)

INSTRUCTIONS:

1. Study all of the tips in this lesson.
2. Decide on what you'll demonstrate.
3. Prepare a rough outline of your speech by using the **Speech Planner** (page 100).
4. As you prepare, check off each step on the **Check-off Tip Sheet** (page 103).
5. Present your speech in class.
6. After your speech, complete Assignment 7: **Self-Evaluation.**

TIPS:

The tips in this lesson are much more detailed and extensive than those you'll get for your later speeches. That's so you'll be sure to get off to a good start on your first speech. Further, these are basic tips that you'll be using, building, and extending on all of your future speeches.

Some of these tips may seem to you to be quite simple, even childish. But they might be the very tips that the student sitting next to you thinks are quite important. On the other hand, some of these tips may appear to be rather complex or advanced for you. Yet someone else in the class may find those same tips to be very helpful. Once you've given a few speeches, you'll have much greater insight into which tips are most valuable for you.

1. Tips for the CONTENT of Your Demonstration Speech

1.1. Your Speech Should Actually Inform the Audience How to Do Something, Not Just Tell Them How Something Is Done

An example will clarify this distinction. A speech on "How to Select a Good Tape Recorder" would be an appropriate subject because you probably could get most of the students in this class to do that.

But a speech on "How Tape Recorders Are Manufactured" would be only a speech *about* the subject. It would be an unsuitable subject for this assignment because after you gave your speech, the audience could not be expected to be able to manufacture tape recorders.

Other *suitable subjects:*

How to Make a Perfect Taco
How to Use a Car Jack Correctly to Change a Tire
How to Fix a Leak in a Rain Gutter
How to Get Started in Quilting
How to Save Time Washing Dishes
How to Reinforce a Weak Gate
How to Barbecue Safely
How to Make Your Own Placemats
How to Color Hair
How to Appeal a Traffic Ticket
How to Select a Lawyer
How to Plan a Nutritionally Balanced Meal
How to Execute Three Self-Defense Moves
How to Put out Three Types of Fires
Unsuitable subjects:
How Our Traffic Courts Work
How an Electronic Watch Works
How Doctors Revive the Dead
How Sara Lee Bakes Cakes
How to Design a Boat

Thus you need to select as your subject for this speech some activity—a process, technique, procedure, task—that your audience realistically could be expected to do after hearing your speech. To put it another way, tell and show your audience how something is made, done, functions, or operates.

1.2. The Subject Should Be Appropriate for the Audience and Your Speaking Time

Your subject should be worth knowing how to be done by this audience. Remember, your speech is to be designed for the students in your speech class; do not assume you are speaking to some other audience. Look around at your fellow students. Think through the things they likely can do already. Then select as your speech subject something they do not know how to do already.

For example, "How to Enroll at This College" might be appropriate for a local high school audience of seniors about to attend your college, but your classmates in this speech course obviously have enrolled; they already know how to do what you propose to tell them.

There might be exceptions. Perhaps a *new* enrollment procedure is to be introduced next semester—but then you're giving the speech too far in advance to be of much real help to your audience. Or you could give a "humorous" speech on enrolling at a college. But check the statement of this assignment: While a humorous speech may be appropriate for some later assignments, here you are to actually inform the audience how to do something. (A speech to inform can be humorous or serious, but a warning: being funny is very difficult indeed. See Lesson 16, Entertaining.)

Also consider the brief length of time you have to present your speech. Don't attempt a subject that is too involved, complex, or lengthy.

On the average we speak at about 125 words per minute. That means your speech will be about 500 to 625 words—little more than the weekly essay written in many high school English classes.

By carefully selecting your subject and then including in your speech only material that will contribute directly to your speech purpose, you'll have no trouble with the time limit.

On the other hand, don't pick a subject that is too limited. Granted, there might be some subjects that meet all the criteria for this assignment and require only a minute or so, or even less, to present. But then you are not giving yourself an opportunity to apply the speech format in detail or to get sufficient experience in speaking.

1.3. Use a Visual Aid: The Actual Item, a Model, or a Drawing

Your speech will be much more effective if you make good use of a visual aid. The aid will make it easier for you to organize your talk, to remember the points you want to present, and to be somewhat more relaxed. You'll have something concrete on which to concentrate your attention.

Even more important, a visual aid helps your audience in three ways. First, it will add interest to your talk. An aid will also make your points clearer, more understandable, and apparent to your listeners. Finally, an aid helps your audience remember what you've said.

1.4. When Appropriate, Provide Each Member of the Audience with Materials to Practice With

You'll never get an audience to learn how to tie a necktie unless they can practice. Solution: Bring enough ties so each member of the audience can practice with one as you present a step-by-step explanation.

However, not all subjects for a demonstration speech require that the audience practice during your speech. Example: how to select an honest weight-control salon.

1.5. When Appropriate, Show Your Demonstration Item in Various Stages of Preparation, to Speed Demonstration and to Increase Clarity of Explanation

If your subject is "How to Make Artificial Flowers out of Facial Tissue" (and I've heard several really good speeches on this), it would be particularly effective to have some flowers already partially made, others completely made. Then, during the speech, time need not be taken to add each little petal, each leaf; one or two demonstrations usually make these repetitious procedures clear enough to most in the audience.

"How to Bake a Cake" is another subject for which it is effective to prepare the visuals before speaking. Do the actual baking ahead of time, at home, then concentrate in the speech on each of the steps of preparing, mixing, blending, etc. Conclude by showing the already baked, finished product.

1.6. When Appropriate, Have Someone in the Audience Help in Your Demonstration

Showing how to put on false eyelashes, how to set hair, how to apply a splint, etc., are subjects usually presented more effectively if you demonstrate on someone else rather than try to give the speech and do the thing on yourself at the same time.

In getting someone to help you, there are two options: ask for a volunteer or plant someone (arrange with a classmate ahead of time).

Which do you think is better? _____

Why? _____

Almost all professional speakers who need someone to help them in their speeches arrange for such assistance ahead of time.

Two problems can and usually do arise in asking for volunteers. One, you ask for a volunteer and someone rushes right up. Often that's the person who will ham it up, gag it up, try to embellish your speech, attempt to help you more than you want, or try to distract, confuse, and interrupt your speech.

Your other potential problem in asking for a volunteer: sometimes no one comes forward. Then you're forced to coax someone, and that puts you in an uncomfortable situation before your audience.

Therefore, what's the best way to get someone to help in your speech? _____

_____

The hazards of asking for volunteers should lead you to decide it is best to arrange with someone ahead of time.

1.7. When Appropriate, Lead the Audience in Practice

This is obviously not necessary if your subject is something like "How to Reduce Your Gasoline Bills." On the other hand, if your subject is "How to Write Common Greetings in Japanese" or a similar subject, your audience will indeed need practice—led by you during your speech—if you are to be successful in getting them to acquire that skill.

1.8. Include Personal Stories and Examples

When you hear the other students in your speech class present their demonstration speeches, notice how much your own interest and attention—and that of most other members of the audience—perk up when a speaker says such things as:

▶ I was showing a friend how to do this the other day and all of a sudden he found that he . . .

▶ How I got into doing this kind of thing really shocked me. One day I was walking along the docks and I noticed that . . .

People are interested in people. Make the steps, the procedures, and the techniques you present in your demonstration speech more interesting, more memorable, by including incidents, experiences, and stories that are related to what you're demonstrating.

2. Tips for the ORGANIZATION of Your Speech

The basic format for a speech, which you learned in Lesson 2, applies to this demonstration speech, just as it does to most speeches. The following tips, therefore, take that basic format and add specific applications of it to a demonstration speech.

2.1. Begin with an Effective Attention-getter

Do not begin your speech with "Today I'm going to tell you how to. . . ."

Such a statement gives the audience the opportunity to decide strictly on its own whether or not to listen to you. Some in the audience may think, "Oh boy, a speech on how to select chewing gum—just what I always wanted to know!" Others will think, "Who wants to hear *that?*" and they will tune out.

Your job, in the very first words you utter, is to try to capture the attention and the interest of your listeners. You should lead them to wanting to hear what you have to say. Simply stating "Today I'm going to talk to you about . . ." leaves the decision to listen or not to listen up to the audience.

Here are some examples of effective attention-getters from recent speeches by students in this course:

▶ A few weeks ago I got tired of having to pay out so much money so often for all the parking tickets I'd been receiving.
▶ If you see someone holding a hand up near an eye and blinking like crazy, don't think this person is trying to flirt with you. The person is just putting in contact lenses.
▶ I get tired of taking a date to a football game and answering the silly questions she asks about the game. But in listening to the chatter by guys in the stands nearby, I find that a lot of men don't know much about the game either.

For many more tips on how to get your listeners' attention, see Lesson 11, Designing Introductions.

2.2. State Exactly What the Audience Is to Learn to Do and Why It Is Important

The second point in your speech, AFTER you've got the attention of the audience, should tell them in specific terms what your subject is.

Here are examples for those three attention-getters you just read:

▶ So I've worked out a new system for parking; it saves me money, and it can save you money, too.
▶ Many people who don't wear contact lenses often ask me some pretty weird questions about them, so let me show you how to use them.
▶ Therefore, here is a list of five tips on how to watch a football game intelligently.

Don't be a "fog machine"—giving out a lot of vague or irrelevant ideas or words before you state exactly what your subject is. One student speaker started a demonstration speech with a small joke about a fellow who found a worm in an apple. Then the speaker talked about the importance of farmers in growing apples (an obvious point, but, as it turned out, with little significance for the subject he was talking toward). Next he wandered through some ideas about how raising your own apples "saves money and provides you with more healthful food." Then he talked about his views on the "ineffectiveness of health inspections of apples." Finally he got to his subject: how to select good apples.

Sometimes, as part of the exact preview of your subject, it may be necessary to state why what you are demonstrating is important to know. Often it is best to present this point through a story, illustration, example, or such. That's usually more effective than saying something such as "You should know this because. . . ."

Here are some examples of effective statements on the importance of the subjects of demonstration speeches. These would be stated after the attention-getters, as part of the previews of the subjects.

- You may be wondering why you need to know how to enter a burning building. But can you be positive that as you drive home after this class today, you will not drive past a flaming house?
- The legal details I'm about to tell you can be very important to you if, for example, you're stopped by the police for driving a "stolen" car, but you're really just driving a car a friend lent to you.

2.3. Present a Step-by-Step Explanation of How to Do It

Break down what you are demonstrating into a series of steps. Usually two to five steps are plenty. Remember that it's difficult for many listeners to keep in mind more than about five steps.

One way to make the steps you present more likely to be remembered is to number them. You might say, for example:

- The *first* step in building this unit is to . . . [followed by the details]. Now the *second* step is to . . . [followed by the next details].
- You would continue to number each step in your speech.

2.4. Present the Steps in the Logical Order of Doing Them

You would not believe how many batches of cookies I've heard presented with the points in some such order as this:

- First, get your ingredients together.
- When cooking, be sure the oven is hot enough.
- Next, mix your batter carefully.
- Decorate the cookies only after they are cool.
- Follow the instructions on the package carefully.
- When deciding which kind of cookie to make, be sure. . . .

The point is obvious: Present the steps in the process you are demonstrating—the main points of your discussion—in some logical order. Almost always in a demonstration speech that's the order in which the steps must be done to do the thing you're demonstrating.

2.5. Detail Each Step with Specific Data

Data, you learned in the first lesson, are the facts, statistics, and examples in your speech. In a demonstration speech that includes the details of how to do each step, examples of your experiences in doing it, perhaps stories about the experiences of other people in doing the thing, and costs, time requirements, equipment and tools, and such are needed.

Another type of data in a demonstration speech is, of course, the actual showing of how to do your subject. The emphasis should be on actually showing, demonstrating, not just telling how.

Each point you can actually demonstrate—*do,* rather than just talk about—is likely to be clearer, more easily remembered, and more interesting to your listeners. By working with your audience through senses in addition to hearing—by letting them see and feel (practice) as well as hear—you will be more successful in attaining the purpose of your speech.

Another hazard: Don't let some of your listeners still be mentally trying to figure out your shortcut on threading a needle while you have progressed in your speech to another point, such as how to use that needle in attaching a button. Try to explain each step clearly and completely before moving to the next.

And you should avoid—unless they really do apply—such phrases as "You can figure this part out yourself, it is so easy."

Finally, present a personal story for at least some of the steps. There are two benefits in doing this; what do you think they are?

1. _____

2. _____

As we have said, people are interested in people. They're interested in you, your family, friends, and people you've heard about, read about, or observed. Presenting personal incidents in your speech makes it much more interesting—that's the first benefit of this technique.

And most of us remember points, ideas, and concepts better when we can relate them—tie them in—with a story, example, or incident.

So the benefits of personal stories in a speech are that they add interest and make a point more memorable.

2.6. Conclude by Reviewing Each Step Briefly, in Order

You've already learned in the basic format for a speech to present a review. In a demonstration speech, conclude by going over the same steps, procedures, techniques, etc., you've detailed in the discussion part of your speech.

Be sure to present these review points in the same order as you presented them in the discussion part of your speech. Don't change the sequence, don't add new points, and don't change the wording of your points very much. Often it is a good idea to add variety to your speech, to reword the points, but don't change the wording so much that the audience has difficulty in identifying them as the same points you'd been talking about earlier in your speech.

Here are some examples of effective reviews:

▶ These, then, are the three steps to identify a sailboat. First, count the masts; then, look at the comparative height of the masts; and, finally, look at the placement of the masts.

▶ Now you know how to figure out which course a sailboat is on—close-hauled, reaching, or running.

- Follow those four steps—air your boat, run the blower for five minutes, check for gas leaks, and have safety equipment ready—and you'll have a safe start for all your boating trips.

2.7. Close with a Memorable Statement

To close with a memorable statement is a point you learned when you studied the basic format for a speech. The memorable statement in a demonstration speech might well be a story pointing up the value of what you have just demonstrated or an interesting statistic proving the need for your audience to remember what you've just told them.

Remember the reasons for a memorable statement—to drive home the point of your speech and to give your audience a hook, an interesting tie-in to help them remember your speech. This is your last opportunity to attain your purpose in speaking; therefore, select a memorable statement with care. Here are some examples from student speeches:

- So next time you see someone waving at you from a hotel window, you, too, might be able to save a life.
- Is this really worth all the trouble it may seem to require? Well, I saved just about 13 percent—some $1600—on the last used car I bought.

3. Tips for the DELIVERY of Your Speech

Delivery suggestions were detailed in Lesson 3. Those tips apply to your demonstration speech and to your following speeches:

To review that earlier lesson, the tips on delivery of your speech are:

3.1. Step up to speak with confidence and authority.
3.2. Get set before you start to speak.
3.3. Establish contact with your audience before speaking.
3.4. Begin without referring to your notes.
3.5. Maintain contact with your audience.
3.6. Sound conversational, not as if reading or delivering a memorized speech.
3.7. Limit note cards.
3.8. Refer to your note card only occasionally.
3.9. Avoid *ah, so, ya know, well, 'kay,* etc.
3.10. Stop at the end of an idea; don't hook sentences together with *and, and ah,* etc.
3.11. Maintain good posture; don't lean, cross legs, etc.
3.12. Don't play with pencil, notes, clothes, etc.
3.13. Dress to help, not hinder, your speech.
3.14. Speak loudly enough to be heard easily.

4. Tips for the PREPARATION of Your Speech

Preparation tips are a combination of the suggestions for preparing notes and practicing presented in this lesson. The tips are useful for all your speeches, not only for this first speech.

The main steps in preparing are as follows:

4.1. Complete the **Speech Planner** (described below).
4.2. Prepare 3 × 5-inch note cards.
4.3. Practice your speech about three to six times.
4.4. Tape-record two of your practices.

4.5.   Listen objectively to your recordings.
4.6.   Practice using your aids.
4.7.   Time your speech as you practice.
4.8.   Don't write out your speech word for word.
4.9.   Don't memorize your speech.

By now, it is hoped, you've started to think about a subject—or several possible subjects—for your demonstration speech. You'll find it helpful now to get quite specific in your thinking.

If you've firmly decided on a subject, complete the following sentence:

After hearing my speech, the audience will be able to_____

_____

_____

That sentence should state exactly what you are to demonstrate.

If you have not decided as yet on your exact subject, start coming to a decision by listing, below, some of the possible subjects you might—just might—be able to demonstrate. Consider this listing as exploratory—simply a listing of possibilities. You're not getting committed to any of these subjects. Later you may want to reject all of them as a totally different subject comes to your mind as just right for you. But at this particular moment, list some possible demonstration subjects you *might* speak on:

1. _____

2. _____

3. _____

More? _____

When you are firmly committed to a subject for your speech, prepare a rough outline of what you're going to talk about, using the **Speech Planner** presented a bit later in this lesson.

To help you still more, on page 101 is an example of a completed **Speech Planner.** It has, you'll notice, the introduction and the last point of the conclusion written out as full sentences, while the rest of the outline is presented briefly, in key words and phrases.

But one speech professor wrote to me, "English teachers get bent out of shape when you teach students to mix forms"—that is, some teachers say you shouldn't use sentences and key words or phrases in the same outline.

Well, when you're first learning to outline, it is a good technique to keep outlines to sentences only, or to key words only, or to phrases only. That's helpful as a learning aid to maintaining consistency in your outlining—your thinking. Once you've developed some skill in outlining, mixing sentences with key words and phrases is certainly not a crime. There are two essential guides:

1. Keep the points in your outlines as brief as you can—as long as they are sufficiently detailed for you to quickly, easily recall the points as you speak.
2. As we've suggested before, write out the first sentence or so of the introductions to your speeches so that you'll be confident you can begin your speeches with

polished, well-structured statements, and write out the closing sentences of the conclusions to your speeches so you may be sure to end with effectively worded statements.

You are urged to complete the **Speech Planner** as part of your preparation for your speech. If you need some help in preparing the **Speech Planner,** don't hesitate to ask your instructor. But at this point you should be planning your own speech on the basis of your own background. If you're not sure how to fill in all the points on the **Speech Planner,** do your best; later you'll get detailed instructions on outlining a speech. Here, we're just introducing you to this outlining approach to designing a speech.

Because the **Speech Planner** is just for your own planning, you may need additional copies; you are encouraged to make photocopies of the form if you need them.

"Most people have ears, but few have judgment; tickle those ears, and depend on it, you will catch those judgments, such as they are."

Lord Chesterfield,
English statesman and author.

SPEECH PLANNER: SPEECH 1—DEMONSTRATION

INSTRUCTIONS: Complete the following form.

Speech purpose: After hearing my speech, the audience will be able to _____

_____

   I. Introduction

      A.   Attention-getter:

      B.   Preview (subject and why it is important):

   II. Discussion

      A.   First step:

        1. (Example, illustration, technique, etc.)

        2.

      (Etc.)

      B.   Second step:

        1.

        2.

      (Etc.)

      C.   Third step:

        1.

        2.

      (Etc.)

      (Additional steps?)

  III. Conclusion

      A.   Review (summarize steps):

      B.   Memorable statement:

SAMPLE SPEECH PLANNER (OUTLINE) FOR A DEMONSTRATION SPEECH

Speech purpose: After hearing my speech, the audience will be able to identify the 4 main types of sailboats.

I. Introduction
   A. It seems strange that here in one of the world's most beautiful seaports, with hundreds of boats sailing in and out each month, few of the local residents can tell one sailboat from another.
   B. Here is an easy 3-step way to identify sailboats. This ability can make you a kind of local expert.

II. Discussion
   A. First step: count the masts
      1. If 1 mast: sloop (SHOW PHOTO)
         a. Most frequently seen
         b. Usually 2 sails: main, jib
         c. Story of inlander asking if boat drying laundry (sails)
      2. A few rare other boats have 1 mast: catboat, dinghy
         a. Open, little gear
         b. Carried on car top or on trailer
   B. Second step: check height of masts if more than 1
      1. If 2nd (aft, rear) mast taller: schooner (SHOW PHOTO)
         a. Typical old movie pirate ship
         b. Rare today
         c. Story of *TeVega* wrecked
      2. If 2nd mast shorter: 2 possible types of boats, so go to
   C. Third step: check location of aft mast
      1. If forward of steering, waterline, or rudder: ketch (SHOW PHOTO)
      2. If farther aft: yawl (SHOW PHOTO)
      3. Confusing even to old salts
      4. Sometimes hard to tell even when close broadside
      5. For cruising mostly

III. Conclusion
   A. Follow these 3 steps to identify most sailboats:
      1. Count masts: if 1—sloop
      2. Check mast heights: if aft taller—schooner
      3. Check mast location: forward—ketch; after—yawl
   B. By remembering this simple process, you'll stand out over many people who have spent their entire lives here on the coast and still can't tell one sailboat from another.

Now that you've completed—or at least got some of your ideas down on—the **Speech Planner,** it is time to move into detailed preparation of your speech.

The next page is a **Check-off Tip Sheet** for your demonstration speech. As you complete each tip, check it off. That will give you a visual presentation of what you still need to do to prepare this speech.

You need not do these points in the order presented. Rather, read through all of the points first, then check each off as you complete it.

Write "NA"—meaning "Not Applicable"—in front of any item you are convinced does not need to be included in your speech or in planning for your speech. However, only a very few of the items should be so marked. If you're marking quite a few as "NA," you should rethink your planning or perhaps your selection of your subject to ensure that you are preparing an appropriate demonstration speech.

Objective

After completing each item of this guide, you should have prepared an effective demonstration speech.

Again, we are defining an effective demonstration speech as one that gets at least 80 percent of your audience (your classmates) to do something that they could not do before your speech and that "something" is relevant, valuable, and significant to them.

DEMONSTRATION—SPEECH #1: CHECK-OFF TIP SHEET

INSTRUCTIONS: Check off each item as you prepare your speech

Speech purpose: After hearing my speech, the audience will be able to _____

_____

1. CONTENT

_____ 1.1.   Informs audience how to do something, not how something is done

_____ 1.2.   Is appropriate for audience and speaking time

_____ 1.3.   Uses visual aid: actual item, model, drawing

_____ 1.4.   When appropriate, provides audience with materials for practice

_____ 1.5.   When appropriate, shows item in various stages of preparation

_____ 1.6.   When appropriate, has someone in audience help

_____ 1.7.   When appropriate, leads audience in practice

_____ 1.8.   Includes personal stories and examples

2. ORGANIZATION

_____ 2.1.   Begins with effective attention-getter

_____ 2.2.   States exactly what audience is to learn to do

_____ 2.3.   Presents step-by-step explanation of how to do it

_____ 2.4.   Presents steps in the logical order of doing them

_____ 2.5.   Details each step with specific data

_____ 2.6.   Concludes by reviewing each step briefly, in order

_____ 2.7.   Closes with memorable statement

3. DELIVERY

_____ 3.1.   Steps up to speak with confidence and authority

_____ 3.2.   Gets set before starting to speak

_____ 3.3.   Establishes contact with audience before speaking

_____ 3.4   Begins without referring to notes

_____ 3.5   Maintains contact with audience

_____ 3.6   Sounds conversational, not read or memorized

_____ 3.7.   3 × 5-inch note cards limits

_____ 3.8.   Refers to note cards only occasionally

_____ 3.9.   Avoids *ah, so, ya know, well, 'kay,* etc.

_____ 3.10.   Stops at end of idea: doesn't hook sentences together with *and, and ah,* etc.

_____ 3.11.   Maintains good posture: doesn't lean, cross legs, etc.

_____ 3.12.   Doesn't play with notes, pencil, clothes, etc.

_____ 3.13.   Dresses to help, not hinder, speech

_____ 3.14.   Speaks loudly enough to be heard easily

4. PREPARATION

_____ 4.1.   **Speech Planner** completed

_____ 4.2.   Note cards prepared

_____ 4.3.   Speech practiced three to six times

_____ 4.4.   Tape recordings made of two practices

_____ 4.5.   Recording listened to objectively

_____ 4.6.   Use of visual aid practiced

_____ 4.7.   Speech timed

_____ 4.8.   Speech not written out word for word

_____ 4.9.   Speech not memorized

PRESENTING A SPEECH IN CLASS

INSTRUCTIONS:
1. Complete the information asked for at the top of the **Evaluation Form** on page 107.
2. Put that **Evaluation Form** inside your **Diagnosis Folder,** which you prepared in Lesson 1.
3. Before class begins on the day that you are to speak, give your **Diagnosis Folder,** with the **Evaluation Form** inside, to your instructor.
4. At the end of the class period in which you speak, pick up the folder and form from your instructor.
5. Remember: your instructor may give you other instructions on using *Evaluation Forms,* and of course you should follow them.

Early in the course, your instructor will establish a procedure for you to sign up for the specific day on which you'll present your speech.

After you present your speech, you'll receive comments about its effectiveness. Those comments may be in any one—or, more likely, a combination of—five forms:

1. *Check marks* on the rating scale—pluses ("+") to indicate your strengths, minuses ("−") to suggest criteria you need to improve on.

   Only those points that your instructor feels are most important to YOU will be marked. That is, not every point on the form will be checked. Thus, you may well receive evaluations on different points than some of your classmates will be evaluated on.

   You can assume that on the points not marked you were probably adequate, about average, or equal to the average of the points that *were* marked.
2. *Written suggestions* on the back of the **Speech Evaluation Form.** Examples: "Your use of the visual was especially effective." "Try to speak up just a bit louder." "Good examples of how your audience can benefit from your demonstration."
3. *Spoken suggestions from your instructor*—during class, right after you speak, or perhaps at the end of the class period, after all students speaking that day have completed their talks.
4. *Spoken suggestions from your classmates*—many instructors encourage general class discussion of at least some student speeches.
5. *Individual conference* with your instructor.

One of the biggest concerns of many students in speech classes is that the comments they'll get will concentrate on the weaknesses in their speeches. The fact is that most students give pretty good speeches right from their first in-class talks. And most instructors know that students learn more—become better speakers faster—from comments emphasizing the strengths in students' speeches rather than from comments about their weaknesses. Most instructors will point out, say, four or five positive, effective qualities in your speeches and only two or so weaknesses. Most of your fellow speech students will also probably quickly recognize the value of positive feedback and their comments, too, will most likely be generally encouraging.

But it seems to be the nature of most of us to *hear* more—worry more, concentrate more—about the negative feedback. You need to be objective in receiving comments about your speeches; don't let some minor, casual comment destroy or reduce your self-image. Talk with your instructor and the other students in your class individually—out of class, privately—to be sure you understand their comments and realize the significance of their evaluations. Most important, you need to be sure you know—especially from your instructor—exactly what action you can take to capitalize on your strengths and perhaps minimize some of your weaknesses.

Alert! ➤ **GRADING:** *NOT* every criterion on your **Evaluation Form** will be graded. Usually just three to five of your major strengths will be marked with a "+" (plus sign). Those criteria on which you should work to improve will be marked with a "−" (a minus sign). Criteria not marked are equal to whatever grade you earned on your speech.

The following guides are the basis on which I assign grades to speeches. Your instructor may use other guides, and of course you should follow them.

A means superior content, outstanding organization, and distinctive delivery. An *A* speech gets almost everyone in the audience thinking, excited, concerned, really wanting to hear more, read more, and *do* something about what you said. And most in the audience remember most of what you said.

B means significant content, good organization, and memorable delivery.

C means pertinent content, adequate organization, and clear delivery. A *C* speech is . . . OK, pleasant, nice, harmless. This is the speech you've heard so many times already—and you'll hear hundreds more during your lifetime. The audience listens, at least now and then. Sometimes they hear some little point that is new, creative, something they have not heard or thought about before. But most of the speech is dull, often repetitious, could have been said in about half the time. When it is over, most in the audience are left with the feeling "So what?" A couple of hours later, few can remember much more than the general subject the speaker almost had in mind.

Evaluating speeches is a delicate process. Your speech instructor will no doubt give you additional guides on how he or she will evaluate your speeches.

Representative Maxine Waters . . .

. . . is perhaps the most outspoken speaker in Congress.

She "brings to her work a wrath that is almost palpable, and an insistence that she will assert herself regardless of protocol," according to *The Almanac of American Politics 1996.*

Democrat Waters says, "I don't have time to be polite." Still, she does get results.

While in the California legislature she led passage of bills covering minority rights, women's rights, tenants' rights, limits on police strip searches, and more. While in Congress she has focused on Community Reinvestment Act racial quotas, job training and counseling for unemployed young men 17 to 30, a Center for Women Veterans within the Department of Veterans Affairs, preference to low-income veterans in purchasing foreclosed properties, and more.

Representative Waters was born August 31, 1938, in St. Lewis, Missouri, moved to California in 1961, raised two children while working in a garment factory, and earned her degree in sociology at California State University.

After the infamous 1965 Watts riot in Los Angeles, she became an assistant Head Start teacher. In 1976 she won a seat in the California Assembly and since then has risen rapidly to become "probably the most prominent freshman in the 102nd Congress" according to Internet biography in *Politics Now.*

DEMONSTRATION SPEECH—SPEECH 1: EVALUATION FORM

INSTRUCTIONS: Complete the top section of this form, put it in your **Diagnosis Folder,** and give the folder to your instructor on the day you are to speak.

Speaker: _____   Audience: Speech class   Date: _____

Speech purpose: After hearing my speech, the audience will be able to _____

_____

1. CONTENT

_____ 1.1. Informs audience how to do something, not how something is done
_____ 1.2. Is appropriate for audience and speaking time
_____ 1.3. Uses visual aid: actual item, model, drawing
_____ 1.4. When appropriate, provides audience with materials for practice
_____ 1.5. When appropriate, shows item in various stages of preparation
_____ 1.6. When appropriate, has someone in audience help
_____ 1.7. When appropriate, leads audience in practice
_____ 1.8. Includes personal stories and examples

2. ORGANIZATION

_____ 2.1. Begins with effective attention-getter
_____ 2.2. States exactly what audience is to learn to do
_____ 2.3. Presents step-by-step explanation of how to do it
_____ 2.4. Presents steps in the logical order of doing them
_____ 2.5. Details each step with specific data
_____ 2.6. Concludes by reviewing each step briefly, in order
_____ 2.7. Closes with memorable statement

3. DELIVERY

_____ 3.1. Steps up to speak with confidence and authority
_____ 3.2. Gets set before starting to speak
_____ 3.3. Establishes contact with audience before speaking
_____ 3.4. Begins without referring to notes
_____ 3.5. Maintains contact with audience
_____ 3.6. Sounds conversational, not read or memorized
_____ 3.7. 3×5-inch note cards limits
_____ 3.8. Refers to note cards only occasionally
_____ 3.9. Avoids *ah, so, ya know, well, 'kay,* etc.
_____ 3.10. Stops at end of idea; doesn't hook sentences together with *and, and ah,* etc.
_____ 3.11. Maintains good posture; doesn't lean, cross legs, etc.
_____ 3.12. Doesn't play with pencil, notes, clothes, etc.
_____ 3.13. Dresses to help, not hinder, speech
_____ 3.14. Speaks loudly enough to be heard easily

Over for comments

4. COMMENTS:

Grade: _____

ASSIGNMENT 7. DEMONSTRATION SPEECH: SELF-EVALUATION

 ACTION: Submit a self-evaluation of your first speech.

OBJECTIVE:
On completion of this assignment, you should have a very specific basis on which to build your improvement in public speaking.

INSTRUCTIONS:
Please write on computer, typing, or binder paper an answer to each of the following questions. Be brief, but specific; that is, give examples, particulars. The questions are, you will note, restatements of objectives for this lesson.

1. List at least three of your major strengths as a public speaker.
2. List at least three of your major weaknesses as a public speaker.
3. Describe the feelings you experienced and the actions you displayed that revealed your confidence as a speaker and those that revealed your concerns about speaking in public.
4. Do you now feel more comfortable—less concerned and more confident—about your potential as a speaker? What has helped you feel this way? How might you be helped to be still more at ease about your speaking?

To answer these questions, draw from the following sources for specifics:

1. Your tape recordings of your speech.
2. Your own thinking back to your designing and delivering of your speech.
3. Your previous experiences in speaking.
4. Comments of your fellow classmates after you gave your speech.
5. The **Evaluation Form** on the speech your instructor may have completed.

Turn in this self-evaluation to your instructor for comments and suggestions that may help you further.

Now, with your first formal speech in this course completed, you're ready to move on to study more sophisticated details of designing and delivering a speech.

"Have something intelligent to say" is the single most important element of an effective speech, according to *Garrison Keillor,* humorist, host of the syndicated radio show *A Prairie Home Companion,* and best-selling author.

L E S S O N 5

Selecting Speech Subjects

OBJECTIVES ▶ Complete this lesson and you'll be able to:

1. Name the three main aspects, and at least four factors for each aspect, that should be included in a useful analysis of a speaking situation.
2. Write a useful analysis of any speaking situation you might face.
3. Use analyses of speaking situations to select appropriate subjects for your speeches.
4. Select appropriate subjects for your speeches.

RELEVANCE ▶ The *last* place to start looking for subjects for your speeches is the library. Some students, with a speech coming due, wander through the library stacks, hoping they'll stumble on an interesting topic. Occasionally some do. But a speech should be more than a report on an interesting article or a fascinating book.

A speech should present the speaker's own views or interpretations. Certainly a speech can include facts and ideas from minds other than the speaker's. Of course, most

SELECTING YOUR SPEECH SUBJECT:

"You're halfway there [in planning your speech] once you decide that you know what you're going to talk about. The rest is just putting it together."
Barbara Jordan, Professor at the University of Texas and former Congresswoman, wrote that in her book *Barbara Jordan, a Self-Portrait.*

speakers need to research for additional details to document or explain their ideas. But the first—the MAIN—source for your speech subjects should be your own mind. After you've picked a speech subject from your own interests, experiences, findings, background, then—and only then—should you start research.

We get into situations in which we are to give speeches either because we volunteer or because someone else asks or orders us to. In either case, we usually select the subjects for our speeches pretty casually, often without much real thought.

This lesson will teach you how to select the subjects for your speeches on the basis of logical thought and planning.

The need for such planning is clear-cut. Consider the situation in which you are asked—or required—to give a speech.

Many beginning speakers are surprised to learn that the typical invitation or order to give a speech very often does NOT give them much of an idea of exactly what they are to speak about. Many invitations to speak are worded something like this:

> "So that was a pretty good conference you went to, huh? Tell you what—why don't you give a little talk to our group about it. OK?"

"OK?" Sure, you'll speak; can't turn down the boss. But what EXACTLY are you to talk about? What should be the point, the view, the emphasis of your speech? Start a list of what you might cover in your speech and you'll quickly realize you've got a problem. Jot down a few of the possibilities here:

1. _____
2. _____
3. _____

Some of the possible subjects your speech might cover are:

1. What happened at the conference
2. What you learned about what other companies are doing
3. What you found out about new equipment
4. Ways your company needs to improve
5. How your company is ahead of others
6. Problems that may be coming
7. The value of the conference
8. Why the entire staff should attend the next conference . . .

Sometimes you're asked or told to give a speech with even less of a basis on which to select your subject. In the previous example, you at least had the advantage of having been to a conference and having been asked to speak "about it." But you may be asked to give a speech and be left entirely on your own to select your subject. Consider these examples:

▶ You're new at school, a new member of a club, new in the community or on the job, and you're asked, "Tell us something about yourself." Do you talk about:

Why you're here?

Where you came from?

What you've done in the past?

Your plans for the future?

. . . ?

- You've helped develop an innovative plan or product, and you are asked or directed to give a speech about it. Do you talk about:

  Its importance?
  The need for it?
  How it came about?
  Its main features?
  ALL that? (Too much to cover?)
  . . . ?

- You are taking a class, belong to an organization, attend a church, or are participating in some such group in which the instructor or leader assigns or expects you to make an oral report, be a member of a discussion panel, make a presentation, give a talk or speech.

Remember, in those examples you were asked or told to give a speech. Now consider typical situations in which you volunteer to speak.

- You're unhappy with a decision made by the student council, the city staff, or the leaders of some organization, and you feel you just have to speak up to try to get a change.
- You've made a trip, attended a meeting, taken part in an event, or helped on a project, and you want to share your experience with others.
- You have information you believe other people need—about your hobbies, jobs, experiences, studies, interests, whatever—and you offer to speak about what you know.
- You've had a funny or unusual experience, or you are able to look at a situation and draw humor from it, and you are moved to entertain people with a speech about your observations, comments, feelings, ideas, reactions.

Since the subjects for our speeches come from situations in which we find ourselves, many speakers simply say to themselves, "Well, what I'd like to, or have to, tell them is. . . ." Thus the subject of a speech is often selected in a pretty casual, unstructured manner.

Here's how to make such decisions—how to select subjects for your speeches.

ANALYZE THE SPEAKING SITUATION

There are three aspects of a speaking situation that should be analyzed. They are:

1. Audience
2. Occasion
3. Speaker

Several factors need to be considered for each aspect.

1. Audience

1.1. Experience and Knowledge of Subject

What can you assume the audience knows about the subject of your speech before you speak to them?

For example, a speech about some aspect of migration would—should—be different to a group of recently arrived residents than to a group of law makers. That does *not* mean you'd take a different stand. It does mean that you should probably select different data—statistics, examples, stories, etc.—and perhaps a different emphasis, points, reasons, logic.

Why? Because of the different knowledge of the subject held by the two audiences.

The point is that your speech should be designed to build on your audience's previous knowledge about your subject. There is no point for you to simply present information the audience already has. Thus, your job is to try to determine just what knowledge about your subject your audience—at least most individuals in your audience—probably has before you stand up to speak.

Probably the best source for information about your audience is the person who invited you to speak. Ask him or her what the group may already know about the subject. Have they had other speakers on the same topic? Do they have a study or action committee concerned with the subject? What made them ask you to speak on that subject? Are there experts on the subject in the group? And . . . well, you get the idea.

If the group you are to speak to is a chapter or part of some national association, you can get an idea of the audience's knowledge of your subject from their national activity, interest, emphasis, or concern about your topic. The group might have a regular publication—a monthly magazine, for example—you could skim to get an insight into what members might already know or think about the subject.

Further, there might have been news reports about the group that could give you an indication of the members' knowledge of your topic. They might have sponsored a recent clinic or workshop on the topic, which you might read about.

Certainly, when speaking to governmental agencies, for example, you need to know how members voted in previous considerations of problems related to your topic. News reports may be good sources for such information. Or look up the official minutes of public agencies before you speak to them.

You might be planning to speak to the board of your college, trying to get them to provide more stands for parking bikes. You should know, as you plan your speech, how the board voted on other such expenditures and how paying for the stands would be decided by the board. Many speakers often lose acceptance of their proposals by taking the attitude that how to finance their recommendations is not their concern, and so they leave that part of the decision out of their speeches. There is no easier way for an agency to refuse a proposal than to say that they endorse the idea, but without financing recommendations, the proposal just can't be accepted now. If you know such facts about your audiences as you start to plan your speeches, your presentations can include those points and thereby be more successful.

1.2. Attitude Toward Subject

Before you speak, is your audience for your viewpoint or against it? Are their minds already made up or are they there to really listen to what may be a different point of view? Will they be favorable, neutral, or hostile toward your subject, toward your opinion?

Suppose you were to speak to a group of police officers to present your views on one side or the other of legalizing marijuana. And suppose that you found out, after you'd accepted the invitation to speak to them, that at their last meeting they'd already voted to take an official, group position on the subject. Your speech, to be effective at all, would indeed have to take into consideration whether they voted for or against your viewpoint.

Again, that difference in your speech would not be a change of your view, but a change in how you present your view and what you use to support that view, as determined by the audience's attitude toward your speech subject.

1.3. Attitude Toward Speaker

Do you think you'll have the audience's respect, that they'll be ready to believe you, as you start to talk? Or will you have to overcome some antagonism against you?

For example, if you're 5'5" and weigh 200 pounds, you'll have difficulty overcoming their doubt about you if your speech subject is how to get into good physical condition. On the other hand, if you weighed 300 pounds a few months ago, they just might listen to you.

1.4. Occupation

If the audience is made up mostly of structural engineers or elementary school teachers or travel agents or any other group that would have experiences, education, and interests in common, your speech can build on the audience's common background.

On the other hand, many audiences are composed of people with a wide variety of occupations. This makes it more difficult for you to pick a specific speech subject and material that would appeal to, or build on, the common backgrounds of your listeners. Consider these questions:

What's an occupation that perhaps all, or most, of your audience might have that would make it difficult for you to give a speech for requiring all cars to get at least 40 miles per gallon of gas? _____

What's an occupation that would make an audience be rather receptive to a speech on that same subject? _____

Think through your answers. Are they based on any facts or actual specific experiences you may have had with such audiences? Or might your judgment be based on just one or two experiences with just one or a few members or that occupation? Decide for yourself; do you really have enough information about that occupation, about that audience, to make such a judgment? What additional facts might you need? Most important, how could you get them? Well, how could you?

Suppose you were to speak on one side or the other on year-round schools to the Parent-Teacher Association of the junior high school nearest your home. How could you get information about their occupations so you could design a better speech?

_____

_____

Well, you could ask questions of whoever invited you to speak. You could telephone, or call on, the president of the group. You could ask someone you may know who is a member. You could read a few copies of the state and the national PTA magazines.

The point is—yes, you do need to dig around for specific answers to such questions as these if you are to design an effective speech.

1.5. Economic Status

By this stage, I rather imagine you yourself can start identifying some of the factors that are part of an audience analysis.

For instance, how would the economic status of your audience influence your design of a speech on capital punishment?

Specifically, if you were to speak to a low-income audience, how might their economic status influence your speech design? _____

_____

_____

_____

If you were speaking to a high-income audience, how might their economic status influence your speech design?_____

_____

_____

_____

In answering those questions, you may have already begun to think about the next point. Would not you and I agree that while we may make a few tentative, partially correct generalizations about different attitudes of low-income and high-income audiences concerning educational standards, economic status is not really a clear-cut indication of an audience's position on this subject?

But suppose you were speaking on the need for revisions of tax laws. Then the differences in economic status would be much more relevant, rather clear-cut, and more important to the design of your speech.

Consider the capital gains allowance—a special tax arrangement for those wealthy enough to take high risks in investing, on the chance they will get greater income if their investments are successful. Such special tax allowances are indeed looked on differently by high-income and low-income audiences. High-income listeners often believe such tax breaks are needed if there are to be sources of money to develop new products, companies, etc. Low-income listeners may look on the capital gains allowance as a loophole through which those with money do not have to pay some of their taxes.

On the other hand, some audiences might feel that investment money should come from the government, not from individuals, while still others would point out that government money in fact comes from individuals. Hence, attitudes of audiences are often complex, conflicting, and confusing.

Yet without knowing at least a little about the basis of an audience's background—in this case, about their economic status—you may well be presenting a speech that has little chance for success.

1.6. Educational Status

Are all or most of your listeners college graduates? High school students? Do they have about the same education you have? Or considerably more? Or less?

The point should be obvious that you'd use different examples, different wording, different emphasis if you were talking about your views on employment opportunities to a group of junior high school dropouts as compared with speaking to seniors in college.

Again, this is not to suggest that you should change your point of view according to who is in your audience. Rather, this is to urge you to consider your audience very carefully, to ensure that your speech will include material, ideas, examples, and stories appropriate to their education.

1.7. Cultural Status

Are most in your audience likely to be regular readers of such magazines as *The New Yorker, Atlantic, Harper's?* Or might they usually read *National Enquirer* or *Modern Romances?*

Do they watch television every night or attend the latest foreign film screening every Friday?

1.8. Ethnicity

Probably the most important factor to consider in analyzing an audience is ethnicity—the shared background of people who are of a particular heritage, race, religion, nationality, or such.

More than one out every four Americans is non-White. If all your audiences were "average," 13 percent would be Black, 11 percent Hispanic, 4 percent Asian and Pacific Islanders, 1 percent American Indian, Eskimo, and Eleuts.

Of course it is extremely doubtful that any of your audiences will ever be exactly "average." Often you'll be speaking to groups that are mostly of one ethnic group or another. More frequently, your audiences will be of diverse backgrounds.

But you need to consider your listeners' ethnicity quite carefully. For example, suppose you were planning a speech about traveling abroad. If your listeners were mostly college students who had never been out of the United States before, your speech should of course be quite different from the speech you would delivery to college students who had come to your school from different countries.

1.9. Sex

An all-male audience? All-female? Or a mixed group?

Again it should be obvious that if you were speaking to men about to go to a military base overseas you could—should—use examples, emphasis, and strength of wording different from those for a group of Girl Scout leaders.

1.10. Age

Are your listeners young? Old? Middle-aged? Varied? What range of ages might you expect in your audience? You might be talking about traveling in Europe, and if your audience is mostly senior citizens, they can't be expected to be receptive to a speech about how to select youth hostels.

1.11. Number

Will your audience be a small group or a large gathering?

With a small audience, you may decide it would be more effective to create an informal speaking situation, to present your speech as you sit in a circle with them. On the other hand, you may want to present yourself as one who strictly observes existing laws. Then you might take a rather formal stance before the audience, using a lectern most or all of the time, structuring the speech with rather formal, specific points, using data that are largely not from personal experience but from available research, quotations of authorities, etc.

Your job, then, is to get as much information about your audience as you can, so you can design a speech that effectively utilizes the audience's background to achieve your speaking purpose.

Review

We have now completed a list of 11 details of the audience that should be considered in an analysis of a speaking situation. You still have—remember how many more?—two more aspects to an analysis of a speaking situation. They are:

1. Audience

2. _____

3. _____

Got them? If in doubt, turn back a few pages to where we listed them just before we started studying this section. Find them? Good.

But we urge you to check back anyway to be sure that your responses above are correct and to reinforce your learning. The answers: audience, occasion, speaker.

Now, here are the points you need to consider in your analysis of the occasion.

2. Occasion

2.1. Purpose of Meeting

Is it a business occasion, a community conference, a celebration of a holiday or anniversary, or a cultural event?

Will the audience take a vote to establish their position as a group for or against your subject after you speak? I've even spoken to a group—county educators in southern California—that had voted to take a position on the subject of my talk, educational television, just *before* I was introduced to speak. To know *that* while I was planning my speech certainly would have influenced what I intended to say. Indeed, it probably would have influenced my decision even to bother to speak there.

2.2. Location

Will you be speaking in a typical classroom? A meeting hall, dining room, auditorium, small conference room?

Is the location noted for any historic or symbolic event that you might refer to in your speech? For example, our city council meets in the same room in which the state's first constitution was signed. This gives speakers who are proposing a variety of new programs, ideas, or plans the opportunity to note in their speeches something such as "a major, historic, new step was taken in this very room well over 100 years ago, and now, tonight, you council members have the opportunity to take another significant step forward...." I'm sure that such historic references can easily be overused and overemphasized. Yet it is an approach that many speakers do seem to find effective at times.

2.3. Facilities

Will there be a lectern? Public address system? Chalkboard? Chairs set in rows or chairs you can have moved into a circle, for example, for a more informal speaking situation?

Will the room be air-conditioned? If your speech is given late in the summer, will that air conditioner make the room uncomfortably cool for your audience? Will it be noisy, making it hard for your audience to hear you?

What other facilities—equipment, furniture, seating, and such—could influence the effectiveness of your speech?

2.4. Time of Day and Amount of Time for Speech

Will you speak to the group at the end of their work day, when they're tired and eager to get home?

Most faculty meetings are after school, with many of the teachers often thinking about how they're going to get those papers graded for first period tomorrow and what they're going to have for dinner. Yet this is often the time they have their planning sessions and have guest speakers—you, a student, or an educational consultant trying to present some new idea.

And how long do you have to speak? Will you have only 5 minutes in which your points must be clear-cut, specific, direct? Or do you have 20 minutes or more, so you can be more detailed and comprehensive in your presentation?

2.5. Other Events

Will there be a business meeting, with financial reports, voting on whether or not to send a delegate to some meeting, and other details to be considered by your audience at the same meeting at which you are to speak?

Will there be entertainment?

In essence, are there other things on the program that, if presented before your speech, may set a mood that either enhances or detracts from the potential effectiveness of your speech?

Or after your speech might there be a tempting highlight-announcement of the winner of a drawing, selection of a delegate to a conference in Hawaii—that could keep the audience tuned out of your speech, looking forward to its ending?

2.6. After Your Speech

Will there be questions from the audience? Other speakers presenting the opposite viewpoint? A fine dinner they all want to get to as soon as you're finished speaking?

Will they vote after your speech to officially endorse your proposal? Will they vote immediately after you speak or at some subsequent meeting? All these should, of course, influence what you decide to say in your speech.

You've just completed studying a list of the six items to be analyzed about the *occasion* in which you are to give a speech. The occasion, you'll remember, is one of the three aspects of a speaking situation that you are urged to analyze in order to determine your speech subject. The occasion was the second aspect you've studied; earlier in this lesson you studied the first aspect, the audience. Now, what's the third, the final, aspect of a speaking situation that should be analyzed?

Right—it's the . . .

3. Speaker

3.1 Knowledge of Subject

Do you know enough about the subject? Can you find all the additional information you might need?

For example, I have my own opinion on legalizing marijuana. It is not a snap decision; I came to it after considerable reading, talking to a few doctors, and listening to a great many students, some of whom had—and some who claimed they had—used marijuana.

But I do not have enough knowledge of the subject to give a speech. I could research it—dig out what I have read before in *Time* and some FBI reports a police science teacher lent to me and talk again to people who have used marijuana. But after all that research, it would still not be *my* subject; while I have my opinions, they are, at this time at least, not firm enough to be presented in a speech.

3.2. Time to Prepare

Students in speech courses often give the impression that they are the only speakers who have time pressures when speeches are due. Not so.

Even the president of the United States, as he and his staff prepare a speech, has a deadline; he must be ready when the time comes for that address to Congress, speech to a conference, or such.

You should agree to give a speech only after you've made a realistic estimate of the time you'll need, adding, say, 25 percent as a safety factor, and considered your other obligations. If you don't have time to prepare properly, you might consider asking for a later date or not giving the speech at all. But in a classroom or in real life, you rarely have the luxury of putting off a scheduled speech. Better simply get to work.

3.3. Interest in Subject

Do you really want to talk on the subject you've selected, been assigned, or been invited to present? If not, you may well be in trouble.

Of all the guides to effective speaking, one rule stands out as most hazardous to break:

> **YOU MUST BE SINCERELY INTERESTED IN THE SUBJECT OF YOUR OWN SPEECH**

It is true that some very polished professionals can fake interest—act as if they were interested in a subject in which they really are not. The greatest opportunity for this is in the field of delivering radio and television commercials. Yet professional after professional has repeated time and again—in personal interviews, trade meetings, business conferences, and such—that he or she actually uses every product. Many announcers insist on touring the company, talking to sales personnel, even interviewing customers, before announcing for a new product.

Certainly not all announcers and professional sales speakers are that meticulous. But many are. The reason: With such a background of information about the product, they can communicate much more effectively a sincere interest in it.

3.4. Reputation and Credentials

Are you, or will you be during and right after your speech, accepted by your audience as knowledgeable or as an authority on the subject?

Many student speakers respond, "I'm not an authority on anything!" But is that true? Certainly some rather detailed research on the problems of atomic power plants will not make you an authority. But are you not now—or couldn't you easily, quickly become—an authority on your own feelings, impressions, attitudes toward or against the need for atomic power plants?

Your credentials, your reputation for having your ideas accepted might include experience during a summer trip, training on a job, participation in a hobby, reading, studying, and such.

In other words, sticking to subjects you are already informed on—your hobbies, trips, personal experiences—is one general field of speech subjects on which you indeed do have your own personal reputation. Further, you more than anyone else, have a reputation as the authority on your own ideas, views, feelings, attitudes, and opinions.

These, then—subjects that are yours already—should be the basis of your speeches. Then you can add to your basic fund of information through additional reading, studying, observing, and research. But you should avoid speaking on subjects about which you cannot be considered to be at least somewhat authoritative.

Review:

Now let's reinforce your learning of these points.

We've established that there are three aspects of a speaking situation that you should analyze in order to have a basis on which to select the subject of your speech. What are those aspects?

1. _____
2. _____
3. _____

If you're in doubt, check back over the last few pages to find the correct responses.

If you're sure you know them—after writing them down in the blanks above—then check back over the last few pages anyway to confirm and to reinforce your learning of them.

In the objectives at the beginning of the lesson, we said you would be able to name at least four factors to be analyzed for each of the three aspects. Try listing them.

Audience

(1)_____
(2)_____
(3)_____
(4)_____

Occasion

(1)_____
(2)_____
(3)_____
(4)_____

Speaker

(1)_____
(2)_____
(3)_____
(4)_____

How well did you do?

Actually, you were presented with 11 factors to be analyzed about your audience, 6 factors about the occasion, and 4 factors about yourself as a speaker. That's total of 21 items, so remembering just 12 of them (4 for each aspect) seems like a realistic task.

Check your answers by referring to the previous pages as often as you may need until you can write them out correctly, without referring back.

Your next objective in this lesson is to be able to write out an effective, useful analysis of a speaking situation.

ASSIGNMENT 8. ANALYSIS OF SPEAKING SITUATION

 ACTION: Submit an Analysis of Speaking Situation for your next speech.

OBJECTIVE:

After completing this assignment, you should be able to prepare an analysis of a speaking situation that would be of value in helping you design your speeches. Specifically, your analysis will help you determine:

1. Your exact speech subject
2. Your specific purpose in speaking
3. The main ideas you'll present
4. The data you'll include
5. Your style of delivery

INSTRUCTIONS:

1. Complete the four pages of **Analysis of Speaking Situation** on the form that appears within a few pages.
2. Prepare the analysis for use in designing your next speech. It will ask you to speak to your classmates as if they were some other specific audience; your speech is to try to achieve a specific purpose with that particular audience.

    If additional details about that next speech assignment would help you prepare this analysis, check the specifics for it, which are presented at the end of the next lesson.
3. Be sure to assume a *specific* audience—and an audience other than your speech class.
4. Submit your analysis to your instructor for evaluation.

SUGGESTIONS:

> BE SPECIFIC IN YOUR RESPONSES

1. On the first line, "Audience," state *exactly* the name of the group about which you are preparing this analysis. Do *not* name a general audience such as "local businessmen."

    Identify a particular group, such as "Monterey Small Business Association" or "San Francisco Small Business Association." It should be obvious that your analysis of these two audiences should be different because of the different business problems, procedures, and services of the two distinct groups.

2. On the second line, state the *specific occasion* for which you are preparing the analysis. Is it a regular weekly luncheon meeting? Annual installation of officers? Opening of a new campaign for improved services? For each of these occasions, your analysis should reveal distinct features that would be important to keep in mind as you later prepare your speech.

3. The "Speaker," of course, is you.

4. "Subject" should establish a *specific topic,* not a broad, general area such as "sales" or "growth" or "new developments." Your statement of your proposed subject should be specific so that as you proceed through your analysis, your responses can relate back to just what it is you are intending to speak on.

   Remember that here you are naming a subject; later, on the basis of the completed analysis, you will establish a specific purpose for your speech.

   Possible specific subjects might be "How to Increase Sales," "Is Your Business Growing Too Fast?" or "New Developments for Saving Money for the Small Business."

5. In the details of your analysis, continue to be quite specific.

Now let's look at a sample of part of an effective analysis of a speaking situation. Note that the responses are specific, relevant, and insightful—yet brief.

Audience: Jefferson High School Multicultural Club
Occasion: Regular monthly meeting
Speaker: Matilda Gomez (student at nearby Charles College)
Subject: Should You Go to College?

1. Audience
   1.1. Experience, Knowledge of Subject:
      Most have been told often by parents, teachers, and friends that they should go to college, but they continue to wonder if college is for them.
   1.2. Attitude Toward Subject: Questioning, doubtful.
   1.3. Attitude Toward Speaker:
      Admiration, because she is—like most in the audience—a recent arrival in the area, came from a comparable background, and is a successful college student.

Well, you've got the idea. BE SPECIFIC.

Proceed now to complete the following form for an Analysis of Speaking Situation, using the audience you intend to speak to for your next speech. That will probably be your next speech in this course—Assignment 10. In general, that assignment asks you to present a speech in class designed as if you were to speak before some other, specific audience. You can pick any realistic audience and speak to them on any subject you consider appropriate. For further detailed instructions for that speech, you may want to skip ahead and study that assignment (page 125) before you prepare your **Analysis of Speaking Situation.**

Ebonics . . .

. . . also called Black English, Black Dialect, Black Idiom, African American Vernacular English, has been debated strongly from diverse viewpoints.

The word "ebonics" has been formed from "ebony" and "phonics." Examples of ebonics include: "He be here soon." "I'm not gonna do dat no more." "They in de store."

"The debate is interesting because it reflects the ideological division we have in this country between those who believe ethnic or racial minorities should totally assimilate into 'American' culture, and those who celebrate the ethnic diversity they view as constituting American society," said Dr. Steven Ybarrola, professor of anthropology, Central College, Pella, Iowa.

"Black English is a bonafied language system with its own rules of grammar, vocabulary, and structure," according to linguist Joycelyn Landrum-Brown. Others say it degrades established English and limits the achievement of its speakers.

"Supporters say the idea is to catch those students who don't fully comprehend mainstream English or tune out because they feel the language of their community is being ignored," wrote Michelle Locke, Associated Press reporter.

But critics don't like that idea. "It's a racist afront against people who have struggled for decades to be a part of the American fiber," said Steven Gooden, honorary youth chairperson at the Republican National Convention in San Diego.

"I don't want [Ebonics] to be an excuse to lower the standards for African American children," said California's Superintendent of Schools Delaine Eastin.

ANALYSIS OF SPEAKING SITUATION

❶ ACTION: Submit the following as part of the planning for your next speech.

Audience: _____

Occasion: _____

Speaker (your name): _____

Subject: _____

1. AUDIENCE

    1.1. Experience, knowledge of subject before you speak:

    1.2. Attitude toward subject before you speak:

    1.3. Attitude toward speaker before you speak:

    1.4. Occupation:

1.5. Economic status:

1.6. Educational status:

1.7. Cultural status:

1.8. Ethnicity:

1.9. Sex:

1.10. Age:

1.11. Number:

2. OCCASION

   2.1. Purpose of meeting:

   2.2. Location:

   2.3. Facilities:

   2.4. Time:

   2.5. Other events:

   2.6. What the audience will do after your speech:

3. SPEAKER

3.1. Knowledge of subject:

3.2: Time to prepare:

3.3. Interest in subject:

3.4. Your reputation and credentials:

Now that you've completed a detailed **Analysis of Speaking Situation,** you should be able to make such an analysis for the speeches you may give in the real world—outside this speech class—quite quickly and easily. For most speaking situations, you won't have to write out a complete analysis. All you usually will have to do is think through each point.

To help you analyze speaking situations you'll face in the future, you can use the **Check-off Tip Sheet** on the next page.

Importance of Speech

"Speech is civilization itself. The word, even the most contradictory word, preserves contact—it is silence which isolates."

German novelist *Thomas Mann* wrote that in his 1924 novel **The Magic Mountain.**

ANALYSIS OF SPEAKING SITUATION CHECK-OFF TIP SHEET

INSTRUCTIONS: To help ensure you consider all the relevant points, check off each of the following as you select a subject for a speech.

Possible Speech Subject: _____

_____

1. AUDIENCE

____   1.1.   Experience and knowledge of subject

____   1.2.   Attitude toward subject

____   1.3.   Attitude toward speaker

____   1.4.   Occupation

____   1.5.   Economic status

____   1.6.   Educational status

____   1.7.   Cultural status

____   1.8.   Ethnicity

____   1.9.   Sex

____   1.10. Age

____   1.11. Number

2. OCCASION

____   2.1.   Purpose of meeting

____   2.2.   Location

____   2.3.   Facilities

____   2.4.   Time

____   2.5.   Other events

____   2.6.   After your speech

3. SPEAKER

____   3.1.   Knowledge of subject

____   3.2.   Time to prepare

____   3.3.   Interest in subject

____   3.4.   Reputation and credentials

L E S S O N   6

Pinpointing Speech Purposes

OBJECTIVES ▶ After finishing this lesson, you will be able to:

1. Name the general purposes a speech might have.
2. Name the criteria for an effectively worded speech purpose.
3. Determine if a given speech purpose meets the criteria for an effectively worded speech purpose, and if not, state why.
4. Write effectively worded speech purposes.
5. Use effectively worded speech purposes as the basis for designing speeches.
6. Present in class a 4- to 5-minute speech that is:
    6.1. Based on an effectively worded purpose.
    6.2. Designed for an audience other than this class.
    6.3. Effective—that is, the speech incorporates at least 80 percent (i.e., 30) of the concepts and techniques studied in this course so far, the 38 points listed on the **Evaluation Form** for this speech.

SPEECH PURPOSE:

"Don't confuse what you want to achieve in giving the speech with your own motivation for doing so. 'What do I want the audience to do, feel or think as a result of hearing my speech?' Your answer to that question is your purpose."

That's the recommendation of television personality *Ed McMahon,* as stated in his book ***The Art of Public Speaking.***

 What do you consider the one most important step in designing speeches? Please state your opinion here: _____

_____

_____

Since your opinion was asked for, of course your reply is correct—you certainly know what your own view is. In MY opinion the single most important step in planning speeches is the title of this lesson: pinpointing your speech purpose.

Why is that so important? Because once you've figured out the specific purpose of a speech—*decided precisely what effect you want that speech to have on your listeners*—then ALL of your other decisions about the speech can be made on a rational, logical basis quickly and easily.

This lesson urges you—teaches you how—to design your speeches by using this 2-step process:

1. Pinpoint a specific, measurable purpose for the speech.
2. Use that specific purpose to make all other decisions about the speech—about its content, organization, and delivery.

Frankly, many students are not impressed with this concept the first time they meet it. I'm challenged frequently. Students growl, "What's the big deal about that?"

My reply tries to emphasize its value. "Learn that concept, accept it, and use it, and your speeches will be *greatly* improved. And designing your speeches will become almost a cinch."

Still students express doubt. "How can it be so important? It's so simple!"

"I didn't say it was difficult; I said it was important."

"But *why* is it important?"

"Because it gives you an objective, concrete, exact basis on which to determine everything—everything!—else about your speech."

"How?"

"Check the concept again. Two steps. First, you write out exactly what your speech is supposed to do *for your audience.* In other words, you describe—in words that can't be twisted or used to cover a lot of different points—just what your speech is to accomplish. That's the first step."

"And then?"

"Then you use that statement of your speech purpose as the basis for making all your remaining decisions about your speech. Every time you find a fact and wonder, 'Should I include this?' every time you try to figure out, 'Is this the best way to say this?' all you have to do is check it against your speech purpose. If the point you're wondering about will help you meet your speech purpose, include it in the speech. If what you're questioning does not contribute directly to the purpose of your speech, leave it out."

Students take time to think that over.

The skeptics soon hit me again.

"If that concept is so important and so simple and so clear as you seem to make it, don't most speakers already use it?"

"No, very few do."

"Why?"

"Because it's as much an attitude, an approach, as it is some hard, exact tool or technique for designing a speech."

That silences most doubters. For a moment. Then one student will express the thought of most.

"Huh?"

Pause.

"I said that what we're studying in this lesson is as much an attitude. . . ."

"I heard that. But what's it mean?"

Let's try it this way.

Human beings speak because they want some specific reaction from their listeners.

You say "Hi!" or "Hello" or some such greeting to a classmate, an instructor, or a friend because you want to obtain some particular response or result. Consider these examples:

- From the classmate, you may want a response to your "Hello" so that a conversation may be started that may lead to your getting the details for a class assignment you missed last week.
- You may express a greeting to an instructor as the first step in your campaign to get him or her to reconsider that low grade your received on your last report.
- Your purpose in saying "Hello" to the friend may be part of your effort to build a favorable image of yourself, preparatory to asking him or her for a date.

In every instance, we human beings speak only to achieve a purpose; we speak because we want to communicate something to someone.

What about when you're alone, working on your car, the wrench slips, a finger gets a good cut, and you yell, "Ouch!" or you swear or cry out, "Why won't this thing work?!?"

Still, we are really speaking with a purpose—to relieve tension or to express frustration. The only difference is that in this type of situation we are communicating for the purpose of having an effect only on ourselves.

So we all speak for some particular purpose.

What, then, are the purposes a speech might have?

GENERAL PURPOSES OF A SPEECH

These are the three general purposes a speech might have:

1. To inform
2. To persuade
3. To entertain

On the blank to the left of each of the following examples, name the general purpose the statement indicates the speaker had in mind.

_____ 1. The audience will be able to adjust a car so that greater gas mileage will be obtained.

_____ 2. The audience will enjoy some stories of my trip to Europe.

_____ 3. The audience will contribute to the college's scholarship fund.

_____ 4. The audience will be able to name three advantages of owning a sailboat.

_____ 5. The audience will vote for the next tax plan.

Answers:

1. To inform
2. To entertain
3. To persuade
4. To inform
5. To persuade

If you missed any of those purposes, think through each one again to try to figure out why this author classified each the way he did. The following, more detailed discussion of these general purposes should clarify your questions.

1. To Inform

"To inform" is your purpose in giving a speech when you want your audience to:

1. Acquire or improve a skill, their ability to do something.
2. Acquire knowledge of a subject new to them.
3. Learn more about or increase their understanding of a subject they already know something about.
4. To know something new to them.

Read carefully these examples of specific purposes for a speech to inform:

- To have the audience able to read correctly the danger symbols appearing on a navigational chart.
- To have the audience able to name three recent research findings about the impact of television commercials.
- To have the audience able to select a career appropriate to each individual based on five specific criteria.

In the first example, the purpose is to have the audience acquire a skill. In the second, the purpose is to have the audience learn something they presumably did not already know. In the third, additional information is being provided, on the assumption that each listener has already made at least some tentative selections of a career.

You could easily check the effectiveness of speeches given for each of those specific purposes by testing listeners on what they learned.

2. To Persuade

"To persuade" is your speech purpose when you want your audience to:

1. Modify or change their attitudes or opinions.
2. Accept or approve your point of view.
3. Be motivated to take some specific action.

Consider these examples of specific purposes for a speech to persuade:

- To have the audience impressed with the importance of the opening of a new bank in town.
- To have the audience agree with your three main reasons for voting for more funds for space research.
- To have the audience volunteer to work four or more hours next Saturday to help plant gardens around the new school.

You will notice that in these examples there is a considerable range of response you want to elicit from your audience.

In the first example, the speaker is developing merely an impression, an imprint of an idea, a notion, concept, or attitude.

The third example illustrates the other end of the range of speeches that have persuasion as their general purpose. Here the audience is expected to take specific and observable action—work in the gardens.

The middle of the range of possible audience responses to a speech to persuade is illustrated by the second example, in which the speaker's goal is to have the audience accept or agree with particular points, but they need not then take any action, such as voting, petitioning, etc.

Thus there are three possible "levels" of a speech to persuade:

2.1. To Impress

An example of a speech to impress—some prefer to call it a speech to inspire—would be the typical college commencement address, for which the purpose may be to have the graduates impressed—or inspired—with the importance or significance of the occasion. Other examples of this type of speech include sermons, eulogies, and memorials.

At this level of the speech to persuade, your purpose is little more than to get your audience to strengthen, reinforce, or reemphasize a particular opinion, concept, attitude, viewpoint.

Determining if your speech was effective is indeed difficult, often impossible. Reason: The changes you desire in your audience are mental, affective, and subtle rather than outward, apparent, and demonstrable.

2.2. To Convince

An example would be a speech you might present when you are a member of a panel discussion. Your goal is to change minds, to get acceptance, support, or perhaps even endorsement of your plan or idea.

You might determine your success in meeting your speech purpose by asking for a show of hands or by giving a short questionnaire to the audience before and after your speech. You might ask a question such as "Do you intend to vote for the new educational plan?" which you were proposing.

Obviously, such a questionnaire is not practical to give in many speaking situations, and the results would be very rough indeed. Some in your audience might not want to reveal their true convictions, while others might want to "help" the speaker by slanting their responses with more enthusiasm than really resulted from the speech. And, with such a polling, you would be approaching the next level of the speech to persuade.

2.3. To Activate

Examples of a speech to activate include a sales manager urging a staff to increase the number of orders for a product, a candidate soliciting votes, or a fund-raising appeal.

The desired response from an audience is an overt, specific, and measurable action.

The success of such speeches can usually be identified more easily than that of the other levels of speeches to persuade. If, after a sales manager urged increased efforts by a sales staff, more orders were placed for the product, the sales talk seemingly met its purpose. If the candidate solicited votes and then did get more votes, the speech was evidently productive. If more money was received after a fund-raising appeal, the intent of the fund-raising speech was apparently achieved.

Still, in many speaking situations, even when you are seeking overt actions from your audiences, firmly demonstrated results may be difficult to identify.

Now don't get confused. What we've just been considering are various levels within the general speech purpose of . . . .

Well, let's make sure you know where you are in all this.

So far, we've established that there are three general purposes of a speech. They are (write them out, please, to reinforce your learning):

1. _____

2. _____

3. _____

The general purposes a speech might have—as we hope you've just written out correctly—are to inform, to persuade, or to entertain.

The second general purpose, to persuade, has three "levels," three degrees of overtness or activity expected from the audience. Those levels of the speech with a purpose to persuade are (please write them out below):

Most overt response: _____

Least overt response: _____

Midlevel response: _____

You've answered, we hope, that the most overt response of the speeches to persuade is the one to activate, the least overt is to impress, and the one in the middle is the speech to convince.

3. To Entertain

Now let's consider the third general purpose a speech might be designed to achieve. "To entertain" is the purpose of your speech when you intend to provide pleasure or amusement through your remarks. This is the speech that, for example, comedians present as monologues. The humorous speech and the joking introduction of a guest speaker are other examples of speeches that have entertainment as their purpose.

Examples of specific objectives for such speeches would be:

- To have my audience enjoy some stories about unusual places I have visited in Europe.
- To have my audience entertained with examples of strange ways some professional performers have broken into show business.

The speech to entertain is used in rather specialized speaking situations that relatively few public speakers face. One such situation is the after-dinner speech in which humor is used to be a kind of entertainment, almost a show business kind of presentation. Another situation typically calling for a speech to entertain is a celebration of the completion of a group task, such as a dinner at the end of a semester of study, after the launching of a boat, to conclude a group's work on a joint study, at the end of a trip taken by a club. To be the speaker at such specialized situations is a task that comes to relatively few of us.

The success of a speech to entertain is generally quite obvious. If listeners laugh, the speech was effective. Of course, some speeches to entertain are intended to get the audience to be pleased without laughing out loud; evaluating those speeches may be less precise, but listeners may come up to the speaker later and say such things as "Really enjoyed your unusual comments."

Combinations?

Might a speech have more than one general purpose?

Might, for example, a speech have as its purpose both to inform and to entertain?

Consider, as an example, a speech on the subject of shopping in the marketplaces of Nigeria. Included in the speech are such points as how to shop, how to bargain, and how the markets are scheduled. The general purpose of the speech would be _____.

It should be obvious that since the audience would be acquiring new information, the general purpose would be to inform.

Now assume that in presenting those points about the Nigerian markets, the speaker presented some funny stories about his or her experiences in such markets. Does the speech now have a different, or an additional, general purpose? Because humorous stories are included, does the speech also have the general purpose to entertain?

No. The humorous stories are used to make the basic points of the speech more interesting and more memorable. But the speaker would still have as the basic main purpose that the audience would be more informed on how to shop in Nigeria.

Another example: Your speech instructor presents a demonstration on how to outline a speech. The general purpose would be _____.

While showing you how to outline, having the general purpose to inform, the instructor might at the same time include some points designed to persuade you that outlining is important. Further, since outlining is probably a bit of a bore to at least some students, the instructor might try to use a few humorous examples to keep more students interested. But the general purpose—the primary, basic purpose—of the speech remains to inform.

Thus, while a speech has but one basic general purpose—to inform, to persuade, or to entertain—techniques or types of content that are considered typical of other speech purposes might be included.

Why only one general purpose for a speech?

First, the time for your speech is limited, even if you have an hour. You can't cover all bases—purposes—in a speech effectively.

Second, you need to concentrate your speech content on achieving the purpose of your speech. Additional purposes require you to broaden your speech, consequently weakening your effectiveness by spreading your speech more thinly, shallowly.

A third reason a speech should concentrate on only one general purpose is that most individuals in an audience can absorb and concentrate on only a limited, direct goal through a speech. An exception is the typical college lecture. It can cover a great many points and have several purposes because the audience knows it is in a concentrated listening situation and usually is prepared, mentally and physically, to take notes or record the lecture.

Review:

So far in this lesson you have learned, first, that there are three *general purposes* a speech might have:

1. To inform
2. To persuade
3. To entertain

The various levels of the speech to persuade—to impress, to convince, and to activate—are all, in effect, different degrees of the basic general purpose "to persuade."

Those three levels merely help clarify the range of activity you may expect to elicit from an audience—all under the *general purpose* "to persuade."

Second, you have learned to identify the general purposes a speech might have. Prove that to yourself. What's the general purpose of each of the following specific speech purposes?

_____ 1. To have the audience able to read a stock market report with accuracy.

_____ 2. To have the audience show up at next week's dance.

_____ 3. To have the audience contribute a recipe for publication in the school's international cookbook.

_____ 4. To have the audience able to repeat correctly "Good morning," "Good evening," and "Good bye" in three languages other than their own.

_____ 5. To have the audience support the school's intercultural club.

_____ 6. To have the audience able to bake a cake.

_____ 7. To have the audience convinced that they should take part in local government.

_____ 8. To have the audience join the local antipollution campaign.

_____ 9. To have the audience able to state why more modern training for the local police is needed.

_____ 10. To have the audience amused by some mathematical tricks.

Jesse Jackson. . .

. . . is one of the most dramatic, effective, recognized speakers in America.

He is a Baptist minister and a Democratic leader.

In 1971, as an activist in the Civil Rights movement, he founded PUSH—People United to Save Humanity—a highly successful program to advance the interests of Blacks and other disadvantaged groups.

He made a strong bid for the Democratic presidential nomination in 1984, becoming the first African American to make a serious run for the office. He ran again in 1988, on a platform calling for "economic justice," won 30 percent of the delegates and was the runner-up to nominee Michael Dukakis.

Jackson was born in Greenville, South Carolina, October 8, 1941.

While attending North Carolina Agricultural and Technical State College he was active in the Civil Rights movement. After graduating in 1964, he enrolled in the Chicago Theological Seminary.

In the early 1960s he was a leader in the SCLA—Southern Christian Leadership Conference—headed by Martin Luther King, Jr. Jackson was selected by King to head the SCLA's program of Breadbasket in Chicago, which obtained jobs and services for African Americans.

In the 1970s, Jackson spoke throughout the United States in a campaign for education and against drug abuse and gangs.

His autobiography, *A Time to Speak,* was published in 1988.

Answers

1. To inform	6. To inform
2. To persuade	7. To persuade
3. To persuade	8. To persuade
4. To inform	9. To inform
5. To persuade	10. To entertain

Miss more than two? If so, please restudy this section. Remember your goal: to achieve 80 percent or higher on each lesson.

Now we move from *general* purposes to developing your skill in writing *specific* purposes for speeches.

DEFINITION OF A SPECIFIC PURPOSE

A *specific* purpose is a statement—a complete sentence—expressing exactly what you want your speech to achieve.

Be clear on the difference between a general purpose—what you've just been studying—and a specific purpose, which we're into now. A *general* purpose is a broad, collective expression of the general intent of your speech. Your general purpose, as you know, is simply to inform or persuade or entertain.

Your job now is to move from that general statement or idea of the goal of your speech to writing a specific, exact, precise statement of what your speech is to achieve.

CRITERIA FOR A SPECIFIC SPEECH PURPOSE

There are *three criteria for a speech purpose* that is correctly, effectively worded. Such a speech purpose is:

1. Worded from the audience's viewpoint
2. Specific
3. Attainable

Let's detail those a bit more. A good specific speech purpose is:

1. *Worded from the audience's point of view.* A statement of what the *audience* is to be able to do or think or believe or enjoy after they hear your speech.
2. *Exact, specific, precise wording.* The wording is so clear that, if it were feasible, you could actually measure or test your audience after your speech to determine if your speech purpose had been achieved.
3. *An attainable goal.* The specific purpose is a realistic, practical goal, one that might in fact actually be achieved by your speech.

Important: In the view of this book's approach to becoming an effective speaker, **the one most important step in designing a speech is establishing the specific purpose.**

Pardon that and the following repetitions, but this point is so critical it cannot be overemphasized.

And you should continue to remember *why* so much emphasis is put on this really simple step. The reason: *Your statement of your specific speech purpose should be the basis for ALL of your remaining decisions about the design of your speech.*

That means you should use your specific speech purpose to help you decide how to organize your speech, what would make a good attention-getter, if you should use a particular statistic, if you should present a chart or a diagram, your style of delivery—*all* such decisions about *all* aspects of your speech can best be made by turning to your specific purpose as the single most valuable source for your answers.

Clearly, your speech purpose must be worded carefully, precisely, thoughtfully.

WORDING THE SPECIFIC PURPOSE

First think through what you want your speech to achieve in general, broad terms. Is your speech to inform? To persuade? To entertain?

Then write out a sentence to state your specific speech purpose.

Consider an example from a recent student speech—an example of an *ineffective* speech purpose:

 ♦ The purpose of my speech will be to tell my audience about sailboats.

It is hoped you're starting to get ahead of me by already spotting at least some of the weaknesses in that speech purpose.

How does it meet the criteria for a speech purpose we've established above? Let's see.

Worded from the Audience's Viewpoint?

In that example you'll note that the speaker has decided that his speech purpose will be "to tell" the audience something. His speech can be successful, even if not one person in the audience listens. All the speaker intends to do—all he wants to achieve—is "to tell." He needs no listeners to do that. More important, his listeners need do nothing—they need not become informed at all.

But this course maintains that you should design your speeches so that something actually takes place in the minds or abilities of the listeners. The purpose—and consequently the speech—should be listener oriented, not speaker oriented.

Why?

Because in all human speaking, in even our everyday, casual conversation, we speak, as we've already established, because we want to have some particular effect on the listener. We do this without thinking about it as we participate in our usual, conventional talking with one or a few people. This course is trying to get you to carry that same approach over to the designing of your talks to an audience of many listeners, in speaking situations that are more formal than conversation.

So a speech purpose using the words "to tell" describes what the speaker does, not the listener. The emphasis should be just the reverse; that is, the speech purpose should establish what it is that the audience, not the speaker, does. An effective speech purpose should not center on the speaker and his or her actions, thoughts, etc.; it should center on the audience.

A specific speech purpose that would be correctly worded on this first criterion—worded from the audience's viewpoint—would start with such words as these:

 ♦ After hearing my speech the audience will . . .
 ♦ The purpose of my speech is to have the audience . . .
 ♦ To have my audience . . .
 ♦ After my speech the listeners will . . .
 ♦ The audience will, after listening to me speak . . .

Now let's return to our first example of a speech purpose, that poorly worded statement.

▶ The purpose of my speech will be to tell my audience about sailboats.

To correct that speech purpose—to word it from the audience's point of view—it should state . . . _____

_____

_____

Your response should include the word "audience" or "listeners" or some other reference to those who are to hear your speech. And your response should be worded so that it expresses something that the audience, not the speaker, should be able to do.

Here are two examples of improved responses you might have made. Remember, at this point we are concentrating only on the first criterion for an effective speech purpose, that of wording it from the audience's viewpoint.

▶ After hearing my speech, the audience will know about sailboats.

> **Comment:** It still has some weaknesses (we'll get to them later), but it is at least worded from the audience's point of view.

▶ The purpose of my speech is to have the audience informed about sailboats.

> **Comment:** This now meets the criterion of being worded from the audience's point of view. (We'll consider the other two criteria in a moment.)

And of course there are other possibilities that you might have written. Now, about the second criterion for a correctly worded speech purpose.

Specific?

None of the examples of a speech purpose concerned with the sailboat is specific.

Our initial example uses the word "about" to try to describe what the speech is to do—"to tell my audience about sailboats." Certainly the word "about" is vague, indefinite, nonspecific.

The two examples of improved speech purposes suggested by your author are correct in wording the purpose from the audience's viewpoint, but they, too, use vague words, "know" and "informed." These are indefinite, useless words to try to pinpoint just what it is the speech is to accomplish.

So let's look at our *second criterion* for a speech purpose: being *specific*.

Suppose your speech purpose is one of those already suggested:

▶ After hearing my speech, the audience will know about sailboats.

> **Comment:** Again—perhaps a bit redundant, but to be sure all our students are with us—that purpose meets our first criterion, that of being worded from the audience's viewpoint.

That purpose says that the audience will "know" something. How might a speaker determine that his or her speech was successful?

If you had the opportunity, for example, to talk with your audience after a speech, how could you find out if they now "know" what you wanted them to know?_____

_____

_____

_____

Some students respond with something such as "Ask them." OK, ask them what? Point: need to be a bit more specific than that.

Some students respond with something such as "Ask the audience some questions about the speech." That's getting a bit more specific.

Let's accept that reply, even though others are, of course, possible.

Now, just what would you ask your audience so you'd find out if they now "know" about sailboats? _____

_____

_____

_____

_____

Well, to answer with any specificity you have to start, in effect, defining "know," wouldn't you? You could ask that audience to name the main types of sailboats or to summarize how they work or to describe the different cuts of sails or to list the main parts of a sailboat or some such question. But whatever you ask, you'll need words that are more specific than the general word "know."

Hope you didn't respond with some further generalized words that only seem to be more specific but actually are not. For example, some reply that the audience should "understand," maybe "understand how sailboats work." But what exactly does "understand" mean? How would you determine if your audience "understands" what you've been talking about?

Another error is to suggest that the audience should "really know" or "really understand." Again, you can spot these—can't you?—as just further generalizations.

On the next page is a guide that will help you select effective, specific words for your speech purpose. It lists words you should not use in a speech purpose and words you should use to help make your speech purpose state a specific objective.

KEY WORDS FOR SPEECH PURPOSES

AVOID vague words, such as:

acquaint	consider	know	think
appreciate	convince	knowledge	understand
aware	familiar	recognize	
believe	interest	see	

USE more specific words, such as:

Inform	**Persuade**	**Entertain**
analyze	accept	amuse
compare	agree	enjoy
contrast	argue	entertain
define	attend	excite
demonstrate	buy	laugh
describe	contribute	like
design	cooperate	please
determine	debate	smile
discuss	defend	welcome
document	disagree	
explain	follow	
identify	help	
list	join	
name	lend	
plan	move	
prepare	offer	
quote	participate	
recall	react	
repeat	select	
restate	serve	
show	share	
state	suggest	
summarize	support	
tell	switch	
	volunteer	
	vote	

But in addition to vague wording, there's another way in which a speech purpose can be so indefinite that it is not useful to you in planning your speech.

Consider this example:

▸ After hearing my speech, the audience will vote for new laws concerning drugs.

This speech purpose is correctly worded from the audience's viewpoint. And it is specific in stating an action that the audience is to take; the speaker wants the audience to "vote for." That's about as specific an action as you can describe.

But what are they to vote for? The speech purpose states "new laws concerning drugs." What new laws? Will the laws be more liberal? Or more strict? Are they local, city, or state laws? Is the speaker proposing national regulations?

The point is clear: The *subject* of this speech purpose is too vague and generalized.

How would you word that speech purpose about drug laws so it would meet our criteria for being specific? _____

_____

_____

_____

Again, there are several possibilities. But check your response against our criteria.

Is your statement worded from the audience's viewpoint? _____ (yes or no?)
Is your statement specific in stating what the audience is to do? _____ (yes or no?)

To check your answer to that last question, consider this. Could you, if you had the opportunity, measure, test, or observe what you expect your audience to do, think, feel, or act as the result of your speech? _____ (yes or no?)

OK, pinpoint it still further: *How* might you, if the situation were appropriate, check up on your audience? _____

_____

_____

Here are some correctly worded speech purposes—of course, not the only ones you could write out—to further specify that purpose concerning drug laws.

▸ After my speech, the audience will vote for a law allowing cities to set up their own regulations to control drugs.
▸ After my speech, the audience will vote for the repeal of all laws against drugs.
▸ After hearing my speech, the audience will vote for establishing strict national laws to outlaw the use of all drugs other than those for medical purposes.

If you have any doubt about our answer, you can (1) check over the previous pages again for possible further insights to help you answer, (2) check your answer with a fellow classmate, or (3) ask your instructor.

How does this speech purpose, again from a student's speech, meet our criteria?

▸ After hearing my speech, the audience will be able to summarize in their own words how a sailboat works.

Does it meet our criterion on being worded from the audience's viewpoint?

_____ (yes or no?)

Certainly you and I would agree that it does.

Does it meet our criterion on stating specifically what action the audience is to take?

_____ (yes or no?)

We agree again, don't we? "Able to summarize in their own words" is very specific; it does meet our criterion.

Does it meet our criterion on stating specifically what the subject is?

_____ (yes or no?)

Are we in agreement? "How a sailboat works" is rather broad. The speech could include material or points on how sails work, how different-shaped hulls influence a boat's sailing, the principles of physics on which a sailboat works, and other specific areas of information. So such a broad subject statement as "how a sailboat works" does not meet our criterion because it does not help the speaker determine just what he or she is to present in the speech.

We have one more criterion to writing an effective, specific speech purpose. Do you remember it?

Attainable?

Again, let's start with an example:

> ◗ After my speech, the audience will be able to sail a boat.

Hope you've already rejected that speech purpose. Worded from the audience's viewpoint? Yes. Specific? Yes. Attainable? Hardly. Practice in a boat, on the water, would be needed in order to be able to sail a boat. No speech by itself could make an audience qualified in such a complex skill.

Yet I've heard students attempt to give five-minute speeches on how to play chess. One might be able to give a speech so the audience would be able to move the pieces in a chess game, but that's distinct from being able to play.

Some other *un*attainable purposes for a speech:

> ◗ To have my audience able to summarize the main features of the national budget.
>
> > **Comment:** Far too complex, lengthy, and involved subject. Unless the speaker defines "main features" in very limited terms, they should be named, specified, in a speech purpose like this.

> ◗ After hearing my speech, the audience will agree to join the ecology activists.
>
> > **Comment:** Unless the audience is composed of people who have already decided to consider volunteering, this purpose would seem to be unattainable. That is, giving a speech to an audience composed of a cross section of young adults is not likely to get them to take such a giant step as joining activists.

> ◗ After my speech to the County Republican Committee, the audience will agree to vote for the Democratic candidate.
>
> > **Comment:** Again, expecting quite a bit from one speech, unless, of course, there is some solid background of experience held by that audience that has most of them already at least somewhat inclined to that change of party allegiance. The point is that while a speech realistically might be expected to change the minds of some, as well as raise considerable doubts in the minds of most, it is doubtful that a speech alone will produce such a complete change in the minds of the audience.

Review

This lesson has presented these points so far:

1. General purposes a speech might have.
2. Criteria for an effectively worded speech purpose—a specific purpose.
3. How to determine if a speech purpose meets those criteria.

Got them?
Good.

Let's try a self-test. Do you first want to take a look back through this lesson to make sure you get 80 percent (24 points) or more on the self-test?

ASSIGNMENT 9: SPEECH PURPOSE: SELF-TEST

❶ ACTION: Take the following self-test.

1. Name the general purposes for which a speech might be designed.

2. Name the criteria for an effectively worded specific speech purpose.

State whether each of the following is a correctly worded specific speech purpose or not. If it is not, state briefly why not.

3. After hearing my speech, the audience will be able to list three reasons for the increasing inflation.
   Correctly worded? _____
   If not, reason:

4. My speech will tell the audience how to improve their skills in using a VCR.
   Correctly worded? _____
   If not, reason:

5. I'll give the audience details on how to pick a good hotel in a foreign country.
   Correctly worded? _____
   If not, reason:

6. After hearing my speech, the audience will know how to tie three knots—overhand, figure eight, and bowline.
   Correctly worded? _____
   If not, reason:

7. After listening to my speech, the audience will be able to summarize in their own words what I consider to be the three main advantages of going to college.
   Correctly worded? _____
   If not, reason:

8. After my speech, my listeners will agree with my viewpoint.
   Correctly worded? _____
   If not, reason:

9. After hearing my speech, my listeners, members of a pacifist group, will vote to outlaw guns.
   Correctly worded? _____
   If not, reason:

10. During my speech, the audience will laugh with me at descriptions of some of the humorous events that happen at a typical gas station.
    Correctly worded? _____
    If not, reason:

11. After hearing my speech, the audience will understand the need for shopping carefully for a new car.
    Correctly worded? _____
    If not, reason:

Assume you are to speak at the following situations. Write out a correctly worded specific speech purpose for each.

12. *Audience:* Board of trustees of your college
    Occasion: Regular monthly meeting
    Specific speech purpose:

13. *Audience:* Local Boy Scout troop
    Occasion: Meeting to award honors to outstanding scouts
    Specific speech purpose:

Check your answers in the page after the next.

Longest Filibuster

For 22 hours, 20 minutes, Senator Wayne Morse (D, Oregon) talked nonstop, setting a record and blocking all action by the Senate. He spoke about a Tidelands Oil Bill, on April 24–25, 1953. His speaking is noted in *The Guinness Book of Records.*

ANSWERS:

1. Inform, persuade, entertain.
2. Worded from audience's viewpoint, specific, attainable.
3. Yes.
4. No. Not worded from audience's viewpoint; uses words "will tell," which describe speaker's actions, not audience's.
5. No. Not worded from audience's viewpoint; uses wording "I'll give," which describes speaker's actions, not audience's.
6. No. Not specific; uses the vague word "know"; should state something such as "will be able to tie (those knots)."
7. Yes.
8. No. Not specific; "my viewpoint" does not state a specific subject.
9. Yes.
10. Yes.
11. No. Not specific; uses the vague word "understand."
12.,13. Your speech purposes should be statements of a subject appropriate to the designated audience, occasion, and speaker (as you learned in the previous lesson) and should be worded from the audience's viewpoint, be specific, and be attainable.

SCORING:

You can get up to 30 points on this self-test.

Questions 1, 2:	3 points each, 1 for each correct statement.
Questions 3–11:	2 points each, 1 for your correct evaluation of each statement and 1 for the correct reason for each.
Questions 12, 13:	3 points each, 1 for each criterion your purposes fulfill correctly.

If you got 24 or more points correct, you've reached your goal of 80 percent—congratulations!

If you got fewer than 24 points, please restudy this lesson. You'll need to be sure you have attained at least 80 percent correct on this self-test because you'll now be writing speech purposes for all your coming speeches in this course.

To start, here's your next assignment.

ASSIGNMENT 10: SPECIFIC PURPOSE SPEECH: SPEECH 2

 ACTION: Deliver in class a 4- to 5-minute extemporaneous speech that is designed for an audience other than this class and that fulfills the objective of this assignment.

OBJECTIVE:

Your speech should demonstrate your effective use of at least 80 percent of the concepts and techniques of public speaking studied in this course so far in each of the three aspects of speaking—content, organizations and delivery. Effectiveness will be determined on the basis of the 38 points listed on the **Evaluation Form** for this speech, which appears on page 165 with those points as defined in this and previous lessons in this course.

In essence, your speech should:

1. Be based on a useful analysis of the speaking situation.
2. Be based on a correctly worded speech purpose.
3. Present appropriate points and data.

4. Be delivered effectively.
5. Follow the basic format for a speech.

INSTRUCTIONS:

1. Be sure to design and deliver your speech as if you were speaking before an audience other than this class. (You will not be asked to actually give this speech to that other audience.)

2. To pick a subject, consider this speech assignment your opportunity to give that speech you always wanted to. Some students respond with such answers as "I always did want to tell our city council that they just have to do something about the parking problem downtown" or "If I just had a chance to talk to the management of that company, I could sure point out a few things they need to do to improve their service."

   Think through some of the problems or topics that are of greatest interests to you, then ask yourself, "Who else—what audience and in what kind of a speaking situation—is or should be interested in that subject?" Students in previous classes have given speeches for this assignment such as:

   Gun control, as if speaking to a state crime committee.

   A college student's view of religion, as if speaking to the congregation of a church.

   Education needs, as if speaking to the faculty of a college.

   Problems of the nearby shopping center, as if speaking to the local chamber of commerce.

   Smoking, as if speaking to a class of junior high students.

   Car insurance, as if talking to a meeting of the area's insurance agents.

3. Select a particular audience. Do not select some generalized audience such as a "city council," but rather, select a particular council, such as the Centerville City Council. Reason: By now you should be sensitive to the fact that a speech to the Centerville City Council should not be the same as a speech to the San Francisco City Council. While you might be presenting the same basic subject, points, or data, your speech design, delivery, emphasis, and such should be different for those two very different cities.

4. Complete the **Check-off Tip Sheet** for this speech, which is on page 167. Its purpose, of course, is to help you to be sure to observe each point on which this speech will be evaluated and, even more important, to help you remember the techniques for effective content, organization, and delivery of a speech.

5. Just before you begin to present this speech, the other students in your class will need to know what audience you've designed your speech for. You have two options:

   5.1. Your instructor can announce—by reading from the **Evaluation Form** you will have turned in—just what audience you are speaking to.

   5.2. Or your instructor may prefer that you get a bit of practice in greeting audiences. In that case, take a look at the tips on presenting greetings, on page 00.

6. Finally, for those of you using a **Diagnosis Folder,** before you speak, remember to fill in the appropriate spaces, the information about your date of completion, and your grade for each previous assignment, and the summary of the strengths and weaknesses of your first speech.

A l e r t ! ⮕ All appropriate, relevant tips and techniques suggested for the previous speech—your demonstration speech—should continue to be followed. It will now be up to you to review them, either by recalling them or by looking back through the previous lessons.

The point is that you are now expected to start on your own to apply and utilize speaking techniques already presented, without their being relisted or reviewed for you in subsequent lessons.

For example, even though they are not listed in this lesson, you should use the preparation tips you've already studied—preparing a rough outline (we'll study outlining techniques in detail later), preparing a note card, practicing, etc.

1. Tips on Content

1.1. Base Your Speech on an Accurate Analysis of Your Speaking Situation

You learned how to do that in Lesson 5, you'll remember. If you need to refresh some details, look again at that lesson.

1.2. Be Sure Your Specific Speech Purpose Is Worded Correctly

How? As you studied earlier in this lesson.

1.3. The Subject Should Be Appropriate, Relevant, and Interesting to Your Designated Audience

If your analysis of your speaking situation is correct, then your subject should be appropriate, relevant, and interesting to your listeners. But suppose, as you plan your speech, you think that perhaps your listeners, as they hear you speak, might wonder, "So what?" Their "So what?" implies, of course, that they're either not interested in your subject or are wondering what it has to do with them.

If their "So what?" comes because they are not interested in your topic, the problem may be a faulty analysis of the speaking situation. Redo the analysis. Perhaps you have selected a poor subject for the speaking situation.

If you reexamine your analysis and decide that the subject is indeed appropriate, but you still feel your listeners may wonder "So what?" then you may need to state in your speech quite specifically exactly what your subject has to do with them. Right after you preview your subject, you might use such wordings as these:

- ⯈ Why am I speaking to you about the problems of far-off Nigeria? Consider these facts of how involved you actually are with the affairs of that country . . .
- ⯈ Let me tell you a story that will help you see just how important the gold standard is today.
- ⯈ The importance of this subject was emphasized recently when three different national magazines each published an article that said, in effect, . . .

Now remember what we've been talking about here has been the *subject* of your speech. Turn now to considering that . . .

1.4. The Points and Data Should Be New and Significant to Your Audience

And to meet that criterion, we urge you once again to turn to our two-word question: "So what?"

As you consider each of the two to five main points you'll present in the discussion part of your speech, and then as you consider each of the bits of data—the statistics, stories, quotations, etc.—you'll present to support those points, ask yourself "So what?" For example, ask yourself:

- *So what* does this point have to do with my speech subject?
- *So what* makes this point important to my audience?
- *So what* makes this point new to my audience?
- *So what* makes this fact significant to my audience?
- *So what* makes this story relevant to my audience's background?
- *So what* makes this quotation interesting?
- *So what . . . ?*

Answer such questions to yourself for each point and each piece of data so you'll always be able to say to yourself, "Yes, it does seem to me this is relevant." Or new. Or significant. And each time you wonder if a bit of data or a point might not be relevant, significant, or new, continue to think and to search for a replacement.

1.5. Include Personal and Human Interest Stories in Your Speeches

- Just a few hours ago two students in last semester's class came up to me, yelling and claiming that . . .
- The new neighbors who moved in next door faced the problem of ghosts by . . . .
- But listen to what the ship's captain said just before the fire broke out.

Most people in an audience will listen to you with greater interest whenever you tell a story or give an example about people. It bears repeating: People are interested in people. Think about your own reactions when you hear personal stories in the speeches given by others; almost always you become more interested in what they are saying.

By "personal and human interest stories" we do not mean that they have to be incidents that you yourself have experienced. They can be stories about people you know or stories you've read or heard. They can also be hypothetical—ones you invent as representative of actual events. But in general, each point of your speech should include one or more personal or human interest stories, to add interest, to make your points clearer or more memorable, or to explain the meaning of your basic points.

1.6. All Material Should Clearly Contribute to Your Specific Purpose

With one speech under your belt, your experience both as a speaker and as a listener should tell you by now how very important it is that everything you say in your speech contributes to the specific purpose of your speech.

First, as a speaker, you don't have the luxury of time in the brief 4- to 5-minute speeches you're now giving in this class to expend words on material that may not help you get the effect you want on your listeners. Even when you get into a speaking situation (not in this course) in which you have perhaps 20 minutes or longer to speak, your time will be better used giving more data to support your case rather than wandering into slightly related or nonrelated material.

Second, remember how you react as a listener when, for example, a speaker talking about population control in India wanders into facts about India's transportation,

elections, geography, etc. Many listeners quit listening to such a speaker. Some drop out mentally for only a short time, until the speaker gets back to the subject. But often a speaker loses many listeners entirely as they mentally refuse to join the speaker again.

So keep the specific purpose of your speech foremost in your mind; use it as your guide to deciding what to include in your speech. Leave out of your speech any bit of material, no matter how interesting or unusual, that does not contribute clearly and directly to your speech purpose.

1.7. Get to the Point Quickly—Don't Overdetail Data or Points

The Lord's Prayer consists of only 56 words. The Declaration of Independence has but 1,322 words. But there is a federal regulation on olives that goes on for 11,400 words.

You've heard speakers whom you can outguess—that is, you can figure out the point they are trying to make faster than they state it. Such speakers tend to spin out their stories, explain their meanings, tell three stories when the first one made the point.

Then there are speakers—again undesirable because they are detracting from their effectiveness—who show you a chart of statistics and proceed to tell you the figures, which you've already read before they get to them.

Finally, there's the speaker who summarizes the plot of a movie by including what seem to be more details than the director had in the script from which the film was shot.

In brief, don't insult your audience and lose their attention by being too detailed. Get to the point.

1.8. Present Your Own, Original Ideas, Structure, or Interpretation

There's no point in presenting a speech that is in essence a summary of a magazine article or a TV documentary or another speech.

"But that article says just what I want to tell this audience," a student will proclaim. And she may well be right. But why not simply distribute copies of the article? Why take the time of the audience to tell them what someone else has already written?

Further, there is the more basic consideration of the moral obligation a speaker has to express his or her own ideas, rather than merely mouth—in effect, steal—those of someone else.

You as a speaker should be presenting at least some aspect in your speech that is distinctive, that is of yourself alone. It might be a different interpretation of a problem, a different way of stating the problem, a different solution, different proof of its significance, different relating of it to the interests of the audience.

1.9. Use Visual or Audio Aids When Appropriate

The demonstration speeches illustrated the value of using aids effectively. But in those speeches you and your classmates spoke mostly on subjects that were visually oriented.

Think, then, how important it is to use visual and audio aids when the speech subject is an idea or a concept. These subjects are in even greater need of visualization so that more of your audience might be informed, persuaded, or entertained. Your job in such subjects is to attempt to move them from the verbal, the thought, to the specific, the actual, the here-and-now.

But again we are still working on your early speeches. The point here is to urge you to use aids. How to choose them is detailed in Lesson 7, on selecting your data. How to use aids is presented in Lesson 9, on polishing your delivery. You can skip ahead and skim those lessons if you'd like some specific help on selecting and using aids now.

Remember, aids not only add interest and variety to your speeches; aids also help you and your listeners remember your speech.

1.10. Emphasize the Organization of Your Speech Enough to Help Your Audience Remember Your Points

This is done such techniques as illustrated by these quotations from recent speeches:

- There are three reasons why we need this new law. First, . . .; second, . . .; and third, . . .
- Now that we've considered the cause of the disaster, let's look at what we can do to prevent such calamities in the future. The cause and then the solution are the focus of our concern here today.
- Think of the designing of this new product as roughly parallel with the design of your own body. You have, and it has, a head, a body, and extremities, hands and feet.

Anything you can say or do (gestures, visuals, demonstrations) to help your audience remember your points will increase the chances that you'll fulfill the purpose you've established for your speech.

2. Tips on Organization

By now you should realize that to be effective, a speech must be structured much more carefully than the usual class reports kids used to give back in elementary school. Then, about all you had to do was stand up and summarize something you'd read, for example. A student would say little more to the class than "This is what I found out about this subject" and then proceed to repeat a few main points from what he or she had read someplace.

Magazine articles, essays, and other written materials are also usually organized quite differently from speeches. Here are a few of those differences:

1. In an article, the points generally are not repeated, as they often are in each of the three parts of a speech—introduction, discussion, and conclusion.
2. In an article, "hooks" are often used to lead the reader from one paragraph to the next. In a speech, it's usually more effective to lead your listeners to your next paragraph by summarizing the point you just made, then stating a short transition—such as "There's another reason we should vote for this"—then previewing (stating briefly) your next point.
3. In an article, the points may be presented in a sequence that is different from a speech.
4. In an article, the organization is often designed to get readers to think independently as they read. Speeches are generally more successful when organized to lead listeners to think along with the speaker.

So now *one more point* will be added to your **Check-off Tip Sheets** and **Evaluation Forms** (following pages) in the section on organization:

> *2.8. Uses the structure of speech, not of old-style class report or article*

3. Tips on Delivery

The tips given for your demonstration speech apply to this and all other speeches. If you'd like to review them, see Lesson 3, Delivering Speeches.

4. Tips on Preparation

These were presented in Lesson 4, Preparing to Speak. Use the **Check-off Tip Sheet** on note cards and practicing your speech.

So now you're ready to do your detailed planning for your next speech—a speech designed to achieve a specific purpose with a designated audience other than your class. To guide your planning, use the **Check-off Tip Sheet** on the next page. To get an evaluation of your speech, use the form on the subsequent page.

SPECIFIC PURPOSE—SPEECH 2: CHECK-OFF TIP SHEET

INSTRUCTIONS: Check off each item below as you plan your speech.

Audience: _____ Speech purpose: _____

_____

_____

1. CONTENT

_____ 1.1. Based on accurate analysis of speaking situation:
  - _____ 1.1.1. Audience
  - _____ 1.1.2. Occasion
  - _____ 1.1.3. Speaker

_____ 1.2. Speech purpose worded correctly:
  - _____ 1.2.1. From audience's viewpoint
  - _____ 1.2.2. Specific
  - _____ 1.2.3. Attainable

_____ 1.3. Subject appropriate, relevant, and interesting to audience

_____ 1.4. Points and data new and significant to audience

_____ 1.5. Includes personal and human interest stories

_____ 1.6. All material clearly contributes to purpose

_____ 1.7. Gets to point quickly—does not overdetail

_____ 1.8. Presents own, original ideas, structure, or interpretation

_____ 1.9. Uses visual or audio aids when appropriate

_____ 1.10. Emphasizes organization enough to help audience remember points

2. ORGANIZATION

_____ 2.1. Begins with effective attention-getter

_____ 2.2. Previews subject or viewpoint specifically and clearly

_____ 2.3. Presents 2 to 5 specific points

_____ 2.4. Arranges discussion points in logical order

_____ 2.5. Supports each discussion point with data

_____ 2.6. Reviews subject, viewpoint, or discussion points

_____ 2.7. Concludes with memorable statement

_____ 2.8. Uses the structure of speech, not of old-style class report or article

3. DELIVERY

_____ 3.1. Steps up to speak with confidence and authority

_____ 3.2. Gets set before starting to speak

_____ 3.3. Establishes contact with audience before speaking

_____ 3.4. Begins without referring to notes

_____ 3.5. Maintains contact with audience

_____ 3.6. Sounds conversational, not read or memorized

_____ 3.7. Uses, few 3 × 5 note cards

_____ 3.8. Refers to note cards only occasionally

_____ 3.9. Avoids *ah, so, ya know, well, 'kay,* etc.

_____ 3.10. Stops at end of idea; doesn't hook sentences together with *and, and ah,* etc.

_____ 3.11. Maintains good posture—does not lean, cross legs, etc.

_____ 3.12. Does not play with notes, pencil, clothes, etc.

_____ 3.13. Dresses to help, not hinder, speech

_____ 3.14. Speaks loudly enough to be heard easily

Your Personality?

Were you an early talker—saying five or so words before you were a year old?

Then chances are you are intelligent, restrained, somber. When you were in high school, likely you were known as an egghead. By the time you're 30 years old you will be—or are—practical, prudent, and conservative.

Or were you a late talker—not speaking until after you were 15 months old?

Then you are—if typical—active, uninhibited, perhaps rebellious.

If you first spoke when 12 to 15 months old, you probably grew up to be conventional.

Such are the claims of a study reported in the book *American Averages,* written by *Mike Feinsilber* and *William B. Mead.*

SPECIFIC PURPOSE—SPEECH 2: EVALUATION FORM

INSTRUCTIONS: Complete the top section of this form, put it in your **Diagnosis Folder,** and give it in the folder to your instructor on the day you are to speak.

Speaker: _____ Audience: _____ Date: _____

Speech purpose: _____

_____

_____

1. CONTENT

_____ 1.1.   Based on accurate analysis of speaking situation:
- _____ 1.1.1.   Audience
- _____ 1.1.2.   Occasion
- _____ 1.1.3.   Speaker

_____ 1.2.   Speech purpose worded correctly:
- _____ 1.2.1.   From audience's viewpoint
- _____ 1.2.2.   Specific
- _____ 1.2.3.   Attainable

_____ 1.3.   Subject appropriate, relevant, and interesting to audience

_____ 1.4.   Points and data new and significant to audience

_____ 1.5.   Includes personal and human interest stories

_____ 1.6.   All material clearly contributes to purpose

_____ 1.7.   Gets to point quickly—does not overdetail

_____ 1.8.   Presents own, original ideas, structure, or interpretation

_____ 1.9.   Uses visual and audio aids when appropriate

_____ 1.10. Emphasizes organization enough to help audience remember points

2. ORGANIZATION

_____ 2.1.   Begins with effective attention-getter

_____ 2.2.   Previews subject or viewpoint specifically and clearly

_____ 2.3.   Presents 2 to 5 specific points

_____ 2.4.   Arranges discussion points in logical order

_____ 2.5.   Supports each discussion point with data

_____ 2.6.   Reviews subject, viewpoint, or discussion points

_____ 2.7.   Concludes with memorable statement

_____ 2.8.   Uses the structure of speech, not of old-style class report or article

3. DELIVERY

_____ 3.1.   Steps up to speak with confidence and authority

_____ 3.2.   Gets set before starting to speak

_____ 3.3.   Establishes contact with audience before speaking

_____ 3.4.   Begins without referring to notes

_____ 3.5.   Maintains contact with audience

_____ 3.6.   Sounds conversational, not read or memorized

_____ 3.7.   Uses few 3 × 5 note cards

_____ 3.8.   Refers to note cards only occasionally

_____ 3.9.   Avoids *ah, so, ya know, well, 'kay,* etc.

_____ 3.10. Stops at end of idea; doesn't hook sentences together with *and, and ah,* etc.

_____ 3.11. Maintains good posture; does not lean, cross legs, etc.

_____ 3.12. Doesn't play with notes, pencil, clothes, etc.

_____ 3.13. Dresses to help, not hinder, speech

_____ 3.14. Speaks loudly enough to be heard easily

Over for comments

4. COMMENTS:

Grade: _____

SPEECH PURPOSE: CHECK-OFF TIP SHEET

PROCESS:

_____ 1.   Pinpoint a specific, measurable purpose for the speech.

_____ 2.   Use that specific purpose to make all other decisions about the speech—its content, organization, and delivery.

GENERAL PURPOSES OF A SPEECH:

_____ 1.   Inform

_____ 2.   Persuade

      _____ 2.1. Impress (inspire)

      _____ 2.2. Convince

      _____ 2.3. Activate

_____ 3.   Entertain

CRITERIA OF A SPECIFIC PURPOSE FOR A SPEECH:

_____ 1.   Worded from the audience's viewpoint

_____ 2.   Specific

_____ 3.   Attainable

Gesture!

"Suit the action to the word, the word to the action."

*William Shakespeare, **Hamlet***

L E S S O N 7

Selecting Data

OBJECTIVES

After completing this lesson, you will be able to:

1. Name the types of data.
2. Given examples of data, identify the type.
3. Name the main methods of misleading an audience.
4. Use data effectively in your speeches.

RELEVANCE

"Don't confuse me with facts—my mind's made up!"

Few members of your audiences will admit that statement is their creed. But some people act and think as though a closed mind is their proudest possession.

The purpose of this lesson is to help you achieve your speech purpose with such listeners and with the majority of your audience who will accept your ideas and viewpoints more readily if they are effectively documented.

How to document your points is the subject of this lesson: how to select a variety of types of data and how to present them effectively in your speech.

SELECTING DATA:

"The stories and facts should be chosen carefully so that they further strengthen the argument you're trying to make. If you throw in irrelevant stories or figures, your audience will immediately pick up this flaw and decide, 'This guy is disorganized!'"

That advice is from the book **Public Speaking for Private People** by *Art Linkletter,* formerly one of the most famous, persuasive, and effective interviewers on radio and TV.

Using data effectively in a speech won't guarantee you will sell a bad idea. But using data effectively can increase the likelihood that your listeners will accept those of your viewpoints that have merit or validity of their own.

On the other hand, if you use data poorly, the chances are you'll not win many of your listeners over to your viewpoint.

SOURCES OF DATA

As a student in this course, you are probably already pretty skilled in finding data in a library. But there are other valuable sources of information to find data for your speeches. Consider:

1. Your Computer

America Online, Internet, World Wide Web, and other such computer services can get you to gold mines of data you can incorporate in your speeches. (For more tips on using your computer to research your speeches, see Lesson 13, Using a Computer to Design Speeches.)

2. Reference Librarians

Many public, as well as school, libraries have specially trained professionals available to help you find specific information.

Many libraries accept phone calls from patrons asking research questions—if the questions are specific and the answers brief. That service is a big help to speakers who have specific questions like "How many Hispanics live in the United States?" But of course you should not phone a reference librarian to ask broad questions such as "What can you tell me about immigration trends?"

3. Computerized Library Search

Many college, university, and community libraries have computers through which you can search expanding resources for data for your speeches. And many of those library computers can be accessed from your home, via your own computer. For example, I can, from my home office, use my computer to contact the computer at the main library in this area, then search on-line for particular books, magazine articles, and information about local organizations.

4. Local Organizations

Your town's historic society, museum staff, amateur radio club, business person's association, etc. usually have members who can often provide useful information.

To find such groups, your library can often help—many libraries maintain files of local groups, including names, addresses, and phone numbers of people to contact. You can also find many such groups listed in the yellow pages of your local phone book.

5. State and National Organizations

The public relations departments, customer service representatives, sales staff, marketing personnel, advertising agencies, and such of many businesses, companies, manufacturers, trade and industrial associations, government agencies, etc. are often eager to provide information—they figure your speeches might help promote their products and services.

In addition, a surprising number of states, cities, towns, and tourist attractions have their own chambers of commerce, tourist information bureaus, travel centers, etc. that exist just to disseminate information about their particular features. Most of them love to provide information to speakers—student or professional. Increasingly, you can contact these institutions by using the Internet.

6. Correspondence

E-mail, fax, write, or phone to experts, leaders, companies, businesses, and such, asking for both general information and answers to specific questions; many will respond quickly.

7. Professors at Your College or University

Preparing a speech about some specific aspect of Asian culture? About Black leaders? About the life of Verdi? Many professors (like most people) enjoy being interviewed and asked about their fields of knowledge. Sometimes they can also refer you to colleagues who may have additional specifics. You of course don't have to be in their classes; just use your college catalog as another reference book to help you find specialists in the subjects of your speeches.

8. Community Experts

Preparing a speech about Mexican cooking? Interview a local chef. Planning a talk about safety checks on a car? Interview a local mechanic. For a speech about preservation of forests, you might get some interesting insights by talking with the manager of a local lumber yard.

To find such authorities, consult your phone book, the local resources files at your library, area newspapers, ask friends, phone organizations concerned with the subject— in essence, dig around your community's own backyard.

9. Build Your Own Library of Basic References

Some of the references good students have on their own book shelves include—not listed in order of importance, usefulness, value, etc.:

9.1. A Really Good Dictionary

"Really good" means, in this case, a dictionary you are comfortable using, is up to date, and extensive.

Be sure you know the features of your dictionary. For example, some dictionaries list the most popular meaning of a word first, while other dictionaries list the oldest meaning first. And there are other differences between dictionaries that you need to know in order to use them most productively.

Again, consult your reference librarian; she, or he, can point you to reviews of dictionaries and reference books that will help you select the dictionary that can help you most.

You can also buy dictionaries for use via your computer. But be sure to check them out before you invest—some require that you leave the document you are writing in order to look up a word; that is often time-consuming, awkward, frustrating.

9.2. A Really Good Thesaurus

Some students prefer a thesaurus listing words alphabetically; others favor listings by contrasting topics—hot and cold, fast and slow, etc. Before you buy one, be sure it is organized in a way that will help you most in finding words.

Many word-processing programs have a built-in thesaurus, and you can also buy separate software providing listings of words. But some of those programs have much more limited selections than some of the books; be sure to audition your computerized thesaurus before you buy.

9.3. A Good Style Manual, such as **The Chicago Manual of Style** or **Associated Press Stylebook and Libel Manual.** Such books will answer your bothersome questions about grammar, word usage, and such.

9.4. The Elements of Style, by William Strunk, Jr., and E. B. White.

This reference does not simply duplicate the material in the previous two books; it is a gem of brevity and specificness, and fun to read, too. It details elementary rules of usage, principles of composition, form, commonly misused words and expressions, and more.

9.5. A Good Dictionary of Quotations

Here, "good" means it is comprehensive and has an extensive cross-referenced index to help you find appropriate quotations quickly, easily.

9.6. A World Almanac

There are several good ones on the market. Skim them, select the one that seems to have the most material of interest to you. Since they come out yearly, it is wise to get a new one at the start of every year. Sure, that's a bothersome expenditure, but an almanac on your own bookshelf comes in real handy Sunday evenings, for example, when most libraries are closed and your need one or more bits of facts for your Monday morning speech.

9.7. Specialized Reference Books

Audiences like statistics that are presented through comparisons and contrasts, and they usually remember such statistics longer. And listeners like stories, examples, unusual facts, and such. To find those kinds of information my own library includes *American Averages, Guinness Book of Records, Famous Firsts, Book of Days, Facts About The Presidents, Nautical Dictionary, Books of Lists,* and others.

Now wait a moment—don't panic. Don't think I'm suggesting you should rush out right now to buy a stack of books for your own library. Rather, consider the words of English essayist and statesman Augustine Birrell:

> "Libraries are not made; they grow."

(No, that quote was not stored in my memory—computer or human; I just dug it out of one of my quotation books.)

PURPOSES OF DATA

You know, of course, that data can be used as proof—as evidence, documentation. For example, consider a speaker attempting to convince a city council that it should take some specified action about expanding the local airport. To prove her case the speaker might well present such data as the estimated cost, the experience of a comparable city, and the recommendation of a transportation expert.

Each of these three kinds of data would help the speaker substantiate her viewpoint. But data can also be used for other purposes. Another speaker might say, in another speaking situation:

> Next, I believe we should expand the use of educational television because it is efficient. By that I mean that educational television can release those kids in room 12 at Dewey Elementary School who are saddled with a teacher who is still attending evening classes to learn how to teach, to get her credential. Educational television can bring to those youngsters the top teacher in the entire state.

That is a use of data to clarify a point. In that case, the speaker used one type of data, an example, to explain what his basic idea meant. So a second use of data is to help a speaker make his points understandable, explicit, and unmistakable.

A third purpose of data in a speech is illustrated by this statement:

> Now I know you college students are years beyond your teenage fun of spending hours on the telephone. Therefore I know you're not very interested in listening to tips on how to use a phone correctly. But what if I told you that for about half an hour's work a day you could easily earn $150 or more a month—just by using your phone? That works out to $10 per hour, and you wouldn't even have to get out of bed!

That's using data to make a point interesting, to get the audience alert, thoughtful, involved, and observant.

Finally, the fourth use of data . . . . Huh? Do I hear a student calling, "Wait—how do you make that kind of money on a phone?" Provide a wake-up service, the speaker suggested.

Now for the fourth purpose of data. I used to speak frequently about educational television; often I would include this statement:

> Educational television is economical. Now many educators immediately scoff at that statement. Some even know the figures—to operate the typical community television station costs 10 to 15 million dollars a year. But when you consider the number of students who learn from educational television, the cost figures out to less than what many students spend in a year on just paper and pencils.

Those figures made that point memorable. After that speech, many in the audience would mention their surprise, then their doubt, then their checking those figures and finding them correct.

In summary, then, you now know the four purposes for which data might be used in a speech. They are (see if you can remember them):

1. _____

2. _____

3. _____

4. _____

The purposes of data in a speech: to prove, to clarify, to add interest, and to make memorable. As you'll soon see, it's important for you to know these four purposes.

Now let's look at the various types of data you can use.

TYPES OF DATA

There are eight main types:

1. Examples
2. Stories
3. Quotations
4. Definitions
5. Comparisons
6. Contrasts
7. Statistics
8. Audiovisual aids

Here are suggestions for using each of them.

1. Examples

Examples are one of the most frequently used, and misused, types of data. It is an example when a speaker says:

▶ Our library is right on the ball. The other day I was in there and asked for some material on space travel. And there, stacked on a special shelf, was a variety of references all ready to go.

USING EXAMPLES:

"I do not consider myself a trend setter. But I'm still the only member of Congress who goes to work on a motorcycle, hates neckties, and is never accused of using the Senate barber shop."

Colorado Senator *Ben Nighthorse Campbell,* speaking at the Republican National Convention.

An example is a "typical, representative, or illustrative instance or case," to quote our friend Webster again.

An example is valid and effective to meet three, but not all four, of the purposes of data in a speech. An example can be used to clarify, to add interest, or to make memorable. *But an example is NOT valid proof!* You've heard speakers say something such as:

▶ The army is unfair in how it treats new soldiers. I know because of what happened to my brother in the army.

Your brother is only one of thousands of "new soldiers" in the army each year. What happened to him *proves* nothing, unless—*unless*—you show that your brother is in fact typical, representative, in the qualities or experiences under consideration. Your brother, to be used as proof, must be established as just about the same as at least half of all those other new soldiers.

It is indeed legitimate to tell of your brother's experiences as an example that might *explain* or *clarify* what you mean by some specific statement. It is effective to tell of your brother's experiences so your point will be more *interesting* to your listeners— people always like to hear about people. And it is correct to tell of your brother's experiences to help your audience *remember* your speech or a point in your speech.

But an example—an isolated, individual case—does not *prove* anything unless— again—the example is shown to be typical, average, representative, usual for at least most, if not all, of those people or situations or experiences or whatever the example is drawn from.

2. Stories

Stories are accounts of events or incidents. Here are two examples:

▶ A small child waits, thumb in mouth, doll in hand, with some impatience, the arrival home of a parent. She wishes to relate some small sandbox experience. She is excited to share the thrill she has known that day. The time comes, the parent arrives. Beaten down by the stresses of the work place the parent so often says to the child, "Not now, honey, I'm busy, go watch television."

> Robert Keeshan, *"Captain Kangaroo";*
> *Speech at Fourteenth National Abe Lincoln*
> *Awards Ceremony, Southern Baptist*
> *Radio-Television Commission,*
> *Fort Worth, Texas*

▶ A minister was giving a children's sermon the Sunday before Thanksgiving using a large cornucopia overflowing with fruit. The minister asked the children to imagine the cornucopia empty so they could fill it with whatever they liked. The children responded with items like popcorn, pizza, and mayonnaise. He asked them to respond with their favorite toys or games. Then he suggested putting in something which was invisible—something from God. One small child answered, "Natural gas!" I congratulate my colleagues at the American Gas Association.

> L. R. Wallis, *Health and Physics Consultant,*
> *General Electric Company;*
> *Speech at Waste Management Conference,*
> *Tucson, Arizona*

One of the main values in telling stories in your speech is that people like to hear about the experiences of others. Some of your stories should be selected from incidents

you may hear or read in your research. But at least some of your stories should usually be of your own experiences.

Not only is an audience interested in stories, but most listeners tend to remember stories, especially when they are told vividly. But that leads us to one of the major, most frequent weaknesses in storytelling—overdetailing, rambling, stretching the story far beyond its significance or its interest value.

Don't be the speaker who tells a story in words such as:

▶ So, like I say, he got in the car. And he started the motor—you know, he turns the key on, and then he puts it in gear, and he goes. So we drive away, and then we turn, and then we go up this street, and then he looks like maybe he doesn't know where he's going. So I start getting a little nervous—cause I noticed, back there when he was starting this car, and putting the key in, and getting ready to go, I noticed then that as he drives he . . . .

"Come on!" I yell mentally at such a speaker. "Get to the point!!"

But there's really little need for such a reaction. Most in the audience usually have already tuned out such a speaker.

3. Quotations

Quotations are statements by persons who are usually authoritative or experienced in the subject. You've heard and used quotations. They range upward from the very informal—"Must be true because I was standing in line at the snack stand this morning and overheading a guy say. . . ." You know, too, the weakness of a quotation. You

USING A QUOTATION:

"As I stand before the American people and think of the honor this great convention has bestowed upon me, I recall the words of Dr. Martin Luther King, Jr., who made America stronger by making America more free. He said, 'Occassionally in life there are moments which cannot be completely explained by words. Their meaning can only be articulated by the inaudible language of the heart.' Tonight is such a moment for me."

That effective use of a quotation was presented by *Geraldine Ferraro,* former U.S. Ambassador to Japan, in her speech accepting nomination as candidate for Vice President, Democratic National Convention, San Francisco.

can almost always find someone else to quote with a statement presenting the exact opposite view.

Essentially the value of a quotation depends largely on the source—his or her reputation as knowledgeable, objective, and honest.

A major problem with using quotations is that some listeners reject the statements of experts largely because of apparent lack of objectivity due to vested interests. For example, when talking about nuclear safety, it has been fashionable in recent years to reject statements made by nuclear scientists.

At the same time, many listeners believe, without questioning, statements about nuclear safety made by people who are inexperienced, untrained.

To reject the words of all specialists is as unjustified as to accept the words of all novices.

As a speaker, your problem is to select quotations that are most likely to influence your particular listeners. The decision should be based on three factors:

1. Your impression of the validity of the quotations
2. The reputation, experience, knowledge, and authority of the individuals whom you quote
3. The impact the statements may have on your listeners

However you select the quotations you are to use in your speeches, your decisions should be based on facts about the sources of the statement rather than on feelings, emotions, or opinions about those sources.

Here are some examples of quotations used in speeches:

▶ When Harry Truman was notified, on the death of Franklin D. Roosevelt, that he we now President of the United States, he said, "I felt like the moon, the stars, and all the planets had fallen on me." While I don't actually feel that way, I now understand more than ever how Mr. Truman could have said it.

L. Patrick Gray, III, *then Acting Director, Federal Bureau of Investigation; Speech to Thomas More Society, Washington, D.C.*

▶ President Clinton has said: "America has flourished for over 200 years because of our willingness to cultivate the human spirit."

Jane Alexander, *Chairwoman of the National Endowments for the Arts; speech to Economic club of Detroit*

"How do you find quotations?" some students ask.

There are two main sources. First, your library has quite a selection of books containing hundreds of quotations. The most well known of these books is *Familiar Quotations* by John Bartlett. Especially valuable is its detailed index, some 600 pages covering just about every topic you might need for your speeches.

The second major source of quotations is via your computer. It provides several options. Get on the Internet and enter the words "Software AND Quotations." One document, titled "Quotation Collections on the Internet" lists 23 collections so diverse they include:

"Blackboard Quotations" by Bart Simpson

"Mathematical Quotations"

"Memorable Sayings of Aristotle"

"Quotes About Libraries and Librarians"

"Quotations About Tea"

"Quotations from TV and Movies"

"Some Unclassified Funny Quotes"

Another route: go to the home page "Quotations." At this writing it contains 11,168 entries, and more are added regularly. You'll not be alone—it gets several thousand "hits" per day.

▶ To look for quotations by a particular individual, consult "Really Miscellaneous," a listing alphabetical by person.
▶ To search for quotes on a specific subject, bring up "Quotations by Topic."
▶ To hunt for statements containing a key word, go to "Search Tool."
▶ To check specialized listings, you can go to:
  • Great Leaders
  • Miscellaneous Malapropisms
  • Proverbial Wisdom
  • Quotes by Women
  • Quotes from Poetry
  • Sarcasm
  • Selections from William Shakespeare

Or you might go to what are probably the two most well known, frequently used sources for quotations:

"Bartlett's Familiar Quotations": http://www.columbia.edu/acis/bartleby/bartlett
"Famous Quotes": http://www.noord.bart.nl/~bfm/quotes/quote.html

Other options via your computer include CD-ROMs, disks, and software. For example, the software called "Correct Quotes" includes more than 5,000 quotations indexed by author and subject. It's part of the "WordStar, Writing Tools Library." And of course there are many other such sources.

"But how do you deliver a quotation?" students often ask. "Do you have to say 'quote'? And what about 'unquote'; is that OK to use?"

Most of the time a speaker should be able to indicate simply by a pause or by a slight change of voice—inflection, tone, pace, or placement—that the words are from some-one else. That does not mean the speaker should become an actor and try to project a completely different voice or try to imitate or impersonate the person who is being quoted. Rather, a slight change in delivery will usually let the audience know that you're presenting a quotation.

A further signal that you're going into a quotation is using such phrases as "In the words of . . ." or "As so-and-so said recently . . ." or "Listen to what one expert reported . . . ."

Thus, you seldom need to use those troublesome words "quote" and "unquote." However, if you want to point up or add emphasis or significance to a quotation using the word "quote" will help. Further emphasis is usually added by saying something such as "And let me give you this expert's words directly—quote . . . ."

Now what do you say to complete a quotation introduced by "quote"? In most speaking situations, "unquote" is certainly acceptable. Sure, there are some so strict about the niceties of expression that they object to that word. Some claim "unquote" is not in the dictionary; it is in my copy of Webster, and the word is not even noted as slang, but as just a good, usable word.

But if you are in doubt how your audience might accept "unquote," you can go for-mal and close a quotation with the words "end of quote" or "close of quote." To me, they are awkward, overformal phrases, but I'd probably use them if I were speaking, for example, before the New England English Teachers Association.

4. Definitions

Definitions are statements of the meaning of words or ideas.

In a speech, using a definition can help prove a point but is usually presented to make a point more understandable. For example:

▶ Our world is heading toward marketing internationalism. By my term "marketing internationalism" I mean the two-way flow across national boundaries of marketing thought, marketing practice, and marketing people.

John G. Keane, President, Managing Change, Inc.; Speech at First Brazilian Marketing and Commercialization Congress, Rio de Janeiro, Brazil

▶ My subject is "The Future of Capitalism." When I speak of the future of capitalism I mean the future of competitive capitalism—a free enterprise capitalism.

Milton Friedman, Professor and Economist, University of Chicago; Speech at Pepperdine University, Los Angeles, California

Presenting a definition:

"I know the last few years we have heard a lot about something called 'family values.' And like many of you, I have struggled to figure out what that means, and since my accident, I have found a definition that seems to make sense. I think it means that we are all family. And that we all have value."
Christopher Reeve, speaking at National Democratic Convention.

▸ The title of this talk [Third World Development] and many of the terms which I will use may well offend some purists, but in the interests of clarity, some definition is necessary. The "Third World" is generally perceived as consisting of what is left over after the nations of the "First World"—the industrialized democracies—and the "Second World"—the centrally planned socialist economies of eastern Europe—have been accounted for.

Sean M. Cleary, *Consul General of South Africa; Speech at the Town Hall of California, Los Angeles, California*

The major value of a definition in a speech is to establish with the audience a common basis for views. Listen carefully to two or more of your friends arguing vigorously, each having opposing viewpoints. If you can keep from getting involved, you frequently will identify the one basic point of the disagreement as simply the difference about the definition of some key word, phrase, or idea. So to prevent the possibility that some in your audience may start objecting to a viewpoint you present in a speech, it may be helpful to offer a definition.

COMPARISON:

"Reagan and Bush borrowed more money and ran up more debt in 12 years than all the presidents in the previous 205 years of our history combined."

That vivid comparison was presented by Congresswoman *Maxine Waters* (California) when she spoke to the National Newspaper Publishers Association.

5. Comparisons

Comparisons present characteristics, features, or qualities that are similar.

Comparisons help clarify the unknown by referring to the known. The speaker refers to ideas, processes, actions, events, or such that the audience already knows, and the speaker uses those points as a basis for developing the audience's knowledge or acceptance of a new idea, proposal, etc.

Here are a couple of examples of comparisons:

▶ Today the government is spending about $1.20 for every $1.00 it takes in taxes.

President Bill Clinton;
Radio Address from the White House

▶ To succeed in pollution abatement or surfing, you've got to ride the crest of a good wave. Too early, and you can't get going. Too late, and you're swamped. In pollution control today "the surf is up" for resource conservation. It, indeed, is an idea whose time has come.

Joseph T. Ling,
Vice President, 3M Company;
Speech at National Conference on Treatment of
Disposal of Industrial Wastewaters and Residues,
Houston, Texas

In using comparisons in a speech, it is important that the features being presented are relevant. Comparisons can be made between virtually any subjects, but the points that are compared may not be appropriate. For example, you could claim that sailing a boat from California to Hawaii is like driving a car from California to New York because you'd go about the same distance. But the distance traveled is not a significant quality; rather, there are great differences in the pivotal features—the time needed to complete the journeys, the presence of others along the route, the availability of assistance, the dependence of the traveler on his or her own resources, the complexity of keeping on course, and such. Therefore, equating those two trips would be an ineffective comparison.

Comparisons can often be humorous, thereby making the point vivid and memorable as well as enjoyable. One national political speaker was especially adept at humorous comparisons, including in his speeches lines like these:

> ◗ Our economy is like a tired old racehorse that was a great old racehorse but now has arthritis in his legs.
>
> ◗ Our government consumes 25 percent, or one-fourth, of our gross national product. My question is, do you think you're getting your money's worth? Isn't that sad? You bought a front-row seat in the box, and you're seeing a fourth-rate vaudeville show from the balcony.

Ross Perot;
*Speech to Better Govemment,
Washington, D.C.*

6. Contrasts

Contrasts of course present qualities, features, or characteristics that are different.

Examples of contrasts are in the quotations from speeches in the following two photo captions.

PRESENTING A CONTRAST:

"In his speech from San Diego, Senator Dole offered himself as a bridge to the past. Tonight, Bill Clinton and I offer ourselves as a bridge to the future."
Al Gore, candidate for reelection as Vice President, speaking at the National Democratic Convention.

PRESENTING A CONTRAST:

PRESENTING A CONTRAST:

"Democracies do not war against one another. Democracies make better partners. Democracies do not ignore the environment, shelter terrorists, or spawn refugees. Democracies honor human rights."

Statement before the Foreign Affairs Committee, U.S. House of Representatives, by *Bette Bao Lord,* Chairwoman, Freedom House, New York; writer and prodemocracy and human rights activist.

7. Statistics

A statistic is, of course, a numerical fact or figure.

Statistics are boring to many people. But a good speaker can do much to make statistics interesting, comprehensible, and likely to be remembered.

Suppose you're designing a speech on some specific aspect about crime. You find this statistic that you could use in your speech:

◗ Each year about 24 percent of Americans are the victims of crime.

Presented in a speech, that statistic might be rather impressive because it is such a high percentage. But that fact could be worded much more powerfully. How would you suggest it be stated in a speech so it would have greater impact on your listeners? Your answer, please:_____

_____

_____

There are, of course, several possibilities. You could personalize that percentage a bit by stating it this way:

◗ Each year one out of every four Americans is the victim of a crime.

You could make it still more personal by relating it to your audience. You might say something such as:

◗ If this audience is typical of America, one out of every four of you here in this audience today will be the victim of a crime this year.

Another way to express that same fact is to change that percentage to the actual number. You could look up the nation's total population (248,709,873) and compute 24 percent of that. Then you could say:

◗ Each year about 59,690,369 Americans are the victims of crime.

That might get more attention because as a number, it may be more impressive than the percentage. Further, because it is a number representing individuals, it may seem more personal than the percentage.

On the other hand, sometimes it may be more effective to use a percentage rather than numbers. For example, it would *not* be effective to present those figures in a statement such as:

▶ Each year, of the 248,709,873 Americans, some 59,690,369 are the victims of crime.

Obviously, few listeners will remember such figures. Besides, many in an audience may have trouble understanding the importance of numbers at the time they hear them in a speech. Consequently, some may continue to ponder the statistics as the speaker goes on to the next point, resulting in some listeners missing the following statements as well.

A technique to increase the likelihood that your audience will grasp and remember the statistics you use in speeches is to round off the numbers. The statement "more than half a million dollars" is more likely to be remembered than the unnecessarily cluttered exact figure "$527,737.00." Indeed, some listeners may doubt statistics that seem overprecise. The stock example of this:

▶ The average American family has 2.3 children.

Some listeners respond with the old quip, "But I've never seen one-third of a child!"

Generally, large figures presented in a speech are usually more memorable if they're rounded off. More of your listeners might remember the crime statistic if it were stated this way:

▶ Each year nearly 60 million Americans are the victims of crime.

But it can be expressed still more interestingly. Got a suggestion? _____

_____

_____

Again, there are several possible answers. You might, for example, look up the population figures for various states. Then that same basic fact could be presented in these words:

▶ Each year nearly as many Americans are the victims of crime as the total number of residents in all three of our most populated states—California, New York, and Texas.

Or you could present that same crime figure this way:

▶ Each year more Americans are the victims of crime than the total number of all the residents in 30 of our states.

Indeed, you might present that bit of data in an especially striking fashion by naming each of those states—Wyoming, Alaska, Vermont, North Dakota . . . and on through the entire list.

Let's look at a few more examples of how statistics can be presented dramatically in speeches. Assume you're working on a speech about the poor condition of the roads in our nation today. You could point out that:

▶ Back in the mid-1970s, when the United States was at its peak in building roads, each year enough roads were built to go around the world three times. In three years, that's equal to building a road from here to the moon.

"Other nations spend significant portions of their budgets to encourage visitors to their shores. The Bahamas spend about $125 per visitor. We, in the United States, rank 56th and spend a dismal 5 cents per visitor. While Italy spent over a billion dollars in 1990, the United States spent $14 million."

Those statistics were presented by U.S. Senator *Daniel K. Inouye* (Hawaii), speaking to the Hawaii Chamber of Commerce.

Comparing statistics with other easily visualized facts is a particularly effective technique in speeches. Another example: If you were preparing a speech about safe driving, you'd likely include this fact:

▸ This year some 40,000 people will die in auto wrecks in the United States.

That figure can be stated more impressively by presenting this comparison:

▸ This year 30 percent more people will die in auto wrecks in the United States than the total number of American soldiers killed during the entire 25 years of our country's involvement in the Vietnam War.

Here's another example of adding impact to the number of people likely to be killed in auto accidents this year:

▸ This year the number of people who will die in auto wrecks in the United States will be more than the total population of such well-known cities as Poughkeepsie, New York, or Monterey, California, or Wheeling, West Virginia, or Bremerton, Washington.

Another way to make statistics more interesting is to present them in a creative illustration. In his book *Future Shock*, Alvin Toffler wrote:

▸ If the last 50,000 years of man's existence were divided into lifetimes of approximately 62 years each, there have been about 800 such lifetimes. Of these 800, fully 650 were spent in caves.

But it is popular in some circles today to reject statistics completely. Someone said, "Figures can lie and liars can figure." That's a clever turn of words, but it is so broad a generalization that it has little value in helping a speaker or a listener decide whether to use or accept a particular statistic.

It is as ridiculous to reject all statistics as it is to accept all. You have to develop your own standard for using statistics in a speech, just as you should for accepting them as a listener or reader. If a figure meets your test of credibility, if it seems honest and not misleading, if it seems to make sense, then you should use and accept it. Just because I've heard one government statistic that was incorrect, I thereafter have not rejected all government statistics. If the figure is questionable and also important to me, I will make an effort to check it. If I have no basis to question the statistic—if I have no other information or no experience of receiving a faulty figure from that source before—I accept it.

To review, these are the major techniques to make statistics in a speech more interesting, memorable, relevant, valuable:

1. Personalize.
2. Relate to your audience's interests or situations.
3. Change percentages to numbers.
4. Change numbers to percentages.
5. Round off large numbers.
6. Compare with other statistics.
7. Compare with easily visualized facts.
8. Develop creative illustrations.

All these techniques won't work on all statistics or in all speaking situations. A technique may be effective for some purposes and not for others.

8. Audiovisual Aids

There are 8 main types of audiovisual aids:

1. Objects
2. Models
3. Overhead projections
4. Chalkboards
5. Graphs, charts, diagrams, maps, etc.
6. Slides, motion pictures, video recordings
7. Audio recordings
8. Computer-generated graphics

The advantages of using audiovisual aids as data to support a point are:

1. Aids make a point clearer.
2. Aids make a point more memorable.
3. Aids emphasize a point.
4. Aids add interest to a speech.
5. Aids concentrate the attention of the audience.

In essence, aids allow you as a speaker to present your case through an additional communication channel—the visual channel—as well as help you expand your audio communication.

Even presidents of the United States use visual aids in their speeches: Presidents Clinton and Bush have both used charts, diagrams, maps, and such in their speeches.

The main features of the various types of audiovisual aids are:

1. *Objects.* Rather than merely trying to describe a two-way radio or simply talking about one, it would be much more interesting and clearer to your listeners if you showed them an actual unit.

2. *Models.* For a speech about oil wells, you might be able to borrow a small replica of an oil well from the public relations department of a petroleum company or from the engineering department of your school; for a speech about the brain, you might borrow a plastic recreation of a brain from a local medical center or perhaps from a doctor.

   Even a very modest model, cut from colored cardboard, for example, could have a greater impact on your listeners than no visual at all.

3. *Overhead projections.* Because overhead projections are easy, fast, and inexpensive to make, they are highly recommended.

   And they have several significant advantages: You can write on the aid as you talk—adding statistics, for example; you can face your audience as you write; the room in which you speak need not be darkened when overhead projectors are used.

   But a warning: I've had students watch other speakers using overhead projections and become so impressed that they drew up their own charts on regular graph paper, for example, and then tried to use those charts on an overhead projector directly. They failed to note one drawback of overhead projections: The original drawings must be run through a machine to make a transparency—a sheet of plastic you can see through. However, such equipment is available today in almost every school, college, and office; even many libraries are now providing the equipment. So the transparencies can be prepared readily, and they take but a few seconds.

4. *Chalkboard.* Here are a few suggestions for using this familiar aid.

   If you are to draw a rather extensive or complex visual, such as a detailed map, don't take to much speech time with the act of drawing. Consider drawing it on the board before you speak, perhaps covering it with a sheet of paper until the time you need it in your speech.

   Also, if you have not used a chalkboard before, you'll need to practice just a bit unless you are a somewhat skilled artist. Chalkboard drawings seem so easy that many speakers skip any preparation, and consequently their scribbled key words, rough graphs, etc. may detract more than contribute to their speeches.

   You've probably noticed one frequent hazard in using a chalkboard: the tendency of so many speakers to talk to the board, not to their audience. Of course, you pretty much have to turn your back to your audience during the time you're writing on the board. But while you're writing—with your back to your listeners—you shouldn't go on giving your speech. **Worse:** Speakers who continue talking to the board after they've completed writing. **Better:** When you're putting material on the board, pause in your speech; when you're finished writing, then turn again to your audience and resume your speech.

5. *Graphs, charts, diagrams, maps, etc.* Keep them simple. Don't, for example, use a detailed street map of Los Angeles, which is covered with tiny blocks and minute names, to show a route that is only a few blocks long. Rather, draw a large version of just that portion of the map you are talking about.

   Further, don't clutter such visuals with more information than is needed. Round off figures; don't label all items in full sentences; use abbreviations or symbols whenever they will improve clarity, understanding, and communication.

6. *Slides, motion pictures, video recordings.* Often used in what otherwise would be straight speeches. The color, the impact, the emphasis, and the motion add much to a speech.

7. *Audio recordings.* CDs, cassettes, etc. can present mood or background music that would enhance a talk about Hawaii, for example. If you're presenting quite a few quotations in a speech, you might have some friends read them onto a tape; then you could play the simulated expressions of the people you're quoting.

8. *Computer-generated graphics* (CGGs): If you're skilled in using a computer, you can rather quickly and easily design quite a variety of diagrams, pie charts, bar graphs, drawings, and other such visuals—in a variety of colors—to use as data to support points in your speeches.

After you get a printout of your visual, you can take it to the audiovisual department of your school or to almost any photocopy service, and they should be able to convert your paper copy into a transparency for projection on an overhead projector.

Among the several software programs now on the market to help you design CGGs are:

"Corel Presentations": The manufacturer says, "It's easy to learn and use and integrates fully with other applications." Among its features:

- "The Show Expert," which asks you questions about your audience and what you want to present, then helps you structure your speeches.
- "The Outliner," which helps you create and organize your speeches.
- You can change the sequence of slides by clicking on them, then dragging them to a new position.
- Objects and text can be made into 3-dimensional effects.

"Great Presentations": published by "Expert Software," which says you can "get your message across with perfect overheads, slides, and handouts." Its features include:

- "Auto Content Wizard," which helps you design your speeches.
- More than 25 background templates for your visuals, plus help in designing your own backgrounds.
- A selection of 57 chart styles.
- 42 transition effects —wipe, dissolve, fade, etc.—to make your moving from one visual to the next appear smooth and professional.

"PowerPoint": A Microsoft program "for everyone who can't wait to get a good idea across," according to its manufacturer. It has features such as:

- A multimedia CD-ROM disk so you can add sound, video clips, clip art, and such to your speeches.
- "Answer Wizard," which lets you type in a question about using the software, then gives you the answer.
- "AutoClipArt," which suggests images for your speeches; "AutoContent," which automatically corrects your misspellings and typos; and "StyleChecker," which checks your punctuation.

In addition, as this is being written, computer companies are expanding in the production of attachments that can link visuals on your computer's screen with various projection equipment, some specially designed for use by speakers.

The advantages of CGGs include ease of designing; the variety of formats available; the facility to try different colors, shapes, sizes, formats, and labels; the greater impact of color; and the increased power of visuals prepared especially for your particular audience.

Those tips are intended to help you select audiovisual aids for use as data in your speeches. Now, here are a few suggestions on:

Designing Your Aids

1. *Use aids that are large enough to be seen easily and clearly by all in the audience.* But how large is large enough? Best guide: Try out a rough, preliminary version of the aid in the actual room in which you are to speak or a room comparable in size.

2. *Make aids precise and neat.* Avoid aids that are cluttered with detailed explanations or labels you're going to talk about anyway. In general, details that you're going to mention need not be on the aid. Rather, the aid should communicate something that is better seen than heard. Use straight, traditional block lettering; avoid fancy scroll or specialized lettering.

3. *Make aids visually interesting.* Use cartoons, symbols, drawings, and such to make your speech vivid and memorable, as long as these add to rather than detract from the effectiveness of the aid.

4. *Use an aid only when it shows what you want it to.* Too often a speaker will use a map, for example, and present a feeble apology such as "This gives you a rough idea of the area I'm talking about, although a good part of the land doesn't quite show on this particular map." The solution, of course, is to get a map that does show what you want to show; don't bother using an aid simply because it happens to be available.

5. *Get skilled help in preparing aids.* Many schools, from elementary through university, and many businesses, government agencies, etc. now have their own graphic artists or visual aids department. If you're speaking for or to such a

USING A VISUAL AID:

A man was hit by a soda bottle thrown by someone in the stands in a New York stadium. The injured man sued the concessionaire who sold the soda. The vendor claimed there was nothing he could have done to prevent the injury. Throughout the trial, the lawyer for the injured man kept on his courtroom desk a strange brown bag. The bag became a fascination to the jurors. Not until the lawyer presented his closing argument did he open the bag and dramatically take out—a paper cup. "*This* is what they could have done to protect my client," the lawyer announced. He won the case.

The lawyer was *Harry Lipsig,* "perhaps the winningest liability lawyer in America," according to ***Time*** magazine.

group, you could get help from the staff. Or perhaps you have a friend who is an art major or who is talented in such work.

6. *The elaborateness of the aid should be appropriate to the speaking situation.* Just as it can be out of place to offer too formal an introduction to your speech if the situation is rather small or casual, aids also can be too formal.

For your speeches in this course, we are much more interested in your using aids often, for practice, than we are in seeing elaborate, extensive aids that might be time-consuming and expensive to prepare. Just a simple graph on a binder page is sufficient for your in-class practice in this speech course. It will be good enough to give you experience in selecting, designing, and using an aid. After all, you've signed up for a speech course, not an art course. But do use aids whenever they can add to your speech.

REVIEW

Now let's start to bring together what you've learned so far—as a review, not as this lesson's self-test. Let's consider the first objective you were to achieve in this lesson.
Name the types of data:

1. _____
2. _____
3. _____
4. _____
5. _____
6. _____
7. _____
8. _____

To check your answers, look back through this lesson.

Now, how about the second objective for this lesson.

Identify the type of data in each of the following examples.

1. In California, between 1980 and 1990, the Asian population increased by 3.1 million.

   Type of data: _____

2. Let me tell you about a friend of mine who faced such a decision. He'd been sailing his boat through heavy fog for more than three hours. By then, he should have sighted land, but he had not. He sailed on for another hour. Still no land. Finally, he decided he had but one alternative—he had to radio to the Coast Guard.

   Type of data: _____

3. It's popular in Hawaii to say, "Go for it!"

   Type of data: _____

4. Our federal government needs to stay within its budget for the same reasons we here at this meeting today need to stay within our own personal budgets.

Type of data: _____

5. A great many humans are collectors—of shells, money, books, stamps, miniatures, paintings, antiques, possessions of all kinds.

Type of data: _____

6. Amateur radio operators must pass examinations testing their technical knowledge and operating skills; on the other hand, operators of CB—Citizen Band—radios do not have to take any tests.

Type of data: _____

Check your answers with those on the page after the next.

"Half the world is composed of people who have something to say and can't, and the other half who have nothing to say and keep on saying it."

Robert Frost, poet.

Answers

1. Statistic
2. Story
3. Quotation
4. Comparison
5. Examples
6. Contrast

By now you should have attained the first two objectives of this lesson. You should be able to name the types of data, and you should be able to identify the type of data in a given example.

But as you have probably observed as you listened to some speakers, data can be used not only to support a point or prove an idea, but data can also be used to mislead an audience.

MISLEADING DATA

There are 3 main methods of misleading an audience. They are bias, lie, and propaganda.

POINTING TO MISLEADING DATA:

"The indictment drawn up by the army against Lieutenant Calley stated in six separate charges that he did at My Lai murder four 'Oriental human beings'—murder not less than 30 'Oriental human beings'—murder an unknown number of 'Oriental human beings' not less than 70—and so on, numbering 102. Thus, the army did not charge him with the murder of human beings as presumably would have been the case had Caucasians been involved, but instead charged the apparently lesser offense of killing mere 'Oriental human beings.'"

Keynote address at the Thirtieth Anniversary of the West Los Angeles Japanese American Citizens League, by *Patsy Takemoto Mink,* member of the U.S. House of Representatives (D, Hawaii) and attorney.

1. Bias

Bias is defined as unreasoned or unfair distortion in favor of or against a person, idea, proposal, or such.

In essence, bias most often exists when only the information that supports one particular view is presented or when information is withheld even though it is crucial to a point.

2. Lie

Another way to mislead an audience is to tell a simple, straightforward *lie.*

But in some circles today, particularly in government, politics, and bureaucracies, old-fashioned lies get awarded with new—almost glamorous—names. For example, a lie today is sometimes called "misinformation"—apparently in the belief that a 14-letter word is somehow more politically correct than the 3-letter term "lie." Recently lies have sometimes been called "strategic misrepresentation," "misspeak," "mislead," "withholding information," and other exotic terms.

As a speaker, you have a moral responsibility to be sure you do not present lies in your speeches—to be positive that every statement in your speeches is true.

3. Propaganda

The third way to deceive your listeners is by using *propaganda.*

Traditionally, propaganda has been defined as the use of facts, ideas, or allegations that are distorted, slanted, incomplete, or otherwise misleading. While that definition is still valid, today analysts of propaganda define propaganda in more sophisticated terms. In their book *Age of Propaganda,* psychology professors Anthony R. Pratkanis and Elliot Aronson wrote that propaganda means "mass 'suggestion' or influence through the manipulation of symbols and the psychology of the individual. Propaganda is the communication of a point of view with the ultimate goal of having the recipient of the appeal come to 'voluntarily' accept this position as if it were his or her own."

Until recently, many communication researchers and theorists said propaganda uses a variety of specific techniques such as card stacking (unfair statistic), glittering generality (vague feature described attractively), flag waving (undeserved appeal to patriotism), and such. While those techniques continue to be used by some speakers (and a great many advertisers), much of today's propaganda is considerably more complicated.

But be perfectly clear: of course this brief section about misleading data is not to teach you how to use lies, bias, and propaganda in your speeches; rather, the purpose is to guide you *not* to use these methods.

STATING THE SOURCES OF DATA

Students—indeed, experienced speakers—often ask, "Should I say in my speech where I got my information?"

Answer: Depends.

In most speaking situations, there's no need to make such a statement as "According to **The World Almanac and Book of Facts 1997,** page 375, in the section titled 'Noted Personalities,' in the listing headed 'Original Names of Selected Entertainers,' in the right-hand column, in the eighteenth entry down the list, Whoopi Goldberg's real name is given as Caryn Johnson." All you need to say is "Whoopi Goldberg's real name is Caryn Johnson."

Nearly always your listeners will accept what you say as reliable. Hence, usually you need not state in a speech the sources of your data.

But if you are presenting a statement that many of your listeners might doubt, then you should mention the source. Example: "Despite popular belief, automobile driving is actually far safer now than it was just 25 year ago. Nearly eleven thousand more people were killed in auto wrecks in 1970 than in 1995. That means that there are now more than 24 percent fewer deaths by car wrecks than there were just a quarter century ago. That's according to the latest figures available as reported in the *1997 World Almanac.*"

The major advantages of stating the sources of your information are adding an impression of authenticity, factualness, and reliability. The major disadvantages of stating the sources of your data include presenting uninteresting details, unnecessarily lengthening your speech, telling your listeners more than they might be able to remember comfortably, and detracting from your basic information.

Now, when you're ready, start studying the next lesson for tips on how to outline your speeches.

Long Speeches

"Speeches measured by the hour die with the hour."

Thomas Jefferson

ASSIGNMENT 11: SELECTING DATA: SELF-TEST

 ACTION: Take the following self-test.

1. Name the types of data.

2. Name the main methods of misleading an audience.

In the blank to the right of each of the following, name the type of data.

3. The world's longest sailboard is 165 feet.   _____

4. According to *Time,* the problem is "how to strike an acceptable balance between employment and inflation."   _____

5. While listening for a signal on my amateur radio gear one day, I was suddenly surprised to hear a station calling from a country seldom heard on the air. I talked with the caller briefly, then telephoned several of my friends who are hams so they, too, could talk with this rare station. Turned out all my friends had long ago been in contact with this "rare" station several times.   _____

6. Only two nations are smaller than Nauru—the Vatican and Monaco.   _____

7. Throughout the world, virtually all wealthy people live where they have almost unlimited choices of what they can buy, but while every citizen of Nauru is exceptionally wealthy and expected to be a millionaire in a few years, they have nearly nothing on which to spend their money.   _____

8. We know educational television works. In Chicago, students can earn community college degrees by television. In Philadelphia, students can earn high school diplomas by TV.   _____

9. You can see the results from this chart.   _____

10. By "criticism," I mean the strengths as well as the weaknesses of the plan.   _____

11. Watching TV is generally passive—the viewer usually just sits and looks; on the other hand, reading a book is typically active—the reader customarily involves his mind, his imagination, his own creativity.   _____

Representative Patsy Mink . . .

. . . speaks in the United States House of Representatives for the interests of Hawaii.

It's a fascinating area. It includes all of the state except the near-metropolis of Honolulu. Thus she is concerned with the farmlands north of Pearl Harbor, the huge cattle ranches on the island of Hawaii, the fastest-developing island of Maui, and Kauai, the island devastated by the 1991 hurricane.

Democrat Mink was born in 1927, on Maui, is married, has one child. She attended the University of Nebraska, got her bachelor's degree at the University of Hawaii, and earned her doctor of jurisprudence at the University of Chicago Law School in 1951.

She was a practicing attorney, a lecturer at the University of Hawaii for seven years, served in the Hawaii House of Representatives for two years, in the Hawaii Senate four years.

Congresswoman Mink is "exuberant and enthusiastically liberal," according to *The Almanac of American Politics 1996.* And "she helped feminism grow from a fringe cause to one of the main rallying cries for Democrats." She sponsored a gender equity act, women's health-care measures, and many other innovations.

She is a committed activist, and when her party lost in the 1994 elections, she said, "I will not like having to just wait for the other side to make their move in order to get something done."

Answers

1. Types of data:
    1.1. Examples
    1.2. Stories
    1.3. Quotations
    1.4. Definitions
    1.5. Comparisons
    1.6. Contrasts
    1.7. Statistics
    1.8. Audiovisual aids
2. Main methods of misleading an audience:
    2.1. Lies
    2.2. Bias
    2.3. Propaganda

3. Statistic
4. Quotation
5. Story
6. Comparison
7. Contrast
8. Examples
9. Audiovisual aid
10. Definition
11. Comparison

Scoring

Give yourself credit as follows:

Question 1:   8 points, 1 for each type of data you named correctly.

Question 2:   3 points, 1 for each type of misleading data you named correctly.

Questions 3–9:   1 point for each correct identification you made.

Thus, if you got all your answers correct, you'd earn 20 points. Your goal, you remember, is to get at least 80 percent or more correct, so you should have 16 or more of your responses correct. If you have, and if you are maintaining your **Grade Record Form,** give yourself "credit." If you didn't get 16 or more correct answers, please restudy and retest yourself until you do.

Your final objective for this lesson is to use data effectively in your speeches. To evaluate your attainment of that objective, *these four new points will be added to your Speech Evaluation Forms:*

> *1.11. Includes variety of data—statistics, quotations, etc.*
> *1.12. Data seem accurate, honest*
> *1.13. Points seem valid conclusions from data presented*
> *1.14. Includes examples to clarify, add interest, etc., not to prove points*

SELECTING DATA: CHECK-OFF TIP SHEET

PURPOSES:

_____ 1. Proof

_____ 2. Clarify a point

_____ 3. Make a point interesting

_____ 4. Make a point memorable

TYPES:

_____ 1. Examples

_____ 2. Stories

_____ 3. Quotations

_____ 4. Definitions

_____ 5. Comparisons

_____ 6. Contrasts

_____ 7. Statistics

_____ 8. Audiovisual aids

_____ 8.1. Objects

_____ 8.2. Models

_____ 8.3. Overhead projections

_____ 8.4. Chalkboards

_____ 8.5. Graphs, charts, diagrams, maps, etc.

_____ 8.6. Slides, motion pictures, video recordings

_____ 8.7. Audio recordings

_____ 8.8. Computer-generated graphics

MISLEADING DATA:

_____ 1. Bias

_____ 2. Lies

_____ 3. Propaganda

The First Speaker . . .

. . . to address an organization by radio was *Dr. Weir Cadyle Ketler,* president of Grove City College, in Pennsylvania, on April 20, 1920. He talked to the Rotary Club in New Castle, 25 miles away.

L E S S O N 8

Outlining Speeches

OBJECTIVES ▶ After you've finished this lesson, you will be able to prepare a speech outline that is useful and technically correct. By technically correct, we mean that the outline incorporates correctly 80 percent (32) or more of the guides for outlining presented in this lesson.

RELEVANCE ▶ This lesson will teach you the *technical* aspects of speech outlining—layout, symbols, and such. The *creative* aspects—selecting points, patterns, data, etc.—are presented in Lessons 10, 11, and 12, the lessons on how to design the discussion, introduction, and conclusion of a speech.

"But I can already do an outline that means something to *me*. Why do I have to learn another way?" some students say.

There are two reasons. First, the outlining techniques presented here are those that most speakers have found most helpful in preparing for most speaking situations. These tips are not offered as the "only way" to outline, but in learning and applying these techniques, which have been successful for other speakers, you may be able to improve your own speaking.

OUTLINING A SPEECH:

"First of all, I refresh my memory of my earlier thinking on the subject. . . . I then take a large yellow pad and, under the heading 'Random Notes,' put down whatever new thoughts come into my mind in whatever sequence they occur, almost like that of free association. I may cover many pages with such random notes."

"My next step is to examine these notes and decide which points are related to one another and how they are related to form a major unit of the speech. With this in mind, I then put down on paper a brief skeletal outline of the speech in topical form, indicating what should be covered in the introduction, what should constitute the three or four major sections of the speech, and what should be left for the peroration or conclusion."

Mortimer J. Adler, philosopher, teacher, author, gave that description of how he outlines a speech in his book ***How to Speak, How to Listen.***

There is a second reason. In this speech class, your outline has an additional duty beyond merely being helpful to you. It communicates to your instructor what you have in mind for the structure of a speech so that he or she can help you further improve your speech designing.

An outline is to a speech what a blueprint is to a house, a chart is to a cruise, an agenda is to a meeting. An outline tends to ensure that your speech has an effective form (like a house) and direction (like a cruise) and that everything that you want to present is included (like a good meeting).

But note, that last sentence said that an outline "*tends* to ensure." An outline, even an especially good one, will not guarantee results. Even with a good blueprint a carpenter can build a poor house; even with an accurate chart a sailor can . . . . I'm sure you get the point.

The value of an outline is that it tends to ensure that you'll have a logical presentation of the points and data in your speech. An outline is a tool for planning. It is a visual representation of the ideas and the data through which you want your audience to be informed, persuaded, or entertained.

Alert! ➤ **Difference Between Speech Format and Speech Outline:**

A speech **format** is a broad plan or guide for the design of speeches in general.

A speech **outline** is a specific plan for a particular speech.

Study the speech outline on the next page carefully. It is a typical effective outline, suitable for a five-minute speech such as you usually present in a class in public speaking. For a longer speech, you would simply add more specifics to build a more detailed, powerful, convincing case. This outline illustrates all the techniques of outlining.

But don't worry that such a long list of techniques "sounds overwhelming, looks overwhelming," as one speech professor put it. You are certainly not expected to memorize all those 40 techniques. You're only to become skilled in *using* them. Many of those techniques you already know; most will quickly come to your mind automatically as you prepare your outlines. And, of course, there is absolutely no reason why you can't look at the list as often as you need to, as you work up your outlines.

EXAMPLE OF A SPEECH OUTLINE:

Audience: New York School Boards Association
Speech Purpose: After hearing my speech, the audience will agree that schools should guarantee their instruction.

I. Introduction
   A. Would you buy a new brand X car if you knew that half those cars broke down in one year or less? Yet that's just what we do when we "buy" a college education.
   B. Schools should guarantee their instruction
II. Discussion
   A. Need for guaranteed learning
     1. Half of students who enter college never become sophomores
     2. Some graduate from high school with only a fourth-grade reading level
     3. We spend an average of more than $4770 per year per student, yet have no assurance of what that money will produce
   B. How guaranteed learning works—4 steps:
     1. Community and school set broad goals
     2. Teacher establishes specific, measurable objectives, stating:
       a. What the student is to do to show he or she has "learned"
       b. How he or she is to show it—conditions
       c. Levels he or she is to achieve
     3. Teacher then designs instruction to attain those objectives
     4. Teacher tests effectiveness of instruction, redesigns to ensure learning occurs
   C. Successes of guaranteed learning
     1. Gary, Indiana: entire K–6 school, 400 students
     2. Texarkana, Texas: First in nation, reduced dropout rate significantly
     3. More than 200 projects across country
III. Conclusion
   A. Guaranteed learning should be provided by all schools
     1. It is needed
     2. It is a clear, specific 4-step process
     3. It works
   B. We guarantee cars, orange juice, cough drops, dishwashers, a wide variety of our products—why not education?

There are 40 techniques for outlining. Every one is used in the above outline.

Now study the next page, which lists those guides, and then the following page, which illustrates the use of those guides in this same speech outline.

OUTLINING GUIDES:

Points marked with an asterisk are illustrated on the next page.

1. Organization
   - *1.1.   Name specific audience for whom speech is designed
   - *1.2.   State specific purpose for speech
     - *1.2.1.   Worded from audience's point of view
     - *1.2.2.   Expressed in specific terms
     - *1.2.3.   Realistically attainable
   - 1.3.   Maintain consistency of speech purpose with:
     - 1.3.1.   Preview of subject (point I.B.)
     - 1.3.2.   Main points of speech (points II.A., B., etc.)
     - 1.3.3.   Review of subject (point II.A.)
   - *1.4.   Start with attention-getter as point I.A.
   - *1.5.   Preview speech as point I.B.
   - *1.6.   Present 2 to 5 points in the discussion
   - *1.7.   Present discussion points that are logical parts of the subject
   - *1.8.   Arrange discussion points in logical order
   - *1.9.   Support discussion points with data
   - *1.10. Review speech as point III.A.
   - *1.11. Review main points of discussion under point III.A.
   - *1.12. Present memorable statement as point III.B.
   - 1.13. Don't make outline too short—too brief to communicate specifics
   - 1.14. Don't make outline too long—approaching a full script
   - 1.15. Don't make outline too general—lacking in specifics
   - 1.16. Don't make outline too involved or overstructured
2. Content
   - 2.1.   Appropriateness of material to:
     - 2.1.1.   Audience
     - 2.1.2.   Occasion
     - 2.1.3.   Speaker
   - 2.2.   Relevance of material to audience
   - 2.3.   Significance of material to audience
   - 2.4.   Accuracy of facts
   - 2.5.   Justification of conclusions, opinions
   - 2.6.   Stating of sources, when appropriate
3. Mechanics
   - *3.1.   Identify main parts of speech with Roman numerals (I., II., III.)
   - *3.2.   Identify main points with capital letters (A., B., etc.)
   - *3.3.   Identify subpoints (usually data) with Arabic numerals (1., 2., etc.)
   - *3.4.   Identify sub-subpoints with lowercase letters (a., b., etc.)
   - *3.5.   Place periods after each identification (for example, I. Introduction; A. Need for guaranteed learning)
   - *3.6.   Name main parts of speech (Introduction, Discussion, Conclusion)
   - *3.7.   Indent lower points under superior points
   - *3.8.   Line up start of second line of a statement directly under start of first line of that statement
   - *3.9.   Have two or more points whenever indenting

ILLUSTRATION OF USE OF OUTLINING GUIDES:

(1.1.)

Audience: New York School Boards Association. (1.2.2.)

(1.2.) *Speech Purpose:* After hearing my speech the audience will agree that schools should guarantee their instruction. (1.2.1.)

(3.6.)

(1.2.3.)

I. Introduction

(3.1.)   A. Would you buy a new brand X car if you knew that half those cars broke

(1.4.) (3.5.)   down in one year or less? Yet that's just what we do when we "buy" a college education.

(3.9.)

(1.5.)   B. Schools should guarantee their instruction

II. Discussion

(3.2.)   A. The need for guaranteed learning

1. Half of students who enter college never become sophomores

2. Some graduate from high school with only a fourth-grade reading level

(1.9.)   3. We spend on average of more than $4700 per year per student, yet have no assurance of what that money will produce

B. How guaranteed learning works—4 steps:

(1.6.)
(1.7.)   1. Community and schools set broad goals

(1.8.) (3.7.)   2. Teacher establishes specific, measurable objectives, stating:

a. What the student is to do to show he's "learned"

(3.4.)   b. How he or she is to show it—conditions

c. Level he or she is to achieve

3. Teacher then designs instruction to attain those objectives (3.8.)

4. Teacher tests effectiveness of instruction, redesigns to ensure learning occurs

C. Successes of guaranteed learning

(3.3.)   1. Gary, Indiana: entire K–6 school, 400 students

2. Texarkana, Texas: first in nation, reduced dropout rate significantly

3. More than 200 projects across country

(1.10.) III. Conclusion

A. Guaranteed learning should be provided by all schools

(1.11.)   1. It is needed

2. It is a clear, specific 4-step process

3. It works

(1.12.)   B. We guarantee cars, orange juice, cough drops, dishwashers, a wide variety of our products—why not education?

Explanation of Outlining Guides

1. Organization

1.1. Name a Specific Audience for Whom the Speech Is Designed

In Lesson 5 you studied the importance of this step in the preliminary planning of your speech. If you don't remember that clearly, take a moment now to check back through that lesson.

In outlining, the importance of naming a specific audience is twofold.

First, written out at the top of your outline it will serve as a constant reminder to you that it is those people for whom you are designing this speech. As we've established, their knowledge, interests, backgrounds, etc. should help guide your every decision as to what goes into your speech.

Second, to receive help on further improving your speech design, you may be turning in some of your speech outlines for review by your instructor. The effectiveness of what your outline proposes you'll say in your speech cannot be evaluated unless you identify the audience the speech is designed for.

1.2. State a Specific Purpose for the Speech

Again, to guide you as you develop your outline, and then to serve as the basis on which your instructor will evaluate your outline to determine its effectiveness, a statement of just what the speech is to do is the best reference point. That specific purpose should be worded, as we've established, from the audience's viewpoint, be expressed in specific terms, and be realistically attainable.

If you have any questions on this, go back to Lesson 6, on how to pinpoint your speech purpose.

1.3. Maintain Consistency in Your Outline

To evaluate an outline, compare the speech purpose with these three points in the outline:

1. Preview of the subject—point B of part I of the outline.
2. Main points of the discussion part of the speech—points A, B, C, etc., of part II of the outline.
3. Review of the speech—point A of part III of the outline.

Those three statements in an outline should express the same idea, viewpoint, concept, subject, concern, etc. as the speech purpose claims the speech is intended to present.

The consistency should be in *content,* not necessarily in wording. Check our sample outline for a good illustration of consistency.

1.4.–1.12.

These are all the points in the basic format for a speech. You've studied them in detail and used them in the two speeches you've presented. They start with attention-getter and go right on to end with memorable statement. If in doubt, review Lesson 2.

1.13. Don't Make Your Outline Too Short

For the typical 4- to 5-minute speech, it is difficult to be sufficiently specific in an outline that is only half a page or so in length.

Your outline needs to be long enough and detailed enough to remind you as the speaker just exactly what ideas, points, and data you are to present. That is the main value in not having too short an outline.

A second value—less important in the world beyond the classroom, but indeed important in class—is that the outline needs to communicate to your instructor just what you have in mind, if you are to receive much benefit from his or her review and comments.

1.14. Don't Make Your Outline Too Long

Your outline should not approach the completeness of a full script.

The example of a speech outline that accompanies this lesson is about as long as an outline needs to be for the typical 5-minute speech.

One good way to check the length of an outline that may seem too long is to read it aloud word for word and time yourself. If reading the outline takes half or more of the time allocated for your speech, the outline is probably too long and detailed or you are trying to cover too much material.

1.15. Don't Make Your Outline Too General

This is one of the major weaknesses in the outlines of many beginning speakers. Here is an example of an outline that is far too general—so broad in its statements that it is of little help to the speaker.

   I.   Introduction
        A. Joke
        B. Energy today
  II.   Discussion
        A. Cost
        B. Dangers
        C. Future
 III.   Conclusion
        A. Concerns about energy
        B. Emphasize importance

Those simple, brief, vague headings in an outline do little to help you plan your speech. Later, when you are giving the speech, such a generalized outline will not be of much help in remembering what you want to say.

You'll find your outlines are much more helpful if the statements in them are specific. Some teachers prefer students to write full sentences in their outlines; others find specific phrases are sufficient. Whichever you use, they should be far more specific than the mostly one-word points in the above outline. For example:

"Joke"—that one word, written in an outline, may not remind you of just which joke you want to tell. Better: Write out at least the first sentence or key phrase of the joke so you can be sure to deliver the very first words of your speech smoothly, effectively.

"Energy today" is far too broad a subject for a speech, whether it's for the typical classroom assignment of just 4 to 5 minutes, or for a full, formal presentation of say 40 minutes or more. Better: State in your outline precisely what aspect of "energy today" you'll be talking about. For example, that point I.B. in the above outline would be better stated as "Energy today—most pressing problem" or "The problems of our energy today are fast becoming overbearing" or such.

"Cost," as a heading to remind you of the first point in the discussion part of your speech, would be much more valuable to you if you wrote out a complete sentence expressing exactly what about "cost" you want to say. In your outline you might write:

Cost is now too much for many people.

Or:

Cost is increasing faster than many can afford.

Or you could write key phrases to remind you of the specifics, such as:

Cost too much
Cost rising too fast

Further, under each of the main points of the discussion part of your outlines, you should include brief statements of the specific data you are to present. Under that point about cost, for example, you should include specifics such as:

A.   Cost
  1.   In our area, increased some 6% each of the last 3 years
  2.   Now takes an average of $85 per month per home
  3.   One nearby family collects trash newspapers to burn to try to keep warm

All of the other statements in that outline are also far too broad, indefinite, and lacking in supporting data to be of real value in planning and presenting a speech.

1.16. Don't Make Your Outline Too Involved or Overstructured

In general, an outline usually has to include subpoints down to the third level—the level identified by Arabic numerals—1, 2, etc. These usually identify the specific data of your speech—the examples, statistics, etc.

Sometimes you need to go to the next level of subpoints, the level identified by lowercase letters—a, b, etc. Typically this level of detail in an outline is used to document or credit sources of data. An example is the following excerpt of part of an outline for a speech on the problems of the Philippines:

II.   Discussion
  A. Martial law needed
    1.   More than half of food supply lost to summer floods
    2.   Bank robberies common
      a.   Newspapers reported more than one per day
      b.   Armed guards stationed both in and outside banks
  B. Shipping in confusion

That excerpt is an effective outline; it follows the guides we have presented in this lesson.

But consider another example, a portion of an outline for a speech on decreasing effectiveness of a particular school district:

II.   Discussion
    A. The cause of the problem: finances
        1. Tax returns were down
            a. In the 1970s, average yearly tax revenue: . . .
            b. In the 1980s, average was . . .
            c. In the 1990s, average of . . .
        2. Costs were up
            a. Salaries:
                (1) Administration rose to . . .
                (2) Faculty rose to . . .
            b. Equipment:
                (1) More units needed
                    (a) Computers increased . . .
                    (b) Desks rose to . . .
                (2) More sophisticated types used
                    (a) Television, costing some . . .
                    (b) Computers, costing up to . . .
                    (c) Projection systems, costing . . .
                        ((1)) Classroom systems, costing . . .
                      ((2)) Special use systems, costing . . .
    B. None of the three possible solutions accepted

That is indeed an overstructured outline.

2. Content

2.1.–2.3.

These points have been detailed for you in previous lessons, particularly in the tips for the speech assignment in Lesson 6, Pinpointing Speech Purposes.

2.4.–2.6.

These points were covered in Lesson 7, Selecting Data.

3. Mechanics

3.1. *Identify the Main Parts of Your Speech with Roman Numerals*

In your outline you should actually write down Roman numeral I to identify the introduction part of your speech, II to identify the discussion, and III to identify the conclusion.

The reason is simply to serve as a learning lever. By always writing out those same symbols to identify each part of the speech, you'll be more likely to include those parts and then to think for a moment of what goes into each part.

It is simply a memory-jogging technique.

3.2.–3.6.

The explanation is the same as for 3.1.

3.7. *Indent Lower Points Under Superior Points*

Reason: to greatly improve the clarity of the visual presentation of your outlines.

This is related to the next point, so there we'll present an example to help illustrate the value.

3.8. *Line Up the Start of a Second Line of a Statement Directly Under the Start of the First Line of That Statement*

Confusing? Consider these examples.

Don't line up the points this way:

I. Introduction
    A. To get an idea of the magnitude of our federal budget, compare it with the number of grains of sand on the beach at Waikiki. If you had one dollar for each grain, you could cover that beach for as far as . . .
    B. Let's consider today what the individual can do to control the gigantic federal budget and thereby solve our nation's greatest problem.

Do *indent* and *line up* continuing statements this way:

I. Introduction
    A. To get an idea of the magnitude of our federal budget, compare it with the number of grains of sand on the beach . . . .
    B. Let's consider today what the individual can do to control that gigantic federal budget and thereby solve our nation's greatest problem.

You can see that the second example is much easier to read. And if you are still writing your outlines by hand, the clarity resulting from these two guides—indenting and lining up—is more visible.

Huh?

No, I didn't proceed to do the calculations of spreading the federal budget out on that beach. Maybe some math major in class will work it up for us. But the beach at Waikiki is smaller than a lot of people think, and the federal budget is larger than . . . again, you're ahead of me.

3.9. *Have Two or More Points Whenever Indenting*

In outlining, indenting *means that the point above is being divided*—into parts, to present data, or for further explanation or amplification. And you can't divide anything—not an apple, not a pie, not a point in an outline—without getting two or more parts.

Consider this excerpt from an outline:

A. Costs are rising
    1. Telephone up 8%
    2. Mail up 12%
        a. Amount of mail up 10%
        b. Weight of mail up 14%
B. . . .

"Telephone" and "Mail" are indented under "Costs" because they are data intended to prove that "Costs are rising." The indentation is a visual presentation of that relationship. Similarly, under "Mail" two additional facts are presented ("Amount" and "Weight") to document the point "Mail up 12%."

"But *why* indent?" students ask. Because by *definition*—by custom, tradition, convention, if you prefer—indenting in an outline *means* that the previous point is being divided. And, remember, you can't divide anything without getting two or more parts.

"But suppose I don't want to present two points. Suppose I have just one bit of data to offer about a statement?" many students ask. Perfectly acceptable. You do not need to have two subpoints under every statement. Certainly there are times when you want to present only one bit of amplification about a point. But if you have only one subpoint, you are not dividing the idea above; you are simply explaining it further or adding just one more fact or idea or consideration. If, for example, your speech is to state only that costs are up, and you want to document that with just one bit of evidence, the fact that telephone costs are up 8%, that would be presented in an outline this way:

A.   Costs are rising: telephone up 8%
B.   . . .

It *should not* appear in an outline as:

A.   Costs are rising
    1.   Telephone up 8%
B.   . . .

Without a point 2 under A, you are not in fact dividing the idea above ("Costs") but merely adding one more fact.

Confusing? Not really if you accept that by *definition* an indentation in an outline means you are dividing the statement above, and it is impossible to divide anything without getting two or more parts.

Getting Started

To start your outline you need at least most of the points and data for your speech. They can be down on notes or stored up there in your mind.

Some books urge you to get all of your materials together first and then start to organize it by outlining. But that procedure prevents you from benefiting from some of the main values of outlining.

First, outlining will help reveal to you just what holes you may have in your logic. Outlining makes vivid to you where you may have too little or too much data. Finally, outlining helps show you where you are being vague and indefinite.

The next step, then, is simply to . . . well, to start outlining.

Let's get to it with a self-test.

Sounds of Speech

There are about 45 "different units of sound [in English] . . . such as the *m* in *man* or the *ou* in *house*" you can use in your speaking; Italians have 27, Hawaiians 13. That's according to *Peter Farb's* book **Word Play.**

ASSIGNMENT 12. OUTLINING: SELF-TEST

 ACTION: Take the following self-test.

OBJECTIVE:

After completing this assignment, you will have determined for yourself your skill in outlining.

INSTRUCTIONS:

1. Outline as a speech the text on the following page.
2. Start by reading carefully the complete text.
3. Then go back over it, making notes, marks, etc., to indicate the main parts of the speech, then the main points, then the data, subdata, etc. You can write directly on the printed text; it has been double-spaced so you'll have room for your notations.
4. Once you've got it all pretty much noted and in mind, write out on page 211 your version of the complete outline.
5. It's tempting to cheat on this self-test. But since no class average or comparison of grades is made on this assignment, you would be simply cheating yourself. Peek at the answers if you must, but then you won't know if you are really ready to do a good job outlining on your own.

SPEECH FOR OUTLINING SELF-TEST:

Audience: Richmond Troop of Boy Scouts preparing for study trip to U.S. Navy ship-yard, Norfolk, Virginia.

Speech purpose: After hearing my speech the audience will be able to summarize in their own words the main types of ships that make up the strength of the U.S. Navy.

A famous statesman once said, "A nation is only as powerful as her fleet." How powerful, then, is the United States? How strong is her navy? We will answer those questions by telling you about some of the many different types of ships that give the navy of the United States its power and its strength. The navy's ships are classified into two main groups: the combatant ships and the auxiliary ships. Aircraft carriers are the largest of the combatant ships. In fact some of the newest ones are too big to go through the Panama Canal. These giant ships carry a crew of more than 5000 men. Another feature is that several are nuclear powered. Another type of major combatant ships is submarines. Today they are larger than World War II destroyers. They can operate underwater for months without surfacing. Cruisers are important fighting ships, too. They specialize in using guided missiles. One of their main tasks is protecting carriers. Frigates are combatant ships that are growing in importance. They are a new type of escort vessel for the giant carriers. Frigates have strong antisubmarine capabilities. Several other types of ships are also considered combatant ships. Auxiliary ships are generally either supply ships or repair ships. Examples of supply ships are food transports, ammunition ships, and tankers. It is upon these many kinds of navy ships that the strength of the United States is dependent. And, we must always remember, America must keep her fleet if she is to keep her power.

INSTRUCTIONS: Write on this page your outline of the material on page 214.

Answers:

I. Introduction:
  A. A famous statesman once said, "A nation is only as powerful as her fleet."
    1. How powerful, then, is the United States?
    2. How strong is her navy?
  B. The many different types of ships that give the U.S. Navy its power and its strength.

II. Discussion
  A. Combatant ships
    1. Aircraft carriers
      a. Largest combatant ships
      b. Some of newest too big for Panama Canal
      c. Crew of more than 5000
      d. Several are nuclear powered
    2. Submarines
      a. Larger than World War II destroyers
      b. Operate underwater for months
    3. Cruisers
      a. Specialize in guided missiles
      b. Protect carriers
    4. Frigates
      a. Growing in importance
      b. New escorts for carriers
      c. Strong antisubmarine capabilities
    5. Others
  B. Auxiliary ships
    1. Supply
      a. Food transports
      b. Ammunition ships
      c. Tankers
    2. Repair

III. Conclusion
  A. It is upon these many kinds of navy ships that the strength of the United States is dependent.
  B. America must keep her fleet if she is to keep her power.

If more than five items in your outline are different from the correct outline above, you should restudy this lesson or confer with your instructor for additional help.

The next step: designing an outline for your own speech.

ASSIGNMENT 13. OUTLINE OF COMMUNITY PROBLEM SPEECH: SPEECH 3, USING DATA

ACTION: Submit an outline for your next speech.

OBJECTIVE:

After completing this assignment, you are expected to be able to outline a speech effectively, that is, to use correctly at least 32 (80 percent) of the 40 techniques you've just studied.

INSTRUCTIONS:

1. Prepare and submit to your instructor an outline for your next speech.
2. That speech, which is detailed at the end of the next lesson, should:
    2.1. Be designed for a specific local organization (but you'll deliver the speech in class)
    2.2. Be about a community problem
    2.3. Use data effectively
3. Your SUBJECT should be one in which you gather the data firsthand by getting out in your community to experience or observe a problem that is new to you. For example:
    3.1. Live for three days on the money a typical welfare mother receives to feed one person.
    3.2. Spend a few days doing the rounds of meetings and such with your mayor, police chief, school principal, minister, etc.
    3.3. Work for a day or so as a volunteer assistant to a teacher of the handicapped, a hospital nurse, bus driver, or such.
    3.4. Follow up a complaint—yours or a friend's—with a repair shop, store, city agency, etc. until you get a refund, replacement, adjustment, blank wall, or complete frustration!
    3.5. Compare the prices charged by various stores for the same brands of a television set, toothpaste, tennis racquet, or other product.
    3.6. Attend a church service of a faith quite different from your own.
    3.7. Travel with an insurance adjuster, process server, collection agent, police officer, home nurse, or such.
    3.8. Take an article that needs repair, such as a tire, toaster, or radio, to several shops to compare charges, time required, customer relations, etc.
4. Be sure to state at the beginning of your outline the SPECIFIC AUDIENCE for whom the speech is designed and the SPECIFIC PURPOSE of your speech. For example:
    4.1. After hearing my speech, my audience—the local taxpayers' association—will agree that the town's police force needs more money.
    4.2. After listening to my speech, my audience—a meeting of local merchants—will be able to name four copouts often used by complaint departments and how each one turns customers against the firm.
5. If you want additional suggestions on how to organize your speech, you are urged to skip ahead to Lesson 10, Designing Discussions, which gives you guides on various patterns you might use.

6. Submit your outline to your speech instructor for evaluation well before you are to speak; then there will be sufficient time for your outline to be returned to you so you can use whatever comments your instructor offers to improve your outline and thereby improve your speech.

To Speak, or Not to Speak?

"Let thy speech be better than silence, or be silent."

Dionysus the Elder (430–367 B.C.)

OUTLINING: CHECK-OFF TIP SHEET

INSTRUCTIONS: Check off each item as you outline your speech.

1. ORGANIZATION

_____ 1.1. Name specific audience for whom speech is designed.

_____ 1.2. State specific purpose for speech.

    _____ 1.2.1. Worded from audience's point of view.

    _____ 1.2.2. Expressed in specific terms.

    _____ 1.2.3. Realistically attainable.

_____ 1.3. Maintain consistency of speech purpose with:

    _____ 1.3.1. Preview of subject (point I.B.)

    _____ 1.3.2. Main points of speech (points II.A., B., etc.)

    _____ 1.3.3. Review of subject (point III.A.)

_____ 1.4. Start with attention-getter as point I.A.

_____ 1.5. Preview speech as point I.B.

_____ 1.6. Present 2 to 5 points in the discussion.

_____ 1.7. Present discussion points that are logical parts of the subject.

_____ 1.8. Arrange discussion points in logical order.

_____ 1.9. Support discussion points with data.

_____ 1.10. Review speech as point III.A.

_____ 1.11. Review main points of discussion under point III.A.

_____ 1.12. Present memorable statement as point III.B.

_____ 1.13. Don't make outline too short—too brief to communicate specifics.

_____ 1.14. Don't make outline too long—approaching a full script.

_____ 1.15. Don't make outline too general—lacking in specifics.

_____ 1.16. Don't make outline too involved or overstructured.

2. CONTENT

_____ 2.1. Appropriateness of material to:

    _____ 2.1.1. Audience

    _____ 2.1.2. Occasion

    _____ 2.1.3. Speaker

_____ 2.2. Relevance of material to audience.

_____ 2.3. Significance of material to audience.

_____ 2.4. Accuracy of facts.

_____ 2.5. Justification of conclusion, opinions.

_____ 2.6. Stating of sources, when appropriate.

3. MECHANICS

_____ 3.1. Identify main parts of speech with Roman numerals (I., II., III.).

_____ 3.2. Identify main points with capital letters (A., B., etc.).

_____ 3.3. Identify subpoints (usually data) with Arabic numerals (1., 2., etc.).

_____ 3.4. Identify sub-subpoints with lowercase letters (a., b., etc.).

_____ 3.5. Place periods after identification.

_____ 3.6. Name main parts of speech (introduction, discussion, conclusion).

_____ 3.7. Indent lower points under superior points.

_____ 3.8. Line up start of second line of a statement directly under start of first line of that statement.

_____ 3.9. Have two or more points whenever indenting.

Fastest Speaker

The fastest speaker in public life is said to have been President *John Fitzgerald Kennedy,* when, in a speech he delivered in December 1961, he zoomed to more than 300 words per minute.

The present world's record for fastest speaking is 637.4 words per minute, held by *Steve Woodmore,* of Great Britain, attained during the TV show ***Motor Mouth*** on September 22, 1990.

Those records are reported in the current edition of ***The Guinness Book of World Records.***

But most of us speak around 150 to 175 words per minute, and few can speak clearly at more than 300 words per minute.

L E S S O N 9

Polishing Delivery

OBJECTIVES ▶ Complete this lesson and you will be able to:

1. Deliver an extemporaneous speech with appropriate style, confidence, enthusiasm, and sincerity.
2. Incorporate effectively in your speech the concepts and techniques studied in this and previous lessons. To be evaluated as effective your speech should use correctly 80 percent or more of the criteria for the three aspects of a speech—content, organization, and delivery—listed on the **Speech Evaluation Form** at the end of this lesson.

RELEVANCE ▶ Now that you have delivered two speeches in this class and are about to present your third, it is time for you to polish and improve your delivery.

DELIVERY TECHNIQUE:

"Select one or two people in the room—regardless of how many people are there—and seduce them. Talk to them in a normal conversational tone."

So said *Willie Brown*, Mayor of San Francisco, when he was asked about his speaking techniques by a writer for the magazine *San Francisco Focus.*

This lesson builds on the 14 basic techniques for delivering a speech that you acquired in Lesson 3, Delivering Speeches. Now 19 new tips will be presented, for a total of 33 guides to delivering a speech.

Studying a text is not the most productive way to improve your skills in delivering a speech. You'll learn far more from:

1. Listening to and analyzing tape recordings of your practices and in-class speech presentations.
2. Observing and analyzing speeches presented by your classmates and speeches by professional speakers you're hearing in lecture courses, church activities, organization meetings, etc.
3. Studying the evaluation forms you receive after your speeches in this class and your notes of your classmates' comments about your speeches.
4. Working earnestly to incorporate in your speaking those techniques that observers tell you are effective in your speeches and also working diligently to reduce or eliminate weaknesses.

But first, please take a few moments to think about your feelings and speaking skills at this stage of your speech course.

Write out brief but specific replies to the following questions. Your answers should help you and perhaps your instructor plan your next improvements in speaking skills.

How do you feel about your speaking abilities right now?_____

_____

In what ways do you feel your speaking abilities have improved? _____

_____

In what ways do you feel your speaking skills may have deteriorated?_____

_____

What might YOU do about your feelings about speaking and your speaking abilities?

_____

What might your instructor do to help you further improve your feelings about speaking and your speaking skills? _____

_____

If talking with your instructor might help, you have two channels of communication to him or her. You can ask questions in class. But many students are not comfortable talking in front of their classmates about their feelings and speaking skills. So consider the second channel: make an appointment with your instructor to discuss your concerns about speaking. You will probably find, as most speech students do, that talking with your instructor will be very helpful.

Now let's look at tips for improving your speech delivery.

GUIDES FOR EFFECTIVE DELIVERY

Let's restate **the 14 techniques you've already mastered**—those presented in Lesson 3, Delivering Speeches. They're repeated here to reinforce your memory of them and so you'll have the full list—the essentials and the more advanced tips of this lesson—

together in one presentation. If you're not clear on any of them, do check back for a quick refresher of Lesson 3.

Before you speak

1. Dress to help, not hinder, your speech.
2. Limit the number of note cards you use.
3. Step up to speak with confidence and authority.
4. Get set.
5. Establish contact with your audience.

While you're speaking

6. Maintain contact with your audience.
7. Begin without referring to your notes.
8. Refer to your note card only occasionally.
9. Sound conversational, not as if reading or delivering a memorized speech.
10. Avoid *ah, so, ya know, well, 'kay,* etc.
11. Stop at the end of an idea: don't hook sentences together with *and, and ah,* etc.
12. Maintain good posture: don't lean, cross legs, etc.
13. Don't play with notes, pencil, clothes, etc.
14. Speak loudly enough to be heard easily.

Now the new, additional tips on delivery. We'll pick up our numbering system and begin with 15.

15. Use Aids Effectively

Here we are concerned with how you handle and display your aids. Suggestions on designing aids are presented in Lesson 7, Selecting Data, because aids are one of the types of data.

Again, we're on a subject that isn't at all as complex as the following rather detailed tips might suggest. Yet there are several little techniques that can do much to make your speeches more effective.

15.1. Make Sure Your Model or Item Works

Obviously! Yet we've already pointed to professional speakers on television getting caught on this.

Perhaps some of your classmates had problems during the demonstration speeches?

15.2. Be Sure You Know How It Works

Childishly simple? Sure. But try asking a salesperson sometime what that lonely button way down at the bottom does. Your audience, too, might ask such questions.

15.3. Get Your Aids in Place Before Speaking

Set those charts on the easel, hang those maps on the wall clips, pin your graphs to the display board, and draw your visuals on the chalkboard *before* you start to deliver your speech.

It's usually best to attend to such details before the meeting starts. Cover your visuals with a blank piece of paper—you can even tape a newspaper sheet, for example, over your chalk drawings—until the point in your speech at which you want to refer to them. Otherwise, the audience will be studying your aids before and during your speech. Every time the program gets a bit dull, they'll stop listening and start looking. So don't give your audience additional distractions.

15.4. Use a Pointer to Direct Your Listeners' Attention to Particular Parts of Your Visuals

A pointer is more dramatic and has greater impact than pointing with a finger, and you appear to be a more polished, professional speaker as you use it.

More important, pointing with a finger—which most speakers need to support with a big extended arm—puts a lot of your body between your visual and your audience. A pointer will hide far less of your aid.

15.5 Remove Your Aids as Soon as You've Finished the Point They Support

Leaving the aid up lets the listeners keep thinking about it if they want to. But you've moved on to another point, and you want to keep them with you.

It is especially important to remove aids when you've finished your speech—particularly if the subject is at all controversial or if you're in a discussion or debate situation. There's probably no better way for someone with a viewpoint opposing yours to win a case than to use your aids to support the opposite view.

Example: A few years ago, before the board of trustees of a college in southern California, I watched the chairman of a citizens' committee make an elaborate, well-documented case for building a new college at a particular location. He supported his case with a fine map and a visual that listed his reasons and the key data supporting each reason. When he finished, the board seemed convinced.

But one new speaker asked to address the board before they voted. As he stepped up, the previous speaker—the one with all the fine visuals—started to move them aside. "That's all right," said the newcomer, "just leave them; they're not in the way." They were left and were then used to build a point-by-point case of why a different location for the new college should be selected. The map that had illustrated the desirable nearness of the existing library was now used to show the traffic problems that would result from such centralization of buildings. Each point on the visual now served to focus attention on the reverse of the point.

The well-documented case was lost.

15.6. Talk to Your Audience, Not to Your Aid

Certainly it is acceptable to turn away from your audience occasionally. What we are concerned about here is the speaker who uses a visual for quite a bit of a speech and ends up talking to it, with his or her back to the audience or head turned away from them for much of the time.

Hard to point without getting in front of your aid? Then either point from the other side of the visual or point backward.

Hard to draw details, add numbers, etc. without turning your back on your audience? Two options: Take the few moments it requires to learn how to stand to one side and write backward, or pause in your speech, write what you need to, then turn back to your audience and continue speaking.

15.7. Avoid Holding Visuals

Speakers who hold charts, diagrams, pictures, or such for their audiences to see often turn the visuals from one side of the audience to the other, trying to give everyone a view. Such speakers often keep those visuals in motion, giving their listeners little time to see clearly.

You'll be much more effective in showing visuals if you place them on an easel, on a table, in the tray of the chalkboard, or such. Your audience will be able to see them with greater ease and attention.

15.8. Do Not Give Material to the Audience While You're Speaking

For years, a nationally recognized insurance company has had its sales representatives speak to college faculties about the latest provisions of its policies. The representative who came to our college always began his speeches by distributing copies of a brochure to his audience. That brochure listed just about everything he presented in his talks. Know what his listeners did while he spoke? Right! We all studied the brochure, trying to find benefits we'd lost, details that were going to cost us more, searching for other points to question. All that speaker did was give us about 20 minutes—the length of his talk—to prepare to challenge him.

Giving materials to your listeners and then continuing to speak simply divides their interest. If you must distribute something, don't go on talking while it is being passed around; just pause in your speaking until everyone has a copy. Then give your listeners time to look it over before you continue. And don't distribute material that just repeats what you are going to say before you present your talk. If you want to hand out such material so your listeners will have a summary to take with them when they leave, do so after your speech.

It's also distracting to give your audience just one of something—a model, a sample, or such—to pass around as you continue to talk. Some listeners may wonder if they'll get to see the thing before you finish speaking; others may not get the point of what you're saying until they've seen the visual and you may lose them; still others may stop listening while they worry about its being dropped or getting marked up before it gets to them. Again you've divided your audience's attention.

It's better to hold the aid up so your listeners can see what you're talking about, then invite them to come up after your speech to get a better look. Or have enough copies so everyone can look at the item at the same time. Or perhaps a photo or drawing would communicate the point just as well.

16. Gesture Effectively

You'll remember that we gave you some tips on gesturing in Lesson 4, Preparing to Speak. Now it's time for you to start working diligently on improving your gesturing.

When speech classes start working on gestures, students often ask, "What do I do with my hands while I speak?"

"Just leave them there at the end of your arms!" is my reply.

That's not just a flip put-down. Learning to ignore your hands is indeed the first step toward effective gesturing, but if you are "hand conscious," like many students, forgetting about them may be difficult. Try to let your hands just "be." Forget them; they'll stay in place.

Then start moving them around as your mood dictates.

"My mood says 'Don't move!'" says the shy one.

"Try it, you'll like it," I reply.

Gestures have three great values. First, they help you relax. Most speakers find that once they start gesturing, they feel more comfortable and confident.

Second, gestures help your listeners relax. That's important because it seems that when an audience is comfortable with a speaker it is more likely to accept what is said.

And, third, gestures help a speaker emphasize what he or she says.

Gestures include not only movements of your hands and arms. A nod of your head can emphasize a point. A smile can communicate your agreement. A glance at the floor can express doubt. Sometimes even your feet can be used to gesture. Fast, sure movements can suggest assurance, concern, or anger, depending on the words you are saying. Slow, plodding movements may indicate caution, hesitancy, or questioning.

"I know I don't gesture, but I want to. How do I start?" is a frequent question of beginning speakers. Remember the tips we offered earlier:

1. Practice when you are alone.
2. Practice exaggerated gesturing.
3. Practice gesturing in general, but don't practice specific gestures to be used with particular wording.
4. Practice in front of a mirror *only* if you're sure it will help *you*.

You'll find that gestures will help you, too, speak more effectively. And once you start gesturing, you'll likely become quite polished and relaxed.

17. Use Your Face to Add Interest

We mentioned facial expression as a form of gesture, but we want to emphasize its importance. Smile. It won't hurt. Or if you are speaking about a serious subject, then let your face show your concern.

The point here is not to urge you to portray your feelings through any rehearsed facial expressions. Rather, the point is simply to urge you to let your face do its thing—to communicate what you feel.

Many student speakers try to hide their emotions. Even today's television network newscasters no longer appear to work at being "the great stone face." Follow the lead of professional speakers and let your face, along with your voice and your words, communicate your feelings.

18. Move About—Get Out from Behind the Lectern

You can use your entire body to gesture, much as you wave a hand and nod your head. You can emphasize a point, clarify your ideas, add interest and variety to your presentation by moving about.

It's a big first step for most beginning speakers to get out from behind that lectern. Lecterns seem to serve as a kind of fortress behind which speakers somehow feel safer. But once you have taken that first move out of that apparent stronghold, you will likely agree with the majority of speakers who say, in effect, "Getting out there and going down to talk right with the audience—that makes speaking a lot easier!" That's difficult to believe, many beginners point out.

One reason novice speakers like to stay behind their lectern, they claim, is so they can be near their notes, "In case I need them, I want to be right there to take a fast look at them." But there are two considerations that deny the validity of that.

First, most good speakers do not really look at their notes very much. Mostly notes provide a safeguard, a feeling of assurance that help is handy if needed.

Second, when you do need to check your notes after you've stepped away from the lectern, you can, of course, just pause in your speaking, calmly take the few steps needed to return to the lectern, and find the material. That does not take anywhere near

MOVING ABOUT:

"Now, you know tradition in that speakers at the Republican National Convention remain at this very imposing podium. But tonight, I'd like to break with tradition. For two reasons. One, I'm going to be speaking to friends, and secondly, I'm going to be speaking about the man I love and it's just a lot more comfortable for me to do that down here with you."

After saying that, *Elizabeth Dole* delivered the rest of her very effective speech wandering amongst the greatly impressed delegates.

as much time as many speakers feel it does. Besides, listeners like pause in speeches, so they have a moment to think through what the speaker has said.

So, move away from the lectern. Move down closer to your audience. Do what you can to eliminate the physical block of a lectern standing between you and your listeners. Some speakers go right into the audience—moving up an aisle, stopping to speak to an individual, but still addressing the entire audience.

You'll soon find that as hard as you may feel it is to take those first steps away from the lectern, your movement will actually relax you. Moving around a bit while speaking helps you build your own confidence and thereby improves your speaking effectiveness.

19. Don't Pace

"Like a caged lion" is the way some listeners describe the speaker who paces a set path.

Pacing, because it is so predictable once it is started, is distracting to many listeners. Even the speaker who has a significant and stimulating message loses many in the audience by pacing. Some listeners will mentally start projecting the speaker's movements with greater intellectual involvement than they devote to the speaker's ideas.

20. Appear to Enjoy Speaking

Audiences can usually tell if you truly want to talk with them, if you are enjoying your opportunity to express your ideas, if you're pleased with your own speech.

How do you communicate this? Mostly it is through your attitude.

It is difficult to fake enjoyment. If, in fact, you do not want to speak, if you are not happy with your own ideas and your expression of them, if you are not comfortable with what you are saying, it is very difficult to project the opposite image.

The time to solve this problem is certainly not as you get up to speak or during your presentation. The basis for projecting enjoyment must be back when you select your subject, purpose and content of your speech. If you're not comfortable with your speech as you prepare it, you'll very likely project those concerns when you speak. There's only one safe way out: solve the problem during your preparation.

This concept of enjoying yourself as you speak is quite closely related to the next point.

21. Seem to Care That Your Audience Listens

Two questions arise. First, how do you know if you are projecting an "I-don't-care" image? Well, one of the advantages of a speech class is the honest and open evaluation by class members; they'll soon tell you if this is one of your weaknesses.

The second question is how do you overcome this weakness? Again, it is largely a mental attitude. Use the old IBM slogan—"THINK." Think about your audience. Think of them as individuals. Really want them to listen.

And again, it is an attitude that is difficult to fake. Your concern for your audience usually has to be real, or many listeners will spot, and be turned off by, counterfeit caring.

22. Speak with Enthusiasm

"Nothing great was ever achieved without enthusiasm," wrote Ralph Waldo Emerson. Many listeners would include speeches in that statement, pointing out that most successful speakers communicate enthusiasm.

However, a speech course is not going to change the shy, shrinking violet into a sparkling, dramatic, powerful speaker. Projection of enthusiasm must really be based largely on a positive attitude toward your subject and a sincere concern that your listeners receive what you have to say.

Some students who are low in enthusiasm, when urged to "fire up" a bit, often feel they are being told to "yell at the audience." Not so. First, volume does not necessarily communicate enthusiasm.

Some speakers speak quietly and still convey enthusiasm—news commentator David Brinkley, for example. Second, it is difficult for many quiet, low-key speakers to recognize that they sound unenthusiastic; they often think they are speaking with the fire of a sandlot sportscaster.

To find out for yourself just how enthusiastic you sound, watch and listen to tape recordings of your speeches. If your instructor and classmates have been telling you to sound more enthusiastic, try to spot on those tapes just what it is that they feel you are lacking. Is it volume? Projection? Speed? Or, is it a problem of attitude? Is your unenthusiastic delivery coming from your not getting yourself involved in your speech subjects or from your lack of concern that your listeners receive you?

If it's problem of attitude, try to select speech subjects that are of greater real interest to you. Then try making an absolute commitment to yourself to really get your listeners interested.

23. Appear Confident and Relaxed

The fact is that speakers almost always appear much more confident than they claim to feel. You'll confirm this repeatedly in class with your fellow student speakers.

Speaker after speaker will say, "But my knees were shaking!" "I was so nervous I could hardly hold my notes." "Didn't you see me sweating?"

The response from the audience is almost always "No." "You looked cool to us." "Nerves hardly came through a bit."

We go back to your attitude again—if you'll *think* you're confident, you'll be more confident. If you'll think relax, you'll tend to relax.

Some techniques help. Breathe deeply. Be concerned about your listeners, not yourself. Clear your mind of thoughts other than the content of your speech. Go to bed early the night before you speak.

But the main help is recognizing that you do actually appear pretty confident up there—at least much more confident than you feel.

Then there's that greatest teacher of all—experience. The more you speak, the more you will come to understand, accept, and adjust to speaking. Few speakers become completely relaxed and confident. But during this course most students do get on top of this problem. Bet you will, too.

24. Speak with, Not at, the Audience

Some speakers project an image that they are only throwing words and ideas at the audience, for them to catch as they can. The better speaker talks *with* the audience rather than at them.

Once again, it is largely a mental attitude on the part of the speaker. Look at individuals in your audience, think of them as individuals. Want them to listen and to be informed, persuaded, or entertained.

Strangely, some of the more fluent, smooth, polished speakers project the image that they are only speaking *at* their listeners. In talking with some such speakers, as we jointly try to analyze why they seem to project such an image, I have noted that many are so convinced of the value of what they are saying, so sure of their facts, or so convinced of their viewpoints, that they have developed a kind of aloofness. They feel their words will certainly, unquestioningly, unhesitatingly be endorsed and acted upon.

On the other hand, there are speakers who just do not care at all. I've had some students say that "if an audience wants to listen, it will, it's up to them." The point is that it is not "up to them." Rather, it is the speaker's obligation for at least 50 percent of the responsibility to try to ensure that the listeners do receive the message.

So work at talking *with* your audience. Look at them, think of them as individuals.

25. Don't Look at the Floor, out the Window, over Audience's Heads, at the Back Wall, Etc.

The reason is apparent.

Look your audience straight in the eye. About as bad as talking to the floor or out the window is talking to just one or a few selected individuals in the audience. Make everyone in your audience feel that you are talking with him or her as a person.

26. Vary Your Speaking Rate and Don't speak Too Fast or Too Slow

You've heard the speaker who plods along, thinking of the next word so slowly that you can often figure out what he or she is going to say next. You've heard, too, the mile-a-minute rattler who bombards you with words faster than you can absorb them. As a listener, you've probably been turned off by both extremes.

Ideal is the speaker who speaks neither too fast nor too slowly and also varies the rate of delivery. On some points, you should slow down, and then, for variety and impact, you should at times speed up, speak with a quickness and fluency of both your tongue and your mind.

Overdoing either—just as overdoing any other specific characteristic in speaking—is distracting. But variety, an intermixing of techniques, is especially effective.

27.   Vary Your Voice Pitch and Volume

Here the concern is the loudness of your speaking and the highness and lowness of your voice.

Vivid examples in the misuse of volume by speakers have been experienced by every student. Think of some of your class periods as they draw to a close. Some students get restless. They get noisy as they pack up their belongings, preparing to depart. Is it not true that many teachers, as a class gets noisier, begin to speak louder and louder?

But observe, especially during in-person appearances rather than during television programs, your most talented comedians, singers, and actors. To quiet an audience they do not speak louder—they do just the opposite. They drop the volume of their expression. Some will suddenly go down to just above a whisper.

You, too, to be an effective speaker, can use such professional techniques.

28.   Enunciate Clearly

To enunciate means to articulate, to utter your words clearly and distinctly.

Poor enunciation includes dropping the *g* at the end of words, for example, "com*in'*," "go*in'*," "wish*in'*" instead of "com*ing*," "go*ing*," "wish*ing*."

Slurring over consonants, or even syllables, in the middle of words, is another example of failure to enunciate.

What can you do about it?

Move your lips, tongue, and jaw. Here's a drill that will help. Count aloud from one to ten slowly, *over*enunciating as much as you can. For the word "one," start by push-

VOICE:

"Once you start listening to your own voice, you risk becoming trapped into affectation. The speaker's last concern should be how he sounds. The listener, not the speaker, should be aware of how the voice sounds. The speaker should be concerned with what he seeks to communicate by the sound of his voice."

Acclaimed as "one of the great actors of our time," renowned for his distinctive voice, *James Earl Jones* gave that advice in his autobiography, ***Voices and Silences.***

ing your lips forward into an exaggerated kissing form—as if the person you were to kiss remained a couple of inches in front of you, and you're trying to reach him or her by moving only your lips. Now complete the word "one" by letting your jaw pull down and open—open far enough to get in four or more fingers.

Should you speak with such extreme movements? Of course not; this is an exercise. It is much like the example we gave you earlier of the baseball player who practices his swings using two or three extra bats or weights. It is practicing your enunciation by *over*articulating.

For more practice, run through the alphabet, again moving your lips, tongue, and jaw just as far as you possibly can. After half a minute, if the spot where your jaw joins your skull is not feeling it, possibly even creaking or hurting, then you're still not extending yourself enough.

Surprisingly, such practices done just twice a day for only about three minutes each time will significantly improve your enunciation in just ten days. Sounds like a commercial for some high-powered product, but try it and see. Actually, I've had classes that have pointed out students whose enunciation improved—pointed them out without knowing that the student was indeed practicing. The results come quickly for most who practice seriously (and who do not have a physical handicap which inhibits enunciation).

There's another old established drill that is somewhat helpful, too, in improving clarity of speech—practicing with tongue twisters. You've heard many of the old reliables:

- She sells seashells by the seashore.
- Rubber baby buggy bumpers.
- A big black bear ate a big black bug.
- Grass grew green on the graves in Grace Gray's grandfather's graveyard.
- The sixth sheik's sixth sheep's sick.

If you practice conscientiously and regularly, for just a few minutes a day, twice daily, results will be apparent in only a few weeks.

There's one more source for practice material for enunciation. That is to select or to write a poem or paragraph that becomes your own lifetime enunciation practice material. Years ago I settled on this bit from a Gilbert and Sullivan operetta:

> To sit in solemn silence
> In a dull, dark dock;
> In a pestilential prison
> With a life-long lock;
> Awaiting the sensation
> Of a short, sharp shock,
> From a cheap and chippy chopper
> On a big, black block.

Whenever I feel or am told that my enunciation is getting sloppy, I run through those old lines maybe half a dozen times, several times a day.

Does it help?

Try it and find out for yourself.

29. Pronounce Correctly

This speech characteristic is closely related to the previous one.

Enunciation refers to saying words clearly. Pronunciation refers to saying words correctly.

It is surprising, at least to me, how many speakers do not pronounce correctly even the subject or main point of their speeches.

If in doubt, look it up.

"But I can't figure out what the dictionary is trying to tell me on how to pronounce a word," some brave but honest students say. True, without regular use of a dictionary it is a struggle for many of us to try to determine what those symbols and signs and marks mean.

Another solution seems more practical for many—ask someone. But ask someone authoritative. Many students will turn to another student who may have the same lack of knowledge and can give only an incorrect version of how to pronounce the word.

This incorrect pronunciation of any word, but especially a key word, in your speech signals carelessness or laziness in your preparation, if not ignorance of your subject.

30. Hide, Don't Emphasize, Your Goofs

Listen carefully some evening to a top newscaster such as Diane Sawyer or Dan Rather. You'll find that they, too, fumble a word now and then, occasionally even a phrase. Every speaker goofs now and then. Professionals have developed skill in minimizing such errors.

Beginning speakers often repeat the fumbled word with special or additional emphasis, making the error stand out more than needed. Beginners often sound angry or disappointed as they correct themselves.

Professionals, on the other hand, correct their goofs with only casual or usual emphasis. They will often smile at, or even laugh off, an error. They will not call attention to it through some expression—either words or inflection—of concern or anxiety.

There's also a difference between how amateurs and professionals continue after correcting an error. Amateurs tend to speed up to hide the error, perhaps to get away from the distasteful event. But professionals slow down to get control of their speaking, to try to ensure against additional errors. Professionals know that once they have made one fumble, the chances are greatly increased that they will soon make still another one. Amateurs, on the other hand, by speeding up, will likely work themselves into more fumbles.

31. Don't Pack up Early

Don't start to gather your notes, juggling them into a nice neat pile, pocketing them, while you're still speaking.

Remember the importance of the conclusion of your speech. It sums up in a few succinct words the essence of your speech, and if presents a statement worth remembering. Therefore, don't give your audience any more excuse than they may already have for getting restless. Stay up there before them and hold their attention.

32. Move out with Confidence

Conclude your speech, utter your last words, take a slight pause with a right-in-the-eye look at the audience, give a modest smile or a nod of your head if it is appropriate to your speech and your style, and then, as a drill sergeant says, "Move out smartly!"

Don't be the picture of a disappointed speaker, taking up your notes in a gruff manner, shaking your head, shuffling back to your seat.

Keep projecting your confidence—even a false confidence if you must—as you return to your seat and through any discussion about your speech that may follow.

After concluding a speech, most of us feel we "could have done better." And most of us could have "if only . . . ." Speakers can find a million excuses to complete that phrase. If only we had more time, more material, practiced more, prepared more, worked more, and on and on. Yet all of us—the president himself, with all of his staff of speech writers, researchers, and technicians to help his preparation and practice— "could do better if only . . . ."

So take pride in what you have offered your audience. It *was* the best that you could bring yourself to present under the conditions that existed for you at the time. If it was in fact "not good enough," then still express confidence and resolve, sincerely, to do better next time.

33. Time Your Speech Accurately

In general, your speech should be within 10 percent of your allotted time. That means for your usual 4- to 5-minute class speech, generally you should not speak less than about $3\frac{1}{2}$ minutes nor longer than about $5\frac{1}{2}$ minutes. That gives you a 25 percent margin for error—certainly realistic, generous, fair. A shorter speech is often difficult to present in an effective speech format and can be hard to evaluate. A longer speech may well bore your listeners and is unfair to speakers who are to talk after you.

The solution is obvious: Time your speeches during your practices. But be warned: Many beginning speakers find they speak more quickly and express their ideas more briefly when they are before a live audience than during their practice sessions. And there are also those speakers who truly love to talk—they may get caught up in the excitement of the speech setting and add details, points, wander into material they'd not planned to talk about.

WATCH YOUR LENGTH

"President Clinton . . . will do the nation and himself a big favor if he remembers Shakespeare's words of wisdom: 'Brevity is the soul of wit.'"

That was the advice in an editorial in the *San Francisco Chronicle* pointing out that Clinton "broke all records (with his 1995 'State of the Union' speech) with an 81-minute" address.

Earlier, when Clinton nominated Michael Dukakis to be the Democratic presidential candidate at the 1988 convention, he talked for 32 minutes, nearly double his allotted time. He got his biggest ovation when he said, "In closing . . . ."

So there you are with 19 new tips to help you improve the delivery of your speeches. They've been added to the 14 tips you started with on your earlier speeches in this course, for a total of 33.

There's little value in memorizing the list. But there's considerable benefit to keeping in mind those tips that are especially important to you because they are either your special strengths or weaknesses. Take a moment to go back over the previous pages and then list below the techniques you feel you've already mastered most effectively and those you need to strengthen.

Delivery techniques I'm best at:

1. _____

2. _____

3. _____

4. _____

More? _____

_____

_____

Delivery techniques I should improve on:

1. _____

2. _____

3. _____

4. _____

More? _____

_____

_____

And one thing more. Make a mental note, right now, to really go to work on the techniques on that second list, the ones on which you should improve. See if you can move one or more from your list of weaknesses to your list of strengths. But don't slight your strengths—capitalize on them, improve them even more.

Now start preparing your next speech so you can demonstrate your improvements— your improvements not only in delivery, but also in content and organization.

ASSIGNMENT 14. COMMUNITY PROBLEM SPEECH: SPEECH 3, USING DATA

 ACTION: Deliver in class a 4- to 5-minute extemporaneous speech on a community problem, demonstrating your skill in using data effectively. Design the speech for a local group concerned with the subject.

OBJECTIVES:

On completion of this assignment, you are expected to be able to present a speech that is effective in that it:

1. Uses data effectively, as detailed in Lesson 7.
2. Is delivered with appropriate style, enthusiasm, and sincerity, as detailed in this lesson.
3. Is based on an effective outline, submitted to your instructor well before you present the speech so that it can be evaluated and returned to you in time for you to make possible improvements on the speech.
4. Includes the speaking skills you attained in your first two speeches in this course, that is, it:
   4.1. Is based on a useful analysis of the speaking situation.
   4.2. Is based on a correctly worded speech purpose.
   4.3. Presents appropriate points and data.
   4.4. Follows the basic format for a speech.

EVALUATION:

To be effective the speech should demonstrate the correct use of at least 80 percent of the guides for each of the three aspects of speaking as studied thus far in this course. Those guides are listed on the **Evaluation Form** at the end of this lesson. You now have 55 guides:

14 guides to *content*
8 guides to *organization*
33 guides to *delivery*
Emphasis on evaluation will be on your use of data.

INSTRUCTIONS:

1. Deliver a 4- to 5-minute extemporaneous speech on a topic of direct concern to the residents of this area.
2. Design the speech for a specific local organization that is concerned with or responsible for the subject.
3. Deliver the speech in class, but as if you were speaking to that particular audience.
4. Remember that this speech is to be based on the outline you prepared and submitted for Assignment 13.
5. To select a *subject*, see the instructions for that outline, starting on page 217.
6. In planning the speech, use the **Check-off Tip Sheet** on the next page.
7. To receive from your instructor comments and suggestions about your speech, use the **Evaluation Form** on pages 239–240.

Once again, no need to try to memorize all those guides; your goal is just to use them—effectively.

Are you Speaking English?

Not always.

Chipmunk, pecan, skunk, and *squaw* are but a few of the words we have taken from various Native American languages.

Admiral, almanac, harem, and *mattress* are from the Arabic language.

Catsup, silk, tea, and *tycoon* are from the Chinese.

Geisha, karate, and *kimono* are Japanese.

Bamboo, gingham, orangutan, and *sarong* are Malay.

Shish Kebab and *yogurt* are Turkish.

COMMUNITY PROBLEM—SPEECH 3, USING DATA: CHECK-OFF TIP SHEET

INSTRUCTIONS: Check off each item as you prepare your speech.

Audience: _____   Speech purpose: _____

1. CONTENT

___ 1.1. Based on accurate analysis of speaking situation

___ 1.2. Purpose worded correctly: from audience's viewpoint, specific, and attainable

___ 1.3. Subject appropriate, relevant, and interesting to audience

___ 1.4   Points, data new, significant to audience

___ 1.5. Includes personal and human interest stories

___ 1.6. All material contributes to purpose

___ 1.7. Gets to point quickly

___ 1.8. Presents own, orginal ideas, structure, or interpretation

___ 1.9. Uses audiovisual aids when appropriate

___ 1.10. Emphasizes organization enough to help audience remember points

___ 1.11. Includes variety of data

___ 1.12. Data seem accurate, honest

___ 1.13. Points valid conclusions from data

___ 1.14. Includes examples to clarify, add interest, etc., not to prove points

2. ORGANIZATION

___ 2.1. Begins with effective attention-getter

___ 2.2. Previews subject or viewpoint

___ 2.3. Presents 2 to 5 specific points

___ 2.4. Arranges points logically

___ 2.5. Supports each point with data:

    ___ 2.5.1. Example

    ___ 2.5.2. Story

    ___ 2.5.3. Quotation

    ___ 2.5.4. Definition

    ___ 2.5.5. Comparison

    ___ 2.5.6. Contrast

    ___ 2.5.7. Statistic

    ___ 2.5.8. Audiovisual aid

___ 2.6. Reviews subject, viewpoint, or discussion points

___ 2.7. Concludes with memorable statement

___ 2.8. Uses structure of speech, not of old-style class report or article

3. DELIVERY

___ 3.1. Steps up to speak with confidence

___ 3.2. Gets set before speaking

___ 3.3. Establishes contact before speaking

___ 3.4. Begins without referring to notes

___ 3.5. Maintains contact with audience

___ 3.6. Sounds extemporaneous, not read or memorized

___ 3.7. Uses, few 3×5 note cards

___ 3.8. Refers to notes only occasionally

___ 3.9. Avoids *ah, so, ya know, well, 'kay,* etc.

___ 3.10. Stops at end of idea: doesn't hook sentences together with *and, and ah,* etc.

___ 3.11. Maintains good posture

___ 3.12. Doesn't play with notes, clothes, etc.

___ 3.13. Dresses to help, not hinder, speech

___ 3.14. Speaks loudly enough to be heard easily

___ 3.15. Uses aids effectively

___ 3.16. Gestures effectively

___ 3.17. Uses face to add interest

___ 3.18. Moves about

___ 3.19. Doesn't pace

___ 3.20. Appears to enjoy speaking

___ 3.21. Seems to care that audience listens

___ 3.22. Speaks with enthusiasm

___ 3.23. Appears confident and relaxed

___ 3.24. Speaks with, not at, audience

___ 3.25. Doesn't look at floor, etc.

___ 3.26. Varies speaking rate; not too fast or too slow

___ 3.27. Varies voice pitch and volume

___ 3.28. Enunciates clearly

___ 3.29. Pronounces correctly

___ 3.30. Hides goofs

___ 3.31. Doesn't pack up early

___ 3.32. Moves out with confidence

___ 3.33. Time: _____

Speak!

Speech was made to open man to man, and not to hide him; to promote commerce, and not betray it."

David Lloyd, British Biographer

COMMUNITY PROBLEM—SPEECH 3, USING DATA: EVALUATION FORM

Speaker:_____ Audience: _____ Date:_____

Speech purpose:_____

_____

1. CONTENT

___ 1.1. Based on accurate analysis of speaking situation

___ 1.2. Purpose worded correctly: from audience's viewpoint, specific, and attainable

___ 1.3. Subject appropriate, relevant, and interesting to audience

___ 1.4. Points, data new, significant

___ 1.5. Includes personal and human interest stories

___ 1.6. All material contributes to purpose

___ 1.7. Gets to point quickly

___ 1.8. Presents own, original ideas, structure, or interpretation

___ 1.9. Uses audiovisual aids when appropriate

___ 1.10. Emphasizes organization enough to help audience remember points

___ 1.11. Includes variety of data

___ 1.12. Data seem accurate, honest

___ 1.13. Points valid conclusions from data

___ 1.14. Includes examples to clarify, add interest, etc., not to prove points

2. ORGANIZATION

___ 2.1. Begins with effective attention-getter

___ 2.2. Previews subject or viewpoint

___ 2.3. Presents 2 to 5 specific points

___ 2.4. Arranges points logically

___ 2.5. Supports each point with data:

    ___ 2.5.1. Example

    ___ 2.5.2. Story

    ___ 2.5.3. Quotation

    ___ 2.5.4. Definition

    ___ 2.5.5. Comparison

    ___ 2.5.6. Contrast

    ___ 2.5.7. Statistic

    ___ 2.5.8. Audiovisual aid

___ 2.6. Reviews subject, viewpoint, or discussion points

___ 2.7. Concludes with memorable statement

___ 2.8. Uses structure of speech, not of old-style class report or article

3. DELIVERY

___ 3.1. Steps up to speak with confidence

___ 3.2. Gets set before speaking

___ 3.3. Establishes contact before speaking

___ 3.4. Begins without referring to notes

___ 3.5. Maintains contact with audience

___ 3.6. Sounds extemporaneous, not read or memorized

___ 3.7. Uses, few 3 × 5 note cards

___ 3.8. Refers to note cards only occasionally

___ 3.9. Avoids *ah, so, ya know, well, 'kay,* etc.

___ 3.10 Stops at end of idea; doesn't hook sentences together with *and, and ah,* etc.

___ 3.11. Maintains good posture

___ 3.12. Doesn't play with notes, clothes, etc.

___ 3.13. Dresses to help, not hinder, speech

___ 3.14. Speaks loudly enough to be heard easily

___ 3.15. Uses aids effectively

___ 3.16. Gestures effectively

___ 3.17. Uses face to add interest

___ 3.18. Moves about

___ 3.19. Doesn't pace

___ 3.20. Appears to enjoy speaking

___ 3.21. Seems to care that audience listens

___ 3.22. Speaks with enthusiasm

___ 3.23. Appears confident and relaxed

___ 3.24. Speaks with, not at, audience

___ 3.25. Doesn't look at floor, etc.

___ 3.26. Varies speaking rate—not too fast or too slow

___ 3.27. Varies voice pitch and volume

___ 3.28. Enunciates clearly

___ 3.29. Pronounces correctly

___ 3.30. Hides goofs

___ 3.31. Doesn't pack up early

___ 3.32. Moves out with confidence

___ 3.33. Time: _____

4. COMMENTS:

Grade: _____

DELIVERY: CHECK-OFF TIP SHEET

BASIC TECHNIQUES LEARNED IN LESSON 3, DELIVERING SPEECHES:

Before you speak:

_____ 1. Dress to help, not hinder, your speech.
_____ 2. Limit the number of note cards you use.
_____ 3. Step up to speak with confidence and authority.
_____ 4. Get set.
_____ 5. Establish contact with your audience.

While you're speaking:

_____ 6. Maintain contact with your audience.
_____ 7. Begin without referring to your notes.
_____ 8. Refer to your note card only occasionally.
_____ 9. Sound conversational, not as if reading or delivering a memorized speech.
_____ 10. Avoid _ah, so, ya know, well, 'kay,_ etc.
_____ 11. Stop at the end of an idea: don't hook sentences together with _and, and ah,_ etc.
_____ 12. Maintain good posture: don't lean, cross legs, etc.
_____ 13. Don't play with notes, pencil, clothes, etc.
_____ 14. Speak loudly enough to be heard easily.

Additional Tips Taught in This Lesson:

_____ 15. Use aids effectively.
         _____ 15.1. Make sure your aids work.
         _____ 15.2. Be sure you know how they work.
         _____ 15.3. Get your aids in place before speaking.
         _____ 15.4. Use a pointer to direct your listeners' attention.
         _____ 15.5. Remove your aids as soon as you've finished the point.
         _____ 15.6. Talk to your audience, not to your aids.
         _____ 15.7. Avoid holding visuals.
         _____ 15.8. Do not give material to audience while you're speaking.
_____ 16. Gesture effectively.
_____ 17. Use your face to add interest.
_____ 18. Move about—get from behind lectern.
_____ 19. Don't pace.
_____ 20. Appear to enjoy speaking.
_____ 21. Seem to care that your audience listens.
_____ 22. Speak with enthusiasm.
_____ 23. Appear confident and relaxed.
_____ 24. Speak with, not at, the audience.
_____ 25. Don't look at the floor, out the window, over audience's head, at the back wall, etc.
_____ 26. Vary your speaking rate; don't speak too fast or too slow.
_____ 27. Vary your voice pitch and volume.
_____ 28. Enunciate clearly.
_____ 29. Pronounce correctly.
_____ 30. Hide, don't emphasize, your goofs.
_____ 31. Don't pack up early.
_____ 32. Move out with confidence.
_____ 33. Time your speech accurately.

Speak Up!

Concerned about being heard by your audience? Well, the furthest the typical male voice can carry in still air is 600 feet. Still, there is one report that a fellow was heard—over still water, at night, under ideal conditions—10.5 miles! Such is the claim of the current edition of *The Guinness Book of Records.*

L E S S O N   10

Designing Discussions

OBJECTIVES After completing this lesson, you will be able to:

1. Name the most frequently used patterns for organizing the discussion part of a speech.
2. Given various lists of logically organized main points, identify the pattern of organization.
3. Distinguish between a logically organized list of main points and one that is not, and state a correct basis for your decision.
4. Select appropriate main points for speeches.
5. Organize those points in a logical and clear pattern.
6. Incorporate in your speeches parallel wording, smooth transitions, and balanced lines.

RELEVANCE We have established in previous lessons that your goal is to design and deliver an effective speech, and we have defined an effective speech as one that, among other characteristics, is *organized* clearly and logically.

This lesson teaches you how.

Mend your speech a little,
Lest you may mar your
fortunes.
William Shakespeare wrote
that line in his play
Othello.

Specifically, we are concerned here with the selection and organization of the main points of your speech—the divisions of the basic topic or subject of your speech.

You'll remember that the discussion is the main part of your speech, usually about 80 percent of its length. In the discussion you present the substance, or main points, of your speech and the data to prove, explain, or make memorable the main points.

The problem is that listeners usually remember only a small percentage of what speakers say. According to Professor Ronald Salafia of Fairfield University, "A person's short-term memory can only handle seven separate pieces of information at one time."

There are a few exceptions. In specialized speaking situations such as college lectures, listeners may retain more of what they hear, primarily because of two factors. First, listeners often take notes in clearly instructional situations; the act of note-taking increases their memory of ideas and specifics. Second, even if they do not take notes, listeners often remember more because they either want to or know they are expected to remember what they hear.

In general, you can count on your listeners' remembering only that which you as the speaker successfully implant in their memories. Arranging your discussion points in a clear and logical pattern will help considerably.

Here's how to do that.

SELECTING YOUR MAIN POINTS

For purposes of illustration, assume the following set of circumstances. Look at them carefully, because we'll be working with this situation for some time in this lesson.

Assume that you consider many television programs to be childish, poorly presented, a waste of time. In the words of a student I worked with recently, helping him to design a speech on this subject, "There should be a lot more programs of quality—programs about art, music, and dance; programs on really important issues; programs for adults, not for child-minds."

Assume also that you belong to a local action group.

Assume you've heard that television network officials do listen and react to thoughtful, constructive criticism.

You put all these together—your concern about television, your membership in an action group, the fact that executives listen to viewers—and you decide to present a speech to your fellow members in the action group. The speech purpose:

> ◗ After hearing my speech, the audience will agree to send letters of complaint about television programs to the president of each of the three networks.

Assume, too, that you have gathered together quite a few specifics about television programs you consider poor. You've made summaries of several childish programs that were designed for adult audiences; you've found some figures on what seem to be pretty high costs for producing shows; and you have a couple of studies about the many programs showing violence and about the numerous commercials.

So, you've got your (1) speech purpose and (2) your data. Now you need the points for the discussion part of your speech. These are your specific ideas on your general topic of "complaints about television programs."

Where do you get these points?

Some points you already have in mind. They came to you as you thought about your topic. You found others as you gathered your data. Some points occurred to you as you read the research studies.

Now you should prepare a *prospectus*.

PROSPECTUS

In our program for designing a speech, a prospectus is a list of the points you might want to present in your speech.

Simply write down all the points concerning your speech that come to your mind. At this stage, don't bother—don't inhibit your thinking—by trying to determine which points are most valid or which points are not worth writing down. What you want now is a good long list of possible points from which you can select later.

While our focus at this stage of your speech preparation is on selecting the main points, many speakers find it helpful to also include in their prospectus bits of data that relate to their speech. By doing so, their prospectus will be more complete, more useful, than if they prepare two prospectuses—two lists—one of main points and another of data.

In preparing a prospectus, following these four brief guides will help:

1. Start Well Before You Begin to Outline

You should make every effort to develop your prospectus over a period of at least a few days. Preparing a prospectus immediately before you start outlining your speech will usually detract seriously from the completeness, validity, and logic of your planning. Your ideas, points, and data need time to run through your mind so they can be more effectively evaluated, pruned, selected, worded, sequenced.

2. Include at Least 15 to 20 Points

You'll remember that your speech itself will usually include just two to five points. But now, in the early planning of your speech, preparing a much longer preliminary list of points, and of data, will be of significant help to you in the next step of preparing your speech. Then, as you struggle to narrow your list down, you'll find it easier to select only the very best, most potent, relevant, valuable points for your speech.

3. Keep Your Prospectus Open for Adding More Points for Several Days

This will facilitate your adding ideas as they occur to you—a much more productive process than simply sitting down one time and trying to pull from your mind the best material for your speech.

Don't be concerned about listing points that overlap or repeat other points. Don't worry about wordings, and don't worry about possibly mixing points with data. Your prospectus should merely be a working list from which you'll later select the best material.

4. Write Down Your Possible Points Rather Than Trying to Remember Them

If your mind works anything like mine, when you've got a speech coming up, you're thinking about what to include in that speech a great deal of the time—while driving to work or school, while standing in a shopping line, when waiting for TV commercials to conclude so you can get back to the football game, while brushing your teeth, trying to fall asleep—virtually always! And some of your best thoughts—well, some of my best thoughts—come to mind during those periods.

Trying to remember those passing thoughts later can chew up a lot of time. That's why it is much more productive to keep your prospectus handy so you can quickly, easily add your latest ideas to your list. If you do not jot down a point when you first think of it, later you may "feel" you had a really good point in mind earlier in the day, but now you can't quite remember what it was.

Now, let's try developing a prospectus for that speech on television. Your listing might look like this:

Prospectus: TV Complaints

1. Too much violence
2. Not enough culture
3. Need more programs on art, music, etc.
4. . . .

Well, why don't you step in and add some of your own suggestions. Remember, this is a listing of possible points—to be thinned out, reworded, structured later.

1. _____
2. _____
3. _____
4. _____
5. _____
6. _____
7. _____
8. _____
9. _____
10. _____
11. _____
12. _____
13. More?_____
    _____
    _____

Your prospectus might include such points as:

1. Networks spend too much
2. Adult mind not programmed for
3. Daytime soap operas especially wasteful
4. Good plays usually aired only as occasional specials
5. Game shows chew up morning hours
6. Children conned into asking for cheap toys
7. Some good ideas come out on talk shows, but shows far too sleazy
8. Cartoons a major wasteland
9. Studies show audience watching hour after hour
10. Movies, repeated frequently, just cheap way to fill in between commercials
11. Some of the longest-running shows are the worst
12. Current Broadway plays rarely seen except on pay or cable stations
13. Commercials repetitious, childish, irritating
14. Educational programs rare on commercial stations

Now review that list to balance your data with your ideas. Your thinking might go like this:

> Well, I really dislike those commercials. That should be a big point in my speech. Let's see, what proof do I have? (Flip through note cards containing your data.) Here's that study on number of commercials, length, etc. That's part of it, but how do I show commercials are distasteful? I don't remember finding any data on that. Could check library again. No, better I watch some TV and make notes on the commercials I see.
>
> Well, what's another big point in my prospectus? Those talk shows—I really want to point to them. Sure a lot of wasted talk, but still, some good, solid ideas come through now and then. Maybe I can find articles, data on them.
>
> On the other hand, it's those daytime shows—the soap operas—that really waste the air time. With no classes this semester on Tuesday mornings I tuned in a few days. Wow! Unbelievably bad. Hospitals and divorces and crime and phone calls back and forth between the dumb characters telling this guy what that guy said about some other guy. I really have to talk about those in the speech.

Eventually, through such mulling over in your mind, some points become more dominant. From the above meditation these points might appear:

1. Commercials
2. Talk shows
3. Daytime soap operas

Now it's time to check back to the speech purpose you established earlier to make sure you're still heading toward a speech to fulfill it. Reread your speech purpose carefully, considering its implications word by word:

> ▶ After hearing my speech, the audience will agree to send letters of complaint about television programs to the president of each of the three networks.

Let's see, it says the letters your audience will send will be about "television programs." That means you should be talking about—using as your examples, illustrations, and such—television programs. Check again the three most likely points of the speech we've arrived at: (1) commercials, (2) talk shows, and (3) daytime soap operas. Two of those points are concerned with programs, but the first one centers on commercials.

Check back to your speech purpose. Remember that there is nothing sacred about it; you certainly can change it as you plan your speech. But what would you change it to? Commercials and programs? Commercials only?

How to decide? Some considerations would be, Do you have enough time for a speech about both? Do you have enough data on commercials? On talk shows? On soap operas? Will speaking on both spread your speech too thin? Are the programs or the commercials worthy of a speech individually?

And, of course, there are other considerations—your own preferences, interests, and concerns. But most of all, you should keep thinking back to that audience, trying to decide not what you want to say, not what they want to hear, but what might have the most positive, productive influence on them. For this, you go back to that **Analysis of Speaking Situation** you prepared at the very start of planning your speech.

Now you are at the stage of deciding just how to organize whatever main points you finally do decide to present in your speech. What are your options here?

PATTERNS FOR THE DISCUSSION

"Pattern" is used here to mean a design, configuration, or sequence. There are four most frequently used patterns for organizing the discussion part of a speech. They are:

1. Time
2. Space
3. Topic
4. Problem-solution

Consider each of these in detail.

Alert! ➤ Note: The following examples are partial outlines of points as they would appear in a complete outline of a speech. They would be identified by capital letters under the main part heading II. Discussion. The outline of the discussion would be preceded by I. Introduction and followed by III. Conclusion.

Also note that the data are not included in the examples.

We are focusing here on the 2 to 5 main points of the discussion part of a speech.

1. Time Pattern

A time pattern is useful for structuring a speech about a process, an activity, or an historical event. For example, the speech about television might present these main points in the discussion:

A. Early-morning programming
B. Midday programming
C. Evening programming
D. Late-night programming

That list of discussion points is effective for several reasons. The time units are those that television itself often uses. The time segments are the logical periods in which people tend to watch television. There are significant differences in programming in the time segments. In sum, the time units divide the subject of television programming into four manageable, related, and logical points—a time pattern.

Consider some other applications of a time pattern.

Your first speech, a demonstration speech, is one for which the time pattern is frequently appropriate. For example, if your subject is changing a tire, your main points might be:

A. Secure by braking and blocking
B. Raise car by jacking
C. Remove damaged tire
D. Replace with spare
E. Lower car

This is a time pattern because the actions should occur in the sequence listed and that would be emphasized by your wording of your speech points.

Another example: Your topic might be that the United States seems to face a crisis every decade.

The points might be:

A. In 1950s, threats from internal and external sources
B. In 1960s, a lingering war
C. In 1970s, economic problems
D. In 1980s, spirit of recovery
E. In 1990s, what can we expect?

If your speech topic were the general subject of how to take a trip, a logical use of the time pattern might present such points as . . . well, what do you suggest?

A. _____

B. _____

C. _____

D. _____

E. _____

There are, of course, many possibilities. One would be:

A. Before the trip
B. Start of the trip
C. During the trip
D. After the trip

A slight variation in structure, with different wording, of a time pattern for that same trip would be:

A. Pretrip
B. During trip
C. Posttrip

Check your suggested list of points by asking yourself:

1. Are my points time segments?
2. Are the time segments about equal or comparable?
3. Are they logical?
4. Are they related directly to the subject?

Consider the negative. Look at the following examples of *poor* uses of the time pattern.

For a speech on hints about operating on-line, one student had these points in this sequence:

A. Check your billing regularly, so you don't run up an expense beyond your means.
B. Pick a screen name that is easy to remember.
C. Leave a chat room when the talk gets rough.
D. Don't go into a chat room and break into the talk before you know the topic being discussed.

Time pattern? Hardly. But the student thought it was a time pattern because "you have to do those things in an order." True—but not in the order presented there. Certainly point C, about leaving a chat room, should come before point D, about entering a chat room. Indeed, other points in that list should be in a different sequence.

Another *poor* use of a time pattern was this speech on selected historical highlights of radio broadcasting:

A. Before 1920s—experimentation
B. 1920s—commercial development
C. 1927—first network
D. Decade of 1935–1945—height of nationwide programs
E. Late 1960s—talk shows develop

This is an *ineffective* use of a time pattern because of the irregularity of the time units presented. For point A, a long period, in effect all the years before 1920. Then a decade, the 1920s of point B. Next a specific year. Then a "decade" that really spans two decades in the usual sense. Finally, a half-decade, "late 1960s." Such variety does little to help your audience remember the points of your speech, follow along with you, and accept your ideas.

2. Space Pattern

A space pattern is useful for organizing speeches presenting subjects concerned with physical, geographical, governmental, sectional, or comparable topics.

For our basic example of a talk about television programming, the main points, organized in a space pattern, could be:

A. Programs in small towns of America
B. Programs in large cities of America
C. Programs in foreign countries

This listing has the defect that the three points are not equal in characteristics of a geographical nature, but this may not be important to the point of your speech. For example, within these points you might document the lack of virtually any local creative programming in small towns, then the banality of large city production. Finally you could compare them both with what is telecast in foreign countries.

If your speech subject were recreation, your points would be in a space pattern if they were these:

A. Recreation in the mountains
B. Recreation at the seashore
C. Recreation in the deserts

If your speech subject were the characteristics of colleges in the United States, and you were to use a space pattern, your points might be . . . well, try listing some:

A. _____

B. _____

C. _____

D. _____

More? _____

Your points could be colleges in the West, Midwest, and East. Or, they might parallel the areas into which colleges are divided for athletics: Ivy League, Pacific Coast, etc.

How about the following use of a space pattern for a speech on how to select a house for purchase:

A. What to look for in a living room
B. Important features of a yard
C. Important features of a kitchen
D. Good qualities to look for in roofing

Would you consider that effective or ineffective? _____

Why? _____

_____

_____

_____

_____

Among the weaknesses you could point to is that the points jump from a room, to outside, back to a room, then to the top of the house—consequently, they are not logical, equal divisions of the subject.

Those points are also weak because they change from "what to look for" to "important features" and then to "good qualities."

3. Topic Pattern

A topic pattern is useful particularly in speeches presenting types, classes, aspects, or qualities. This is sometimes called the "catch-all" pattern, that is, if no other pattern is appropriate, you can always figure out some topical divisions of your speech subject.

Let's return again to our basic example, the speech on television. A good topic pattern would be:

A. Talk shows
B. Soap operas
C. Game shows
D. Situation comedies
E. News programs
F. Dramas

Additional types of programs could be listed, such as educational programs, variety shows musical programs. But remember that in general a speech is more effective if it presents just 2 to 5 points; more than that are difficult for your audience to remember.

Another topic pattern on our television subject would be:

A. Violence
B. Childish programming for adults
C. Lack of programs of significance

This is an acceptable set of main points for the discussion part of a speech, but it does have the weakness that they are not comparable or equal divisions of the basic topic. However, in many speeches the topics cannot always be divided into strictly equal parts.

Try another example of a topic pattern. Assume your speech subject is problems of pollution. You might present these points:

A. Pollution by individuals
B. Pollution by government agencies
C. Pollution by industry

These points are an application of the topic pattern, but they do have the weakness that, even for a rather lengthy speech, they cover quite a bit of ground, probably more than could be presented in any suitable depth. Hence, we're shown one danger in using a topic pattern: designing points that may be too inclusive, too broad.

Assume you are designing a speech on how to select a college. What points might you present in the discussion part of your speech that would be a logical, effective use of a topic pattern?

A. _____

B. _____

C. _____

D. _____

More? _____

Your answer could be any of a great variety of points. To check your reply, answer these questions to your self:

1. Are my points actually topics, as such?
2. Are they all logical, appropriate parts of the speech subject?
3. Are they about equal or comparable divisions of that speech subject?
4. Are they sufficiently restricted—not covering too much?

4. Problem-Solution Pattern

A problem-solution pattern is useful in speeches presenting proposals for change, new procedures, laws, concepts, regulations, and such.

For our speech on weaknesses in television, a problem-solution pattern could present the main points in this way:

A. Problem: poor television programming
B. Solution: action group to write letters of complaint to networks

But there is one problem in those points, a problem we pointed to in one of the previous examples. Can you spot it? What would you suggest that weakness is?

_____

_____

_____

If your answer is that the points are too broad, you're right with us.

But there's a solution. A speaker can divide the points of a speech and present a series of subpoints before getting to the data. For example, the points above might become:

A. Problem: poor television programming
   1. Lack of mature programs
   2. Lack of programs on significant issues
   3. Lack of cultural programs
B. Solution: action group to write letters of complaint to networks

Only now we have another problem: The speech is rather out of balance, with three subpoints under point A. and none under point B. Again there's a solution. The outline could become:

    A. Problem: poor television programming
       1. Lack of mature programs
       2. Lack of programs on significant issues
       3. Lack of cultural programs
    B. Solution: action group to write letters of complaint to networks
       1. Networks do respond to intelligent comments from audience
       2. Networks are interested in improving their programming
       3. Letters from other groups have changed network programming

Now we have a balanced outline—the same number of subpoints under each major point. Outlines need not always have exactly the same number of subpoints for each main point, but they should usually be about equally distributed.

Why?

Glad you asked. If you present several subpoints under one point and only one under another, some of your listeners may assume, perhaps rightly, that you have a strong case for the more detailed point but a rather weak case when all you can offer is one point.

But there are exceptions. You may want to present a point simply to get it on the record. For example, in a speech to doctors you need not detail that there's a shortage of medical service in rural areas; they certainly know that. But you might want to just mention it in order to establish the basis for proposing a new solution to that problem.

Consider another application of the problem-solution pattern. Assume your speech topic is the need to improve college instruction. Your points might be:

    A. Problem: college instruction not sufficiently effective
       1. Need for more individualized learning
       2. Need for better teachers
    B. Solution: more funds to colleges
       1. To keep up with inflation of operating expenses
       2. To provide more and better facilities

On first reading, that outline may seem to be an effective application of the problem-solution pattern. It does present logical points or parts of the speech subject. The points are in a logical order. They are specific enough to be handled clearly and with direction in the speech. And the points are equally distributed, two subpoints for each of the two main points. Finally, the main points and the subpoints are about as equal as they could be in importance.

Yet that partial outline illustrates the most frequent and serious weakness of many speeches. It is a weakness that appears often in speeches that try to get a new procedure or policy adopted. And it is a weakness particularly common in speeches organized in the problem-solution pattern.

That weakness is . . . or are you ahead of me again? What have you spotted as the major weakness in that last partial outline?

_____

_____

_____

Have an extra dessert at dinner tonight if you stated something such as the solution does not necessarily solve the problem presented.

The first aspect of the problem (A. 1.) is the "Need for more individualized learning." Yet neither of the two subpoints presented in the solution is concerned with that. Rather, the solution—"more funds"—is to do two things not pointed to as problems.

Consider the weakness from another angle. It may well be true that more funds are needed to keep up with inflation and to provide facilities. But neither of those particular points is established as a problem earlier in the speech. In the first part of the discussion the problems identified are the need for individualized learning and better teachers.

This weakness—the failure to present a solution that solves the problem presented—is emphasized here for two reasons. First, as a speaker, don't present such a nonrelated solution to the problem you're trying to solve. And second, as a listener, don't be taken in by the many speakers who point to a legitimate problem, offer a realistic solution, but the solution does not contribute directly to solving the problem presented.

This weakness is more a matter of substance than pattern. Our example did satisfy organizational requirements, but it is still inadequate. If you use the problem-solution pattern, be sure your subpoints do have the correct organizational form and do offer a true solution. How could that partial outline be strengthened? One way is this presentation of the solution using the same structure:

A. Problem: college instruction not sufficiently effective
1. Need for more individualized learning
2. Need for better teachers
B. Solution: more funds to colleges
1. To finance the high cost of designing individualized learning
2. To pay for higher salaries demanded by more qualified people

Now the two points of the solution relate directly to the two points of the problem. Further, it is what might be called an "each-to-each" relationship; that is, the first point of the problem is solved by the first point in the solution, and the second point of the problem is solved by the second point of the solution.

This, then, suggests another way for you as a speaker to check on the logic of your outline when you use a problem-solution pattern and also for you as a listener to be alert to the logic and consistency in the presentations of speakers. The solution to a problem is easier to accept, easier to follow and understand, if there is a direct point-to-point relationship between the presentation of the problem and the presentation of the solution. If this is not clear, check again the correct, effective application of this feature in the previous partial outline.

5.   Combination Patterns

Can you use a combination of, say, two patterns in the same speech? Yes, you can, but it is not recommended.

Consider the following partial outlines:

Subject: Ecological Problems of Our Rivers

A. Pollution of eastern rivers
B. Neglect of our central rivers
C. Destruction of western rivers

In what pattern are these points organized? _____

Subject: Ecological Problems of Our Rivers

    A. Eastern rivers are being polluted.
    B. Central rivers are being neglected.
    C. Western rivers are being destroyed.

What pattern are these points in? _____

You can see that the distinction between a topic pattern and a space pattern, for example, may not be clear-cut. The first list of points names topics first—pollution, neglect, and destruction. Whatever is named first tends to be emphasized and remembered. Thus the first list can best be classified as a topic pattern. The second list of points changes the emphasis by naming geographical features first—eastern, central, western. The points are arranged in a space pattern.

But consider one more partial outline.

Subject: Ecological Problems of Our Rivers

    A. Pollution of eastern rivers.
    B. Central rivers are being neglected.
    C. Manufacturing is destroying rivers in the West.

What pattern is used in this listing? _____

You'd have to say it is a combination pattern, wouldn't you? The first point mentions a topic first—pollution. The second point mentions a geographical feature first—central. The third point mentions a topic first—manufacturing.

As you can see, a combination of patterns lacks clarity. Combination patterns make it more difficult for your listeners to follow your points.

Combination patterns do add variety to the structure of your presentation. Such variety is often desirable in written material, such as an article or an essay. But variety in the patterns of the points in a speech tends to hinder, rather than help, your listeners remember the points you present.

Another problem often develops in using combination patterns. You may have noticed that in that last pattern the wording of the points is not at all as smooth as in the first two patterns.

So you should avoid combining patterns to sequence the points in your speeches. Combination patterns are less clear, harder to understand, harder to follow, more difficult to remember, and usually can't be worded smoothly.

LANGUAGE

The language we use in speaking is different from the language we use in writing, as you have no doubt noticed. Knowing exactly what those differences are can help you improve both your speaking and your writing. When we speak we usually use:

1. Shorter words
2. A smaller vocabulary
3. Fewer adjectives
4. More informal words and expressions
5. Shorter sentences

6. A longer complete text—we generally take more words to express an idea when we speak than when we write
7. More statements that are egocentric—about ourselves; examples: "I want to say . . .," "I think . . .," "In my opinion . . .," "Let me add . . ."
8. More partial (fragment) sentences
9. More repetitions, digressions, rewordings, false starts
10. More questions seeking agreement, understanding, etc.; examples: "Right?" "OK?" "Ya know?" "Agree?" "Follow?" "With me?"
11. Less structure

You can easily spot many of those differences yourself by comparing a newspaper's report of an auto accident, for example, with how your friend who witnessed the accident describes it.

WORDING TECHNIQUES

This topic opens the door to entire courses and lifelong practice and experience in the delicate and sensitive selection of words. Here we'll detail only three techniques especially valuable in public speaking:

1. Parallel wording
2. Transitions
3. Balanced line

1. Parallel Wording

Parallel wording is the stating of a series of points or ideas by repeating key, or significant, words. For example, notice the repetition in wording in the following points for a speech about problems of ecology.

A. Rivers are being destroyed.
B. Forests are being destroyed.
C. Beaches are being destroyed.

The repetition of the key phrase "are being destroyed" will strengthen a speech significantly. Notice how much stronger, clearer, and more memorable the points are than

EFFECTIVE WORDING:

"Today, we have a vision of Texas where opportunity knows no race or color or gender. . . . Tomorrow, we must build that Texas.

"Today, we have a vision of a Texas with clean air and land and water. . . . Tomorrow, we must build that Texas.

"Today, we have a vision of a Texas where *every* child receives an education that allows them to claim the full promise of their lives. Tomorrow, we must build that Texas."

That effective wording was presented by former Texas Governor *Ann. W. Richards,* now a frequent public speaker, in her speech on the occasion of her inauguration.

PARALLEL WORDING:

"We must expect the right to a job with adequate wages. Expect it. We must expect the right to adequate health care. Expect it. We must expect the right to affordable housing. Expect it. We must expect the right to education. Expect it."

Those are but a few of the many dramatic uses of parallel wordings in the speeches of *Jesse Jackson,* minister, activist, former presidential candidate, and talk-show host.

the points in our previous examples on the same subject. Essentially the same points are presented, but now the point of the speech will be driven home much more directly, strongly.

Let's return to the speech about television programming. In the section about the time pattern we suggested these points could be used for that reason:

A. Early-morning programming
B. Midday programming
C. Evening programming
D. Late-night programming

That is an effective application of a time pattern. And it also uses parallel wording in that it repeats the word "programming," which is the basic subject of the speech.

Additional parallel wording is used to express the time segments—early morning, midday, evening, late night. This is repetition through comparable, even though not the exact same, wording.

So it is a good listing of points, it follows a specific pattern, is arranged in logical order, and uses parallel wording. But that parallel wording could be strengthened by wording the points this way:

A. Weaknesses in early-morning programming
B. Weaknesses in midday programming
C. Weaknesses in evening programming
D. Weaknesses in late-night programming

Parallel wording is one of the most effective techniques of speech design.

It is, incidentally, one of the ways in which the structure of spoken material differs from written; parallel wording in written material is not at all as effective, as it often appears to a reader as boring and unimaginative. But use parallel wording in your speeches and you'll quickly recognize its value. It not only helps your audience but also helps you, the speaker, remember your points.

Parallel wording was used especially effectively in two noted speeches in recent decades. Both speeches had great impact on their listeners and continue to be remembered.

One of the speeches was presented to an audience of some 210,000 people; millions more heard it on television and radio. That historic speech continues to be an inspiration and has been rebroadcast often. Although you probably have seen television

PARALLEL WORDING:

Dr. Martin Luther King, Jr., used this speaking technique most effectively, as illustrated by the adjacent quote from his most famous speech.

replays of at least parts of this speech, its power comes through in even this brief excerpt:

▶ I say to you today, my friends, that in spite of the difficulties and frustrations of the moment I still have a dream. It is a dream deeply rooted in the American dream.

- I have a dream that one day this nation will rise up and live out the true meaning of its creed: "We hold these truths to be self-evident; that all men are created equal."
- I have a dream that one day on the red hills of Georgia the sons of former slaves and the sons of former slaveowners will be able to sit down together at the table of brotherhood.
- I have a dream that one day even the state of Mississippi, a desert state sweltering with the heat of injustice and oppression, will be transformed into an oasis of freedom and justice.
- I have a dream that my four little children will one day live in a nation where they will not be judged by the color of their skin but by the content of their character.
- I have a dream today.
- I have a dream that one day the state of Alabama, whose governor's lips are presently dripping with the words of interposition and nullification, will be transformed into a situation where little black boys and black girls will be able to join hands with little white boys and white girls and walk together as sisters and brothers.
- I have a dream today.
- I have a dream that one day every valley shall be exalted, every hill and mountain shall be made low, the rough places will be made plains, and the crooked places will be made straight, and the glory of the Lord shall be revealed and all flesh shall see it together.

Dr. Martin Luther King, Jr., *President,*
Southern Christian Leadership Conference;
Speech at March on Washington for Jobs and Freedom,
Washington, D. C.

Parallel wording helped make another speech particularly effective. In 1972 a great many politicians gave a great many speeches. Few are remembered. But this speech moved many Americans. Note its dramatic use of parallel wording.

> So join with me in this campaign, lend me your strength and your support, give me your voice—and together, we will call America home to the founding ideals that nourished us in the beginning.
> - From secrecy and deception in high places, come home, America.
> - From a conflict in Indochina, which maims our ideals as well as our soldiers, come home, America.
> - From the entrenchment of special privilege and tax favoritism, come home, America.
> - From military spending so wasteful that it weakens our nation, come home, America.
> - From the waste of idle hands to the job of useful labor, come home, America.
> - From the prejudice of race and sex, come home, America.
> - From the loneliness of the aging poor and the despair of the neglected sick, come home, America.
>
> Come home to the affirmation that we have a dream.
> Come home to the conviction that we can move our country forward.
> Come home to the belief that we can seek a newer world.

> George McGovern, *former Senator, South Dakota;*
> *Acceptance Speech as Candidate for President,*
> *Democratic National Covention,*
> *Miami Beach, Florida*

Parallel wording continues to be an effective technique for speakers. Here's another example:

> We need you now more than ever.
> - Let us all join together to find some answers.
> - Let's sit down and identify how business, legislators, and the arts can work in concert for the best interest of their communities.
> - Let's make what has been mostly a private commitment an ongoing public responsibility.

> Jane Alexander, *Chairwoman,*
> *National Endowments for the Arts;*
> *Address to the Economic Club of Detroit*

Of course, parallel wording is effective not only in political speeches, but in all types of talks. For example:

> [Control of pollution] must—by necessity—be done in context with three environmental realities:
> - Environmental issues are emotional.
> - Environmental decisions are political.
> - Environmental solutions are technical.

> Joseph T. Ling, *Vice President, 3M Company;*
> *Speech at National Conference on Treatment and*
> *Disposal of Industrial Wastewaters and Residues,*
> *Houston, Texas*

2. Transitions

You will be given some additional tips on transitions in Lesson 11, Designing Introductions, as they are especially important in that part of a speech. They are important in the discussion part of a speech too, but they may take a somewhat different form.

Let's start with what not to do. Don't simply use titles or headings to introduce points; such as:

- Well, now for cost figures
- Next, the roof
- The Internet

Those are the bold-print paragraph heads for an article. They are not effective in a speech. Rather, your job is to find a few words that will lead your audience's thinking from one point to another smoothly so they recognize the logic and the structure of your presentation. Here are some typical effective transitions to replace those poor ones above:

- Now you know what is needed in our new program, but you may be getting concerned about how much all these proposals will cost. Well, let's now look at the cost figures.
- So those are the main things to inspect in the foundation of a used house you may be thinking about buying. Now, before we move inside for more inspection points, let's take moment to look at the other main problem area of the outside of an older house, the roof.
- The Internet is indeed valuable, but there are problems.

As those examples show, you should present a transition that relates the previous point of your speech to the next.

For more complex subjects or speeches that present quite a few points, or when you want to be very sure your audience remembers each point, you can use a specialized type of transition called an *internal summary.*

In essence, internal summaries restate all the points of the speech each time the speaker moves on to the next point. This may be a bit confusing to illustrate in excerpt, but let's try.

In the preview in your introduction, you list, say, three points—need, cost, and effect. (Of course, they would be specific and detailed, but we're condensing the presentation for clarity—OK?) As the first point of the discussion part of your speech, you build your case for the need. As you finish the first point, the usual transition, as suggested above, would link that point (need) to the second point (cost). However, using an internal summary, you would say something such as:

- That, then, is why we need this new program. Now, you'll remember that as I started this speech I told you there were three things I wanted to talk with you about this evening—the need, the cost, and the effect of our new program. Now you know my thinking on the first point—the need—so let us turn to the second consideration, the cost.

After presenting the case for the second point, you might say:

- You can now see our concerns about the cost of this new program. We've talked so far this evening about the need and the cost of our proposal. Now let's turn to that third point I've mentioned, the effect of this program.

These brief summaries, taken out of context of a full speech, may appear to you to be redundant oversimplification, even talking down do the audience. However, many of our best speakers use these internal summaries, because they certainly do help an audience see the direction of a speech, follow along with the sequence in the speech, and remember the points of the speech more precisely and for a longer time.

3. Balanced Line

The typical political speech lasts 20 to 30 minutes and includes about 3000 to 4500 words. But usually only a score or so of those words will end up on national television news programs, to be heard by millions rather than the relatively few who were present when the speech was delivered. Barbara Walters, network television interviewer, has pointed out that many polished political speakers include in their speeches brief statements written especially to be the parts that may be selected for telecasting in the news reports of their speeches.

Often the brief statement that survives is a *balanced line*—a sound bite. A balanced line is the "most quotable of rhythmic techniques" and "is the deliberate writing of a quote," according to former presidential speech writer and word expert William Safire. Here are some examples:

BALANCED LINE:

"The Constitution of the United States mandates equal protection under the law. This is not code language for racism, it is plain speaking against it."

Bob Dole, in his speech to accept nomination as Republican presidential candidate.

◗ Ask not what your country can do for you; ask what you can do for your country.

> John F. Kennedy, *President of the United States;*
> *Inaugural Address, Washington, D. C.*

◗ We can move from the slave ship to the championship!
From the guttermost to the uppermost!
From the outhouse to the courthouse!
From the statehouse to the White House!

> *The Reverend* Jesse Jackson;
> *Speech to Congregation of First African Methodist*
> *Episcopal Church, Los Angeles, California*

Try your mind at writing balanced lines. They're fun to write—and effective in your speeches.

GUIDES

Briefly, just to refresh your memory, here are three essentials you've studied in previous lessons. They're repeated here to make sure you recall them as you design the discussion part of your speeches.

1. The length of the discussion part of your speech should be about 80 percent of the entire speech.
2. The style of your discussion should be the same as that of the introduction and the conclusion of your speech. If the speaking situation calls for a casual, what-the-heck presentation, then maintain that style throughout your speech. On the other hand, if you're in a formal speaking situation, in which the introduction part of your speech is appropriately restrained, then the discussion part of your speech should be formal too. Of course, the conclusion to your speech should also be consistent with the style of the rest of your speech.
3. Now that you've got the discussion part of your speech planned, remember to prepare the note card you'll use when speaking. Your notes on that card, you'll recall, should be in outline form so you can find specifics on it quickly, easily.

Now it's time for you to see how well you meet the objectives for this lesson. But before you take the self-test that starts on the next page, you may find it helpful to review this lesson so that you're sure to attain the goal of a score of 80 percent or higher.

ASSIGNMENT 15. DESIGNING DISCUSSIONS: SELF-TEST

❗ ACTION: Take the following self-test.

1. Name the patterns that could be used for organizing the discussion part of your speech:

   _____

   _____

   _____

   _____

Name the pattern of organization for each of the following lists of points.

2. Subject: Choosing a Sailboat
   A. Appropriate to the area you'll sail it in
   B. Large enough to accommodate maximum number of people you'd likely have aboard
   C. Condition determined by licensed boat surveyor

   Pattern: _____

3. Subject: My Experiences in Snorkeling
   A. In California waters
   B. In Bay of Siam
   C. In Hawaiian waters

   Pattern: _____

4. Subject: Selecting a Rental Car
   A. Great variety in condition of cars
   B. Best way is to rent from a famous, nationwide company

   Pattern: _____

5. Subject: Educational Television
   A. Started in early 1950s
   B. Until about 1960, emphasis on building more stations
   C. Since then, emphasis on program improvement

   Pattern: _____

6. Subject: Getting an Auxiliary Sailboat Under Way
   A. Get sails ready to hoist
   B. Start motor
   C. Cast off
   D. Proceed out channel
   E. When out of traffic, hoist sails

   Pattern: _____

7. Subject: Popular Types of Sailboats
    A. Day sailers
    B. Cruisers
    C. Racers

    Pattern: _____

8. Subject: How the Loafer Prepares Food for a Cruise on a Sailboat
    A. Well before sailing, plan menus
    B. Just before departing, bring food aboard
    C. During cruise, cook as little as possible
    D. Upon arrival, have a big meal at a top restaurant

    Pattern: _____

For each of the following sets of main points for the discussion part of a speech, state if it is or is not organized logically and the reason for your decision.

Subject: Selecting a Car
    A. Checking the motor
    B. Checking the dealer
    C. Checking the body
    D. Checking the equipment

9. Organized logically? (Yes or no?) _____

10. Reason for your decision: _____

_____

Subject: Basis for Selecting a Vacation Spot
    A. Cost
    B. Activities
    C. Location

11. Organized logically? _____

12. Reason for your decision: _____

_____

Subject: Too Much Advertising on TV
    A. The problem of too much advertising on TV is critical
        1. Distracting
        2. Waste of time
        3. In poor taste
    B. Could be solved by establishing government controls
        1. Could improve content
        2. Could ensure products are worthwhile
        3. Could limit the number per program

13. Organized logically?_____

14. Reason for your decision: _____

_____

Subject: Improving High School Teaching of English
    A. Need for more reading assignments
    B. Southern schools behind those in other areas
    C. Senior classes not as good as freshmen

15. Organized logically? _____

16. Reason for your decision: _____

_____

For each of the following speech purposes, name appropriate main points for the discussion part of a speech. Then state the pattern you used.

After hearing my speech, the audience (voters in Virginia in 1860) will vote for Abraham Lincoln for president of the United States.

17. Points:

18. Pattern: _____

After hearing my speech, the audience (tourists from New York) will be able to summarize the main features that should be seen in a visit to California.

Points:

Pattern: _____

Answers:

1. Time, space, topic, problem-solution
2. Topic
3. Space
4. Problem-solution
5. Time
6. Time
7. Topic
8. Time
9. No
10. Not equivalent points. Three points (A, C, D) are concerned with car itself; point B is not.
11. Yes
12. Equal, clear, specific, logical parts of the subject
13. No
14. Proposed solutions do not solve the problems presented. For example, under point A it was not established that there are too many commercials, yet limiting the number is one of the suggested benefits of the solution.
15. No
16. Not equal divisions of the subject and a mixture of patterns. For example, point A is a topic point, point B is a space point, and point C could be either a time or a topic, depending on emphasis.

To evaluate yourself on the remaining questions, compare your replies with the following. If in doubt, check back for specifics in the lesson.

17., 18. Points might be, for the speech about Lincoln:
A. Experienced
B. Popular
C. Understanding
This is a topic pattern.

Or

A. In 1840s, Lincoln did this:
B. In 1850s, Lincoln did this:
C. In 1860s, Lincoln can do this:
This is a time pattern.

Or

A. For his town, Lincoln did this:
B. For his state, Lincoln did this:
C. For his nation, Lincoln can do this:
This is a space pattern.

19., 20. For the New York tourists, your points might be:
A. Disneyland
B. Yosemite
C. San Francisco
This is a space pattern.

Or

A. Scenic spots
B. Historic centers
C. Shops
D. Restaurants
This is a topic pattern.

Or

A. First day, visit . . .
B. Second day, travel to . . .
C. Third day, tour . . .
D. Fourth day, visit . . .
This is a time pattern.

Scoring:

Question 1:	1 point for each correct answer
Question 2–16:	1 point for each correct answer
Question 17:	2 points if perfect, 1 point if almost perfect, 0 points if you miss
Question 18:	1 point
Question 19:	2 points if perfect, 1 point if almost perfect, 0 points if you miss
Question 20:	1 point
Total	25 points

If you got 20 or more points, you met your goal of getting 80 percent or better. If you got fewer, recycle yourself through this lesson again.

That self-test checked you out on only three of the six objectives for this lesson. The remaining three objectives—concerned with selecting appropriate main points for speeches, organizing those main points logically, and using specialized wording techniques—will be evaluated in your coming speeches.

So now, based on the content of this lesson, the following points on your **Speech Evaluation Forms**—points that have already been on those forms—have additional concepts and tips on which they will be graded:

1. Content
   1.4. Points and data new and significant to audience
   1.6. All material clearly related to subject
   1.8. Presents own, original ideas, structure, or interpretation
   1.10. Emphasizes organization enough to help audience remember points
   1.13. Points seem valid conclusions from data presented
2. Organization
   2.3. Presents 2 to 5 specific points
   2.4. Arranges discussion points in logical order
   2.8 Uses the structure of speech, not of old-style class report or article

The following points will now be added to the **Evaluation Forms,** in the section on contents.

> *1.15. Points parallel and equal, as appropriate*
> *1.16. Moves from point to point with smooth transitions*
> *1.17. Includes at least one balanced line*

Closely related to those points are the tips on data, presented in Lesson 7. The tips, techniques, and concepts in both lessons are basic to designing the discussion part of your speech.

To help you pinpoint those tips, use the **Check-off Tip Sheet** on the next page as you plan your future speeches in this class.

When you're ready, move on to the next lesson, on designing the introduction part of a speech.

DISCUSSIONS—CHECK-OFF TIP SHEET

INSTRUCTIONS: Check off each item as you prepare the discussion parts of your speech.

1. PRELIMINARY

_____ 1.1. Some data collected

_____ 1.2. Some points in mind

2. PROSPECTUS

_____ 2.1. Started well before you begin to outline

_____ 2.2. Includes at least 15 to 20 points

_____ 2.3. Available for additions for several days

_____ 2.4. Written, not just mental

3. SELECTING POINTS

_____ 3.1. Logical parts of speech subject

_____ 3.2. About equal in significance

_____ 3.3. About equal in comprehensiveness

_____ 3.4. 2 to 5 points

_____ 3.5. Comparable to each other

_____ 3.6. Related to each other

_____ 3.7. Not too broad

_____ 3.8. Specific

_____ 3.9. Speech purpose checked to ensure points help fulfill it

_____ 3.10. Situation analysis checked for appropriateness of points

4. PATTERN

_____ 4.1. Time

_____ 4.2. Space

_____ 4.3. Topic

_____ 4.4. Problem solution

_____ 4.5. Not a combination

5. DATA

_____ 5.1. Variety of types used (statistics, quotation, illustration, etc.)

_____ 5.2. Each bit of data does at least one of the following:

    _____ 5.2.1. Proves a point

    _____ 5.2.2. Clarifies a point

    _____ 5.2.3. Adds interest

    _____ 5.2.4. Makes point memorable

_____ 5.3. About equally distributed for each point

_____ 5.4. No propaganda

_____ 5.5. No lies

_____ 5.6. No bias

6. WORDING

_____ 6.1. Parallel when appropriate

_____ 6.2. Smooth transitions

_____ 6.3. At least one balanced line included

7. GENERAL

_____ 7.1. Length about 80% of speech

_____ 7.2. Style consistent with introduction and conclusion

_____ 7.3. Note card prepared, in outline form

L E S S O N 11

Designing Introductions

OBJECTIVES ▶ After you have finished this lesson, you will be able to:

1. Name the criteria for an effective introduction part of a speech.
2. Name at least 8 of the 11 techniques for getting this attention of your audience.
3. Decide if a given introduction is effective or not, and state the basis for your judgment.
4. Design effective introductions for your speeches.

RELEVANCE ▶ The introduction of your speech is your first speaking opportunity to start achieving the effect you want on your audience.

When you step up to speak, the spotlight focuses on you. Your very first words do much to establish your position as a speaker—your validity, your empathy, your sincerity, your interest, your value as someone worth listening to wholeheartedly. Hence, presenting an effective introduction is critical to the success of your speech.

ATTENTION-GETTER:

"Begin with something interesting in your first sentence. Not the second. Not the third. The First! F-I-R-S-T. First!"

That's the advice of *Dale Carnegie,* the founder of the leading course in all adult education, the author of the widely read book ***How to Develop Self Confidence and Influence People by Public Speaking.***

THE GREETING

You'll remember that there are two sections to the introduction part of a speech.

A. Attention-getter
B. Preview

Today flamboyant and lengthy openings are rare. A brief "Good evening" is usually sufficient.

Even those few words are often more effective when stated AFTER the speaker has delivered the attention-getter. Remember: Your first task as you begin your speech is to capture the attention of your listeners. Your second task is to let them know exactly what you are going to talk about. A greeting, if appropriate, is secondary in importance. Therefore, work it in so it does not detract from the primary purposes of your introduction.

CRITERIA FOR AN EFFECTIVE INTRODUCTION

An effective introduction meets 4 criteria:

1. It is *relevant*—to your subject, your audience, the occasion, and your own style of speaking.
   You've heard speakers, I'm sure, who open with a joke, then mumble a kind of apology as they point out that the joke doesn't really have much to do with their speech, but they "thought you in the audience would enjoy it." Solution: Find a joke or story that is relevant. You'll learn how in a few pages.
   And you have perhaps wondered about speakers who present a smooth, polished, and precise introduction and then become quite casual, informal, even wandering—changing their style in midspeech. Your speech should have consistency in content, in structure, in delivery. Each aspect of your speech should be relevant to all of the other aspects.
2. It gets your audience *involved*—gets them thinking about your speech; gets them to participate mentally as you talk with them. Again, tips on how to do this are coming.
3. It gets them to think *positively* about your subject—leads them to think with you, not against you. Your introduction should not antagonize your audience, not turn them off, not spark them to think about why they disagree with you. How do you do this? Read on.
4. It *stimulates* your audience—gets them eager, wanting to hear your speech; gets them excited, concerned, happy, or angry (*with* you, not at you); gets them turned on and tuned in.

Those then are the 4 criteria for an effective introduction. You should remember them so you can apply them in designing your own introductions as well as in evaluating the speeches of others. Here's an easy way to remember them. The key words are:

Relevant

Involved

Positive

Stimulate

You want an introduction that **RIPS** into your audience, that is, an introduction that will "slash or slit" into the thoughts of your listeners, one that will "rush headlong" to alert them. Those quotations are from Webster's definition of *rips*. The acronym will help you remember the criteria.

It's time to react, I'm sure you've guessed. So, what are the criteria for an effective speech introduction?

1. _____

2. _____

3. _____

4. _____

Positive? Check above to be sure and to reinforce your learning.

Now let's start applying those criteria as you learn the specific techniques for designing an introduction.

Techniques for Designing an Introduction

Think for a moment about your attitude as you wait for a speaker to begin. Usually you're eager for the speech to start, hopeful that the speaker will be powerful and dramatic, that he or she will have something relevant, significant, valuable for you to listen to.

But your mind is also spinning through many other subjects. If you've just arrived at the hall, you may look around the audience and wonder why so many others came—in this speaker going to be that good? Or you may wonder why the audience is so small—how did you get hooked into thinking this was to be worthwhile? You may think for a moment about someone you saw as you entered. Your thoughts may wander back to your car—did you remember to roll the windows up and did you turn the lights off? Crowded—will you be stuck in a traffic jam getting out of here?

If you've just heard another speaker you may be reviewing what was said, thinking about why your particular pet point was not included, or wondering why anyone would invite that bumbling bore to speak.

The point is that as a speaker steps up to begin, while most in the audience are eagerly hoping to hear something of value, almost every listener is rushing a wide variety of thoughts through his or her mind. As a speaker, then, your task is to clear those minds and to focus them as you begin your speech and to focus them on you and your speech.

How?

Attention-getters

There are 11 basic techniques for getting the attention of your audience:

1. Ask a question.
2. State an unusual fact.
3. Give an illustration, example, or story.
4. Present a quotation.
5. Refer to an historical event.
6. Tell a joke.
7. Use a gimmick.
8. Point to common relationships, beliefs, interests, or opinions.

9. Refer to the occasion, purpose of the meeting, audience, a local event, or some other part of the program.
10. Compliment the audience.
11. Point out the importance of the subject to the audience.

We'll now detail specific tips for each. Remember, you should be able to name at least 8 of these attention-getters and use an appropriate one to open your speeches.

1. Ask a Question

The value in opening a speech by asking a question is that you can immediately focus the attention of your listeners on a particular point, and you can usually do that in a very few words.

Most questions speakers use to open their speeches are *rhetorical questions.* Webster's defines a rhetorical question as "a question asked merely for effect with no answer expected." A speaker uses a rhetorical question when he or she asks an audience such questions as "If you had your life to live over again, what would you change?" Clearly the speaker is not expecting listeners to respond with their views. Rather, the speaker expects each individual to think through what he or she would want to change.

Some speakers find it effective to open their speeches with *genuine questions* that are intended to get actual responses from their audiences. A politician may begin a campaign speech by asking a question such as "Do you want high taxes to continue?" The speaker pauses and the audience roars back "NO!" The speaker often follows with a series of questions evoking the same response: "Do you want government waste to continue?" Audience: "NO!" "Do you want bad planning to continue?" "NO!" "Do you want your present mayor to continue?"

Such questions can help get an audience committed, involved, or emotional.

Questions are easy to design to introduce any subject. *Good* questions are a bit harder. And it's easy to ask a bad question—one that may turn off many listeners. For example, if you ask, "Would you like to earn a million dollars tomorrow?" this type of question is so far from reality that many listeners will mentally—sometimes even audibly—scoff at the speaker asking it.

Another type of distracting question is "How much do you think you spend each year on nonessentials, such as cigarettes, candy, gasoline for nonimportant trips, magazines you don't read, and such?" This may well get your audience thinking, but some may get so involved in trying to compute their answer that they cease to follow along with what you say next in your speech.

You should also avoid asking questions that disparage or embarrass or divide your audience. Such a question would be "How many of you have enjoyed, as I have, a trip to Hawaii?" or "All of you in favor of capital punishment, would you please raise your hands?"

A good question, on the other hand, can quickly lead your audience to think along with you, to become involved with your speech. Examples of effective questions are these:

- What bugs you most about your college classes?
- If you could—or had to—live the life of someone else, whom would you choose?
- What do you think is the biggest concern of multicultural students?
- How long has it been since you visited a wilderness? Heard a bird chirp? Watched a sunset? Wandered alone with not a single person within a mile of you?

2. State an Unusual Fact

Here are some examples:

- Today more people see the typical evening TV show than have seen all of the stage performances of all of Shakespeare's plays in all of the more than 400 years since he wrote them.
- Deadly poisons come not only from some snakes and spiders and fish but also from such supposedly delicate and attractive flowers as sweet peas, morning glories, irises, and at least nine other common flowers.
- In Hawaii during a typical year there were 27 girls who were already widows at the tender age of 14, 43 girls who had been married two times or more and were still only 15 years old, and 15 boys who had been divorced and still were only 14 years old.

The first—about the size of audiences at Shakespeare's plays—could be used to introduce a variety of subjects, including:

Loss of interest in classical drama

Gigantic number of potential customers who watch television commercials

Need for better drama on television

Contrast between the intimacy of the theater and the impersonality of television

The second example—about poisons—might introduce a speech on:

Things are not always what they appear to be

Gardening

How to protect your family from poisons

Dangers in your backyard

The third example—about Hawaii—could introduce a speech on such subjects as . . . well, let's exercise your creativity in using attention-getters.

Name four subjects that might be introduced by those statistics about Hawaii.

1. _____

2. _____

3. _____

4. _____

Now let's reverse course and assume you're seeking a good attention-getter for a speech on each of these subjects you've just listed. And let's further assume that you've just stumbled on those facts about Hawaii. Do they meet our 4-point criteria for an effective attention-getter, appropriate for each of your four subjects?

To answer, first write out the criteria below so you'll have a handy checklist to use. Remember, you're after an introduction which **RIPS** into the minds of your listeners.

The criteria for an attention-getter are:

1. _____

2. _____

3. _____

4. _____

Now to be sure your criteria are correctly stated, take a moment to check back a few pages to compare what you've just written with the text.

Finally, use the criteria to determine if the Hawaii item is appropriate for each of your four subjects.

3. Give an Illustration, Example, or Story

Here are some examples:

- Last night, well after sundown, on a side street with the only light more than a block away, while walking home from the library, I noticed a woman's purse lying on the sidewalk. As I leaned over to pick it up . . .
- You read the headlines in our local paper just last week, as I did. You read about the yachtsman who disappeared from his 45-foot sailboat while out for an afternoon cruise. We read about the search planes, the Coast Guard patrol boats, the volunteer rescue team. We read the interviews with the lost sailor's wife, who said . . .
- If three students meet regularly and seriously to study together, to prepare for tests together, to help each other write reports for a particular class, could they expect to improve their grades? Isn't that just exactly the same thing that is happening when our government . . .

Got your interest?

Why? Or, why not?

No, you don't have to answer here. But you get the point. An audience will listen to a good illustration, example, or story, because people are interested in people.

And it would be interesting to think about just where each of those three introductions led your mind. What's the subject of the speech for each? Obviously, there are many possibilities.

You do want to hear more about each of those stories, now don't you? A well-told story or example or illustration, which unfolds a dramatic, interesting humorous, relevant, or significant situation gets people listening.

4. Present a Quotation

Quotations are a good way to open a speech for two reasons. First, people are always interested in what others, especially the famous, have said. Second, you can almost always find a quotation by someone who supports your view and is enthusiastic or concerned or authoritative about your subject.

But that second reason for using a quotation suggests the major reason for *not* using a quotation. You also can almost always find someone who is an authority or famous or popular, who has made a statement to express just the opposite view.

You know, of course, that finding quotations certainly does not require you to skim through volumes to dig out an appropriate statement. Look at *Bartlett's Familiar Quotations*. There you will find thousands of quotations from the famous throughout history. Or, if you intend to use quotations often, you may find it valuable to buy one of those inexpensive paperback editions of collections of quotations. There are specialized ones on the market just for speakers, teachers, ministers, salespersons, and others.

Then there are the valuable sources for quotations on Internet, several of which are mentioned, with addresses, in Lesson 7, Selecting Data, page 169.

Examples?

Well, we're studying public speaking, so how about a couple from my collection of more than a hundred quotations about speaking:

- He has the gift of compressing the largest amount of words into the smallest amount of thought.

> Winston Churchill,
> *British Statesman*
> [*said* by *him, not* about *him*]

- Let thy speech be better than silence, or be silent.

> Dionysius,
> *Greek Rhetorician*

Obviously the quotation must be relevant. Don't be one of those speakers who states, "Let me start by quoting one of my favorite authors,. . . . Well I always liked that statement and wanted to share it with you, even though it really doesn't have anything to do with what I want to talk about today."

5. Refer to an Historical Event

Here's an example:

- Tonight we meet on an historic battleground—Detroit! Here we successfully defended Dr. Ossian Sweet and established for all time that an American's home, whether he is white or black, was his castle! Here great legal decisions were achieved by Judges Frank Murphy and Ira W. Jane. Here, the famous counsel for the defense, Clarence Darrow, made his closing argument in the NAACP-Sweet case in 1925 and it will live forever as a forensic classic.

> *Bishop* Stephen G. Spottswood, *Chairman,*
> *NAACP National Board of Directors;*
> *Speech at 63rd Annual NAACP Convention,*
> *Detroit, Michigan*

You might check the special books in a library or special columns in some newspapers that list significant events in history that happened on a particular day. Frequently you can find something that you can relate to the subject of your speech—the birth or death date of a famous individual; the signing of some agreement; the start or end of a reign, a strike, a war; the discovery of a land, a scientific principle, or such.

Let's get specific.

As I write this, it is October 20. Looking in the local paper, I find a short column entitled "Today's Almanac." It lists, among other points:

- Today is the 294th day of the year, with 72 days to come.
- On this day in 1859, educator John Dewey was born.
- In 1918 Germany accepted President Wilson's terms to end World War I.
- 1944—American troops started recapture of the Philippines from Japan.
- 1964—Former President Hoover died at age 90.
- 1968—Mrs. Jacqueline Kennedy married Greek shipping magnate Aristotle Onassis.
- 1977—first takeoff by supersonic Concorde airline from New York's Kennedy Airport.
- 1995—Canadian mayors adopted resolution for a United Canada.

Consider the broad range of speech subjects that can be introduced by these varied incidents. For example, the event of the German acceptance of President Wilson's terms to end World War I might well be used as the attention-getting introduction to such varied speech topics as:

Is war inevitable?

What to watch out for when signing a contract.

How prejudices are spread.

The full introductions might be worded like these:

▶ Sixty-six years ago today President Wilson received acceptance of a contract with Germany, ending World War I. Yet not many years later, Germany and America were again at war. Are contracts worthwhile? If two great countries cannot observe the provisions of a contract, how can you, as a consumer, expect the contracts you sign for buying a car, leasing an apartment, purchasing a suit—how can you be sure the contracts you sign are worth the paper they are written on?

▶ On this very day, more than three-quarters of a century ago, the United States and Germany came to agreement on ending World War I. Yet today there are still Americans who characterize Germans as unfeeling, gruff, hostile, even warlike. Such generalizations are the same as many of us have about some other peoples, some occupations other than ours, some characteristics or behaviors or ways of speaking other than our own. Just how can we deal with such prejudices?

The item about the death of President Hoover might be used to introduce such topics as:

Is the United States facing another depression?

President Hoover—his life, his times, his achievements.

90 years—is a lifetime short or long?

How is your health?

Is medicine making-living more than a century possible? Desirable?

Is retiring at age 60 or 65 wasting too many of our productive years?

Can we learn from the lives of former leaders how to identify the leaders of the future?

Leadership—does one earn it or fall into it?

How and why has the role of the president changed?

Now, to exercise your creativity in adapting an incident to be the attention-getter for a speech, please select another of those events listed for October 20 and develop a list of possible related topics, such as the listings above. Select any event other than the two that have just been used as examples.

Event selected from the list for October 20:_____

Possible topics that might be introduced by that incident:

1. _____

2. _____

3. _____

4. _____

5. _____

6. _____

The point is that a particular historical event—just as an unusual fact, a quotation, etc.—can be used effectively as the attention-getter for quite a variety of speech subjects.

6. Tell a Joke

Examples? Well, you have your own favorites.

But we'll remind you again, don't be that speaker who tells the joke about two flying fish and then, after the laughter quiets down, says, "Well, that really doesn't have much to do with what I'm going to talk about today—about the problems of property taxes."

The point is that your joke *should* be directly related to your speech subject. For example, here's one that caught me smiling. It's stolen from Herb Caen (San Francisco's top columnist). The soft drink stand at a theater was taking a straw vote on the national election. When you bought a soda you could select one straw and it would represent a vote for the Democratic candidate for president, or you could choose another straw and it would count as a vote for the Republican candidate. But, someone pointed out, "That survey disenfranchises those who drink straight out of the cup. It only tells how the suckers will vote."

That joke can be related to a wide range of speech subjects. Obviously it ties in with elections, politicians, public opinion surveys, etc.

But could it be used if your subject were . . . well, say, gardening? Or, would you have to end up like so many speakers, apologizing for telling a joke that has nothing to do with your subject? No, it could be used by pointing to the fact that gardening, too, requires you to make selections—selections of what to plant, when to plant, etc.

Is that stretching the point of the joke? Perhaps. Only you, as the creative designer of your speech, can determine as you plan your speech the appropriateness of your attention-getter. Later, of course, when you give your speech, the audience will decide whether or not what you have selected is indeed appropriate, relevant, and interesting—helping you or hindering you from attaining your purpose in speaking. Follow the advice of freelance speech writer Robert B. Rackleff, given in a speech he presented to the National Association of Bar Executives: "If there's any question about whether to use a joke, then there's no question—don't use it."

We've now detailed for you tips on 6 of the 11 techniques for getting the attention of your audience. And remember you are to be able to name at least 8 of the total list of 11. So here—at the halfway point—you should refresh your memory of those we have covered so far. List them below.

1. _____
2. _____
3. _____
4. _____
5. _____
6. _____

Check your responses by referring to the previous pages. Learning those first 6 now will make learning the complete list of 11 a little easier.

OK, let's continue.

7. Use a Gimmick

Gimmicks are novelty openings—distinctive, creative, usually visual. Examples:

Starting a controlled fire to capture attention for a talk on safety

Blowing a whistle to introduce a speech on refereeing

Releasing a pigeon to fly around the room, introducing a speech on how to train birds

Tearing a $10 bill in half, leading to a talk on banking

Those examples are from speeches given by students in my classes. Such openings are usually very effective because they are unexpected, different, and creative. I like such attention-getters; most audiences like them, too.

But there are disadvantages. Consider the examples listed.

Starting a fire may cause more concern than concentration. Some in your audience may be more worried about possible damage or danger than they are interested or involved in the topic of your speech. And, of course, their concern is justified.

Let me tell you about the most spectacular opening of a student's speech I've ever heard. (But please, don't try this one! It makes me worry too much about the small print in my insurance policy.)

A young man stepped up before his audience, holding a can of motor oil in one hand. He dipped his other hand into it. He set the can down on a table, took a cigarette lighter out of his pocket, lit it, held it to the hand that he'd just removed from the can. That hand was now dripping with oil. He proceeded to ignite it, letting the oil burn about his fingers, wrist, up his arm! Suddenly he gave his arm a vigorous jerk, and the remaining oil slipped off, onto the floor, and soon burned out.

He was not hurt because, he claimed (remember, please don't do this!!), the oil burned at a temperature lower than his pain threshold. Apparently, this trick used to be popular among the members of hot rod clubs. But if you try to shake the oil off your hand too soon, it is not sufficiently warmed up to be fluid enough to leave your hand. Or, if you wait too long . . . .

ATTENTION-GETTER:

"Once I was appointed to a mayor's commission to try to bring baseball to Miami. I had to make a speech on it to the City Council, and the Miami City Council is like no other. It has always had a great public attendance, because lots of retired people would go to the meetings for entertainment and to lobby for senior citizens' programs. They'd come for the day, pass out pastrami sandwiches, and if a subject didn't affect them they'd kibbitz among themselves."

"I got up to make my presentation, and not a soul was listening because I was talking about baseball. So I yelled: 'Attention! The head of the American League is in favor of Medicare!' I got a standing ovation."

Larry King told that story about himself in his book ***Larry King.***

There are hazards in the other examples too. Blowing a whistle in the typical small classroom, doors closed, windows and chalkboards making fine reverberation centers, often produces real pain in the ears of some in the audience. Indeed, a student in another of my classes opened a talk on how to start a race at a track meet by firing a starter's gun with its regular blank shell. Much echo, much pain, much confusion in other classrooms. *Not* recommended.

The pigeon flying was interesting—got us so involved that after the speech the audience went outside and watched the bird take off, circle, pick out a direction, and head for home. The speaker and two students, to document the event, took off in a car heading for the pigeon's roost; when they got there, the pigeon, banded for positive identification, was already settled in its roost.

The tearing of money? Illegal. But the speaker worked for a bank, and the bill he used was one the bank was going to replace because of the recall of certain bills.

But don't get me wrong. All gimmick openings are not dangerous or undesirable or illegal. But they may be. Think through any you may dream up. Consider trying it out on friends before you used it in a speech. But even then, first be sure that it is safe and legal. Make it relevant to the speech too.

8. Point to Common Relationships, Beliefs, Interests, or Opinions

Here you attempt to establish a sharing of the views or experiences with your audience.

This opening is often appropriate when you are speaking on a subject on which you and the audience are in rather strong disagreement. This opening might be used by, say, a Democratic candidate speaking to a Republican meeting; a student speaking to the faculty of a college athletic department on why physical education classes should be discontinued; a civilian speaking to the city police board on why policemen should cease carrying guns; a citizen talking with the local veterans' group to urge them to endorse amnesty for conscientious objectors. These are all examples of speaking situations in which this type of attention-getter may be appropriate.

A typical opening would be:

▶ Ladies and gentlemen, you and I both know that at this moment we hold exactly opposite views on the subject of my speech. Yet is it not also true that both you and I agree almost completely on many of the basic considerations behind my proposal?

   Comment: Then you might point to a common desire to save money or create a better community or be fair to all citizens or other equally accepted principles.

The advantage of such as opening is obvious—you can at least start by getting agreement on a few related points.

The disadvantages are also clear. One: It's not really much of a grabber of an audience's attention. Some in the audience may start thinking of reasons why they disagree on those points on which you'd expect to have complete and quick agreement.

In essence, this opening can be successful, but it can backfire, too.

9. Refer to the Occasion, Purpose of the Meeting, Audience, a Local Event, or Some Other Part of the Program

This type of opening is used often. It builds on the audience's pride or previously established interest or knowledge. It is effective because it can be timely and relevant.

Its disadvantage is that it is often overused, trite, obvious, or insincere.

The classic—which, unfortunately, is not just a sad story but has in fact happened—is the traveling candidate who opens his speech with something such as:

> ◆ It is indeed a pleasure to be here this evening in your fine town, which I've admired for so many years, famous as you are, generous in your welcome, here in . . . [and then he has to glance at his notes to make sure just where he is].

As an alert speaker, you should check the paper or listen to a local newscast before presenting a speech. Often you can find a local story, event, or angle to tie in directly with your speech subject.

Indeed, it is surprising how many speakers fail when giving a speech on some debate or discussion topic, simply because they did not consult the latest news outlets, then learned at their speaking engagements that something happened that very day that either supported their view (they should have capitalized on it) or detracted from their point (they should have bolstered their presentation against that latest development).

Local celebrations, anniversaries, upcoming events such as fairs or shows, or other speaking situations—all such events can be used to help you make a more direct relationship between your ideas and the experiences and views of your listeners.

Here are some examples:

> ◆ Just before coming to this meeting, you may have heard on the news, as I did, the government's report that once again food prices rose last month. Of course, we are not surprised by that report. But I daresay we are both disappointed.
>
> **Comment:** Where can your speech go now? Into some specific problem in government; how statistics are gathered or used or misused; broadcasting, news, newscasters, reporters, etc.; how to cope with disappointment—a great many different subjects.
>
> ◆ The installation of your new officers here this evening parallels exactly the purpose of my speech. I, too, am here for an installation—the installation of a new idea, a new concept, which I am suggesting your organization adopt.
>
> ◆ Earlier in this evening's program, as I sat here and enjoyed along with you the beautiful voice of your talented guest singer, I was startled to find that the theme of her song was so similar to the point of the speech I would like to present to you tonight.

10. Compliment the Audience

> ◆ To speak to such a fine-looking group of men and women—just standing here looking out at you I can tell you're going to be a really great audience. . . .

Pretty corny. To me. To most student speakers I know. Yet those television talk show masters twirl that type of tripe from their tongues time and time again. And the audiences love it, react just as the TV stars want.

Why? First, of course, people do like to be complimented—when it's sincere, especially, but at times even when it obviously is not. Second, those professionals on television can and do deliver such lines with apparent sincerity. Or they sometimes give such speeches with just enough humor so the audience knows it's being kidded, but loves it anyway.

Try it if you think you can pull it off. In general I don't recommend it, except in one case: when a compliment is indeed sincerely due. If you are speaking to an audience to ask their participation in some community effort, and they have just been awarded, say, a plaque, or had a story about them in the local paper, or coverage on television news, for their recent successful work on some other community project, then, of course, complimenting the audience may be a good, effective, and appropriate opening for a speech.

But note that last sentence says "may be." The point is to be sure the compliment is appropriate, well worded, deserved, and presented with sincerity.

11. Point out the Importance of the Subject to the Audience

I'm hesitant even to suggest this as an opening for a speech because it is so trite, weak, unsuccessful, and unstimulating. But it is included primarily because so many speakers use it that its weaknesses should be emphasized. Yet those weaknesses should be obvious.

If an audience needs to be told something is important, it probably is either not really important or they already know that it is. Further, just telling an audience something is important gets only the most unthinking listener to accept such a statement. Better to at least *show* the audience the importance of the subject through some other technique—a story that clearly illustrates its importance or a few unusual, dramatic, stimulating statistics.

If you feel that you absolutely must start your speech by informing your audience of the importance of your topic, then at least say something to jazz it up.

So there's your list of 11 techniques for getting your audience's attention. Your job, you'll remember, is to be able to name at least 8 of them. Try it:

1. _____
2. _____
3. _____
4. _____
5. _____
6. _____
7. _____
8. _____

More?

9. _____
10. _____
11. _____

All of them? Congratulations. Check your list by comparing it with the listing on the previous pages. Review and reinforce your learning of them as you may need.

The next section of your introduction is, as you know, the preview of your speech. But you have to design a way to get to it from where you have just been—a *transition* from your attention-getter to your preview.

TRANSITIONS

A transition need be only a phrase, not necessarily even a sentence. It should show or suggest the relationship between your opening and your preview. Do not leave it to the audience to make the connection; do not assume that they will recognize the logic of the sequence of your thinking.

Often this transition is a statement such as:

- That true story illustrates the need for the new tax proposal I want to suggest to you.
- We can laugh at a joke like that, yet that fellow's flip remark makes a good theme sentence for this serious subject I want to present to you.
- Those are the shocking facts of what's happening in some hospitals. Now, what can be done about them? Let me offer some suggestions.
- You may think that incident is rare, but let me now show you just how widespread the problem it reveals has now become here in our community.
- Thus we can see that . . ..
- The point is clear . . ..
- You, too, may have come to realize that . . ..

The transition, then, is to show or emphasize or clarify the relationship between your opening attention-getter and the basic theme of your speech.

PREVIEWS

The preview part of your speech should be clear, specific, and precise. There are only two techniques possible.

1. State the Point of Your Speech—the Central Idea, Viewpoint, or Subject

The statement should be made in just one or only a few brief, direct sentences. Here are some examples of effective previews of speeches:

- Today I would like to explore with you some of the critical issues affecting the professions and examine in detail the way those issues affect the design, engineering, and building field.

> Julia Thomas, *President, Bobrow/Thomas and Associates;*
> *Speech at Annual Convention, Society for*
> *Marketing Professional Services, Coronado, California*

- That's what I want to talk about with you today—I want to look at our society in terms of the threatening world environment we now live in.

> James P. Mullins, *Commander,*
> *Air Force Logistics Command;*
> *Speech to the Joint Caucus of the*
> *Arizona Legislature, Phoenix, Arizona*

Why couldn't those statements be the *first* sentences of speeches? Because they are not attention-getters. The statements are interesting only to listeners who are already interested in the subjects. To others, the topics may be a bore. The statements, if they had been the very first words of speeches, would have left the decision whether to listen or not up to the audience. That's why we've urged you to open your speech with an attention-getter; then introduce your subject clearly, specifically, and exactly.

What's meant by "clearly, specifically, and exactly"?

Here are some previews of speech subjects, selected from recent student speeches. As you read them, notice how you can be left wondering just what the subject is. You may even wonder if the speakers are for or against a particular proposition.

♦ Today, I'd like to talk about multicultural developments. They are growing, we all know that. Lots of those problems are increasing. In some places, at least, more people seem to be working more to help them.

Comment: Just what is the subject of that speech? Multicultural developments? The growth of multicultural developments? Multicultural problems? People working on multicultural developments, or people working on multicultural problems?

Actually, the speaker finally got around to speaking about the academic successes of students of various races. That subject is certainly related to that poor introduction to a speech, but the speaker sure wandered around in his speech before telling his audience the precise subject on which he wanted to focus.

♦ Business is important in America today, and here's why.

Comment: Why WHAT? Why is business important? Why in America? Why today?

There is a second effective way to introduce the subject of your speech.

2. List the Main Points of Your Speech

Here are some examples of the use of this technique by experienced speakers:

♦ I want to consider the following five questions:
How does Pope John Paul II see his mission to the world?
What does he mean by peace?
What in his view are the obstacles to peace?
Should we not give everything to avoid war?
What is his position on armaments and the arms race?

Camilla Mullay, *Former Mother General,*
Congregation of Dominican Sisters of St. Mary of the Springs,
Columbus, Ohio;
Address at Colloquium, Washington, D.C.

PREVIEWING POINTS BY ASKING QUESTIONS:

"There was discussion today about whether the U.N. did or did not reflect the real world. Was what went on there important, or should it be discussed? Did the words in the resolution adopted by the U.N. make any difference? Should they be taken seriously, or should they simply be dismissed as without significance in the real world?"

After presenting those questions in the introduction part of her keynote address to the World Leadership Conference at Wabash College, then-Ambassador to the United Nations *Jean J. Kirkpatrick* answered them as the major points in the discussion part of her speech.

⬧ I will discuss the importance of the U.S.-Japan relationship to both countries, try to identify the major causes of our problems, and make some suggestions for improving this unfortunate situation.

Robert C. Angel, *President,*
Japan Economic Institute of America;
Speech to the Town Hall of California, Los Angeles,
California

⬧ I will begin by outlining in some detail why economic recovery is at hand. I will then focus on what the upturn will look like. Finally, to prove that I am not blindly optimistic, I will seek to identify the legitimate risks and possible surprises that loom on the economic horizon.

Earl Bederman, *Chief Economist, the Permanent;*
Speech in Vancouver, British Columbia

GUIDES

We have listed specific techniques for the two main parts of your introduction, the attention-getter and preview, and commented on the transition between them. Now let's review some more general guides for preparing and delivering your introduction.

1. Don't Apologize

Many speakers begin their speeches with an apology. You've heard this kind of speech opening:

⬧ I'm certainly glad to be here to talk with you people today, but I do want to explain, before I begin, that I'm really sorry I don't have those slides your program chairman told you about last week. It's been a busy week, not only getting ready for this speech, but I also had to. . . .

⬧ I'll try today to give you a lot of the information about this subject, but I just got back from an important meeting and didn't have all the time I wanted to get this speech ready for you.

⬧ I'm sorry about this cough I have today [hack hack]. I hope you'll be able to hear me OK and that [hack hack] you'll bear with me.

Apologies are all pretty much the same. And usually inappropriate.

If you *do* have something legitimate to apologize for, it is better to explain your problem before the program starts, to the chair, or moderator. He or she should take the initiative and explain your problem—offer the apology—for you. You may need to request this be done.

In the example of the missing slides, the speaker should have made every effort to have them; failing that, he should have informed the chair at least a day before the speech and asked the chair to give an explanation to the audience in the introduction of the speaker.

In the case of a cough, if the chair does not offer the apology, you might, but very briefly; don't make it sound as if you just got out of the intensive care ward. Best of all, don't mention it at all until your first cough. Then, without undue emphasis, say something such as "I'm sorry. I may be coughing later in the speech, too, so let me apologize right now, once, for any future coughs which may interrupt our thinking together." Or, if it suits your style, you could use a joke, like TV comic Jackie Vernon's line, "If it weren't for this coughing I'd get no exercise at all!"

2. Don't Be Long-Winded

A good way to kill a speech fast and early is to present a long, rambling, nondirected introduction. Certainly you need to get the attention of your audience, but make your opening joke, story, illustration short and to the point.

There's no need for a detailed explanation of what got you interested in your subject, or how you researched it, or how you found your topic so valuable, or how you're sure your listeners, too, will become fascinated with what you're going to talk about.

Rather, get to it; present your topic specifically, directly and briefly.

3. Don't Antagonize or Offend Your Audience

That's the general guide. But in some special speaking situations, blunt statements may work. Not long ago, America's auto makers were in great trouble—sales low, defects high. Plants which manufactured parts for cars were closing all over the country; nearly a million auto workers lost their jobs. The head of one plant called his workers together and told them, in part:

> ▶ You're going to hear things you're not going to like, but they're true . . . . [The Japanese auto makers] are beating you in quality, and they're beating you in cost. Either we work as a team and do the job, or it will be a case of the last guy out, please turn out the lights.

> Marvin Craig, *Director, Livonia Transmission Plant,*
> *Ford Motor Company;*
> *Speech at Plant, Livonia, Michigan*

At the end of that speech, the workers stood up and applauded. Even though that speech would seem to antagonize the audience, Craig's listeners realized that what he said was true. They accepted his ideas, went to work, and today that plant is pointed to as a model of efficiency.

But I've heard speakers open speeches with such lines as:

> ▶ For far too long you people in the petroleum industry have failed to realize the importance of petroleum.

Unless you intentionally seek to shock your audience, insult them, or present some information or point of view in a startling way, such a line usually won't work. Usually, listeners turn against the speaker.

If you do intend to try to shock your audience, you should attempt to do so only after careful consideration. Even after you have clarified your "real" thinking, some in the audience may well remain skeptical or antagonistic.

One student speaker, in a class for management trainees, opened his speech with what he intended to be a startling statement:

> ▶ You and I, as we prepare to enter the management field, are about to be employed in one of the most useless, unproductive of all fields.

He then went on to give reasons, with examples and other specifics, why "management is of no value." Finally, toward the end of his speech, he made the point that other occupations would be still more "useless"—confused, chaotic, conflicting—if management were not there to provide leadership. But this "reverse twist" came too late in the speech, long after most listeners had decided they didn't agree.

Other statements that are insulting to an audience are ones such as:

- To tell you the truth, I really didn't have time to prepare much of the speech I wanted to give to you, but let me do the best I can with what little I have prepared.

   Comment: That's telling the audience you didn't think them important enough to prepare for them.

- This may seem pretty simple to a lot of you, but take my word for it, this is important.

   Comment: Usually such an opening then leads into something such as telling photographers that using the correct film is important or telling teachers that school is important. Those are "pretty simple" subjects for such audiences, unless you are presenting something new and distinctive or unless you are speaking as a recognized authority, again with special or unique information.

4. Don't Use Irrelevant Material

We've talked about breaking this rule before—by the speaker who opens with a joke about a rainstorm in New York City and then says, "Well, I thought you'd enjoy that little humor, even though it doesn't have much to do with my subject today—how to reduce the costs of funerals."

If the joke or any other type of attention-getter is not legitimately related to your subject, it should be obvious that it is not appropriate for that speech.

5. Don't Start with "Today I'm Going to Talk to You About"

That leaves it all up to your audience to decide if they want to hear your speech or not. Instead, open with an attention-getter designed to lead them to want to hear you.

6. Don't Lead the Audience to Take a Negative Attitude Toward Your Subject

Once you lose your audience with a poor attention-getter, obtaining their interest or agreement later in your speech will be difficult indeed.

Don't ask a broad question such as "Have you ever wondered how oil is distributed?" That may well lead at least some of your listeners to think, "No, and I don't want to know!" They'll then turn their minds to subjects other than your speech, figuring, probably correctly, with that corny question as a starter, your speech will probably continue to be dull.

Another type of poor attention-getter that may lead your audience to think your views are not worth their time is the ridiculously overstated point. One student opened a speech with this line:

- You may not realize it, and you may not agree with me, but actually the most important thing in your life is the color of your tie.

He went on to talk about the importance of color as an indicator of personal attitudes and preferences. But that weak opening line led many of his listeners to think he was making a mountain out of a molehill, and they stopped listening seriously.

7. Do Get the Attention of the Audience First

Do skip *all* preliminary explanations, such as:

- Now before I really get into my speech, I want to take a moment to explain what I mean by . . . .

▶ It will help you to know, before I really start, how I got interested in this subject.

Too late—you've already lost some, and you're losing others fast. *Start* with that attention-getter as the very first words of your speech (the only possible exception is the rare speaking situation that requires a very brief greeting). Incidentally, notice how often "I" ends up as the focus point of such preliminary remarks by so very many speakers.

8. Do Be Confident in Your Attitude

Step up with confidence, speak loudly and clearly, move with assurance, sound authoritative and pleasant. Send out—*think!*—positive vibrations.

9. Do Get Set Before You Start to Speak

You've seen, and been distracted by, the speaker who spends a good part of the introduction, sometimes right down into the discussion part, arranging notes, adjusting the microphone, straightening clothes, moving the lectern to one side or the other, and on and on.

When it's your turn to speak, get all your things set—and go!

10. Do Make Introduction Consistent in Content and Delivery with Rest of Speech

Don't be one of those speakers who opens with, for example, a carefully worded dramatic story, then slips into a jargon-packed informal discussion of your speech topic. Instead, your introduction should use the same style of substance and presentation as that which you'll present later in the discussion part of your speech.

11. Do Be Alert to Tie-Ins

A "tie-in" in an introduction is the use of a few words or an idea from a previous speaker to begin your own speech.

Many speakers make poor use of what is going on around them right before they speak. Instead of listening to a previous speaker or their introduction by the chair, they go over their notes, adjust their clothes, think again about what they plan to say. You are urged, instead, to listen to what's said just before you step up to speak. Often you can pick up a phrase or idea that you can use to make your opening more timely, relevant, or appropriate. Here are some examples of effective tie-ins from student's speeches:

▶ That announcement we heard just before I was introduced—about your Saturday morning ecology trip—impressed me with your concern for our community. My speech, too, relates to your interest in your community.

▶ At the opening of your meeting, as we were led in a brief prayer, my mind focused on one particular phrase your minister used, because it is a good summary of what I'm here to talk about with you today. You may remember that he said . . . .

12. Do Write out Your Opening Sentence on Your Note Card

You'll recall that this suggestion was presented to you in Lesson 4, Preparing to Speak. The value is that writing out your first sentence word for word can give you confidence to speak smoothly as you begin your speech. You'll have something specific to refresh your memory as you start in case you need to. But remember: After that opening, your note card should have just an outline of what you're going to say.

13. Don't Overpractice Your Introduction

Some speakers go over and over and over again the first few sentences of their speeches. Then they practice the rest of their speeches just a few times. Remember that you are urged to practice your speeches in their entirety—as complete packages, not as fragments.

14. Do Make Your Introduction 15 Percent or Less of Your Speech

We've established that the typical introduction to a speech is only about 10 to 15 percent of the length of a speech. That means that at an average rate of 150 words per minute, for a speech of 4 to 5 minutes, the introduction would be a maximum of only 113 words. But note the examples of introductions presented in this lesson: all use fewer than 80 words.

This lesson has been a bit long because the introduction to a speech is so very critical. As you have been shown, it is your job, as you start your speech, to turn that collection of daydreaming, diverse individuals into a concentrating, stimulated, thinking participating audience.

Time now to check yourself on your mastery of the delicate art of designing introductions. Yuppp, self-test time again. Remember that, as for all of the objectives for all the lessons in this course, you are expected to demonstrate your achievement of them without referring back to the lesson or to any notes or source other than your own memory.

ASSIGNMENT 16. DESIGNING INTRODUCTIONS: SELF-TEST

❗ ACTION: Take the following self-test.

1. Name the criteria for an effective introduction for a speech.

2. Name at least 8 of the 11 techniques for getting the attention of your audience:

    (1) _____

    (2) _____

    (3) _____

    (4) _____

    (5) _____

    (6) _____

    (7) _____

    (8) _____

    (9) _____

    (10) _____

    (11) _____

Identify which of the following examples of introductions are effective and which are not. State the basis for your decision.

Las Vegas comedian Alan King tells a story about a teenager who's been trying to run away from home for months. But every time the kid's about to go out the door, the phone rings! It is indeed true that phones have become decision-makers in our lives. But here's a list of five ways in which you can become master of your phone instead of letting it be the ruler of you.

3. Effective or not? _____

4. Reason:_____

    _____

    _____

It is an unusual subject I speak about to you today. It is subject that is very important to you—life insurance.

5. Effective or not? _____

6. Reason:_____

    _____

    _____

What order are the following numbers in? 8, 5, 4, 9, 1, 7, 6, 3, 2, 0. Give up? They are in alphabetical order. Order is also needed in the classification of automobile tires, and I'm here to suggest how to bring that about.

7. Effective or not? _____

8. Reason:_____

_____

_____

Importance of Speech

"A man's character is revealed by his speech."

Greek poet *Menander* (343–292 B.C.)

Answers:

1. Relevant, Involved, Positive, Stimulate.
2. (1) Ask a question.
   (2) State an unusual fact.
   (3) Give an illustration, example, or story.
   (4) Present a quotation.
   (5) Refer to an historical event.
   (6) Tell a joke.
   (7) Use a gimmick.
   (8) Point to common relationships, beliefs, interests, or opinions.
   (9) Refer to the occasion, purpose of the meeting, audience, a local event, or some other part of the program.
   (10) Compliment the audience.
   (11) Point out the importance of the subject to the audience.
3. Effective
4. Reason: Attention-getter is relevant, interesting, transition to preview is clear, logical: subject is stated specifically, briefly.
5. Not effective.
6. Reason: Attention-getter is uninteresting; transition is routine; subject is stated specifically but without any attempt to get listeners interested.
7. Not effective.
8. Reason: Attention-getter may get audience to continue to try to figure out the gimmick; transition is a somewhat big leap; subject has but slight relationship to the attention-getter.

Scoring:

Your answers are worth:

Question 1:	1 point for each of the 4 criteria named correctly
Question 2:	1 point for each of 8 techniques recalled accurately (you didn't have to remember all 11 techniques, but if you did, take a bonus of 2 points)
Question 3–8:	2 points for each correct evaluation and 4 points for each correct reason
Total:	30 points
Needed to pass:	80%, or 24 points

If you missed, the same old line is here again: Restudy.
If you passed, congratulations!

DESIGNING INTRODUCTIONS: CHECK-OFF TIP SHEET

INSTRUCTIONS: Check off each item as you prepare the introductions for your speeches.

1. CRITERIA

_____ 1.1. Relevant

        _____ 1.1.1. To subject

        _____ 1.1.2. To audience

        _____ 1.1.3. To occasion

        _____ 1.1.4. To speaker

_____ 1.2. Involves audience

_____ 1.3. Positive audience thinking initiated

_____ 1.4. Stimulates audience

2. ATTENTION-GETTER

_____ 2.1. Question

_____ 2.2. Unusual fact

_____ 2.3. Illustration, etc.

_____ 2.4. Quotation

_____ 2.5. Historical event

_____ 2.6. Joke

_____ 2.7. Gimmick

_____ 2.8. Common relationships, etc.

_____ 2.9. Occasion, etc.

_____ 2.10. Compliment

_____ 2.11. Importance of subject

3. TRANSITION

_____ 3.1. Connects attention-getter with preview

_____ 3.2. Brief

4. PREVIEW

_____ 4.1. States subject or central idea

_____ 4.2. Lists main points

5. GUIDES

_____ 5.1. Don't apologize

_____ 5.2. Don't be long-winded

_____ 5.3. Don't antagonize or offend

_____ 5.4. Don't use irrelevant material

_____ 5.5 Don't start with "Today I'm going to talk to you about"

_____ 5.6. Don't lead the audience to take a negative attitude

_____ 5.7. Do get the attention of the audience first

_____ 5.8. Do be confident in your attitude

_____ 5.9. Do get set before you start to speak

_____ 5.10. Do be alert to tie-ins

_____ 5.11. Do make introduction consistent with rest of speech

_____ 5.12. Do write out opening sentence on note card

_____ 5.13. Don't overpractice introduction

_____ 5.14. Do make introduction 15% or less of speech

You Know People Like This?

"To speak much is one thing, to speak well another."

Sophocles, Greek dramatist, about 400 B.C.

LESSON 12

Designing Conclusions

OBJECTIVES ▸ After you have completed this lesson, you will be able to:

1. Decide if a given conclusion to a speech is effective or not, and state the correct basis for your judgment, applying the suggestions of this lesson.
2. Design effective conclusions for your speeches.

RELEVANCE ▸ Should you ever give a speech that is important enough to be covered by television or the papers, you should know of a special technique used in covering such events. Usually they will be especially alert for the conclusion of your speech. They know that it is in your conclusion, if ever, that you'll bring together all the basic points of your

CONCLUDING WITH A MEMORABLE STATEMENT:

"You know, it is customary to end an address with a pledge or saying that holds a special meaning. And I've chosen one that we all know by heart, one that we all learned in school. And I ask everyone in this great hall to stand and join me in this. We all know it."

"'I pledge allegiance to the flag of the United States of America and to the republic for which it stands, one nation under God, indivisible, with liberty and justice for all' Thank you. God bless you."

That's the conclusion presented by *George Bush* in his speech accepting nomination to be a candidate for President of the United States.

speech. As you go into your conclusion, many good reporters will be taking their most detailed notes, and cameras will likely be focused most intently.

Of course, most of our speeches are not newsworthy. Nevertheless, the conclusion is important because it is your last chance to attain the purpose of your speech. Consequently, while the tips on how to design a conclusion are relatively few, they are truly important.

PURPOSES OF THE CONCLUSION

You've heard speakers who end their speeches with what you can't really call a "conclusion," but merely "last words." They seem to simply stop talking. But the conclusion is a main part of the speech with specific purposes. It can't be left out of an effective speech.

You'll remember that your conclusion should consist of two sections:

A. Review
B. Memorable statement

These two sections have the following 3 purposes:

1. To emphasize the point of your speech
2. To climax your speech
3. To help the audience *remember* your speech

In addition, when your speech is any kind of a sales talk, there's one further purpose to be achieved in the conclusion. In such speeches, you also want to *get action* from your listeners.

CRITERIA FOR AN EFFECTIVE CONCLUSION

Do you remember the acronym we offered for the criteria for a good attention-getter for the introduction to your speech? Right—**RIPS.** Remember what **RIPS** is supposed to bring to mind? Right again:

Relevant to the speaking situation

Involves the audience

Positive thinking by audience

Stimulates audience

RIPS into the mind of your audience—that's what a good opening should do. The conclusion should meet the same criteria—a good conclusion also **RIPS** into your listeners' minds.

TECHNIQUES FOR DESIGNING A CONCLUSION

Once again, think of yourself as a member of an audience. The speaker has been talking for a half-hour or so. The speech has become less than thrilling. For the last few moments you've been only half-listening. But now the speaker finally seems to be ready to end. You figure you'd better become alert again, better start listening more carefully, just in case something important is said in the conclusion.

Unfortunately, that scenario fits far too many speeches. And that's why the conclusion is such an important part of your speeches. The conclusion is your last chance to attain the purpose of your speech. Techniques you use here can save a sagging speech or make a successful speech truly memorable.

Reviews

1. Summarize Your Subject or Viewpoint

In just a few words, present a brief, an abstract of the subject or viewpoint of your speech. You've heard many examples:

- Thus, I have built the case for eliminating billboards along our highways.
- Now you can understand my concern about the lack of controls on bicycle riders.
- Those, then, are my reasons for urging you to vote for federal licensing of all boat operators.
- And so, you can now recognize how very different Thoreau's thinking was from that of the antiwar activists of the 1970s.
- Such is the true background of this man whose writings are so critical of others.

A summary can be presented in either of two forms.

You can *repeat* word for word the statement of your speech subject or viewpoint just as you presented it in your preview. The idea is that the audience is more likely to remember words, sentences, and concepts that they hear repeated.

You can *rephrase* your preview, stating the same content or idea in different wording. The advantage is the variety of the expression. Some listeners might tune out when they begin to hear the same words over again but may listen alertly to a new, different statement. There is also the possibility that some listeners did not understand or accept your initial statement, so changing the words might capture those listeners now at the ending of your speech.

2. Repeat Your Main Points

In this techniques for the conclusion, you repeat or rephrase the two to five main points you presented in the discussion part of your speech. For example:

- These, then, are the three keys to successful savings—commitment, regularity, and growth.
- Thus we have examined the evidence on what caused this tragic plane crash and the effect the crash had on both the passengers and the company.
- And so a writer progresses from thinking to doing, to evaluating, to finally mailing her manuscript.
- Four reasons, ladies and gentlemen, stand out as to why we must not let the incumbent mayor continue in office. He must not continue because he is dishonest. He must not continue because he is prejudiced. He must not continue because he is hard to work with. And he must not continue because he is out of date.

Like a summary, a review of your points can *repeat* them exactly as you stated them earlier in your speech or *rephrase* them. Which is better is generally arbitrary, depending really on your own feeling and style.

Note the parallel construction used in the last two examples, about the writer and the mayor; such repetitive phrasing is often particularly effective in the conclusion.

3. Combine a Summary with a Repetition

Many speakers find it most effective to combine the two techniques and to present both a summary of the main subject or idea of their speeches and a repeat of the main points.

A few examples:

> ◆ Those, then, are the three reasons that have led me to invest in mutual funds. First, they provide safety in diversity; second, they provide participation in the growth of our nation's industry; and third, they provide me with money.
>
> ◆ Think again of our candidate's background—her training, her experience, her achievements. Then certainly you'd vote for her with enthusiasm.
>
> ◆ And so in this way—through the research, then the expedition, and finally the analysis of all of the evidence—we now know positively that Columbus's ship lies here, at this very spot on our chart.

The examples illustrate both repeating and rephrasing. They also use parallel construction to emphasize points, to add interest, and to make points more memorable.

Memorable Statements:

1. Use One of the Attention-getter Techniques

For your memorable statement you can use any of the 11 techniques for getting the attention of your audience in the introduction of your speech. You remember them:

1. Ask a question.
2. State an unusual fact.
3. Give an illustration, example, or story.
4. Present a quotation.
5. Refer to an historical event.
6. Tell a joke.
7. Use a gimmick.
8. Point to common relationships, beliefs, interests, or opinions.
9. Refer to the occasion, purpose of the meeting, audience, a local event, or some other part of the program.
10. Compliment the audience.
11. Point out the importance of the subject to the audience.

In using these in the conclusion, apply the same general guides that you learned for using them in your introduction.

2. Return to the Theme of Your Attention-getter

It is particularly effective in closing a speech to present again the same story, incident, quotation, joke, etc. that you used as your attention-getter, but now with a different ending or an additional line or perhaps another insight or explanation.

Consider these examples:

> ◆ And so we see the need for learning how to farm our oceans. You'll remember that family in Hawaii that I told you about as I started this speech. You'll remember that I quoted the father as saying to the U.S. federal farm adviser, "Mahalo—thanks—for showing us how to sow our lands." But what I didn't tell you was that our farmer said that way back in the 1920s. Now, more than half a century later, that farmer's son may soon be able to repeat his father's words, saying "Mahalo—thank—for showing us how to sow our seas."

▶ Those, then, are some special, insider's tips on how to make a good speech. Remember the two simple guides I suggested at the opening of this speech—to give a good speech, have a good beginning and have a good ending. There's one more tip—keep them close together!

3. Look to the Future

Both President John F. Kennedy and his brother Robert often closed their speeches with these words, written by poet Robert Browning:

▶ Some men see things as they are, and ask, "Why?" I dare to dream of things that never were, and ask, "Why not?"

Pointing to the future extends to your audience the invitation to consider, explore, and think further about your subject. Other examples of speech conclusions that look to the future are:

▶ Thus we have seen the past and the present of our problems of mass transportation. But what of the future? It is in your hands, ladies and gentlemen; you, as our city council, can write the future of mass transportation through the vote you are now about to cast. May your decision not be based on a misty look at the past, not a blurred glance at the present. But rather, may your decision be based on a clear vision of our future.

▶ So far we've covered four points on how to sail a boat for greater speed. And I've been telling you there are five points. So now let's get on to that final point—practice! Your boats are waiting. Let's go.

4. Call for Action

The point of a speech that is a sales talk is to get action—to move the audience to buy, join, vote, march, etc. Consequently, the memorable statement for a sales talk is usually an appeal for action.

A plentiful source of examples for such speech conclusions is television commercials:

▶ So next time you're in your grocery store, pick up a package of . . . .
▶ Call now to get your special invitation. Call this number. Call now!!
▶ You've just seen how truly fast this spray works. Now show your family how fast you can help them get rid of bugs by going out right now to buy a can for your home.

Of course, other types of speeches also present an appeal for action—the minister spurring his congregation to attend a special meeting, the teacher urging you to study, the politician seeking your vote. For example:

▶ Tonight I ask everyone in this chamber—and every American—to look into their hearts, spark their hopes, and fire their imaginations. There is so much good, so much possibility, so much excitement in our nation. If we act boldly as leaders should, our legacy will be one of progress and prosperity. This, then, is American's new direction. Let us summon the courage to seize the day.
Thank you very much. Good night. And may God bless America.

President Bill Clinton;
Address to the Joint Session of Congress,
Washington, D.C.

One hazard of presenting an appeal to action is that of the "overpress"—an appeal for something beyond realistic expectation. Examples include the car salesman pushing for an "immediate decision" on what would become a three-year commitment to payments. Not all uses of the overpress are by salespersons, but my favorite is the announcer on the late-late late show (actually, the early-morning movie along about 2:45 A.M.) whose script had him trying to get me to go down to my grocery store "right now for this new, improved bread."

So, do make an appeal for action when action is needed, but make it a realistic appeal, one that can be fulfilled.

Guides:

1. Don't Merely Stop at the End of Your Material

You should bring your speech to a smooth, polished ending. It is helpful to think of a speech as a package and the conclusion as wrapping it all up nicely and neatly. That is, your speech should have unity. It is the conclusion that brings together all you've presented—your basic subject or viewpoint, as well as the specific points about that subject and the data used to support the points.

Therefore, don't simply present your final point with its last bit of data and then stop. Rather, bring coherence through a well-worded conclusion.

2. Don't Apologize

Don't say such lines as:

- So that's about it, and I'm really sorry I didn't have all the figures for that budget, but there just wasn't time, and I hope you kinda get the idea.
- So let me close by saying how sorry I am that I wasn't able to work this up as a regular speech. But that's about all I wanted to say, and if I left any questions or doubts, I really regret that, only maybe if you have questions I could try to answer them.

Just as we suggested for the start of your speech, we suggest that for your conclusion, if in fact you do have an honest, legitimate apology due the audience, it is usually better to have the chair rather than you express it. On the other hand, the two examples above don't seem to me to be justified; the speakers simply *should* have been prepared.

3. Don't Stretch It Out

The rambling, I-don't-know-when-to-sit-down speaker is one of the most annoying people to listen to. One example is enough.

- Well, that pretty much covers what I wanted to say. I really can't add anything. As I said already, I do think we need to vote for this idea and get it going, even if it costs a lot, as I explained in my speech. I'm not sure, but I hope you feel as I do about this, and—well, that's about all I can say. If you have any questions I'll give them a try. It is important, however, and . . . well . . . so . . . .

Get to your point.
Summarize specific, precise points.
Finish with something we'll remember.
But most of all—finish! Please!!

4. Don't Introduce New Points

Avoid:

- And one thing more I wanted to say was . . .
- Oh, and I forgot to tell you that . . . .

If you did in fact overlook a really critical point, try to ease into the point smoothly. This may happen following a question-and-answer period, in which a question from the audience might uncover a basic point that you had not presented. You might work it into the conclusion you planned to present after the discussion by wording it so that the new point seems to have a relationship with the rest of your speech. For example:

- I've covered these three basic features—location, size, and cost of the new fire station. Let's now add just one more—appearance. Now, of course, we have recommendations on that. And your committee, too, will be invited to help design and suggest appearance features. But they will come later. Right now, the critical points are those of location, size, and cost. So . . . [into a memorable statement].

5. Don't Say "And One Thing More I Wanted to Say"

This point is an extension of the two previous guides: Don't stretch it out and don't introduce new points. It gets its own paragraph because this unpleasant and irritating phrase is used so often.

6. Don't Pack up Early

This is a tip you were introduced to in the lesson on polishing your delivery. You'll remember that you should stay up there before the audience, presenting your ideas until you're finished speaking. Don't give them the idea you've quit thinking about your subject by picking up your notes, putting them in your pocket, starting toward your seat, or otherwise deserting your spot before your audience.

7. Don't Continue to Speak as You Leave the Lectern

This is another tip presented to you when you studied delivery techniques and is repeated here for emphasis. Stay up there before the audience, maintaining contact, until your final words are out. Then, take a slight pause, and move out.

8. Do Work on Your Conclusion Carefully

Remember, the smart listener or the good reporter is most alert during your conclusion. Don't be misled by the shallow, unthinking members of your audience who start to "move out" before you do.

Many speakers are intimidated by the sounds of an audience getting ready to leave as a speaker gets near the end of his or her time allotment. This is especially apparent in lecture classes. But the top students will usually concentrate hardest during those last few minutes, even though many in the class are audibly closing binders, zipping up briefcases, clipping pens into their pockets, sorting books, lowering retractable desk arms, shuffling into their shoes, and such. Even an average lecturer will usually try to present a summary, a review—and very often those are the points that end up as questions on an exam.

9. Do Point up That You Are About to Finish If Helpful

You can signal that you have reached the conclusion part of your speech with such "pointer phrases" as

- And so, in conclusion . . . .
- Now let's restate our three main points . . . .
- To bring this all together, think again of these points . . . .
- And so, what have we said today? First . . . .

These often help quiet a restless audience. (But remember, it is you who got them restless.) These statements often help emphasize your points. Such pointer phrases are sometimes recognized as cues to the weaker minds to tune out, but the better heads usually listen harder.

10. Do Look for Opportunities to Tie in with What May Follow

If the opposing view is to be presented next, try to present some words that will help bridge the gap between your views and the next. For example:

- In a moment, you'll be hearing the reasons against this plan. It might be helpful for you to keep my points—the reasons why we must have this plan—in mind and compare them with those you're about to hear. Remember, we need this plan because, first . . . . If you do make this comparison, objectively, fairly, and honestly, the need for what we recommend will be evident. [Then, into your memorable statement.]

If a question-and-answer period is to follow, you have two options. First, conclude your speech, and then handle the questions. Or second, especially if you're the only speaker, consider the questions as part of the discussion part of your speech. Give a kind of internal summary as you finish the discussion part of your speech, handle the questions, then wrap up your speech and the question period with a regular, structured conclusion.

11. Do Make the Conclusion 10 Percent or Less of Your Speech

Recall the guides for the length of the three parts of your speeches:

I. Introduction	10–15 percent
II. Discussion	80 percent
III. Conclusion	10 percent or less

That means that if you speak at the average rate of 150 words a minute, you have only about 75 words for the conclusion for a 5-minute speech. Clearly, that's not very much. Still, many advertising campaigns are highly successful with televisions commercials of even fewer words. So it's important that you work carefully on the design of the conclusions to your speeches.

Of course that 10 percent or less is only a guide. Sometimes your conclusion can be shorter, such as when the subject is of great interest to your audience. For example, concluding a speech to college students on how to apply for some new financial aid certainly need not be very long. On the other hand, a speech with the purpose of persuading an audience to take some specific action that is undesirable—such as voting to increase their own dues in an organization—may well need a longer conclusion.

The point is that long or short, your conclusion, like the rest of your speech, should be designed on the basis of some rational, specific, calculated judgment on your part.

12. Do Make Your Style Consistent with the Rest of Your Speech

The reason is obvious.

Need for the guide: Because, strangely, quite a few otherwise rather fluent, polished speakers do become quite formal and structured in concluding when just seconds before they were casual and easy. Your conclusion should be presented in the same tone, style, form, and wording as your introduction and discussion.

13. Do Write out the First Sentence of Your Conclusion on Your Note Card

I find it most helpful to write out word for word on my note card the first sentence, or at least the beginning of that first sentence, of the conclusion. It helps me begin my conclusion smoothly and with confidence. As you become more experienced as a speaker, you may well begin to "read" your audience's reaction as you speak. If they seem bored at one spot, you may come to add a joke, an unusual story, a startling statistic. If they seem to be well informed on anther point, you may shorten it considerably. If you have a question period, new and significant points may arise.

To be prepared to bring all these possible variables in my speech together for a unified, skillful conclusion, I write out that first sentence of the conclusion. Then, no matter how far I may roam in my speech, I can always start to bring it all back together. Frankly, I rarely have to refer to that script, because I don't really roam that far. But writing out the sentence gives me the assurance, if I need it, that I can bring it all together.

The rest of your conclusion, like the rest of your speech, should be in outline form on your note card.

And now, to conclude this lesson on conclusions, a look at these conclusions from professional speeches may help.

> Let me conclude:
> Our [foreign] policy is based on an historical vision of America's role;
> It is derived from a larger view of global change;
> It is rooted in our moral values;
> It is reinforced by our material wealth and by our military power;
> It is designed to save mankind;
> And it is a policy that I hope will make you proud to be American.
>
> Jimmy Carter, *Former President of the United States;*
> *Speech at Notre Dame University, South Bend, Indiana*

> Let me close with one thought.
> It is my fervent hope that within my lifetime we will all be competing on a level playing field, no longer being treated differently, and that successfully managed diversity will be so much the norm that there no longer will be the need to hold a conference such as this.
> Then, my friends, we truly will have accomplished something very great and very special, something for which your children will be the beneficiaries.
> Thank you.
>
> Farah M. Walters, *President and Chief Executive Officer,*
> *University Hospitals Health System, University Hospitals of Cleveland;*
> *Speech at the Effective Diversity Management Conference*
> *at Case Western Research University, Cleveland, Ohio.*

Are you now a master of conclusions? Let's find out.

Eccentric English

In our language, blackboards can be blue or green, there is neither pine nor apple in pineapple, and no ham in hamburger. Homework can be done in school, boxing rings are square, tablecloths can be made of paper, most telephones are dialed by being punched or pushed, a woman can man a station but a man can't woman one.

A writer is a person who writes, and a stinger is something that stings—but fingers don't fing, grocers don't groce, hammers don't ham.

If a teacher taught, why doesn't a preacher praught? We recite at a play and play at a recital. Privates eat in a general mess while generals eat in a private mess.

Those and hundreds more such contradictions and confusions are noted in the fascinating book *Crazy English* by *Richard Lederer.*

ASSIGNMENT 17. DESIGNING CONCLUSIONS: SELF-TEST

🛈 **ACTION:** Take this self-test.

INSTRUCTIONS:
For each of the following, state if it is a conclusion that effectively utilizes the tips we've suggested in this lesson or if it does not. State the basis for your judgment.

And so, in conclusion, let us recall the three highlights we've summarized briefly today in the life of Cesar Chavez—his adherence to the principles of nonviolence, his leadership of farm labor, his receiving the Presidential Medal of Freedom. As Cesar Chavez himself said, "We need to help students and parents cherish and preserve the ethnic and cultural diversity that nourishes and strengthens this community—and the nation."

1. Effective or not? _____

2. Reason:_____

_____

_____

_____

Again, the three main reasons I've presented in my speech for the need for this change in law are that the present law is unfair, it is out of date, and it is difficult to enforce. And it's also true that the law is costly to administer. So please be sure to vote for this change at the election next week.

3. Effective or not? _____

4. Reason:_____

_____

_____

_____

So I've talked to you about this new type of motor. Any questions?

5. Effective or not? _____

6. Reason:_____

_____

_____

_____

Now you know a little more about this new motor—its distinctive features and its economy.

7. Effective or not? _____

8. Reason:_____

_____

_____

_____

So that's the third reason for voting against this proposition. Three reasons should certainly be enough for you to make up your mind, first, be sure to vote; second, vote against the proposition; and third, get your friends to vote. We're counting on your vote at tomorrow's election.

9. Effective or not? _____

10. Reason:_____

_____

_____

_____

Well, those are the three reasons for voting against this proposition. First, it is not in the interest of your students; second, it will cost us more; and third, it is poorly written.

11. Effective or not? _____

12. Reason:_____

_____

_____

_____

It seems to me we must start on this project soon. As the old proverb says, "A stitch in time saves nine." With this project, we might save nine times as many students from dropping out of school.

13. Effective or not? _____

14. Reason:_____

_____

_____

_____

We've gone through each of the steps you need to take to get your car checked out. There are just four steps, and they won't take very long. We detailed them, explained them, so you should have no trouble. Remember, as some cartoon character said, "A safe car is a happy car."

15. Effective or not? _____

16. Reason:_____

_____

_____

_____

Picture again that unfortunate family I described to you as I started this speech. A handicapped mother, an unemployed father, and triplets now 8 years old and stricken blind just one year ago. But I didn't tell you the names of those three girls. One is named Grace, one is Joy, the third is Hope. How could their parents have possibly picked such appropriate names eight long years ago—names, words, which I have used today to summarize each of the three reasons for our program of help to needy families. Grace, Joy, Hope—indeed living tributes.

17. Effective or not? _____

18. Reason:_____

_____

_____

_____

In review, then, what I've presented to you today are three things we try to do for students. We help them identify their strengths. We help them identify trades or professions that utilize those strengths. And we help them to identify a technical school or college that would be best for them in turning their strengths into employment skills. I'm sorry I couldn't go into more detail, but there just wasn't time. But the motto of our organization, carved in stone and displayed over the door of our building, says it all, says it to every student: "You can succeed!"

19. Effective or not? _____

20. Reason:_____

_____

_____

_____

Answers:

1. Effective.
2. Reason: reviews subject and main points; presents a memorable statement.
3. Not effective.
4. Reason: introduces new point.
5. Not effective.
6. Reason: merely stops; no review; no memorable statement.
7. Not effective.
8. Reason: no memorable statement.
9. Not effective.
10. Reason: does not review same points as presented in discussion. Note that the first sentence restates a reason for "voting against this proposition," but the next sentence, the review, gives three reasons to vote, not three reasons for the viewpoint.
11. Not effective.
12. Reason: no memorable statement
13. Not effective.
14. Reason: no review.
15. Not effective.
16. Reason: no restatement of points.
17. Effective.
18. Reason: reviews subject and main points, and presents a memorable statement. Note the creative intermixing of review with the memorable statement.
19. Not effective.
20. Reason: includes apology.

Scoring:

Questions 1–20: 1 point for each correct answer
Total possible: 20 points
Needed to pass: 80%, or 16 points

If you got 15 or fewer points, please redo the lesson. If you got 16 to 19 points, congratulations! Perfect score? Supercongratulations!

Now, look through the **Check-off Tip Sheet** on conclusions, which is on the next page. Remember that it is available should you need a reminder or two or more as you plan conclusions for your future speeches.

And on to the next lesson.

DESIGNING CONCLUSIONS: CHECK-OFF TIP SHEET

1. CRITERIA

_____ 1.1. Relevant

    _____ 1.1.1. To subject

    _____ 1.1.2. To audience

    _____ 1.1.3. To occasion

    _____ 1.1.4. To speaker

_____ 1.2. Involves audience

_____ 1.3. Positive audience thinking continued

_____ 1.4. Stimulates audience

2. REVIEW

_____ 2.1 Summarize speech subject or viewpoint

    _____ 2.1.1. Repeat speech preview word for word

    _____ 2.1.2. Rephrase speech preview

_____ 2.2. Repeat main points

    _____ 2.2.1. Repeat points word-for-word

    _____ 2.2.2. Rephrase points

    _____ 2.2.3. Use parallel construction when appropriate

_____ 2.3. Combine summary with repetition of main points

3. MEMORABLE STATEMENT

_____ 3.1. Use attention-getter technique

    _____ 3.1.1. Question

    _____ 3.1.2. Unusual fact

    _____ 3.1.3. Illustration, etc.

    _____ 3.1.4. Quotation

    _____ 3.1.5. Historical event

    _____ 3.1.6. Joke

    _____ 3.1.7. Gimmick

    _____ 3.1.8. Common relationships, etc.

    _____ 3.1.9. Occasion, etc.

    _____ 3.1.10. Compliment

    _____ 3.1.11. Importance of subject

_____ 3.2. Return to theme of attention-getter

_____ 3.3. Look to the future

_____ 3.4. Call for action

4. GUIDES

_____ 4.1. Don't merely stop at the end of your material

_____ 4.2. Don't apologize

_____ 4.3. Don't stretch it out

_____ 4.4. Don't introduce new points

_____ 4.5. Don't say "And one thing more I wanted to say"

_____ 4.6. Don't pack up early

_____ 4.7. Don't continue to speak as you leave the lectern

_____ 4.8. Do work on conclusion carefully

_____ 4.9. Do point up you are about to finish if helpful

_____ 4.10. Do look for opportunities to tie in with what may follow

_____ 4.11. Do make conclusion 10% or less of speech

_____ 4.12. Do make style consistent with rest of speech

_____ 4.13. Do write first sentence of conclusion on note card

"It's not interesting to say (in a speech) 'America loves freedom,' it's interesting to say 'Freedom to us is newspapers that everyone can buy on the street corner, newspapers that get to say just about anything about anybody. . . .' Be specific, personalize. Make it real."

Peggy Noonan, speech writer, in her book **What I Saw at the Revolution.**

L E S S O N   1 3

Using a Computer to Design Speeches

OBJECTIVES

If you can use a word processor, after studying this lesson you will be able to design a speech using a word processor:

If you don't know how to use a computer

1. Well, you might as well skip this lesson.
2. Or, better, much better, learn how to use a computer.

RELEVANCE

A computer can be a speaker's greatest aid—by far!—in preparing a speech. Benefits include:

▶ Convenient and fast compiling of a prospectus of points and data.
▶ Quick and simple entering of points and data in your outline.

IMPORTANCE OF COMPUTERS:

"Students who graduate during this decade (1990s) will be the best equipped if they use these (computer) tools and, as they move into the work place, they'll be innovators, they'll be driving the companies they work for to take best advantage of what's possible."

That's the view of *Bill Gates,* Chairman and Chief Executive Officer, Microsoft, speaking at National Education Computing Conference, Seattle, Washington.

- Speed and ease in adding new points and data.
- Flexibility in changing the sequence of your points and data.
- Not having to repeatedly retype or rewrite your outlines and note cards.
- Always having a smooth, complete, neat, and accurate version of your latest outline for your speech right on the screen—from which, of course, you can quickly, easily get a "hard" (printed) copy.
- Increasing the clarity of your thoughts and organization.

PROCESS

1. Establish, in the Directory of Your Hard Drive, a Folder for Designing Your Speeches

In that folder you should put:

- A file containing a "skeleton outline for speeches"—that is, a partial outline with blanks for you to fill in as you prepare speeches. That skeleton outline is presented on following pages.
- A different file for each of your speeches.
- Data you come across that you might want to use in future speeches.

There are three advantages to establishing that folder:

- You will simplify keeping track of your speech materials.
- You'll be able to borrow information from one speech to include in another speech much easier and quicker.
- You'll be able to compare and contrast the outlines of your various speeches side by side, as well as one after the other—whichever you prefer.

In addition to that folder on your hard drive, you should of course also maintain, preferably on a separate disk, your usual backup of that folder. By designating one disk to store all your speech materials, you'll simplify and speed your finding them when you need them.

2. In That Folder, Establish a File Named SKELETON.DOC

That file name obviously stands for "skeleton outline for a speech." That file name will work for either "Microsoft Word" or "Word Perfect." If that file name is not acceptable to the software you use, then of course give the file some other name that does meet the specifications of your software. Whatever you name the file, it should be one that reminds you that's the place that provides you with a partial outline for a speech, ready for you to fill in as you design a speech.

3. In That File, Enter the Following:

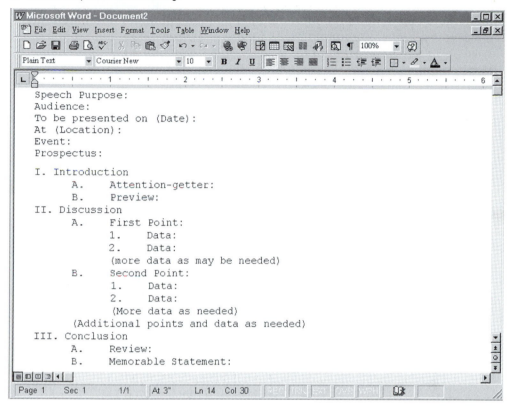

```
Speech Purpose:
Audience:
To be presented on (Date):
At (Location):
Event:
Prospectus:

I. Introduction
      A.       Attention-getter:
      B.       Preview:
II. Discussion
      A.       First Point:
               1.      Data:
               2.      Data:
               (more data as may be needed)
      B.       Second Point:
               1.      Data:
               2.      Data:
               (More data as needed)
      (Additional points and data as needed)
III. Conclusion
      A.       Review:
      B.       Memorable Statement:
```

Computer users call such an entry a *template*. In this case, that's an set form stored in your word processor that you can use by simply filling in the blanks on the form. And that is, of course, what we urge you to do—design your speeches by entering your points and data on that skeleton outline.

You need to create your own template of the skeleton outline for a speech as shown above because while "Microsoft Word," "Word Perfect," and many other word-processing softwares include in their programs templates for other uses—for letters, envelopes, brochures, purchase orders, etc.—no software provides a template of the outline for a speech as you are studying here.

That template contains, as you certainly recognize, the basic format for a speech that you learned back in the second lesson of this book.

4. Before You Start to Design a Speech Using That Template, Make a Copy of It in Another File (on the Same Speech Disk)

This second copy will be the template you'll use to design your speech. You should save that first version of the template (without entries) so it will be available on your speech disk for you to recopy as you may need for designing subsequent speeches.

5. You Should Give that New File Another Name—One That Will Help You Remember Which Speech Is in It

That file name you select must, of course, be one that is compatible with whatever software you're using for word processing.

6. Start Designing Your Speech by Filling in on That Second Template the Basic Specifics of the Speech You're Designing: Purpose, Audience, Date, Location, and Event

Keeping those specifics in front of you, at the top of your speech plan, will help ensure that you'll design a speech that's appropriate for your speaking situation.

7. Enter Specifics in the Section Headed "Prospectus"

Remember—and use—the tips on developing a prospectus that were presented back in Lesson 10, Designing Discussions:

1. Start to make entries in your prospectus before you begin your outline.
2. Include at least 15 to 20 points and data.
3. Work on this list over a period of several days, as ideas come to your mind.
4. Actually enter the points and data rather than trying to simply remember them; you'll lose many if you don't write them down.

Many people designing speeches on a computer find it helpful simply to leave the template you're working on open on the screen of your computer whenever you're around it. (Of course, you should use some kind of "screen saver"—a design that comes on automatically after a few minutes of no action on your screen; that helps preserve the life of your computer's screen.) With the template always before you, it is much more likely that you'll get ideas for your speech and that you'll enter them immediately, before you have time to forget them.

8. From that Prospectus, Select the Material for Your Outline

As you've learned, look through your prospectus and select the most interesting, unusual, specific—the statistic that will shock your listeners, the story that will hold them spellbound, the quotation that will get them nodding agreement. That becomes, of course, your attention-getter.

Continue working your way through your prospectus, moving material from it into your outline.

It is in this process that one of the biggest advantages of a word processor for designing a speech shines through. Computer users call it "massaging"—processing data, moving points and data from one place to another, until you develop what seems to you to be the best possible arrangement. And all the time, you have on your computer screen a smooth, polished, complete, accurate presentation of your outline. Gone are those messy handwritten inserts, sloppy arrows indicating new locations, bothersome crossouts, jumbled reentries, and such.

9. Complete Additional Research

As you probably know, your computer can be a gold mine of information for your speeches. On-line resources seem limitless.

Examples:

▶ Hispanic culture is detailed at gopher://latino.sscnet.ucla.edu.
▶ The search engine "Excite" reported to me there were 4,885,432 documents on public speaking.
▶ news:rec.humor.funny will provide you with stories to help add smiles to your audience's reactions to your speeches.

Digging through the many menus, routes, and sites can be tedious and costly, but often provides valuable information. For example:

Searching for information for your speeches?

Here are some "search engines"—places that will search the Web for information you ask for.

http://galaxy.einet.net/search.html
http://lycos.cs.edu/lycos-form.html
http://webcrawler.com
http://www.altavista.digital.com
http://www.stpt.com
http://www.yahoo.com
http://www.infoseek.com

Or, you might consult two of the biggest basic sources of material for your speeches:

Library of Congress: http://www.w.or/hypertext/DataSources/bySubject/LibraryOfCongress.html

Encyclopedia Britannicia: http://www.eb.com
(At present, this encyclopedia gives you one week free searching; then a charge is made.)

Looking for particular books you don't have and are not in your local libraries?

The address below will get you to what is reportedly the biggest listing of books anywhere. You can search by title, author, or subject, then order the book if you want. Many of the books listed have comments from readers, and some have statements from their authors. (Yes, my comments about this book are there.)

http://www.amazon.com

Seeking Specific Words for Your Speeches?

Roget's Thesaurus: gopher://odie.niaid.nih.gov/77/thesaurus

Webster's Dictionary: http://c.gp.cs.cmu.edu:5103/prog/Webster (But I can find definitions and synonyms faster by looking in a conventional—"hardcopy"—dictionary or thesaurus.)

Hunting for Phone Numbers, Addresses, etc.?

Companies, Services, Individuals: http://www.bigbook.com
Individuals: http://www.switchboard.com
Internet Address Finder: http://www.iaf.net
Products and Services: http://www.niyp.com

NOTE: Following are e-mail addresses, not URL's (Universal Resource Locators) as above.

Looking for Magazines?

Business Week (magazine): bwreader@mgh.com
Christian Science Monitor: oped@reachel.csps.com
Computer World: letters@cw.com
Newsweek: letters@newsweek.com

Scientific American: letters@sciam.com

Time: timeletter@aol.com

U.S. News and World Report: 71154.1006@compuserve.com

And those are but a few examples of the many varied magazines now available through your computer, and of course more publications are being added.

Searching for Newspapers?

Might just as well start with the biggest in the nation:

New York Times: staff.nytimes.com

But a surprising number of local newspapers are also on-line. Just to give you an idea of the range, consider:

Albuquerque Journal: ajoopinion@aol.com

Honolulu Star Bulletin: davids@aloha.net

Las Vegas Sun: thompson@lvsun.com

Orange County Register (California): lmgentry@ocrl.freedom.com

Peoria Journal Star (Illinois): xxnews@heartland.bradley.edu

San Jose Mercury-News (California): sjmercury@aol.com

Want Information About Other Colleges and Universities?

Many schools have web pages providing details about courses, facilities, and such.

Or suppose you were designing a speech about a college topic, such as what problems exist on other campuses, plays other schools are producing, special programs that are available, or such. You might find such material in the newspapers of other colleges and universities. Or you could E-Mail a question, and perhaps it will reach a student editor who might respond. Here's a sampling of campus newspapers:

Brigham Young University (Daily Universe): letters@byu.edu

California, University of, at Los Angeles (Daily Bruin): viewpoint@asucla.ucla.edu

Columbia University (Daily Spectator): spectator@columbia.edu

Kansas State University (Collegian): rjohnso@ksu.ksu.edu

Minnesota, University of (Minnesota Daily): network@edit.mndly.umn.edu

Nevada, University of (Sagebrush): sgbrush@shadow.scs.unr.edu

Pepperdine University (Graphic): thegraphic@pepperdine.edu

Polytechnic University of New York: jsu@photon.poly.edu

San Jose State University (California) *(Spartan Daily):* meagher@sjsuvml.sjsu.edu

Vanderbilt University (The Hustler): hustler@ctrvax.vanderbilt.edu

Washington, University of (The Daily): daily@u.washington.edu

Digging Through Just About All Media?

For an all-in-one media directory, reportedly listing all USA, TV, radio, newspapers, magazines, Black and Hispanic media, syndicates, networks, and more, go to:

http://www.gebbieinc.com

Those are, of course, but a few samples of many sources of information you can access through your computer. More computerized research is being added constantly, and the costs of accessing many of them, as you may have noticed, are becoming more reasonable.

10. Have Your Computer Print out the 3 × 5-Inch Cards You'll Refer to While Speaking

How you do that will, again, of course, depend on the software you're using. It may take you a few trial-and-error attempts to get your outline to the size and placement you want for your note cards, but once you've figured those out, you'll have another step in your speech designing eased by computer.

11. Prepare Visuals

If your software has the capability of producing graphics, you can add visuals to your speeches with surprising ease.

Some conventional word-processing software can be used to create simple statistical charts, bar graphs, pie charts, and such. Or you might want to move up to using one of the truly sophisticated software packages that create "impressive presentations with overheads, slides, 3-D charting, sound, and video clips," to quote one ad for a program currently being featured. And, "it is a cinch" to use, the manufacturer claims.

There are three advantages to computer-produced graphics, according to Jerrold E. Kemp and Deane K. Dayton in their book *Planning and Producing Instruction Media:*

- Increased speed of production
- Ease of revision
- Increased emphasis on design—because colors and structures can be generated so quickly on a computer, a great many formats for each visual can be considered.

Realistically, your most practical use these days of a computer to produce visuals for your speeches (*presentations,* in the verbiage of computerists) is preparing images for overhead projection. Converting a computer's printouts to the transparencies needed for overhead projection is inexpensive and takes little time; your school's audiovisual department or your neighborhood photocopy center can help you.

For more suggestions on preparing visuals, see the section titled "Designing Your Aids" in Lesson 7, "Selection Data."

In sum: It's clear that computers can help you prepare your speeches faster and easier. It is also apparent that both computers and their software are continuing to become much more powerful—another reason why you'd be well advised to start now to use a computer to design your speeches so you can continue to capitalize on their advantages.

USING A COMPUTER TO DESIGN SPEECHES: CHECK-OFF TIP SHEET

_____ 1.   Designate a folder for designing your speeches.

_____ 2.   In that folder, establish a file named SKELETON.DOC.

_____ 3.   In that file, enter the recommended template.

_____ 4.   Make a copy of that template in another file.

_____ 5.   Name that file.

_____ 6.   Enter in that file the specifics about your speech purpose, audience, etc.

_____ 7.   Enter specifics in the "Prospectus."

_____ 8.   From that prospectus, select material for your outline.

_____ 9.   Complete additional research.

_____ 10.   Print out 3×5-inch cards to refer to while speaking.

_____ 11.   Prepare visuals.

L E S S O N   1 4

Informing

After you've completed this lesson, you will be able to:

1. Name 6 techniques helpful in getting your listeners to remember the points of your speeches.
2. Use those techniques in your speeches.
3. Present an effective 4- to 5-minute extemporaneous speech to inform. To be considered effective the speech should incorporate correctly, as detailed in this and the previous lessons, at least 80 percent of the criteria in each of the three features of a speech—content, organization, delivery—listed on the **Speech Evaluation Form.**

RELEVANCE According to an old college line:

▶ A lecture is a process in which information travels from the mouth of a professor to the notes of students without passing into the minds of either.

Too often that's true not only of classroom lectures but also of a great many other speeches to inform. They include speeches by school administrators briefing parents about new programs for their children, talks by government officials telling citizens

INFORMING:

"It's always a shame when a guy with great talent can't tell the board or a committee what's in his head."
Lee Iacocca, former head of the Chrysler Corporation, now author and speaker, expressed that view in his autobiography, ***Iacocca.***

about new regulations, speeches by managers telling staffs about new procedures, and many other speaking situations.

The point of this lesson, then, is to teach you how to give talks to inform that do in fact achieve their purposes. That is, this lesson is to help you not only to present information but to have that information remembered by your listeners.

Back in Lesson 6 you learned the definition of a speech to inform—a speech designed to enlighten or instruct the listeners; to increase their knowledge, skill, or understanding; to get them to know more about a subject or something new.

In this lesson the emphasis is on helping you to unify all of the 58 techniques you've been studying and practicing in your previous speeches in this course. Those techniques apply whatever the general purpose of your speech—to inform, to persuade, or to entertain. In addition, you'll learn six new techniques especially helpful for speeches to inform.

Problems

"Facts are apt to alarm us," wrote an unknown author using the pseudonym Junius. The reasons for such hesitancy are diverse.

Some people simply distrust information itself. English essayist Sydney Smith wrote, "Don't tell me of facts, I never believe facts." Automobile manufacturer Henry Ford said, "History is bunk."

Another problem: Many of us gained much of our knowledge because someone else required that we learn. Consequently, we may have developed negative feelings about new information. Greek philosopher Plato claimed, "Knowledge which is acquired under compulsion obtains no hold on the mind."

Further, new information may challenge what we already believe. That's unsettling for some people: They might have to change their opinions. According to English writer W. Somerset Maugham, there is "an exaggerated stress on not changing one's mind."

There's also the problem of your listeners' lack of concentration on what you say. Columnist Sydney J. Harris pointed out, "The mind tends to wander during lectures in large part because while the brain can absorb information at a rate of about 300 words a minute, normal speech plods along at as little as one-third that rate."

Finally, for many people, in many situations, it's more comfortable, more convenient, to resist new information. English philosopher John Locke wrote, "It is one thing to show a man that he is in error, and another to put him in possession of truth."

Yet that's your job when you design and deliver a speech to inform—to put your audience "in possession of truth."

Clearly, you face some real problems. But they can be solved. Here are some techniques to help you present effective speeches to inform.

Differences Between Introductions and Conclusions

In the introduction to your speeches, your job is to guide your listeners to becoming interested in what you're about to say. In the conclusion to your speeches, your task is to review what you've said, summarize, and most important, guide your listeners to remembering what you have told them.

The introduction is forward looking, the conclusion is a look back.

The introduction builds anticipation, the conclusion implants retention.

The introduction is a "heads-up," a call to be alert, to listen to what's coming. The conclusion is a "wrap-up."

In this lesson, you will learn the techniques for planning effective introductions. In the next lesson, you will learn how to design productive conclusions.

GUIDES

1. Emphasize How Your Listeners Can Benefit from Your Information

Your information might make their tasks easier. It might save them time. It might improve their lives or work or both. It might save them money or bring in more money. Your information might . . . well, just how could your listeners benefit from what you tell them? Let them know as specifically as you can.

For example, a student in one of my speech classes, giving a speech intended for students planning careers as journalists, gave a talk to inform his audience about new developments in word processors. Early in his speech he said:

> ▸ I know that many of you will immediately think that a word processor is too expensive for you. But keep listening and I'll explain just how you can get one for about 15 percent to even 50 percent less than the price asked for in any computer store.

That certainly kept his audience listening! Finally, at the end of his speech, he told them how they could save so much money: by deducting the cost of their word processor as an educational expense from either their own or their parents' income taxes. (Please check with a tax expert before you try this.)

2. Relate Your Information to the Interest of Your Audience

If you're speaking to a group of high school students about efficient study techniques, some may be interested in how to learn faster, but others may be interested only in

RELATING YOUR INFORMATION TO THE INTERESTS OF YOUR AUDIENCE:

Speaking at a National PTA Convention, Secretary of Health and Human Services *Donna E. Shalala* said, "I have a teenage advisory group—17 young people from all walks of life who meet with me about once a month. Whether we're talking about preventing drug use or depression, smoking or sex, they say the same thing: They say that their parents are by far the most influential people in their lives. They say that parents and families can do the most to save them."

getting out of the meeting at which you're speaking. Still, you might be able to get even them to listen to your suggestions if you point out that faster studying will give them more time to do what they really want to do.

Therefore, think through just what it is that might be most relevant to the interests of your particular audience. How to do that, you'll remember, was detailed in Lesson 5, Selecting Speech Subjects, where you studied techniques for analyzing your audience.

3. Create Ways to Get Audience Participation

Be inventive. Here are several possibilities:

1. Ask questions—both rhetorical (which you ask for effect to emphasize an idea, point, or such, and then answer yourself in your speech) and real questions (which your listeners may answer).
2. Distribute a copy of the outline of your speech to help your listeners follow and remember your points. But remember our warning back in Lesson 9, Polishing Delivery: If you distribute an outline that is too close to your speech, you may well lose the attention of some listeners. The solution: Distribute a very brief outline, perhaps one key word per point, so the audience may be motivated to follow your speech more alertly.
3. Give your audience forms to fill out, checklists to complete, quizzes to take as you speak, etc. But be sure such handouts do not distract from what you're saying; do not make them so elaborate they do not listen. Use handouts with short questions, brief statements, simple checkpoints, etc.
4. Have your listeners confer with others sitting nearby to compare what they know about your subject before you speak or to review what you've told them after you speak.
5. Present a statement, then ask them to raise their hands if they've heard it before, believe it, can use it, etc.
6. On an especially nice day, have your audience move out on the lawn to hear you speak.
7. Try having your audience . . . well, what do you suggest?

4. Organize Your Material Clearly and Logically

This point was presented previously, but it deserves repeating for added emphasis. Work hard at structuring the information you want to present so your listeners will receive easy-to-follow, step-by-step bits of information.

5. Include Only Information Easily Communicated in a Speech

Don't forget that *not* all subjects can be presented effectively in speeches. Some legal problems may be too complex, the federal budget may be too lengthy, some personal relationships may be too sensitive, the politics of the Middle East may be too involved. You'll certainly find other topics about which you'd like to speak that simply are not suited to communicating through speech.

6. Get to the Point

Apparently this has been a problem of speakers for centuries. Way back in the 1600s English poet Matthew Prior wrote, "And 'tis remarkable that they talk most who have the least to say." And in the 1700s French writer Voltaire said, "The secret of being a bore is to tell everything."

7. Repeat Your Main Points

In spite of the previous guide—more precisely, along with that last guide—repeating key concepts will help your listeners accept and remember what you say. A few pages further along in this lesson, we'll talk again about internal summaries as a technique for reviewing your main points.

8. Make Your Information Interesting

Use all the tools in a speaker's bag you possibly can, including:

Humor: "Did you hear about the speech professor who . . . ."

Clever comparisons: "If you were to make a pile of all the books a student needs during his educational career, they'd reach up to the . . . ."

Compelling contrasts: "On the one hand, we have the bank president trying to . . .; on the other hand, we have the 14-year-old computer whiz who . . . ."

Curious quotes: "Remember the words of the psychologist who was declared insane. He said . . . ."

Visual aids: "This graph shows you . . . ."

Audio aids: "Listen to this recording I made of what that store manager told me on the phone."

Drama: "There, at midnight, in the center of the cemetery, we all heard . . . ."

Gestures: !!!!!

Movement: "As I step over to this chart . . . ."

Voice: "Softly, quietly, the protesters waited—then suddenly *YELLED*—then *YELLED AGAIN.*"

And any and all the other techniques you can dream up!

In addition to those eight guides just presented, you may recall that your first speech in this course—remember way back then?—your demonstration speech, taught you several techniques that can help you in all types of informational speeches. Here, continuing the list, is a brief review of the most important ones you learned earlier:

9. Be sure your subject is one that your audience can be informed about in the time, in the setting, and under other constraints in which you are to speak.
10. Be sure your speech follows the basic format for a speech—an attention-getter to start, a memorable statement to close, and all those other points you've learned to use in between.
11. When informing about a specific object, such as a tool, a written form, a machine, etc., use the actual item in your speech if possible.
12. When appropriate, provide each member of the audience with the item to practice with.

In a demonstration speech, for example, that would mean if you were showing how to compute some specific figure on an income tax form, you'd give your listeners a copy of the form so they could do the computations along with you. In an informational speech about some particular problem in our tax laws, for example, your listeners probably will be better able to follow what you say if you provide them with a copy of the law for them to read as you talk about it.

13. Early in the speech, state in specific terms exactly what it is you're informing your listeners about.
14. Present your information in brief, clear, and specific steps.
15. Arrange those steps in a logical order.
16. Support each step with specific data—examples, human interest stories, statistics, etc.

In Lesson 7, Selecting Data, you learned some additional guides that are productive in speeches to inform. The most useful ones, added to the above list, are:

17. Use a variety of data: quotations, contrasts, comparisons. Remember all of the seven types of data we presented?
18. Follow the specialized techniques for using the different types of data, such as rounding off large numbers and using examples to clarify, to add interest, and to make points memorable, but *not* to prove statements.
19. Use visual and audio aids. Aids are especially helpful in making your points more interesting, clearer, more emphatic, and more memorable, and they concentrate the attention of your listeners.
20. Using misleading data—bias, lies, and propaganda—is not only dishonest, but can reduce, even destroy your credibility in the minds of your listeners.

Following these guides will greatly increase the chances that your audience will listen to and understand what you say in your speeches. But your goal should be higher: You should also want them to *remember* what you say. Here are some techniques that are especially effective.

Making Your Points Memorable

1. Acronyms

An acronym is a word formed from the first letter or the first few letters of the key words of an idea, phrase, or such. For example, SNAFU is an acronym, standing for the phrase "Situation Normal, All Fouled Up." Snafu is an acronym so popular in American usage that it is now in dictionaries. RADAR is another established acronym, meaning equipment for Radio Detecting And Ranging.

A student in one of my speech classes gave a talk on what she called the **SMART** way to study:

Survey your material.

Memorize the main points.

Analyze the value and meaning of what you're learning.

Review regularly.

Test yourself.

By using that acronym, she made the points of her speech stick in the minds of many of her listeners.

If you're lucky, the key words of the main points of the discussion part of your speech just might happen to fall into a sequence that makes an acronym. Or you may have to be a little more creative; for example, you may have to reword or, if logic allows, reorder your points to form an acronym.

Suppose you are working with a group of junior high school students who are just moving up from arcade electronic games to computers. You're to inform them of your computer club's guidelines when they're working with computers. You've decided that there are just three main points you want them to know:

A. Keep alert to new developments.
B. Ease into more advanced computers as soon as you can.
C. Yell for help if you have a problem.

Look at the first *word* of each of those points, and look at the first *letter* of each word:

Keep

Ease

Yell

Right! You've got an acronym—**KEY!** Not only do you have a word, but it is a word related to the operation of a computer. So you've lucked into an appropriate acronym to help make the points of your speech easier for your listeners to remember.

Obviously, the main points of your speech will rarely fall into such a nice, neat sequence. To then get an acronym you'll have to create. By changing the wording of your points a bit or perhaps by changing the sequence of your points, you may be able to come up with an appropriate acronym.

If you were giving a speech to inform your audience about your ideas on how to stop inflation caused by imports, you might come up with these three points:

Establish more effective tariffs.

Adjust prices of American products to meet or beat prices of foreign goods.

Eliminate waste in production.

Not much of an acronym apparent there. But if you play around with the three points for a while, you might reword them as:

Tariffs are needed.

Adjust prices.

X waste [X as the symbol for eliminating].

Now you have an acronym—**TAX**—directly related to the subject of your speech.

2. Alliteration

Alliteration is the use of two or more words close together that start with the same sound. For example, "Take time to talk thoughtfully" is an alliteration.

Alliteration can help your listeners remember the points of your speeches. If you were giving a talk on planning a safe boating trip, your points might include fuel, food, fathoms, and foresight. A speech to inform an audience about a new program could be more memorable if it covered facts, fallacies, fears, and the future.

As with acronyms a little creative study of your points may lead you to an effective alliteration. For example, in a speech on the advantages of travel, the main points might be that travel:

Will broaden your knowledge.

Doesn't cost as much as you may think.

Will provide you with lifelong memories.

The points could be made more memorable by summarizing each in one word, and there just happens to be a word for each that will give you a nice set of alliterative points. The advantages of travel are:

Educational

Economical

Everlasting

3. Numbering

Telling your listeners the number of points you are to present in your speech and then stating those numbers as you present each point will also help get the points remembered. For example, you are informing your audience about the advantages of a new manufacturing process:

Easier work

Faster production

Reduced cost

Higher wages

The advantages will be remembered more easily if they are numbered as they are presented:

First advantage: easier work

Second advantage: faster production

Third advantage: reduced cost

Fourth advantage: higher wages

Another benefit of numbering your points is that the numbers can help you put a sequence of priority on your ideas. You can lead the audience, number by number, from the most important point to the least important, from the best option to the worst, or such. Of course, you can also reverse the order of priority of your points—guide your audience from the least significant point to the most significant, from the worst solution to the best.

Numbering also has the advantage of allowing you to use, in many cases, parallel wording, an effective technique you'll remember you studied earlier in this course.

But you have probably spotted the two major disadvantages to numbering the points in a speech. First, because so many speakers number the points they present, the technique can sound routine and uninteresting to some listeners. Second, if the speaker before you has presented numbered points, too, then your listeners may find it hard to also remember your numbering. More than one or a few lists of numbers are seldom remembered by many listeners.

Despite these disadvantages, numbering can be an effective aid in making the points of your speech easier to follow and more memorable.

4. Contrasting

After a good attention-getter, a speaker might preview the points of his speech in these words:

 ‣ There are three points I'd like to present to you on how to buy a sailboat. First, shop for what you want, not for what's being sold; then take the boat out for a tryout rather than buying it dockside; finally, have the boat surveyed by a professional, not by your own eager eye.

That "do this" but "don't do that" structure—contrasting—is especially effective in getting your listeners to remember the points you present. You might contrast the positive and the negative or the advantages and the disadvantages. The present and the future, the past and the present, or the past and the future could be contrasted. Contrasting can be built around the expensive and the inexpensive, the long range and the immediate, the prudent and the rash—the possibilities are limited only by your own creativity.

5. Internal Summaries

In addition to previewing the points of your speech in your introduction and reviewing those points in your conclusion, it is sometimes effective to summarize them as you move from one point to another in the discussion.

You learned this technique, you probably remember, when you studied transitions in Lesson 10, Designing Discussions. Because internal summaries can be very valuable, let's review.

Suppose you want to be sure your listeners remember these three steps in gathering material for a magazine article: research, interview, correspond. In the discussion part of your speech, after you present the first point (research) with its data, you move to the second point (interview) by presenting an internal summary, saying something such as:

> ▶ And so now you know the essential steps in how to research for material for an article. But remember I told you there were three steps in gathering material for an article—research, interview, and correspond. Now let's turn to that second technique, interviewing.

Internal summaries, as you read them in excerpt, may seem to be unnecessary repetition. But when presented in a speech, especially a longer or more complex speech, internal summaries can be very effective.

6. Informative Language:

Consider this speaking situation—a real situation, a situation that's a tough task for any public speaker:

Audience: Television talk show hosts, producers, directors, and such.

Occasion: A "Talk Summit" in New York City.

Purpose: To have the audience agree to change their talk shows from sensationalizing issues to informing and instructing. (You are right: That purpose is to persuade, and here we are studying speeches to inform; but the reason for this example being a speech to persuade will be clarified below.)

Speaker: *Donna E. Shalala,* Secretary of Health and Human Services.

Early in her speech she said, in part:

> Every day in America, nearly 1,400 teenagers drop out of school; more than 1,000 give birth out of wedlock; and approximately 25 are infected with HIV.
>
> Every day, 1.2 million young people have at least five alcoholic drinks; about 3,000 start smoking; more than 150 are arrested for drug offenses; and 15 children lose their lives in gun-related accidents, suicides, and homicides.

That's effective informative language. It presents data—in this case, statistics, of course—simply, clearly, directly, unembellished. It's language that names specific topics—"dropout," "birth out of wedlock," "alcoholic drinks," "smoking," "drug offenses," "lives." It does not comment, elaborate, editorialize; it presents facts only. It's clear, brief, to the point. The "sentences"—actually, those phrases between the semicolon—are short, crisp, punchy.

If you use that kind of language in your speeches to inform you increase your chances that your speech purpose will be attained.

How that informative language is different from persuasive language will be detailed in the next lesson, Lesson 15, Persuading.

But of course effective informative language can take other forms, too. Some speakers are good at informing through dramatic story-telling. Others use humor productively. Some combine story-telling and humor—listen to Garrison Keillor, radio's reporter of "all the news from Lake Wobegon," on his long-running show "A Prairie Home Companion." Many speakers present information through language that attracts because it is, or seems to be, highly educated—note the impressive vocabulary and sentence structure of William F. Buckley, Jr., for example.

But don't try to copy the language of some other speaker. Rather, remember the first of the two points in the "Basic Key" to effective speaking we urged on you in the first few pages of this book: "Be yourself."

REVIEW

Now you have studied 6 techniques you can use to help your listeners remember the points of your speech. Without looking back over this lesson, see if you can list them.

How to make points memorable in a speech:

1. _____
2. _____
3. _____
4. _____
5. _____
6. _____

To check your answers, look back over the last few pages.

Your grade? That was a review, not a self-test. Consider the self-test on this lesson to be the speech you are about to present.

Note that while the techniques you learned in this lesson are especially helpful in speeches to inform, these techniques will also help you improve your speeches to persuade and to entertain.

Now let's see how well you can apply those techniques in a speech to inform.

ASSIGNMENT 18. PERSONAL CONCERN SPEECH: SPEECH 4, INFORMING

 ACTION: Design and deliver the following speech.

OBJECTIVES:

After presenting this speech, you will have:

1. Acquired additional experience in designing and delivering a speech to inform.
2. Demonstrated the speaking skills you have now attained.

The effectiveness of your speech will be evaluated on the basis of the 58 criteria now on the **Speech Evaluation Form.** *Particular emphasis* will be placed on what you were to learn in this and the previous three lessons—on designing the introduction, discussion, and conclusion and on techniques for a speech to inform. You should, as throughout this course, incorporate effectively 80 percent or more of the concepts and techniques of speech design and delivery that have been presented in the course so far.

ASSIGNMENT:

Deliver in class a 4- to 5-minute extemporaneous speech to inform the members of your class about a subject that is of deep concern to you.

INSTRUCTIONS:

1. In general, your speech should focus on making the other students in your class more knowledgeable about something that is of considerable concern to you, but about which you feel they do not know as much as they should.

2. The *subject* might be a pet peeve, a hobby, a trip that fascinated you, your concern for or view of the future of your college, city, community, or country. It might be a problem in human relations, family associations, education, law, medicine, government, international relations, or such.

3. One way to select a topic is to think about some of the subjects your fellow students have spoken on in previous speeches and recall the class discussions following them. There might well have been times when you have thought, "Don't they know that . . . ?" Here, then, is your chance to tell these students something about which you have felt their speeches and discussions have revealed their need for more or better information.

4. Use the three **Check-off Tip Sheets** you received in the last three lessons for designing each of the main parts of your speech. Also use the **Check-off Tip Sheet** for this speech, on page 331.

   Notice: These are your last **Check-off Tip Sheets.** From now on, you're on your own. Of course you can go back and review, reuse, or make copies of previous **Check-off Tip Sheets.**

Double-Speak . . .

. . . is language that seems to communicate but really misleads. Don't use it. Avoid such wordings as:

"Revenue enhancement" when you talk about taxes.

"Human kinetics" when you mean physical education.

"Pavement deficiencies" for potholes.

"Fiscal underachievers" to refer to poor people.

"Negative patient care outcome," medical talk for death.

Those are but a few of hundreds of such phrases in the book ***Double-Speak,*** by *William Lutz.*

PERSONAL CONCERN—SPEECH 4, INFORMING: CHECK-OFF TIP SHEET

Speaker: _____   Audience: Speech class   Date: _____

Speech purpose: _____

_____

1. CONTENT

____ 1.1.   Based on accurate analysis of speaking situation

____ 1.2.   Purpose worded correctly; from audience's viewpoint, specific, and attainable

____ 1.3.   Subject appropriate, relevant, and interesting to audience

____ 1.4.   Points, data new, significant

____ 1.5.   Includes personal and human interest stories

____ 1.6.   All material contributes to purpose

____ 1.7.   Gets to point quickly

____ 1.8.   Presents own, original ideas, structure, or interpretation

____ 1.9.   Uses audiovisual aids when appropriate

____ 1.10. Emphasizes organization enough to help audience remember points

____ 1.11. Includes variety of data

____ 1.12. Data seem accurate, honest

____ 1.13. Points valid conclusions from data

____ 1.14. Includes examples to clarify, add interest, etc., not to prove points

____ 1.15. Points parallel and equal

____ 1.16. Uses smooth transitions

____ 1.17. Includes one or more balanced lines or quotable original statement

2. ORGANIZATION

____ 2.1.   Begins with effective attention-getter

____ 2.2.   Previews subject or viewpoint

____ 2.3.   Presents 2 to 5 specific points

____ 2.4.   Arrange points logically

____ 2.5.   Supports each point with data:

    ____ 2.5.1.   Example

    ____ 2.5.2.   Story

    ____ 2.5.3.   Quotation

    ____ 2.5.4.   Definition

    ____ 2.5.5.   Comparison

    ____ 2.5.6.   Contrast

    ____ 2.5.7.   Statistic

    ____ 2.5.8.   Audiovisual aid

____ 2.6.   Reviews subject, viewpoint, or discussion points

____ 2.7.   Concludes with memorable statement

____ 2.8.   Uses structure of speech, not of old-style class report or article

3. DELIVERY

____ 3.1.   Steps up to speak with confidence

____ 3.2.   Gets set before speaking

____ 3.3.   Establishes contact before speaking

____ 3.4.   Begins without referring to notes

____ 3.5.   Maintains contact with audience

____ 3.6.   Sounds extemporaneous, not read or memorized

____ 3.7.   Uses, few 3 × 5 note cards

____ 3.8.   Refers to note cards only occasionally

____ 3.9.   Avoids *ah, so, ya know, well, 'kay,* etc.

____ 3.10. Stops at end of idea: doesn't hook sentences together with *and, and ah,* etc.

____ 3.11. Maintains good posture; doesn't lean, cross legs, etc.

____ 3.12. Doesn't play with notes, pencil, hair, clothes, etc.

____ 3.13. Dresses to help, not hinder, speech

____ 3.14. Speaks loudly enough to be heard easily

____ 3.15. Uses aids effectively

____ 3.16. Gestures effectively

____ 3.17. Uses face to add interest

____ 3.18. Moves about

____ 3.19. Doesn't pace

____ 3.20. Appears to enjoy speaking

____ 3.21. Seems to care that audience listens

____ 3.22. Speaks with enthusiasm

____ 3.23. Appears confident and relaxed

____ 3.24. Speaks with, not at, audience

____ 3.25. Doesn't look at floor, etc.

____ 3.26. Varies speaking rate; not too fast or too slow

____ 3.27. Varies voice pitch and volume

____ 3.28. Enunciates clearly

____ 3.29. Pronounces correctly

____ 3.30. Hides goofs

____ 3.31. Doesn't pack up early

____ 3.32. Moves out with confidence

____ 3.33. Time: _____

Speech is Important

"I've found, during my quarter-century in management, that most successful people have one thing in common: they can speak."

That's the view of *Terrence J. McCann,*
Executive Director, Toastmasters International.

PERSONAL CONCERN—SPEECH 4, INFORMING: EVALUATION FORM

Speaker: _____ Audience: Speech class Date: _____

Speech purpose: _____

1. CONTENT

_____ 1.1. Based on accurate analysis of speaking situation

_____ 1.2. Purpose worded correctly: from audience's viewpoint, specific, and attainable

_____ 1.3. Subject appropriate, relevant, and interesting to audience

_____ 1.4. Points, data new, significant

_____ 1.5. Includes personal and human interest stories

_____ 1.6. All material contributes to purpose

_____ 1.7. Gets to point quickly

_____ 1.8. Presents own, original ideas, structure, or interpretation

_____ 1.9. Uses audiovisual aids when appropriate

_____ 1.10. Emphasizes organization enough to help audience remember points

_____ 1.11. Includes variety of data

_____ 1.12. Data seem accurate, honest

_____ 1.13. Points valid conclusions from data

_____ 1.14. Includes examples to clarify, add interest, etc., not to prove points

_____ 1.15. Points parallel and equal

_____ 1.16. Uses smooth transitions

_____ 1.17. Includes one or more balanced lines or quotable original statement

2. ORGANIZATION

_____ 2.1. Begins with effective attention-getter

_____ 2.2. Previews subject or viewpoint

_____ 2.3. Presents 2 to 5 specific points

_____ 2.4. Arranges points logically

_____ 2.5. Supports each point with data:

    _____ 2.5.1. Example

    _____ 2.5.2. Story

    _____ 2.5.3. Quotation

    _____ 2.5.4. Definition

    _____ 2.5.5. Comparison

    _____ 2.5.6. Contrast

    _____ 2.5.7. Statistic

    _____ 2.5.8. Audiovisual aid

_____ 2.6. Reviews subject, viewpoint, or discussion points

_____ 2.7. Concludes with memorable statement

_____ 2.8. Uses structure of speech, not of old-style class report or article

3. DELIVERY

_____ 3.1. Steps up to speak with confidence

_____ 3.2. Get set before speaking

_____ 3.3. Establishes contact before speaking

_____ 3.4. Begins without referring to notes

_____ 3.5. Maintains contact with audience

_____ 3.6. Sounds extemporaneous, not read or memorized.

_____ 3.7. Uses few 3 × 5 note cards

_____ 3.8. Refers to note cards only occasionally

_____ 3.9. Avoids *ah, so, ya know, well, 'kay,* etc.

_____ 3.10. Stops at end of idea; doesn't hook sentences together with *and, and ah,* etc.

_____ 3.11. Maintains good posture

_____ 3.12. Doesn't play with notes, clothes, etc.

_____ 3.13. Dresses to help, not hinder, speech

_____ 3.14. Speaks loudly enough to be heard easily

_____ 3.15. Uses aids effectively

_____ 3.16. Gestures effectively

_____ 3.17. Uses face to add interest

_____ 3.18. Moves about

_____ 3.19. Doesn't pace

_____ 3.20. Appears to enjoy speaking

_____ 3.21. Seems to care that audience listens

_____ 3.22. Speaks with enthusiasm

_____ 3.23. Appears confident and relaxed

_____ 3.24. Speaks with, not at, audience

_____ 3.25. Doesn't look at floor, etc.

_____ 3.26. Varies speaking rate—not too fast or too slow

_____ 3.27. Varies voice pitch and volume

_____ 3.28. Enunciates clearly

_____ 3.29. Pronounces correctly

_____ 3.30. Hides goofs

_____ 3.31. Doesn't pack up early

_____ 3.32. Moves out with confidence

_____ 3.33. Time: _____

Over for comments

4. COMMENTS:

Grade:_____

INFORMING: CHECK-OFF TIP SHEET

GUIDES:

_____ 1. Emphasize how your listeners can benefit from your information.

_____ 2. Relate your information to the interests of your audience.

_____ 3. Create ways to get audience participation.

_____ 4. Organize your material clearly and logically.

_____ 5. Include only information easily communicated in a speech.

_____ 6. Get to the point.

_____ 7. Repeat your main points.

_____ 8. Make your information interesting.

MAKING YOUR POINTS MEMORABLE:

_____ 1. Use acronyms.

_____ 2. Use alliteration.

_____ 3. Number your points.

_____ 4. Present contrast.

_____ 5. Give internal summaries.

_____ 6. Use informative language.

You Fumbled?

You are not alone.

"I have opinions of my own—strong opinions—but I don't always agree with them," said *George Bush.*

"Facts are stupid things," said *Ronald Reagan,* misquoting John Adams' statement, "Facts are stubborn things."

"If Lincoln were alive today, he'd roll over in his grave," said *Gerald Ford.*

"I stand by all my misstatements," said *Dan Quayle.*

Those and more than a dozen other such slips are reported in **The Book of Lists,** by *David Wallechinsky* and *Amy Wallace.*

L E S S O N   1 5

Persuading

OBJECTIVES After you have finished this lesson, you will be able to:

1. Name the three types of appeals appropriate for speeches to persuade.
2. Distinguish between inductive and deductive reasoning.
3. Name the five groups of needs on which a psychological appeal might be based.
4. Present an effective 4- to 5-minute extemporaneous speech to persuade the members of your class to accept your view about some national problem. To be considered effective, the speech should use correctly at least 80 percent of the criteria on the **Evaluation Form** at the end of this lesson.

RELEVANCE "Speeches to persuade? I'm not going to be a salesperson!"

That's what some students say. They overlook the times they try to get others to help on a project, to accept a viewpoint, or to change their minds about other topics.

PERSUADING:

"Persuasion is achieved when the orator's speech is so spoken as to make us think him credible; when the speech stirs our emotions; when the speaker provides logical arguments."

That was the view of *Aristotle,* Greek philosopher and teacher of rhetoric, born 384 B.C.

We give speeches to persuade when we talk to an employer about a job, try to get a friend to join a group, discuss a controversial issue, propose a change.

In addition, if we know the techniques of presenting speeches to persuade, we may be better able to handle the hundreds of such speeches that bombard most of us every day. They come at us in the form of television and radio commercials. Those ads are, of course, mini-speeches. Most of them use much of the format for a speech and many of the speaking techniques that you've been studying in this course.

The typical commercial is 60 seconds long, but many are much shorter; 20-second, 10-second, and even some 3-second spots are broadcast. (And some speech students complain that they do not have enough time to present their ideas in the usual 5-minute speech assignment!) Yet as brief as commercials are, they still must capture the listeners' attention, present a case for the product or service, and end with a memorable statement—usually an appeal to buy, to vote, to help, to call, or to visit.

Knowing the techniques used in radio and television ads can help you listen to speeches to persuade with greater objectivity. And you can use many of the highly successful techniques of commercials to help you to present your own effective appeals to persuade.

DESIGNING YOUR APPEALS

When speakers of today present speeches to persuade, they use principles of logic first established by early Greek philosophers. Scholars point to Aristotle (384–322 B.C.) as the greatest influence in helping systematize logic, the science of thought, the basis of an effective speech to persuade.

Since the days of Aristotle, communication analysts, speech theorists, philosophers, and speakers generally have classified techniques for structuring a speech to persuade into three types of appeals, or bases, for the development of an argument or a case:

Logical appeal (*logos,* the Greeks called it)
Psychological appeal *(pathos)*
Personal appeal *(ethos)*

Here are tips on how you can use each type of appeal in your speeches.

Logical Appeal:

Using a logical appeal to persuade your listeners means using reasoning. There are two means—methods, processes, systems, they might be called—of logical reasoning that are especially useful for speakers. They are *inductive reasoning* and *deductive reasoning.*

Many people find it difficult to keep in mind which is which. A memory aid that might help is to think of the meaning of the prefix of *in*ductive reasoning. *In* means (among other things) "into or toward." That might help you remember that inductive reasoning gets *into* specifics first and then moves *toward* a general conclusion. Deductive reasoning is the opposite. Deductive reasoning presents the conclusion first, then presents the specifics on which the conclusion is based.

The similarities and differences of inductive and deductive reasoning become clear when you study the following explanations and examples.

Inductive Reasoning:

Inductive reasoning is reaching a decision, conclusion, or viewpoint by starting with specific cases, then using them as the basis for establishing a generalization. Inductive reasoning is presenting your facts, logic, reasons and then stating the viewpoint that you have developed from them. Inductive reasoning is the process most scientists prefer today: From a study of a number of specific situations or events they come to a decision that has broad general application.

Inductive reasoning is especially effective in a speech to persuade when your analysis of the audience indicates that they are probably against your view.

One of history's most memorable incidents produced an outstanding example of the use of inductive reasoning in a speech. On Sunday, December 7, 1941, the Japanese attacked Pearl Harbor. The next day President Franklin Roosevelt spoke to a joint session of Congress to call for a declaration of war against Japan. In his speech he used inductive reasoning by first detailing specifics about the attack on the ships in Hawaii and then stating more facts:

- Yesterday the Japanese government also launched an attack against Malaya.
- Last night Japanese forces attacked Hong Kong.
- Last night Japanese forces attacked Guam.
- Last night Japanese forces attacked the Philippine Islands.
- Last night the Japanese attacked Wake Island.
- This morning the Japanese attacked Midway Island.

▶ Japan has, therefore, undertaken a surprise offensive extending throughout the Pacific area.

INDUCTIVE REASONING:

"Just think about what many parents are responsible for on any given day. Packing lunches, dropping the kids off at school, going to work, checking to make sure that the kids get home from school safely, shopping for groceries, making dinner, doing the laundry, helping with home work, paying the bills, and I didn't even mention taking the dog to the vet. That's why my husband wants to pass a flex time law that will give parents the option to take overtime pay either in extra income or in extra time off, depending upon which ever is best for your family."

Hillary Rodham Clinton speaking at the National Democratic Convention.

But speakers can reverse that sequence of statements as they present their views in a speech to persuade, and then they're using:

Deductive Reasoning:

Deductive reasoning is getting to a conclusion, decision, or a point of view by starting with a general principle or idea and then moving to specifics. Deductive reasoning is stating your point and then giving your facts, logic, reasons. Deductive reasoning was typical of the logic used by early thinkers.

A student is using deductive reasoning when thinking:

- This would sure be a great day to go to the beach.
  - The radio says the surf's up.
  - I don't have any more classes today.
  - The sun sure feels great.
  - I need a break from my studies.

Deductive reasoning is especially effective in a speech to persuade when an analysis of the audience indicates that it is probably receptive to a viewpoint or a new idea as long as it is supported with specifics. For example:

- The president is failing to safeguard the future.
  - We have been blessed by lakes filled with fish. But our children will inherit dead lakes unless we stop acid rain.
  - We have enjoyed this nation's wildlife. But our children will live in a world with one million fewer species unless we halt the extinction process.
  - We have been privileged to hear waterfowl commute on their flyways. But those flyways will be silenced unless we restart wetland acquisitions, coastal zone management, and cooperative wildlife research.

Walter F. Mondale *Ambassador to Japan,*
then Democratic Candidate for President;
Speech to National Wildlife Federation,
Albuquerque, New Mexico

DEDUCTIVE REASONING:

"The economic crisis of the cities is exacerbating in poor neighborhoods so that low-income families don't have access to the necessities the rest of us take for granted. When they want to cash a check, they're forced to go to stores that often charge gouging rates. When they want to shop for groceries, they may have to travel miles to supermarket. When their children go to school, schools often are dilapidated, if not outright dangerous. And when they need a health clinic, they frequently have no substitute but the trauma center of the public hospital."

That's from a speech by *Henry G. Cisneros,* Former Secretary of the U.S. Department of Housing and Urban Development, delivered to the Progressive Policy Institute Conference in Washington, D.C.

Now let's see if you can remember the difference between inductive and deductive reasoning. Consider this example.

A five-year study of crime in 2400 cities in the United States, conducted by the FBI, established that the most probable months for burglaries are December, January, and February. The study also found that most burglaries occurred between 6:00 P.M. and 2:00 A.M. And the most probable day for burglaries is Saturday. One could conclude, therefore, that if you stay at home between 6 and 2 on Saturdays during December, January, and February, you'll be safer from burglars.

Is that inductive reasoning? (yes or no?) _____ Why? _____

_____

Is that deductive reasoning? (yes or no?) _____ Why? _____

_____

It is, of course, inductive reasoning because the thinking starts with the facts, the month, time, day of most burglaries and then states a conclusion based on these data.

However, not all appeals in a speech to persuade are based on inductive or deductive reasoning. Many speakers find their ideas are accepted more readily if they use psychological appeals, personal appeals, mixed appeals, and other techniques.

Psychological Appeal:

When a television commercial tries to persuade you to buy a particular brand of soap so you'll have a "cleaner, more attractive YOU," it is using a psychological appeal.

A psychological appeal works on the audiences' needs, desires, motives, feelings, concerns. That commercial for soap is aimed at your need to be healthy and your desire to be attractive.

But a great many speeches to persuade fail because they focus on the concerns of the speakers who make the appeals rather than on the psychological needs of the audiences who make the decisions.

In Pacific Grove, a small town on the coast of central California, a public hearing was held to consider a proposal to establish a scenic bike path. Speaker after speaker appeared before the 5-member city council and nearly 500 citizens in the audience. Speeches to persuade were presented in favor of the new bike path and against it. Most speakers made such statements as:

- I took a bike trip into four other states recently and bike riding was a lot easier there.
- Now the only place we can ride a bike in this city is on the street.
- Our bike club would like to have a good, nearby place to ride.

Such statements have little influence on listeners. They focus on benefits to the speakers, not to the listeners.

But one student speaker had the foresight to telephone each council member a few days before the meeting to ask, "What specific reasons might prevent you from voting for the proposed bike path?" He then could design a speech to answer each concern of the council members, presenting such points as:

- Problem of maintenance: The local bike club will agree to set up a regular cleanup schedule.
- Problem of safety: The city's planning office was already working on the design of a special fence for the section of the path that passes through a golf course.

♦ Problem of noise: The path could be routed around a short section that was adjacent to several homes.

A speech built on points of major concern to the audience, rather than to the speaker, has a much greater chance of being effective—of persuading listeners to the view expressed.

Studies have established that people are influenced by quite a range of concerns, drives, needs. Such concerns have been placed in various classifications by different psychologists but usually include these groupings, based on the work of humanistic psychologist Abraham Maslow (1908–1970):

Biological drives: hunger, thirst, sleep, sex, and such

Safety needs: being protected from extremes of weather, having enough money, maintaining order, having reasonable assurance that most things will continue as they are or improve, etc.

Affiliation needs: family relationships, love, friendships, membership in organizations, etc.

Recognition needs: success achievement, pride, being consulted, and such

If one or (better) several of these concerns can be integrated—honestly and clearly—with the subject or with specific points in your speeches to persuade, then you'll be much more likely to achieve the purposes of those speeches.

Using psychological appeals in your speeches becomes relatively easy and clear once you accept the concept of considering your arguments more from the point of view of your listeners and less from your own. For example, a speech about the need for more parking spaces on a campus will be somewhat more effective if the speaker emphasizes such points as that it will help the faculty do a better job of teaching because students will arrive in class on time more frequently and will be more refreshed and eager to learn. That's in contrast to such usual arguments for more parking as that students are bothered by having to search for a space or that they don't like to walk so far to their classes.

Speeches for improving jails are likely to be more effective if they argue that the audience would live in greater safety by not further alienating the convicted than if they state the inmates need more comfort. Rather than argue that citizens have to pay more taxes because the money is needed, government officials get their ideas accepted more readily when they point to additional, expanded, or improved services to be provided to fulfill the needs of the voters.

If you were to give a speech to a local Parent-Teacher Association about the need for more police, an effective use of a psychological appeal would be a reason such as:

_____

_____

_____

Your answer should present a reason (1) based on the audience's needs and (2) a specific psychological concern. For example, your answer might have stated that the audience would have greater protection from crime or (better) from some specific crimes, such as mugging or burglary. Your answer would be still better if you stated that the audience would not have to worry so much about specific crimes, such as their children being molested.

In that same speaking situation, an ineffective reason in a speech to persuade that more police are needed would be:

_____

_____

_____

Your answer should be reason of no direct interest or concern to the parents and teachers. For example, arguing that the police are working too hard would be ineffective because it is based on the police's needs, not those of the audience.

Now, just to assure yourself that you are remembering those 4 types of needs, write them out below. The act of writing them down will help implant them in your memory. Try to write them without referring back to the list in the text. If you do need to refresh your memory, take a look, but still write them out to reinforce your learning.

Types of needs for a psychological appeal:

1. _____

2. _____

3. _____

4. _____

Personal Appeal:

A personal appeal is based on the speaker's reputation with or influence on the audience.

Former President Carter used a personal appeal when he told striking farmers in his hometown of Plains, Georgia:

> ♦ I cannot promise that I will solve every problem. I know that is not what you want. And you know that no president and no government can do that. I cannot promise a guaranteed profit, but I have never met a farmer who asked for that. What farmers want is a fair chance, and I do believe we can and have begun to change the policies of this government so that the farm family gets a decent break.

A personal appeal is most effective when the speaker is accepted by the audience as authoritative, knowledgeable, or influential. The speaker's influence may be based on his or her position—chairman of a committee, elected official, holder of a relevant job in industry, business, education, or such. Or it may be based on the speaker's knowledge—acquired through participation in a research project or college study of the subject or other firsthand experience.

Most of us might not be too successful in a personal appeal on many topics, simply because we lack the position, experience, or knowledge to be accepted by many in an audience as authoritative or influential. Still, you as a student certainly can be effective in a personal appeal when you speak on topics on which you really do have authority. For example, your personal appeal could be effective when you try to persuade high school graduating seniors that they should not try to work while going to college if they want to get the most they can from their studies; you might be able to persuade them that your experience in working hard to save money during the summer for work-free study during the college year is better. Or your experiences as a surfer could justify a personal appeal to a city council to assign a lifeguard to a particular beach that does not now have that protection. Your employment in business, industry, or government may well establish the value of your personal appeal while speaking to persuade about some problem related to your career.

Emotional Appeal:

"Hey, you left out one kind of appeal. How about emotion?" some students ask me in almost every class. They point to such speeches as a union leader urging pickets at the main gate to move to block the entrance to delivery trucks. Of course, not all speeches in such situations are emotional appeals, although many are.

An emotional appeal is effective, but usually only in limited situations. The greatest potential for effect is when the purpose of the speech is to get immediate action. The appeal to picket or demonstrate now—not tomorrow or next week—often works when emotions are fired up. The hawker at a carnival wanting to move a crowd to the ticket booth uses an effective emotional appeal when he cries, "The show is starting right now!" But if he tries to sell tickets for a performance to begin an hour later, he knows he must work in some logic, facts, and appeal other than to the emotions.

Consider the situation in which a speech is given to get people to write letters of complaint to their congressional leaders. If you expect your listeners to go home and write their letters, the request should be based on logical, psychological or personal appeals. If you are going to pass out paper and pens at the meeting so that they can write as soon as you finish your speech, an emotional appeal may be more effective.

The point: An emotional appeal may work when your purpose is to get immediate and short-range results. An emotional appeal is much less likely to produce results for action in the future or when a complex subject is being presented.

Another problem with emotional appeal is that their success is heavily dependent on the personality of the speaker. Few of us have the natural or the developed skills of the spellbinder who can move an audience to action through emotions only. The delivery of an emotional appeal requires exceptionally strong drama in voice, wording, movement, and gestures.

Multi-Appeal:

Certainly. A speech to persuade need not, often should not, rely on just one type of appeal.

The principle is the same as for the selection of data for your speeches. Remember, you were urged not to base your entire case on statistics only. While some in your audience may well be impressed with figures, other listeners may be more likely to be persuaded with a moving, well-told story. Similarly, it is usually better to include in a speech to persuade two or even all three types of appeals.

Rely on a logical approach only and some may reject your views with such thinking as "Oh, he must have twisted something in that reasoning." Depend only on a psychological appeal and you run the risk of not having your points accepted by those who are generally distrustful of psychology, psychologists, and the entire field of understanding the mind of man. Build a case on a personal appeal exclusively and there will be some in your audience who do not know or will not accept your personal authority.

Thus your speeches to persuade have a greater chance to fulfill their purposes if you base your view on all three types of appeal—logical, psychological, and personal.

Now, one more criterion will be added to your **Speech Evaluation Forms:**

1.18. Uses Specific Appeals When Appropriate

MULTI-APPEAL (PERSONAL AND EMOTIONAL):

"My mother was raised in the dust bowl's depression. She knew the meaning of work and the full measure of love. I miss her. Mom died of breast cancer when she was 46. I'll never forget the last time we spoke. I sat at her bedside and held her hand in mine. We talked of the future, not of the past."
Indiana Governor *Evan Bayh;* keynote address at the Democratic National Convention.

PERSUASIVE LANGUAGE

Let's return to that tough task for any public speaker that we considered in the last lesson, on Informing. Remember the situation:

Audience: Television talk show hosts, producers, directors, and such.

Occasion: A "Talk Summit" in New York City.

Purpose: To have the audience agree to change their talk shows from sensationalizing issues to informing and instructing.

Speaker: *Donna E. Shalala,* Secretary of Health and Human Services.

You'll remember in that last lesson we quoted an early part of her speech, in which she presented—in effective informative language—facts. Later in that same speech she began to drive directly to the purpose of her speech—to persuade. She said:

"When you're doing a show about drug use, you have a golden opportunity to steer parents and children towards places they can go for help kicking the habit."

"If you're doing a show about HIV infection among young people, you have an opportunity to teach them how to protect themselves and their children against this deadly disease—and where to go for help if they already have it."

"If you're doing a show about teen pregnancy, you have an incredible opportunity to speak to countless teenagers who are not yet pregnant but are at great risk of becoming so."

That's good, strong, convincing, memorable persuasive language. It's language that points to the audience often, by using "you're" and "you" several times. It states specific remedial actions the listeners can take. It uses positive phrases—"golden opportunity," "opportunity," and "incredible opportunity." It's language that repeatedly points to solutions. It uses words of action—"steer," "teach," "speak." It's direct—it does not wander or soft-pedal what the speaker wants the listeners to do.

That's the kind of language that can often help you make your speeches persuade effectively.

Again, just as in using effective informative language, persuasive language can also be presented in various styles or wordings. Some speakers persuade convincingly through quiet, calm, logical language—simple words, brief sentences, one tiny point or statement at a time. Others change the views of their listeners—or at least think they do—by using language that is dramatic, elaborate, often delivered in shouts one moment, followed by almost whispered words. The basic trick for you is to find and polish persuasive language that is productive for you.

"Speech is power: speech is to persuade, to convert, to compel."

Ralph Waldo Emerson,
American poet, essayist, philosopher.

ASSIGNMENT 19. NATIONAL PROBLEM SPEECH: SPEECH 5, PERSUADING

 ACTION: Present the following speech.

OBJECTIVE:

After presenting this speech, you will have had further experience and practice to improve your skills in designing and delivering a speech. Evaluation will be based on the 59 criteria on the **Evaluation Form** for this speech, with particular emphasis on techniques to persuade.

ASSIGNMENT:

Deliver in class a 4- to 5-minute extemporaneous speech designed to persuade your classmates to accept your viewpoint on a national problem.

INSTRUCTIONS:

1. You're getting close to completing this course, so you are more on your own for this speech. That means that by now you should be skilled at selecting a subject appropriate to the speaking situation; narrowing the subject to a specific viewpoint; using a speech format; incorporating effective use of data; presenting content that is new, significant, and relevant to your listeners; delivering your speech effectively.
2. The *subject* for this speech should be a problem currently of concern to all or most of the nation. The emphasis must be on persuading.
3. Do not select a viewpoint that most of your classmates already accept. Remember, your task in this assignment is to show how well you can apply the techniques for a speech to persuade as presented in this and previous lessons. If your audience mostly agrees with your viewpoint before you speak, there is not much reason for your speech, is there? If there *is* a good reason, establish that in the speech. For example, you might be persuading them on the basis of new or additional information.
4. Your classmates will help evaluate your effectiveness on this and on your final speech. You'll find three additional **Evaluation Forms** on the next few pages. Please fill out the top of each of them, just as you do on the form you give to your instructor. There are specific learning values in having students fill out these **Evaluation Forms:**
   (1) You as the speaker will receive additional feedback as to your strengths and weaknesses as a speaker.
   (2) The student evaluators will receive additional experience in analyzing a speech, thereby improving their own skills both in preparing their future speeches and in judging speeches they hear outside the speech class.

First Broadcast of a Presidential Speech . . .

. . . was on February 12, 1924, by President Calvin Coolidge, at a Lincoln Day dinner at the Hotel Waldorf Astoria, New York City. He talked about tax reduction (!) and was heard by some 5 million people listening to radio stations in New York, Schenectady, Washington, D.C., and Providence, Rhode Island.

NATIONAL PROBLEM—SPEECH 5, PERSUADING: INSTRUCTOR'S EVALUATION FORM

Speaker: _____   Audience: Speech class   Date: _____

Speech purpose: _____

_____

1. CONTENT

____ 1.1. Based on accurate analysis of speaking situation

____ 1.2. Purpose worded correctly: from audience's viewpoint, specific, and attainable

____ 1.3   Subject appropriate, relevant, and interesting to audience

____ 1.4. Points, data new, significant

____ 1.5. Includes personal and human interest stories

____ 1.6. All material contributes to purpose

____ 1.7. Gets to point quickly

____ 1.8. Presents own, original ideas, structure, or interpretation

____ 1.9. Uses audiovisual aids when appropriate

____ 1.10. Emphasizes organization enough to help audience remember points

____ 1.11. Includes variety of data

____ 1.12. Data seem accurate, honest

____ 1.13. Points valid conclusions from data

____ 1.14. Includes examples to clarify, add interest, etc., not to prove points

____ 1.15. Points parallel and equal

____ 1.16. Uses smooth transitions

____ 1.17. Includes one or more balanced lines or quotable original statement

____ 1.18. Uses specific appeals when appropriate

2. ORGANIZATION

____ 2.1. Begins with effective attention-getter

____ 2.2. Previews subject or viewpoint

____ 2.3. Presents 2 to 5 specific points

____ 2.4. Arranges discussion points logically

____ 2.5. Supports each point with data:

    ____ 2.5.1. Example

    ____ 2.5.2. Story

    ____ 2.5.3. Quotation

    ____ 2.5.4. Definition

    ____ 2.5.5. Comparison

    ____ 2.5.6. Contrast

    ____ 2.5.7. Statistic

    ____ 2.5.8. Audiovisual aid

____ 2.6. Reviews subject, viewpoint, or discussion points

____ 2.7. Concludes with memorable statement

____ 2.8. Uses structure of speech, not of old-style class report or article

3. DELIVERY

____ 3.1. Steps up to speak with confidence

____ 3.2. Gets set before speaking

____ 3.3. Establishes contact before speaking

____ 3.4. Begins without referring to notes

____ 3.5. Maintains contact with audience

____ 3.6. Sounds extemporaneous, not read or memorized

____ 3.7. Uses few 3 × 5 note cards

____ 3.8. Refers to note cards only occasionally

____ 3.9. Avoids *ah, so, ya know, well, 'kay,* etc.

____ 3.10. Stops at end of idea; doesn't hook sentences together with *and, and ah,* etc.

____ 3.11. Maintains good posture

____ 3.12. Doesn't play with notes, clothes, etc.

____ 3.13. Dresses to help, not hinder, speech

____ 3.14. Speaks loudly enough to be heard easily

____ 3.15. Uses aids effectively

____ 3.16. Gestures effectively

____ 3.17. Uses face to add interest

____ 3.18. Moves about

____ 3.19. Doesn't pace

____ 3.20. Appears to enjoy speaking

____ 3.21. Seems to care that audience listens

____ 3.22. Speaks with enthusiasm

____ 3.23. Appears confident and relaxed

____ 3.24. Speaks with, not at, audience

____ 3.25. Doesn't look at floor, etc.

____ 3.26. Varies speaking rate—not too fast or too slow

____ 3.27. Varies voice pitch and volume

____ 3.28. Enunciates clearly

____ 3.29. Pronounces correctly

____ 3.30. Hides goofs

____ 3.31. Doesn't pack up early

____ 3.32. Moves out with confidence

____ 3.33. Time: _____

Over for comments

4. COMMENTS:

Grade:_____

NATIONAL PROBLEM—SPEECH 5, PERSUADING: STUDENT'S EVALUATION FORM

Speaker: _____ Audience: Speech class   Date: _____

Speech purpose: _____

_____

1. CONTENT

_____ 1.1. Based on accurate analysis of speaking situation

_____ 1.2. Purpose worded correctly: from audience's viewpoint, specific, and attainable

_____ 1.3   Subject appropriate, relevant, and interesting to audience

_____ 1.4. Points, data new, significant

_____ 1.5. Includes personal and human interest stories

_____ 1.6. All material contributes to purpose

_____ 1.7. Gets to point quickly

_____ 1.8. Presents own, original ideas, structure, or interpretation

_____ 1.9. Uses audiovisual aids when appropriate

_____ 1.10. Emphasizes organization enough to help audience remember points

_____ 1.11. Includes variety of data

_____ 1.12. Data seem accurate, honest

_____ 1.13. Points valid conclusions from data

_____ 1.14. Includes examples to clarify, add interest, etc., not to prove points

_____ 1.15. Points parallel and equal

_____ 1.16. Uses smooth transitions

_____ 1.17. Includes one or more balanced lines or quotable original statement

_____ 1.18. Uses specific appeals when appropriate

2. ORGANIZATION

_____ 2.1. Begins with effective attention-getter

_____ 2.2. Previews subject or viewpoint

_____ 2.3. Presents 2 to 5 specific points

_____ 2.4. Arranges discussion points logically

_____ 2.5. Supports each point with data:

    _____ 2.5.1. Example

    _____ 2.5.2. Story

    _____ 2.5.3. Quotation

    _____ 2.5.4. Definition

    _____ 2.5.5. Comparison

    _____ 2.5.6. Contrast

    _____ 2.5.7. Statistic

    _____ 2.5.8. Audiovisual aid

_____ 2.6. Reviews subject, viewpoint, or discussion points

_____ 2.7. Concludes with memorable statement

_____ 2.8. Uses structure of speech, not of old-style class report or article

3. DELIVERY

_____ 3.1. Steps up to speak with confidence

_____ 3.2. Gets set before speaking

_____ 3.3. Establishes contact before speaking

_____ 3.4. Begins without referring to notes

_____ 3.5. Maintains contact with audience

_____ 3.6. Sounds extemporaneous, not read or memorized

_____ 3.7. Uses few 3×5 note cards

_____ 3.8. Refers to note cards only occasionally

_____ 3.9. Avoids *ah, so, ya know, well, 'kay,* etc.

_____ 3.10. Stops at end of idea; doesn't hook sentences together with *and, and ah,* etc.

_____ 3.11. Maintains good posture

_____ 3.12. Doesn't play with notes, clothes, etc.

_____ 3.13. Dresses to help, not hinder, speech

_____ 3.14. Speaks loudly enough to be heard easily

_____ 3.15. Uses aids effectively

_____ 3.16. Gestures effectively

_____ 3.17. Uses face to add interest

_____ 3.18. Moves about

_____ 3.19. Doesn't pace

_____ 3.20. Appears to enjoy speaking

_____ 3.21. Seems to care that audience listens

_____ 3.22. Speaks with enthusiasm

_____ 3.23. Appears confident and relaxed

_____ 3.24. Speaks with, not at, audience

_____ 3.25. Doesn't look at floor, etc.

_____ 3.26. Varies speaking rate—not too fast or too slow

_____ 3.27. Varies voice pitch and volume

_____ 3.28. Enunciates clearly

_____ 3.29. Pronounces correctly

_____ 3.30. Hides goofs

_____ 3.31. Doesn't pack up early

_____ 3.32. Moves out with confidence

_____ 3.33. Time: _____

Over for comments

4. COMMENTS:

NATIONAL PROBLEM—SPEECH 5, PERSUADING: STUDENT'S EVALUATION FORM

Speaker: _____ Audience: Speech class Date: _____

Speech purpose: _____

1. CONTENT

_____ 1.1. Based on accurate analysis of speaking situation

_____ 1.2. Purpose worded correctly: from audience's viewpoint, specific, and attainable

_____ 1.3 Subject appropriate, relevant, and interesting to audience

_____ 1.4. Points, data new, significant

_____ 1.5. Includes personal and human interest stories

_____ 1.6. All material contributes to purpose

_____ 1.7. Gets to point quickly

_____ 1.8. Presents own, original ideas, structure, or interpretation

_____ 1.9. Uses audiovisual aids when appropriate

_____ 1.10. Emphasizes organization enough to help audience remember points

_____ 1.11. Includes variety of data

_____ 1.12. Data seem accurate, honest

_____ 1.13. Points valid conclusions from data

_____ 1.14. Includes examples to clarify, add interest, etc., not to prove points

_____ 1.15. Points parallel and equal

_____ 1.16. Uses smooth transitions

_____ 1.17. Includes one or more balanced lines or quotable original statement

_____ 1.18. Uses specific appeals when appropriate

2. ORGANIZATION

_____ 2.1. Begins with effective attention-getter

_____ 2.2. Previews subject or viewpoint

_____ 2.3. Presents 2 to 5 specific points

_____ 2.4. Arranges discussion points logically

_____ 2.5. Supports each point with data:

    _____ 2.5.1. Example

    _____ 2.5.2. Story

    _____ 2.5.3. Quotation

    _____ 2.5.4. Definition

    _____ 2.5.5. Comparison

    _____ 2.5.6. Contrast

    _____ 2.5.7. Statistic

    _____ 2.5.8. Audiovisual aid

_____ 2.6. Reviews subject, viewpoint, or discussion points

_____ 2.7. Concludes with memorable statement

_____ 2.8. Uses structure of speech, not of old-style class report or article

3. DELIVERY

_____ 3.1. Steps up to speak with confidence

_____ 3.2. Gets set before speaking

_____ 3.3. Establishes contact before speaking

_____ 3.4. Begins without referring to notes

_____ 3.5. Maintains contact with audience

_____ 3.6. Sounds extemporaneous, not read or memorized

_____ 3.7. Uses few 3 × 5 note cards

_____ 3.8. Refers to note cards only occasionally

_____ 3.9. Avoids *ah, so, ya know, well, 'kay,* etc.

_____ 3.10. Stops at end of idea; doesn't hook sentences together with *and, and ah,* etc.

_____ 3.11. Maintains good posture

_____ 3.12. Doesn't play with notes, clothes, etc.

_____ 3.13. Dresses to help, not hinder, speech

_____ 3.14. Speaks loudly enough to be heard easily

_____ 3.15. Uses aids effectively

_____ 3.16. Gestures effectively

_____ 3.17. Uses face to add interest

_____ 3.18. Moves about

_____ 3.19. Doesn't pace

_____ 3.20. Appears to enjoy speaking

_____ 3.21. Seems to care that audience listens

_____ 3.22. Speaks with enthusiasm

_____ 3.23. Appears confident and relaxed

_____ 3.24. Speaks with, not at, audience

_____ 3.25. Doesn't look at floor, etc.

_____ 3.26. Varies speaking rate—not too fast or too slow

_____ 3.27. Varies voice pitch and volume

_____ 3.28. Enunciates clearly

_____ 3.29. Pronounces correctly

_____ 3.30. Hides goofs

_____ 3.31. Doesn't pack up early

_____ 3.32. Moves out with confidence

_____ 3.33. Time: _____

Over for comments

4. COMMENTS:

Student evaluator's name :_____   Grade: _____

NATIONAL PROBLEM—SPEECH 5, PERSUADING: STUDENT'S EVALUATION FORM

Speaker: _____ Audience: Speech class Date: _____

Speech purpose: _____

1. CONTENT

_____ 1.1. Based on accurate analysis of speaking situation

_____ 1.2. Purpose worded correctly: from audience's viewpoint, specific, and attainable

_____ 1.3 Subject appropriate, relevant, and interesting to audience

_____ 1.4. Points, data new, significant

_____ 1.5. Includes personal and human interest stories

_____ 1.6. All material contributes to purpose

_____ 1.7. Gets to point quickly

_____ 1.8. Presents own, original ideas, structure, or interpretation

_____ 1.9. Uses audiovisual aids when appropriate

_____ 1.10. Emphasizes organization enough to help audience remember points

_____ 1.11. Includes variety of data

_____ 1.12. Data seem accurate, honest

_____ 1.13. Points valid conclusions from data

_____ 1.14. Includes examples to clarify, add interest, etc., not to prove points

_____ 1.15. Points parallel and equal

_____ 1.16. Uses smooth transitions

_____ 1.17. Includes one or more balanced lines or quotable original statement

_____ 1.18. Uses specific appeals when appropriate

2. ORGANIZATION

_____ 2.1. Begins with effective attention-getter

_____ 2.2. Previews subject or viewpoint

_____ 2.3. Presents 2 to 5 specific points

_____ 2.4. Arranges discussion points logically

_____ 2.5. Supports each point with data:

  _____ 2.5.1. Example

  _____ 2.5.2. Story

  _____ 2.5.3. Quotation

  _____ 2.5.4. Definition

  _____ 2.5.5. Comparison

  _____ 2.5.6. Contrast

  _____ 2.5.7. Statistic

  _____ 2.5.8. Audiovisual aid

_____ 2.6. Reviews subject, viewpoint, or discussion points

_____ 2.7. Concludes with memorable statement

_____ 2.8. Uses structure of speech, not of old-style class report or article

3. DELIVERY

_____ 3.1. Steps up to speak with confidence

_____ 3.2. Gets set before speaking

_____ 3.3. Establishes contact before speaking

_____ 3.4. Begins without referring to notes

_____ 3.5. Maintains contact with audience

_____ 3.6. Sounds extemporaneous, not read or memorized

_____ 3.7. Uses few 3 × 5 note cards

_____ 3.8. Refers to note cards only occasionally

_____ 3.9. Avoids *ah, so, ya know, well, 'kay,* etc.

_____ 3.10. Stops at end of idea; doesn't hook sentences together with *and, and ah,* etc.

_____ 3.11. Maintains good posture

_____ 3.12. Doesn't play with notes, clothes, etc.

_____ 3.13. Dresses to help, not hinder, speech

_____ 3.14. Speaks loudly enough to be heard easily

_____ 3.15. Uses aids effectively

_____ 3.16. Gestures effectively

_____ 3.17. Uses face to add interest

_____ 3.18. Moves about

_____ 3.19. Doesn't pace

_____ 3.20. Appears to enjoy speaking

_____ 3.21. Seems to care that audience listens

_____ 3.22. Speaks with enthusiasm

_____ 3.23. Appears confident and relaxed

_____ 3.24. Speaks with, not at, audience

_____ 3.25. Doesn't look at floor, etc.

_____ 3.26. Varies speaking rate—not too fast or too slow

_____ 3.27. Varies voice pitch and volume

_____ 3.28. Enunciates clearly

_____ 3.29. Pronounces correctly

_____ 3.30. Hides goofs

_____ 3.31. Doesn't pack up early

_____ 3.32. Moves out with confidence

_____ 3.33. Time: _____

Over for comments

4. COMMENTS:

Student evaluator's name :_____ Grade: _____

PERSUADING: CHECK-OFF TIP SHEET

APPEALS:

_____ 1. Logical

> _____ Inductive reasoning

> _____ Deductive reasoning

_____ 2. Psychological

> _____ Biological drives

> _____ Safety needs

> _____ Affiliation needs

> _____ Recognition needs

_____ 3. Personal appeal

_____ 4. Emotional appeal

_____ 5. Multi-appeal

Senator Daniel K. Inouye . . .

. . . speaks with a moving sincerity that quickly captures the attention of his audiences.

He has been speaking effectively ever since Hawaii attained statehood in 1959, when he was a member of his state's House. Now he is the fifth most senior member in the U.S. Senate, a Democrat who is "a stickler for [the] prerogatives" of the Senate, according to an on-line report by the *National Journal Inc.*

During World War II he was severely wounded in combat while in the U.S. Army, returned home to earn a bachelor's degree at the University of Hawaii, then became a lawyer through study at George Washington University.

In the Senate, his interests and duties are diverse: He's a member of such powerful committees as the Appropriations, Commerce, Defense, Foreign Operations, Labor, Education, Commerce, Rules & Administration Committee, and others.

At the feisty 1968 Democratic National Convention, he was the keynote speaker who brought some stability to the meeting. He was "a tenacious member" of the Senate Watergate Committee and in 1976 the first chairman of the senate Intelligence Committee.

Inouye thinks, looks, and acts far younger than his age in 1998—74—so he may well continue to serve his nation.

L E S S O N   1 6

Entertaining

OBJECTIVES ▶ After completing this lesson, you will be able to include humor effectively and appropriately in your speeches.

RELEVANCE ▶ Let's start by setting your mind at ease. No, you are not about to be required to be funny. You are not about to face an assignment to give a speech to entertain.

But you are urged to include at least a few bits of humor in your speeches. Shakespeare's most dramatic tragedies include humorous dialogue or short scenes of comic relief from tension. Lincoln included humorous stories in almost every one of his speeches except his most famous, the Gettysburg Address. Almost every great speaker is skilled at telling funny stories or coining quick quips.

Humor in serious speeches—speeches to inform and to persuade—helps audiences relax, makes the speaker sound more human, and thereby helps listeners believe and accept the speaker's ideas.

USING JOKES:

"The subject matter of most jokes, sketches, funny films and plays is quite serious. What this suggests is the profound importance of humor. It's by no means something trivial that's hardly worth the attention of responsible people. If it were, the phenomenon would not have so interested the major philosophers."

Steve Allen, head of the Council for Media Integrity, composer, pianist, comedian, and author of 47 books, wrote that in his book *How to Be Funny.*

Still, many speakers avoid humor. English writer Thomas Fuller said, "Some, for fear their orations should giggle, will not let them smile." English statesman Lord Chesterfield said, "Most people have ears, but few have judgments; tickle those ears, and, depend upon it, you will catch their judgments, such as they are."

Here are some tips that can help you tickle the ears of your listeners. But first, consider the difficulties.

PROBLEMS IN USING HUMOR

"Being funny is a very serious business," many a comedian will tell you.

Almost all successful comedians have a staff of writers. Jay Leno and David Letterman do not simply stroll out before the cameras and let the jokes roll out spontaneously. Some of a comedian's jokes come from full-time writers; other jokes come from part-time professional writers who contribute humor either when the gags come to mind or when the comedian asks for "fresh material." Amateurs—fans, would-be writers, etc.—also send jokes to their favorite comedians.

Former President Reagan's staff of speech writers includes specialists in writing jokes. Former President George Bush, Massachusetts Senator Edward Kennedy, Former President Gerald Ford, and other nationally known politicians use joke writers regularly. Senator John Glenn used a team of four joke writers to prepare for just one speech, a talk to the Gridiron Club in Washington, D. C.

All that suggests one major problem in using humor in your speeches: Your jokes have to stand up against some pretty stiff competition.

Another problem: While you probably don't have the time to practice your jokes, remember that comedians tell the same joke over and over, working hard to increase the laugh. They will change the wording of a gag, try a gesture on one word and then another, shift a pause from one spot to another, adjusting and "tuning" a joke until it gets the biggest laugh possible.

Another problem: A speaker's personality may be a much more important factor in the success of a speech to entertain than it is in a speech to inform or to persuade. Certainly most of us can, with practice and experience, become a bit more humorous. But for many of us, when it comes to being funny, it may well be true that "Either you've got it—or you haven't!"

It all comes down to the one big problem that worries both the comedian and the public speaker who tries to be funny: no laughs. But if you know some of the reasons why humor may fail and use the techniques we'll be presenting, then you might be able to overcome some of the difficulties and bring at least a slight smile to some of your listeners.

TECHNIQUES

Since you're not here to learn how to become a stand-up comic (or a sit-down clown, either!), but to develop the essential skills to add bits of humor to your speeches, we'll give you just 4 basic techniques. They are:

1. Use yourself.
2. Use other sources.
3. Change the peg.
4. Build bridges.

USING YOURSELF AS HUMOR:

Republican vice presidential candidate *Jack Kemp* is notorious for his exceptionally long speeches. He capitalized on that well-known weakness by poking fun at himself in the opening of his speech accepting the nomination—and thereby increasing interest and understanding from his listeners.

"To those who have heard me speak before, [this speech] may be somewhat of a disappointment. I understand this is going to be a short Jack Kemp speech. I kind of got a feeling it was going to be short. At lunch today . . . I turned to Bob [Dole] and I said, 'Bob, how long would you like me to speak.' He said, 'Kemp, you can speak as long as you want, but we're only going to be here for five more minutes.'"

Remember, humor is a serious business. So don't expect to read a lot of funny stuff in here for examples, for example. (See, I just told you this wouldn't be very funny!)

1. Use Yourself

One way: Kid yourself. If the chair of a meeting gives you a big buildup in introducing you, you might say something such as:

▶ Gosh, even I can hardly wait to hear what I'm going to say!

Sure that's a stock line used often. Still, it usually gets a laugh or at least a slight smile. (A gentle grin? Light laugh? Casual chuckle? Well, start your own mind to creating comparable comic cracks!)

Listeners enjoy such quips, even though they've heard them many times. Of course new quips are much better. That suggests another way to use yourself as a source of humor.

Most of us have at least a bit of humor in us. We may have the ability to twist words into funny sayings. I'm told I have that skill. Examples? Come on now—I'm not a professional comic. I can't "be funny" on order. Few of us can. But in a given situation, on the spur of the moment, we may be able to turn a word, and then the idea, the fact, the point may come out humorous. If you have such a skill, we urge you to use it not only in your parties with your friends but also in your speeches in public.

Or perhaps you have a mind that remembers jokes. Some people can file jokes away in their mental banks and always seem to be able to pull out an appropriate one—and it's usually one that's new, whatever the subject.

2. Use Other Sources

There are scores of books in your local libraries with such titles as *Jokes for Every Occasion, The Encyclopedia of Humor,* and *Surefire Gags for Speakers.* (Those titles don't sound very funny. Well, again, humor is a serious . . . .)

Some of these books classify jokes by topics—cars, college, candidates, etc. ("Etc." just might be the funniest of all!) Other books of humor just list joke after joke, in no sequence at all. The big problem with using either kind is that you have to read through many pages of modest gags to find even a few bits-of-humor that may fit your speech subject, your audience, or your personality.

The Internet is an especially choice source for finding jokes you can work into your speeches. For example, I went to "Excite," one of the major search engines, entered "Humor" and it reported it found 323,568 documents. I selected "Wesley's Humor Page" because the brief description of it said it included college humor. There "Wesley's" listed 26 types of college humor, including:

209 Ways to Annoy Your Roommate
How to Take Notes
New Required Classes
Creative Science Experiments

To check out the level of jokes, I selected "50 Fun Things to Do in a Final That Does Not Matter" and found such lines as:

- Do the exam with crayons, paint, or fluorescent markers.
- As soon as the instructor hands you the exam, eat it.
- Try to get the people in the room to do the wave.
- Complete the exam with everything you write being backward at a 90 degree angle.

Or you can go all out in your search for funny stuff. A joke writer on the East Coast will sell you made-to-order humor at about $250 per gag. According to an article from the Associated Press, he writes regularly for comedians, politicians, and executives. (PLEASE, no gags about all three of those being the same!)

Whatever sources you turn to for your humor, be sure you don't take material that is already well known. Don't retell that great gag you heard on last night's television special or the fabulous funny you found in this month's *Reader's Digest.* Too many of your listeners also saw the show or read the magazine, so they already know the stories.

By now you've probably figured out that if you are going to joke it up in your speeches, you'll probably have to do some digging. Often you'll find a fresh quip that almost but not quite fits your speech. Don't throw the gag away; try to:

3. Change the Peg

The peg of a joke is the topic. Often the topic can be changed so a joke is related directly to the subject of your speech. Consider this funny story:

- A really dedicated golfer, a strongly religious man, is getting a bit old. He worries about how much longer he'll be able to play his beloved golf. He visits his minister and asks, "When I die, wherever I go, might there be a golf course for me to play?" "Well!" says the minister "I've not been asked that before. Let me check. Give me a few days for prayer and for searching through the Bible, and I'll get back to you." Couple of days later the minister phones the golfer. "About your playing golf after you die—I've got some good news and some bad news." "Tell me, tell me!" urges the anxious golfer. "Well, the good news is that where you're going there are the most beautiful, challenging golf courses you've ever played. The bad news is that your starting time is seven tomorrow morning!"

The peg of that joke can be changed while the humor remains. If you're speaking about the ocean, fishing, boats, or such, the golfer could easily, effectively, be changed into a sailor—"The good news: where you're going there are beautiful boats, magnificent harbors. The bad news: your boat sails at seven!" Or change the topic to basketball—"Great courts; you tip off at seven!" Or to eating—"The good news: great restaurants. The bad news: there's a table reserved for you tonight!"

Changing the peg of a joke is also called by comedians and comedy writers "pulling a switch." Usually there are three variables that can be changed: the *subject* of the joke, the *character,* or the *setting*.

> ▶ A plane takes off with a full load of passengers on a cross-country flight. As soon as it is airborne a voice comes over the public address system: "Ladies and gentlemen, welcome aboard and congratulations! You are the first passengers to fly on this new, completely automated airplane. There are no pilots aboard, no flight attendants, no crew whatever. The plane took off automatically, your drinks and food are about to be served automatically, and the plane will land automatically—all run by a computer. But please do not worry. Be assured that the entire system has been tested thoroughly and checked completely so nothing can go wrong nothing can go wrong nothing can go wrong . . . .

You could pull a switch by changing the setting to an automated grocery store, dentist's office, or bank (which might be especially funny since some banks are getting very close to full automation). The characters could be changed to a group touring an atomic energy plant or a patient in a new hospital, to suggest but two options.

Try it yourself. Take the old Henny Youngman gag, the title of his autobiography, *Take My Wife . . . Please!* Try changing the peg that gag—wife—to fit a speech about education.

How might you rewrite that gag? _____

_____

_____

The switch might be "Take my school . . . please!" or "Take my teacher . . . please!" or "Take my major . . . please!" There are other possible switches too, of course.

Try another one. Suppose you were speaking about our postal service. How might you switch our basic gag, "Take my wife . . . please!" to fit a speech on our mail system?

_____

_____

One change you might have thought of is "Take my mail . . . please!" Another way is to change the first word instead; the joke might then become "Mail my wife . . . please!" If a point in your speech were concerned about lost mail, that line might be a big hit. For a speech on inflation you might try "Take my stocks . . . please!" Or for a speech on renting, "Take my apartment . . . please!"

4. Build Bridges

Another way to make a joke relate to the subject of your speech is to use a transition—to build a bridge from your topic to the joke or from the joke to your topic. That's a technique used frequently by David Letterman as he ties a number of jokes together in his opening monologue. He uses such bridges as:

‣ I guess you heard the news report about . . . .
‣ Well, on my way to the studio today I . . . .
‣ Oh—just last weekend I . . . .

Public speakers can use the same kind of bridges to relate jokes to their speeches with such lines as:

‣ The guy in that joke had his problem, and here's another problem I'd like to talk with you about this evening.
‣ So that's how one person handled a difficult situation; but consider now how this city might deal with . . . .

Such bridges may be built on pretty flimsy foundations at times. But their job is simply to give a sense of unity, not to establish proof. For example, a joke about bugs can be tied to a speech about ecology with the rather obvious bridge, "We laugh at those bugs, but we must take seriously the problems of ecology." It takes a bolder bridge to go from a gag about newspapers to a serious speech about automobiles, but the transition could be made by saying, "Well, remember that, after all, papers are a bit like cars in that they are both in great demand by thousands of people in this city every day."

GUIDES

1. Be Creative

My college roommate, Ollie Bauquier, after graduating, toured as a professional comedian. Now, several times a year, he mails a one-page collection of what he calls "knee-slappers" to his friends. Read the following samples and you may think he should be mailing them to his enemies:

‣ Travel tip: In an underdeveloped country, don't drink the water. In a developed country, don't breathe the air.
‣ I invented a burglar alarm. But someone stole it.
‣ I don't believe in reincarnation, and I didn't believe in it when I was here last time, either.

Of course, the problem with telling you to "be creative" is that, once again, it is largely, but not entirely, a skill most of us either have or find hard to develop. There are entire courses on how to be creative, but in general, most urge you to let your mind go, don't hold back on your thoughts, adapt something that exists. In humor, that translates to taking a gag you enjoy and pulling a switch.

2. Let Your Audience Know You Expect Them to Laugh

Television interviewer Dick Cavett tried to be a comedian for a while, early in his career. Before that he'd had considerable experience writing jokes for Johnny Carson and other hosts of the *Tonight Show*. Cavett's first night as a comedian was a disaster—he got almost no laughs at all. He asked advice from his longtime friend, the great funnyman Woody Allen. Allen asked Cavett how he was introduced. According to his biography *Cavett,* he "didn't want the audience to expect a harsh one-line comic type, so I told the emcee to tell them there was a young man backstage who would like to talk to them." Allen's advice, Cavett wrote: "You have to insist on an intro that makes two things clear: that you are a comedian, and that the audience is expected to laugh."

If an audience knows they are about to hear a speech on a serious subject, they may not know that it's all right to laugh, that they are expected to laugh. When humor is unexpected, it often misses. Among the lines speakers use to alert listeners to a joke that's coming are these:

- There's a funny joke that illustrates that point. It's a story abut a college student who . . . .
- As comedian Don Rickles would say, ...
- I heard a funny story just yesterday that will help you understand this problem. A tourist was . . . .

3. Deliver Humor with Confidence and Pleasure

You've noticed that most comedians tell their jokes with assurance. A great many comedians are in fact shy, but few appear that way in public. Their delivery is usually fast and forceful.

4. Be Yourself

You can borrow a gesture from one comedian, an inflection from another, a theme from a third. But don't try to duplicate the style and material of a particular humorist. Unless you are working at becoming an impressionist-comedian, you'll find it difficult indeed to be funny just by copying someone else. That may spark your listeners to think of the person you're trying to imitate rather than listen to you.

5. Don't Put Down Your Jokes or Yourself

Do not say such things as "I thought this joke was funny, but maybe you won't." With that lead-in, chances are your listeners will agree with you and not find your humor humorous. Again, there are exceptions, but few.

Further, what funnyman other than Rodney Dangerfield has become successful by putting himself down? His identifying line, "I don't get no respect!" works for him, but mostly because it is such a reversal from the routine of most comedians. Joan Rivers also uses a kind of self-deprecating humor, but she delivers it in a fast, confident style. But both of those comedians built their images over years of performing. The public speaker rarely has the time or the inclination for such a gradual development.

6. Do Laugh at Your Own Jokes

An encouraging laugh or a slight smile will cue your listeners that you are about to say something you expect them to enjoy. Of course, it is quite distracting to hear a speaker laugh long and hard before, during, and after his or her own jokes. Still, listeners need to know what is expected of them, and a bit of a laugh from a speaker can tell an audience that something funny is about to be or has been said.

7. Be *Sure* Your Humor Relates to Your Speech Subject

One of the best ways to guide your listeners to not laughing at your humor is to use such lines as:

- Let me tell you this funny joke I heard recently. Although it really doesn't have much to do with the subject of my speech, I thought you might like it.
- Oh—before I go to the next point, let me tell you a good story I just heard, if you don't mind my digressing for just a moment.

Your humor should, of course, support, not digress from, the points of your speech. Your jokes should relate *directly* to your speech.

In sum, you might well follow the guidelines for writers of *Yakov Smirnoff's* weekly radio show, "Only in America." They include:

- Nothing off-color.
- Make the jokes "thought provoking. Many times when Yakov tells a joke people clap as well as laugh."
- Don't write jokes with generalities about "religion, women, or politics."
- All material should focus on things that happen in America—"that someone in Podunk, Iowa, as well as Los Angeles, California, would know about."

TYPES OF SPEECHES TO ENTERTAIN

Thus far we have offered suggestions on how to add bits of humor to your speeches on serious subjects. Now let's look at speeches you might design to meet the general purpose to entertain.

After-Dinner Speeches

The purpose of the after-dinner speech is to offer the audience light, enjoyable remarks. One critic claimed they were delivered by "a kind of poor man's Johnny Carson," but that remark is not very accurate. Some after-dinner speakers are paid $1000 and more yet remain virtually unknown outside their own group of professional speakers.

Usually an after-dinner speech is a back-to-back series of funny incidents, stories, experiences about people and their problems. As in presenting data in other types of speeches, you should continue to use stories about people if you are to hold the attention of your audiences.

After-dinner speeches are, in essence, an extension of the well-known opening monologue popular on talk shows and variety programs. The funny stories about people may be one-liners—short, punchy gags presented in a few words. Henny Youngman, the bald-headed veteran with a violin under his arm more frequently than under his chin, is named by many as the master of this type of humor. At the other range of jokes about people are the long, involved, twisted routes to the punch line of a shaggy-dog story. Skilled at telling this type of humor, for example, are comedians like Ellen DeGeneres.

A full speech of 20 minutes or more of humor is difficult indeed for most of us. Again, skill in such speaking is heavily dependent on an individual's personality. Few of us have the clever mind needed to create that much original humor, or the retentive mind able to store jokes, gags, stories, and such from a variety of sources. But if you are so inclined, then you should certainly try to present such a speech. One of the big advantages of a speech class such as this is the opportunity you have to try your skills without the disasters that may result before a "real" audience.

Travel Talks

One situation for a speech to entertain that most of us can handle is the travel talk. The speaker's job is to entertain the audience by recreating scenes and reliving experiences that he or she has encountered firsthand in traveling. Many of these speeches feature the showing of slides or movies.

The key to making a travel talk effective is to focus on a specific theme. You might center on the range of buildings you saw, the various types of transportation, the problems of dealing with a variety of coins used in different countries, the different styles of tour directors.

One good way to select the theme for such a talk is to think of your basic reason for taking the trip or the main interests you have in the places visited, or some other common factor or events you experienced. For example, a student in one of my classes gave an outstandingly funny speech about the problems of getting reservations for a main show in a big Las Vegas hotel. (If you have never tried to get into one of these shows, don't knock this as the subject for a funny speech; it is often indeed a complex, tortuous routine imposed on all but the high roller by a herd of reservation clerks, phone operators, pit bosses, waiters, maitre d's.)

The travel talk is often effective entertainment when it concentrates on such everyday occurrences. Another student gave a good speech about the difficulties of a college student trying to open a bank account in a new city, relating the humor of the routine questions asked by bank officials he met as he traveled through different areas of our country. Differences in food in sections of our nation as well as in different countries; problems of sleeping in a variety of beds as one travels; how to get your mail forwarded as you travel—many such routine experiences can be made into a funny speech by a creative mind.

But far too often speeches about traveling become a deadly bore because the speaker breaks one basic rule:

> ## Don't tell everything!

The audience need not know what time you left the hotel the first morning, where you stopped for lunch, what villages the tour passed through—unless there is a point of humor or interest in such details. Don't give the old, standard, tired speech about a trip that merely relates events in sequence. Don't tell us that "First thing the first morning we went to breakfast at . . . and we ate . . . and then we got on the bus . . . and rode to . . . where we stopped to visit the . . . ." STOP! Tell us, instead, something of significance, something tied together around a theme, an idea, a viewpoint. Yes, a speech to entertain should, like a speech to inform or a speech to persuade, have a central point, a concept, a position.

Roasts

Back in the 1970s, Dean Martin moved the roast from a private event at parties for comedians to a public event on television. Those shows featured about a dozen famous personalities who, for the evening, turned into put-down artists, heckling some selected star for about 55 minutes, including commercials. Then the recipient got about 5 minutes to heckle back at his or her tormentors.

The format soon moved from television into small-town civic clubs and big-city parties for corporate executives. "Everyone is doing a roast," one newspaper columnist claimed. Many roasts are fund-raising events. Besides, it's fun to kid the local mayor, the state budget director, the president of the widget company.

What may have been the ultimate roast was cooked up at a meeting of news writers in Washington, D.C. President Carter was the target. He was present. Following the tradition of a roast, after enduring all the gibes and jeers, he stood up and gave his own speech to entertain. He said, in part:

> ◆ Last year when I spoke to this distinguished group, I started my speech by smiling. For the life of me, I can't remember what I was smiling about. . . . I have gotten a great deal of advice from you [the press], some of which, unfortunately, I've taken. . . . Some Republicans have said that our foreign policy is a disaster. I just thought that as the administration changed, there ought to be some continuity. . . .

The point of all this detail about the roast as a speech to entertain is that such quotes should encourage any student of speech to speak up.

Theme Talks

Many successful comedians focus most, if not all, of their material on some specific theme. They may wander from their theme for a few jokes, occasionally get off into a totally different target, but soon they return to the focus of their jabs. Such comedians include Brett Butler, Ellen Cheyhorn, Jeff Foxworthy, Martin Lawrence, Eddie Murphy, Roseanne, Gary Sandler, Seinfeld.

If you try speeches to entertain, you'll find them more effective for most audiences if you, too, select a theme. At first thought it may seem easier to find or dream up a gang of gags on a variety of subjects. But in actual practice most comedians and their writers claim that one good joke usually sparks the mind to come up with another one on about the same subject. Think of all the times you've heard comedians say, "And that reminds me of the time that . . . ."

As in selecting a topic for a speech to inform or persuade, it is usually easier and more successful to stick to areas you already know something about. If you, as a college student, decide to try a humorous talk, try picking a theme you're already familiar with. Students have given good speeches—gotten good laughs—on such themes as:

The university library	Dealing with a car dealer
Picking a dorm	How to borrow money
Finding the right roommate	Joggers
Getting rid of the wrong roommate	Nonjoggers

If you seem to have some skill in entertaining, certainly do follow up on it—use it. If you don't feel you have such skill, you should nevertheless work at including at least a few smiles, if not laughs, in your speeches on serious subjects. Humor in serious talks can add much to their effectiveness, to the likelihood that you will attain your specific speech purpose. Therefore, one last criterion will now be added to your **Speech Evaluation Form** for extemporaneous speeches. (But not for your impromptu speeches; asking you to be funny on the spur of the moment is indeed asking a bit much. But then, the surprise of an impromptu joke is especially valuable.) The new criterion:

> *1.19. Uses Appropriate Humor*

On the next page is a **Check-off Tip Sheet** on entertaining, ready to guide you as you add at least a bit of humor to your speeches. You can also use the same tip sheet should you be motivated to try a full-blown speech to entertain.

So here's a slight shove, a nice nudge, a playful push to get you to work some humor into your speeches. You'll relish the reactions of your audiences—laughter when you hit, groans when you miss. Both of those reactions, heard by an alert speaker, can be mighty pleasant. Even slight smiles from just a few of your listeners can encourage you. Most important: Your use of humor can help get more of your listeners to remember more of what you say, and humor can get your listeners to remember what you say for days, weeks, maybe even months longer than they might otherwise. As Greek dramatist Sophocles advised:

> One must learn by doing the thing;
> for though you think you know it,
> you have no certainty until you try.

ENTERTAINING: CHECK-OFF TIP SHEET

1. PROBLEMS

_____ 1.1. Serious business

_____ 1.2. Stiff competition

_____ 1.3. Few opportunities to practice

_____ 1.4. Speaker's personality

2. TECHNIQUES

_____ 2.1. Use yourself.

_____ 2.2. Use other sources.

_____ 2.3. Change the peg.

_____ 2.4. Build bridges.

3. GUIDES

_____ 3.1. Be creative.

_____ 3.2. Let your audience know you expect them to laugh.

_____ 3.3. Deliver humor with confidence and pleasure.

_____ 3.4. Be yourself.

_____ 3.5. Don't put down your jokes or yourself.

_____ 3.6. Do laugh at your own jokes.

_____ 3.7. Be sure your humor relates to your speech subject.

_____ 3.8. Possibility of no laughs.

4. TYPES OF SPEECHES TO ENTERTAIN

_____ 4.1. After-dinner speeches.

_____ 4.2. Travel talks.

_____ 4.3. Roasts.

_____ 4.4. Theme talks.

Speaking Effectively

"It is but a poor eloquence which only shows that the orator can talk."

That was the claim of *Sir Joshua Reynolds*,
British portrait painter (1723–1792).

L E S S O N 17

Speaking Impromptu

OBJECTIVES After you've completed this lesson and participated in the in-class sessions, you will be able to:
1. Feel confident of your ability to give impromptu speeches—to think and then speak on your feet.
2. Present an effective impromptu speech. To be considered effective the speech should incorporate correctly 80 percent or more of the guides in this lesson.

RELEVANCE What Twain meant, of course, was that it takes of lot of thinking—knowledge, interest, and concern about a subject—in order to speak effectively about it on the spur of the moment. Most of that thinking is done long before you face the opportunity to speak. But you also need to develop skill in thinking quickly and productively when you're on

IMPROMPTU SPEAKING:

"It usually takes me more than three weeks to prepare a good impromptu speech."

Those are the words of *Mark Twain,* author, humorist, and frequent public speaker.

your feet giving a speech. This lesson will show you how and then give you some real-life (but in-class) situations in which to practice.

It seems clear that many people speak, then think. More, it often seems, speak without thinking at all—without thinking before, during, or after speaking. As we shall see, they are the verbal ramblers, digressors, "say-nothingers." In this lesson, our job is to help you make sure you are not one of them.

There are two significant values in developing your skills in thinking and then speaking on your feet. First, you'll be better able to present your ideas in class discussions, business meetings, professional conferences, planning sessions, and the various club, organizational, and governmental meetings in which you participate.

Equally important is the fact that training and practice in impromptu speaking is especially valuable in building your confidence in your abilities in all types of speaking situations. Once you see—as you will soon in this course—how effective you can be in speaking on the spur of the moment, then you should be much more assured of your abilities in speaking in more formal speaking situations. Practice in thinking and speaking on your feet will clearly, directly, improve your skill in speaking extemporaneously.

PROBLEMS OF IMPROMPTU SPEAKING

Many beginning speakers approach impromptu speaking with considerable fear. But for most speakers that old line applies—try it, you'll like it. Many students, once they've tasted the success of speaking on a subject on the spur of the moment, quickly come to enjoy, seek, volunteer for more opportunities to give impromptu speeches.

Beginning impromptu speakers also worry about being asked to speak on a subject about which they have little or no information. Often a student will ask something such as "Suppose I get a subject I really don't know anything about. A subject like . . . well, like how Congress works or problems of auto workers—some subject way out of my field. What do I do then?"

Then you don't speak.

But you're not likely to be asked to speak on such subjects, in class or in real-life situations. You're typically asked for your opinions, your ideas, your suggestions, not for specific facts. You're asked to speak on topics about which the instructor, the audience, the chair, or whoever calls on you believes you are informed. That means topics related to your job, your hobbies, your skills, your experiences.

Here is a list of *subjects* typically used in speech classes for impromptu speeches:

What are your views of multiculturalism?

What do you think about interracial adoption?

How might human rights be more effectively assured?

What are your views about working mothers?

How might the gender gap be narrowed?

How has the growing prominence of cable TV impacted your viewing?

What, if any, laws should we have concerning immigration?

Has the Internet changed your life? How?

How do you think problems in Bosnia can be solved?

How do you think problems in Zaire can be solved?

What do you think of TV ratings?

Should marijuana be legalized?

Should the Department of Education be eliminated?

What changes would you suggest concerning student loans?

What do you think about affirmative action?

How can college athletics be improved?

Has cultural shock affected you? How?

What changes, if any, would you suggest for global marketing?

What suggestions do you have for reengineering corporations?

Should euthanasia be legalized?

What has been your most creative act?

If you could have one other talent, what would it be?

Describe the best or worst car you've ever had.

Describe your ideal mate.

Would you like to be superfamous? Why, or why not?

Describe your favorite actor or actress.

What changes do you think this city needs?

What actions would you take if you were president of this college?

Summarize your views about protecting the rights of minorities.

Speaking on the spur of the moment, in class, on topics such as these, will help prepare you for the many impromptu speaking situations most of us face in real-life situations in business, industry, professions, and other fields. Another step in preparing for such speaking is to examine your present concerns about impromptu speaking. Take a moment to think about the following questions, and then jot down your thoughts.

What concerns you most about *giving* an impromptu speech?

_____

_____

_____

_____

What bothers you most about the impromptu speeches you have *heard*? Haven't heard any, you claim? Sure? Think again. Maybe you've heard what was supposed to be a prepared speech, but which came out like a spur-of-the moment presentation. For example, how about one of the college lecture courses—any seemingly impromptu speeches there? How about them? Anything bother you? What? Why?

_____

_____

_____

_____

Now let's look at some of the possible remedies for the concerns you expressed.

PREPARATION

Prepare for an impromptu speech? "I thought that was just what an impromptu speech wasn't—prepared!" many students interject.

True. But there are three steps you can take to remove at least some of the surprise, some of the lack of advance notice, from impromptu speaking.

1. Predict When You May Be Called Upon to Speak

This is one of the two best tips for impromptu speaking (the other is in the section on organization). The reason is obvious: If you predict, with accuracy, when you'll be asked for an impromptu speech, then you'll be able to do at least some preparing, thus taking the edge off the nature of the situation.

How can you predict when you'll be called upon? Consider some examples:

Last year you were a member, in another city, of a church youth group that received national attention for its innovative activities. Tonight you are to attend, in the small town you've moved to recently, a church meeting to plan the formation of a new program for the youth of this church—the first such activity by this congregation.

You've recently returned to college after several years of employment. To pick up some extra funds, you've just got a job for the Christmas season at a small, local department store. Before you came to this town, you worked for one of the nation's most famous chains of major department stores, where you rose from sales clerk to assistant floor manager. Tomorrow you're to attend the first of the series of training sessions for all sales staff at this store you're now with.

You're the mother of two high school students. You've taken a few courses at the local college "to keep up on things," "to see if I can still learn," or perhaps to get a degree. Tomorrow you are to attend a Parent-Teacher Association discussion on how parents can keep up educationally with their children.

Not predicting that you might be called upon for "a few words" in any of those situations seems to me to be foolhardy.

A student in the back of the class is thinking, "OK, so I've predicted I might be asked for an impromptu speech. Now what do I do? Prepare an entire speech?"

No, we certainly do not suggest you proceed to plan a full, detailed, structured, and outlined speech. But we do suggest you think through maybe two or three ideas you may have about each of those situations. THINK through your own viewpoints and also why you have those opinions—what facts, experiences, incidents, etc. led you to them.

Then stop.

You need not start to design a speech. But with your thoughts clearly in mind, you'll find that if—when—you are called upon to speak in an impromptu situation, you'll do a better job, and you'll be confident you can, too.

2. Keep up with Developments in Your Field

The serious student or diligent professional reads regularly both popular and professional publications in his or her field. For example, if your field is sociology, you'd likely keep up by reading the professional journal *Social Problems* or comparable magazines. For the speech major going into television, your choices would likely be the popular *TV Guide* and the business magazine, also a weekly, *Broadcasting*.

Attending seminars, training sessions, workshops, conventions, and such are other typical ways of keeping up with activities in your specialty.

Reading a daily newspaper and a weekly news magazine, viewing one or more daily newscasts, and catching a regular national and a local radio news program are all obvious ways to help keep up to date in your world.

You can take such preparation, such keeping up to date, a bit further should you be facing a situation in which you might be called upon for an impromptu speech. You could take a bit of time for extra cramming on progress, innovations, policies, and procedures new to your field when you think a speech might be asked of you.

3. Have a Few Good Stories and Remarks Ready

You probably know individuals who always seem to have a quick, appropriate response ready for almost any situation. Some people just seem to soak up and remember and unlimited supply of jokes, strange statistics, unusual experiences. But others—often very successful people—collect these kinds of retorts systematically or at least intentionally. These people think ahead, plan ahead, to have stories and remarks ready. If, for example, you're going to a meeting about parking problems, looking up a specific local fact or two ahead of time is, to many successful people, simply good, intelligent preparation.

GUIDES

The following practical and specific tips on impromptu speeches are presented in the three areas you've been working on for your other speeches—content, organization, and delivery.

1. Content

The content of your impromptu speech should follow in general the guides you have learned to use in the extemporaneous speeches you've presented in this course. But the impromptu speech has the added pressure of giving you but a brief time in which to decide what you are going to say. That's true for an impromptu speech given for practice during in-class sessions or for one in real-life situations on your job, in your organizational activities, or such. Therefore, it is more practical to *concentrate on a few key points* to select what you want to say when you're called upon to give an impromptu speech. Here's how.

1.1. Present a Definite Viewpoint Early in Your Speech

As for all speeches, your first words should present an attention-getter. But after that it is especially important in an impromptu speech to state a firm, clear, specific viewpoint. You might say, for example:

- The chair's recommendation should be approved. [Then state your reasons, supporting each with specifics.]
- I just can't agree with the motion to reduce the services of this department. [Then tell why you have that view, supporting your reasons with details.]
- We're overlooking one key point in all this discussion: How will this new activity be paid for? [Then present your suggestions.]

Remember that in almost all situations in which you're called upon for an impromptu speech, you are expected to express your *viewpoint.* Very rarely indeed would you be expected to present a speech to inform about, for example, the historical development of a problem. By stating a definite viewpoint early in your speech, you'll help your listeners understand and accept your ideas. Stating your viewpoint in specific terms will also help you, as the speaker, present a more direct, structured speech. As you think on your feet, your mind will tend to tell you, *Well, now that you've told them your viewpoint, you'd better tell them WHY you think that.* Then it's time for you to:

1.2. Support Your Viewpoint with Reasons and Logic

After stating your viewpoint, give your reasons and the logic that led you to that viewpoint. If you're speaking against a proposal to increase a road from two to four lanes, one of your reasons might be the probability that traffic will not be eased, but may well be further increased. Your logic supporting that reason might be that the wider road will take traffic away from other routes many drivers now use to get to the next town, for example.

That reason and that logic are in contrast with, for example, the many speakers who merely state something such as "I'm against the widening of the road because I don't like it. I think it won't help. I think it's just not a good idea." Such speakers should state, instead of—or in addition to—those vague points, *why* they "don't like it," *why* "it won't help," *why* "it's just not a good idea."

In sum: Back up your viewpoint with reasons and logic that are explicit.

1.3. *Present at Least Some Specific Data*

In an impromptu speech your audience does not expect you to come up with a big supply of detailed data. But you should present some basis, some justification—at least a few statistics, examples, quotations, etc. The suggestions for using data presented in Lesson 7 apply to an impromptu speech just as well as to any other type of speech.

Indeed, specific data often can be especially effective in impromptu speeches, sometimes even more effective than in other speaking situations. The reason: In impromptu speaking you're often talking to a group considering some action—about to vote for a plan, change a previous decision, or such. In such situations, very few of the other speakers who rise to give impromptu statements of their viewpoints ever present data to support their viewpoints. Thus, if you can offer data—even limited data—your speech may well have considerable impact on the audience and on their decision.

To continue our previous example—about the widening of the road—data you might present include your experiences in driving on a road that was widened in another city and quickly became such a popular route that traffic was increased beyond expectations. Further, while you were in that previous city, you may have heard a statement by some traffic expert that might be worth quoting now. Or perhaps you recall some statistics about traffic increase on that other road.

But remember again that the typical impromptu speaking situation usually seeks only your views, opinions, suggestions, and recommendations; rarely, and then usually when you are a recognized authority or highly experienced, does an audience expect a fully documented, informational presentation. So just a few facts can do much in an impromptu speech to make your presentation truly impressive.

1.4. *Tie in with What Has Been Said or Possibly Will Be Said*

Relate your remarks to those of whoever called on you or introduced you. Try also to link your speech to any speeches or comments that may have been presented before yours.

How? Refer to specific points, ideas, and positions expressed by speakers who made statements before yours.

You might also be able to project what some speakers might say after your speech. If, for example, the topic is police attitudes, and you or a previous speaker were rather harsh in criticizing some attitudes of the police, you can expect strong rebuttals if policemen are to speak later. You may be able to help the group reach consensus, help to solve the problem and get corrective action initiated, by pointing to areas where both views are in agreement—the need for exchanging ideas, the need for each side to know the problems of the other better, and such.

1.5. *Don't Apologize*

Many speakers begin an impromptu speech, and many of their other speeches, too, with words such as:

- ◗ Well, I really didn't expect to be called on to speak today.
- ◗ I'm sorry, I'm really not prepared with a speech on this subject today.
- ◗ I don't know what to say—I really didn't . . . .

The audience is not expecting a deeply moving, highly polished, or joyously funny speech. The situation indicates that it is an impromptu speech, nothing more. An apology is a waste of time, nonproductive. So, get to the point of what you are to say.

If, indeed, you have nothing to add to what the audience has already heard, still no apology is needed. A simple statement of that fact is sufficient, such as:

- ◗ I have no additional information.
- ◗ The other speakers have expressed my view.
- ◗ I haven't made up my mind on this as yet.

1.6. Don't Express Surprise

Few are the speaking situations in which it should be a total surprise to you that you are called upon. The general direction of the previous talks, the reactions of the audience, the remarks of the moderator or chairman—one or all of these indicate that you might well be called upon.

Even in the exceptionally rare case that it is a surprise to be asked to speak, stating so adds little and can often detract from your image and your effectiveness in this or possible future communication situations.

Thus, be alert; don't let a speaking situation be a surprise to you. In any event there's nothing to be gained by letting your audience know you are surprised. Again, get on with the content, the point, the idea you are to express.

1.7. Don't Ramble on About the Subject

Impromptu ramblers are as ineffective as prepared ramblers. For example:

I don't really have anything to say about that. The idea doesn't sound too good to me, so I'm against it. I guess, of course, it could work, could be all right, only I don't think so. It doesn't really seem like a good idea to me. So—as I said—I'm against it. I don't know what else to say, but . . . .

What's been expressed? "I'm against it." But the speaker wandered, backtracked, repeated, dulled both the point and the listeners.

Actually, such speakers are often just thinking aloud. They're kicking the idea around aloud, instead of pausing to think before speaking. Result: boring, nonproductive noncommunication.

1.8. Don't Get off the Subject

An example makes this point clear.

- ◗ So about your proposed plan, I'm not really sure if we can afford it or not. I have been treasurer for plans like this in the past. I remember especially that one last winter, up in the snow country. With all that snow and the extra time it took to finish up, we had quite a problem. Lots of problems, actually. For example, we didn't have enough trucks. In fact, there was this one truck—well, let me tell you about it! That truck went and . . . .

Another speaker simply thinking aloud. He feels he has to say something. But he has nothing to say about the subject asked of him—costs. So he lets his vocal cords carry his thinking and by moving the subject through his mind he covers several related subjects—his being treasurer, snow country, problems, trucks—and finally finds something—trucks—he can speak on. Only problem is, that wasn't what he was asked to stand up and speak on. THINK, *then* speak. Don't think aloud.

2. Organization

An impromptu speech, just as your extemporaneous and other types of speeches, should be organized, have structure. Of course, because of the more informal nature of the speaking situation, you are not expected to come forth with a carefully designed, well-packaged oration. But there are some techniques you can use to help present your ideas, even on the spur of the moment, in a clear, logical, organized expression.

2.1. The Brief Key

No matter what the subject might be for your impromptu speech, three words can help you get your thoughts, and consequently what you're going to say, organized. They, we most strongly urge, should be filed away in your mind under the category of "Speech: Impromptu: Always Remember." Those words are:

> **Past**
> **Present**
> **Future**

Caution: These words do not represent the only way to organize an impromptu speech. There are, of course, other ways. (For other organizational patterns, see the lesson on organizing the discussion part of your speech.) But they will serve as an easy-to-remember and quick-to-apply formula for structuring a speech on any subject.

Their application should be apparent:

1. PAST: After a brief attention-getter and a statement of your subject or viewpoint, begin your speech with a brief consideration of past events related to your subject.
2. PRESENT: State the present condition of your subject, how things are at the moment.
3. FUTURE: Present the possibilities for the coming days, weeks, months, or years regarding your subject.

Again, this is not the only way to organize an impromptu speech; for some topics, in some situations, it may well not be the best. But it is one fast, easy, memorable key to organizing a speech when you have to do it quickly.

So imprint the following design in your mind, ready for instant recall when you're called upon for an impromptu speech.

> **BRIEF KEY TO IMPROMPTU SPEECH**
>
> **PAST**
> **PRESENT**
> **FUTURE**

2.2. The Basic Format

Our old reliable, that structure you learned at the beginning of this course, the basic format for a speech, should be used for your impromptu speeches, just as for all your other speeches. Just for the record and perhaps to jog your memory a bit, here it is again:

    I.   INTRODUCTION
        A. Attention-getter
        B. Preview

   II.   DISCUSSION
        A. Main points
        B. Arrange logically
        C. Support with data

  III.   CONCLUSION
        A. Review
        B. Memorable statement

3. Delivery

The situations in which most impromptu speeches are presented usually do not give the speaker much opportunity to think about delivery techniques. Further, by this stage of your progress in this course, most of your skills in delivery are probably established as almost automatic. By now you may not have to keep reminding yourself of little things like "stand up straight" or "speak loud enough to be heard" and such. Still, some of those 33 techniques for effective delivery are a bit more important in impromptu speaking. We'll list them below, but first, there are three special techniques particularly important for impromptu speaking.

3.1. Accept the Invitation with Assurance

Your audience will believe you are every bit as confident as you let them think you are. If you try to beg off from speaking, hesitate with little grace, stall for time beyond a respectable period to think about what you want to say, your audience will become impatient and start to doubt your value as a speaker.

Try to remember back to speakers you have heard giving impromptu speeches. If none come to mind, think about college teachers who had to come up with rather elaborate explanations in response to students' questions. Their answers were impromptu speeches. The teachers have the information; they can organize it to present it as some kind of clear, logical response to a question. But they do not know in advance that they will be called upon to present that information. The result: an impromptu speech.

Consider what your reaction would be to the teacher who tries to beg off from answering questions, saying something such as "I really didn't expect to have to answer that today. Let me think about it, and I'll get an answer for you at the next class meeting." True, sometimes such a reply is justified, for example, when detailed facts are requested. Still, consider how much more authoritative the speaker appears when he or she accepts that question—that invitation to speak—with assurance and promptly proceeds to reply.

3.2. Take Your Time

When you are called upon, do not let the first words that come to mind rush out your mouth. Take a moment to consider *what* you are going to say and *how* you are going to say it.

Remember that your audience recognizes that you are speaking impromptu. They are interested in hearing valid, thoughtful, and helpful comments. *Think,* then speak, rather than doing your thinking aloud.

3.3. Sit Down When You Are Finished!

We've said it before—STOP when you are finished. Blunt and obvious, but a tip far too often overlooked by many speakers with little or nothing to say.

Don't continue to stand up there before the audience, hemming and hawing and seeking ideas by muttering words that contribute little that is specific or valuable.

Not sure of your view? Little to back it up? Don't wish to make a statement?

Then sit.

Promptly.

Those 3 delivery techniques are especially important for impromptu speeches. Here are 11 more techniques, which you have been using, that are particularly helpful in giving impromptu speeches.

1. Step up to speak with confidence.
2. Maintain contact with your audience.
3. Avoid *ah, so, ya know, well, 'kay,* etc.
4. Stop at the end of an idea; don't hook sentences together with *and, and uh,* etc.
5. Maintain good posture; don't lean on the lectern, cross your legs, etc.
6. Speak loudly enough to be heard easily.
7. Gesture effectively.
8. Appear to enjoy speaking.
9. Speak with enthusiasm.
10. Appear confident and relaxed.
11. Hide your goofs.

Review

There, then, are practical, specific tips on giving an impromptu speech. The two best tips—remember them?

1. The first "best tip" is:_____

2. The second "best tip" is:

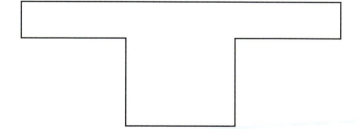

To check your answers, look back through this lesson.

Now let's see how well you can apply these and the rest of the suggestions.

ASSIGNMENTS 20 & 21: IMPROMPTU SPEECHES—SPEECHES 6 & 7

 ACTION: Deliver two brief Impromptu speeches.

OBJECTIVE:

After presenting the following impromptu speeches, you should be more skilled and confident in thinking/speaking on your feet effectively. To be effective these speeches should use correctly at least 80 percent of the 30 techniques presented in this lesson, as listed on the following evaluation forms.

INSTRUCTIONS:

1. Your instructor may have a set of topics for impromptu speeches that he or she would like you to use. You'll receive instructions on how these speech subjects are to be selected or assigned and the procedures for giving these speeches in class. Or:

2. At one of the meetings of your speech course about midsemester, each member of the class may be asked to write out four topics suitable for impromptu speeches. It is suggested that the topics be one in each of the following general fields:

    (1) A national or international topic

    Examples: Should the United States help any foreign country hit by a natural disaster, such as a flood or earthquake?

    Flying saucers—do you think they are fact or fiction?

    Should the federal government control advertising?

    (2) A local or state problem or subject

    Examples: Should California be divided into two states? (And no smart replies, like "Yes, Nebraska and Virginia!")

    How can instruction be improved at your college?

    Should cars be outlawed in resort areas?

    (3) A personal subject

    Examples: Has Christmas lost its meaning for you? Why?

    How should a man pick a wife? A woman pick a husband?

    What have you done—or hope to do—for mankind?

    (4) Wild card (creative, unusual subjects)

    Examples: If you had to pick two living people with whom to spend one year on an island in the South Seas, who would they be? Why?

    If you had one hour with the president of the United States, what would you tell him?

    If you had unlimited resources and only one week to live, what would you do?

3. One day in class you'll be given slips of paper on which to write your suggested topics.

4. These will be collected after you have a few minutes to jot down your suggested topics. They will be put in an envelope, and each student will get to draw two topics.

5. The topic you do *not* want to speak on is to be returned to the envelope. While you may not like that subject, another student may find it ideal.

6. The first student to draw will have 3 to 4 minutes to think through his or her speech. Then the second speaker will draw a topic from the envelope just as the first speaker begins to speak. Thus each speaker will have preparation time for as

long as the preceding speaker is talking and the time for class evaluation of the previous speech.

7. Use the **Evaluation Forms** that appear at the end of this lesson.

REFRESHER:

The main points, again, of an effective impromptu speech:

1. Start with an attention-getter.
2. State a specific subject or point of view.
3. Present reasons, logic, and data.
4. Use some type of speech structure. The structure could be, but not necessarily:

BRIEF KEY TO IMPROMPTU SPEECH

PAST
PRESENT
FUTURE

5. Conclude with a restatement of viewpoint.
6. Close with a memorable statement.
7. Do not apologize, ramble, or get off the subject.
8. Use the good delivery techniques of sincerity, fluency, posture, gestures, clarity and correctness of speech, and audience contact that you've been applying to your speeches.

IMPROMPTU SPEECH 1 (SPEECH 6): EVALUATION FORM

Speaker: _____ Date: _____

Topic:_____

1. CONTENT

_____ 1.1. Presents definite viewpoint early in speech

_____ 1.2. Supports view with reasons and logic

_____ 1.3. Presents specific data

_____ 1.4. Ties in with other speeches

_____ 1.5. Doesn't apologize

_____ 1.6. Doesn't express surprise

_____ 1.7. Doesn't ramble

_____ 1.8. Doesn't get off subject

2. ORGANIZATION

_____ 2.1. Begins with effective attention-getter

_____ 2.2. Previews subject or viewpoint specifically, clearly

_____ 2.3. Presents 2 to 5 specific points

_____ 2.4. Arranges discussion points in logical order

_____ 2.5. Supports each discussion point with data

_____ 2.6. Reviews subject, viewpoint, or discussion points

_____ 2.7. Concludes with memorable statement

_____ 2.8. Uses structure of speech, not of old-style class report or article

3. DELIVERY

_____ 3.1. Accepts invitation with assurance

_____ 3.2   Takes time to organize thoughts

_____ 3.3. Steps up to speak with confidence

_____ 3.4. Maintains contact

_____ 3.5. Avoids *ah, so, ya know, well, 'kay*, etc.

_____ 3.6. Stops at end of idea; doesn't hook sentences together with *and, and ah*, etc.

_____ 3.7. Maintains good posture

_____ 3.8. Speaks loudly enough to be heard easily

_____ 3.9. Gestures effectively

_____ 3.10. Appears to enjoy speaking

_____ 3.11. Speaks with enthusiasm

_____ 3.12. Appears confident, relaxed

_____ 3.13. Hides goofs

_____ 3.14. Sits down when finished

Over for comments

4. COMMENTS:

Grade: _____

IMPROMPTU SPEECH 2 (SPEECH 7): EVALUATION FORM

Speaker: _____ Date: _____

Topic:_____

1. CONTENT

_____ 1.1. Presents definite viewpoint early in speech

_____ 1.2. Supports view with reasons and logic

_____ 1.3. Presents specific data

_____ 1.4. Ties in with other speeches

_____ 1.5. Doesn't apologize

_____ 1.6. Doesn't express surprise

_____ 1.7. Doesn't ramble

_____ 1.8. Doesn't get off subject

2. ORGANIZATION

_____ 2.1. Begins with effective attention-getter

_____ 2.2. Previews subject or viewpoint specifically, clearly

_____ 2.3. Presents 2 to 5 specific points

_____ 2.4. Arranges discussion points in logical order

_____ 2.5. Supports each discussion point with data

_____ 2.6. Reviews subject, viewpoint, or discussion points

_____ 2.7. Concludes with memorable statement

_____ 2.8. Uses structure of speech, not of old-style class report or article

3. DELIVERY

_____ 3.1. Accepts invitation with assurance

_____ 3.2   Takes time to organize thoughts

_____ 3.3. Steps up to speak with confidence

_____ 3.4. Maintains contact

_____ 3.5. Avoids *ah, so, ya know, well, 'kay*, etc.

_____ 3.6. Stops at end of idea; doesn't hook sentences together with *and, and ah*, etc.

_____ 3.7. Maintains good posture

_____ 3.8. Speaks loudly enough to be heard easily

_____ 3.9. Gestures effectively

_____ 3.10. Appears to enjoy speaking

_____ 3.11. Speaks with enthusiasm

_____ 3.12. Appears confident, relaxed

_____ 3.13. Hides goofs

_____ 3.14. Sits down when finished

Over for comments

4. COMMENTS:

Grade: _____

SPEAKING IMPROMPTU: CHECK-OFF TIP SHEET

PREPARING:

_____ 1. Predict when you may be called upon to speak.

_____ 2. Keep up with developments in your field.

_____ 3. Have a few good stories and remarks ready.

GUIDES:

1. Content:

_____ 1.1. Present a definite viewpoint early in your speech.

_____ 1.2. Support your viewpoint with reasons and logic.

_____ 1.3. Present at least some specific data.

_____ 1.4. Tie in with what has been said or possibly will be said.

_____ 1.5. Don't apologize.

_____ 1.6. Don't express surprise.

_____ 1.7. Don't ramble on about the subject.

_____ 1.8. Don't get off the subject.

2. Organization:

_____ 2.1. Use *The Brief key:*

_____ 2.1.1. Past

_____ 2.1.2. Present

_____ 2.1.3. Future

_____ 2.2. Use *The Basic Format:*

_____ I. Introduction

_____ A. Attention-getter

_____ B. Preview

_____ II. Discussion

_____ A. Main points

_____ B. Arrange logically

_____ C. Support with data

_____ III. Conclusion

_____ A. Review

_____ B. Memorable statement

3. Delivery:

_____ 3.1. Accept the invitation with assurance.

_____ 3.2. Take your time.

_____ 3.3. Sit down when you are finished!

Concionative—that's what you're studying in this class.

That means "pertaining to public speaking or preaching," according to the humorous yet authoritative reference book ***Mrs. Byrne's Dictionary of Unusual, Obscure, and Preposterous Words,*** compiled by *Josefa Heifetz* (Mrs. Byrne).

LESSON 18

"And So, In Conclusion . . ."

OBJECTIVES

After completing this lesson, you will have achieved the objective of this course—you will be able to design and deliver effective speeches.

We have established that:

1. An effective speech is one that achieves its specific purpose with a particular audience.
2. A speech is effective when it:
   2.1. Presents points and data that are new, relevant, varied, and significant to the audience.

Tom Brokaw, anchor of the **NBC Nightly News,** on the anniversary of his 30 years with NBC, summed up the basis of his success as a speaker: "The key is preparation."

2.2. Is organized clearly and logically.

2.3. Is delivered with appropriate style, enthusiasm, and sincerity.

3. This course presents 68 criteria on which a speech can be evaluated, listed on the **Speech Evaluation Form.**

4. The criteria cover three general features of a speech:

4.1. Content

4.2. Organization

4.3. Delivery

5. To be evaluated as effective, a speech would use correctly—according to the concepts and techniques presented in this course—at least 80 percent of the criteria.

RELEVANCE ▶

The fable is told of the student who asked, "Teacher, you have indeed given us a great many fine suggestions on how to give a speech. But what is the *one best* recommendation?"

The teacher looked the student straight in the eye and said only one word: "Practice."

"Ahhh," said the student, "that is indeed wise. But after practice, then what is the next most valuable step to becoming a good speaker?"

"Practice!" said the teacher, with added fervor.

"Yes, yes, I understand what you'e saying. Practice and more practice, if you are to be a good speaker. But *after* that, after practice—then what?"

And the speech teacher replied, with the golden voice of all great speakers and with the deep sincerity of all great teachers, "After you've practiced, my child, and practiced again as I have said, there is but one thing left to do to become an effective speaker." And the teacher paused.

The student eagerly pressed on, "Yes, yes—and what is that?"

"Practice," said the teacher.

If you want to research the source of that story, it should be found in the fables of the ancients, with the student robed in toga and sandals. It ought to turn up again, I do believe, in the literature of the Middle Ages, with the student attired in pointed shoes and ruffled shirt. And I myself have been the student in that story, as well as the teacher.

Down through the ages, *practice* has been indeed the one most direct, sure, productive road to success as a speaker. Practice of speech goes back at least as far as the Greek orator Demosthenes, who strengthened his harsh and weak voice by filling his mouth with pebbles and shouting to make himself understandable over the roar of the waves as he strolled on his island beaches in 350 B.C.

Today speakers use elaborate, ingenious, revealing video and audiotape recordings. There are New York and Hollywood companies that specialize in recording airchecks for television personalities and making on-the-spot tapings of speakers in auditoriums, stadiums, churches, and such. Many reporters, commentators, and talk show hosts, as well as trial lawyers, government officials, politicians, executives, lecturers, mediators, board directors, union leaders, evangelists, salespersons, and others subscribe to recording services, Tapes of their speeches are delivered as routinely as the morning paper.

They do study the tapes and they do practice.

Practice is what you, too, now need.

And what you need is what you get.

Depending on what your instructor assigns, you may have just three speeches remaining to complete this course. First, two out-of-class speeches will give you some of the most valuable practice in the course—trying your skills on audiences other than your speech class. Then you will have the final exam speech.

Let's get to them.

ASSIGNMENTS 22 & 23: OUT-OF-CLASS SPEECHES—SPEECHES 8 & 9

 ACTION: Give the following two speeches.

OBJECTIVES:
Delivering these speeches will provide you with experiences to:

1. Identify what additional or different problems you encounter when speaking to an audience not as familiar to you or with you as your regular audience of fellow speech students.
2. Decide how to solve those problems, applying the concepts and techniques presented in this course.
3. Receive additional evaluations of your strengths and weaknesses as a speaker.
4. Practice your skills in public speaking in real-life speaking situations.

ASSIGNMENT:
Deliver two different extemporaneous speeches to any two different audiences other than your public speaking class.

INSTRUCTIONS:

1. *Audiences* may be another college class, a civic organization, government agency, church group, youth club, or such. One of the two audiences may be your family—if you'd be comfortable with them. Many students speak to classes at nearby elementary, junior, or high schools. These audiences and teachers are often especially receptive. Many speech students make arrangements for these speeches with teachers they had when they were in those earlier grades. Some students select classes in which their own children or their younger sisters or brothers or other relatives are enrolled.
2. *Subjects* can be whatever you believe would be appropriate and interesting to the audience you select. Remember the principles of selecting a subject based on an analysis of your audience, as you studied in Lesson 5.
3. The *length* of each speech should be at least 5 minutes, preferably 10 or more minutes.
4. *Arrangements* for the speeches are to be made by you.
5. *Outlines* for the speeches should be turned in to your speech instructor at least one week before you speak. That will allow time for your instructor to offer suggestions for improvement and for you to take action on those suggestions. You are urged to deliver your out-of-class speeches only after your outlines have been evaluated as effective.
6. *After each speech* turn in the following material in a 9 × 12-inch envelope on which you have written your name and class hour:
   (1) An **Out-of-Class Speech Assignment Completion Form** (copies on the following pages). Fill in the information on just the top few lines. Your speech instructor will use the rest of the form to check your material and offer comments. This form should be placed as the first item in this packet of materials.
   (2) Your previously approved speech outline.
   (3) Your corrected version of the outline.
   (4) The note card(s) you used.

(5) **Speech Comment Forms** (copies on following pages) filled out by three members of your audience, including the leader of the group to which you spoke (teacher, president, chairman, etc.).

(6) A statement written by you of some 200 words on:
  [1] Additional or different problems you faced in speaking with this out-of-class audience.
  [2] How you solved these problems.
   Your statement should include specific examples, incidents, feelings, etc. The problems you present should be concerned with designing and delivering your speech, not details of arrangements, schedules, transportation.

7. This assignment must be submitted at least one week before you give your final speech so that your instructor can evaluate your work and return it to you in time to be of value to you as you prepare your final speech.

OUT-OF-CLASS SPEECH 1: ASSIGNMENT COMPLETION FORM

INSTRUCTIONS: Fill in the information above the dashed line.

Speaker: _____ Date: _____

Audience: _____ Number in audience: _____

Location: _____

With whom might your speech instructor check on details of the speech (president, chairman, teacher, etc.)?

Name: _____ Phone: _____

Position: _____

- -

To be completed by speech instructor:

The following material has been turned in:

    1. Previously approved outline: _____

    2. Corrected outline: _____

    3. Note card(s) used: _____

    4. Speech Comment Forms (3): _____

    5. Student statement of problems and solutions: _____

Comments:

Grade: _____

Continue comments on other side

OUT-OF-CLASS SPEECH 1: COMMENT FORM 1

INSTRUCTIONS: To be filled out by a member of the audience.

This student speaker is seriously interested in receiving specific suggestions to help improve her/his speaking. Please be honest, specific, and fair. Your comments will not influence his/her grade in the speech course other than to receive credit for this assignment.

Speaker: _____ Audience: _____

Rated by: _____ Rater's position: _____
(student, teacher, chairman, etc.)

Date of speech: _____ Subject: _____

1. What were the speaker's best qualities?

2. What qualities might the speaker improve on?

3. Would you recommend to your friends that they should have heard this speech? Why or why not?

4. Comments:

Continue comments on other side

OUT-OF-CLASS SPEECH 1: COMMENT FORM 2

INSTRUCTIONS: To be filled out by a member of the audience.

This student speaker is seriously interested in receiving specific suggestions to help improve her/his speaking. Please be honest, specific, and fair. Your comments will not influence his/her grade in the speech course other than to receive credit for this assignment.

Speaker: _____ Audience: _____

Rated by: _____ Rater's position: _____
                                (student, teacher, chairman, etc.)

Date of speech: _____ Subject: _____

1. What were the speaker's best qualities?

2. What qualities might the speaker improve on?

3. Would you recommend to your friends that they should have heard this speech? Why or why not?

4. Comments:

Continue comments on other side

OUT-OF-CLASS SPEECH 1: COMMENT FORM 3

INSTRUCTIONS: To be filled out by a member of the audience.

This student speaker is seriously interested in receiving specific suggestions to help improve her/his speaking. Please be honest, specific, and fair. Your comments will not influence his/her grade in the speech course other than to receive credit for this assignment.

Speaker: _____ Audience:_____

Rated by: _____ Rater's position: _____
(student, teacher, chairman, etc.)

Date of speech: _____ Subject: _____

1. What were the speaker's best qualities?

2. What qualities might the speaker improve on?

3. Would you recommend to your friends that they should have heard this speech? Why or why not?

4. Comments:

Continue comments on other side

OUT-OF-CLASS SPEECH 2: ASSIGNMENT COMPLETION FORM

INSTRUCTIONS: Fill in the information above the dashed line.

Speaker: _____ Date: _____

Audience: _____ Number in audience: _____

Location: _____

With whom might your speech instructor check on details of the speech (president, chairman, teacher, etc.)?

Name: _____ Phone: _____

Position: _____

- -

To be completed by speech instructor:

The following material has been turned in:

1. Previously approved outline: _____

2. Corrected outline: _____

3. Note card(s) used: _____

4. Speech Comment Forms (3): _____

5. Student statement of problems and solutions: _____

Comments:

Grade: _____

Continue comments on other side

OUT-OF-CLASS SPEECH 2: COMMENT FORM 1

INSTRUCTIONS: To be filled out by a member of the audience.

This student speaker is seriously interested in receiving specific suggestions to help improve her/his speaking. Please be honest, specific, and fair. Your comments will not influence his/her grade in the speech course other than to receive credit for this assignment.

Speaker: _____   Audience: _____

Rated by: _____   Rater's position: _____
                        (student, teacher, chairman, etc.)

Date of speech: _____   Subject: _____

1. What were the speaker's best qualities?

2. What qualities might the speaker improve on?

3. Would you recommend to your friends that they should have heard this speech? Why or why not?

4. Comments:

Continue comments on other side

OUT-OF-CLASS SPEECH 2: COMMENT FORM 2

INSTRUCTIONS: To be filled out by a member of the audience.

This student speaker is seriously interested in receiving specific suggestions to help improve her/his speaking. Please be honest, specific, and fair. Your comments will not influence his/her grade in the speech course other than to receive credit for this assignment.

Speaker: _____ Audience: _____

Rated by: _____ Rater's position: _____

(student, teacher, chairman, etc.)

Date of speech: _____ Subject: _____

1. What were the speaker's best qualities?

2. What qualities might the speaker improve on?

3. Would you recommend to your friends that they should have heard this speech? Why or why not?

4. Comments:

Continue comments on other side

OUT-OF-CLASS SPEECH 2: COMMENT FORM 3

INSTRUCTIONS: To be filled out by a member of the audience.

This student speaker is seriously interested in receiving specific suggestions to help improve her/his speaking. Please be honest, specific, and fair. Your comments will not influence his/her grade in the speech course other than to receive credit for this assignment.

Speaker: _____ Audience: _____

Rated by: _____ Rater's position: _____
(student, teacher, chairman, etc.)

Date of speech: _____ Subject: _____

1. What were the speaker's best qualities?

2. What qualities might the speaker improve on?

3. Would you recommend to your friends that they should have heard this speech? Why or why not?

4. Comments:

Continue comments on other side

ASSIGNMENT 24: OUTLINE OF FINAL SPEECH—PROPOSING A CHANGE

🛈 **ACTION:** Submit an outline for your final speech.

OBJECTIVE:

This assignment will provide you with an opportunity to demonstrate your ability to prepare an outline that is useful and technically correct. To be considered useful and technically correct, your outline is to incorporate 80 percent or more of the guides for the three aspects of outlining—content, organization, and mechanics—as listed in Lesson 8 on outlining.

INSTRUCTIONS:

1. Submit this outline at least one week before you are scheduled to speak to allow time for:
    (1) Your instructor to evaluate and comment on your outline and proposed final speech.
    (2) You to act on your instructor's suggestions to improve your final speech.
2. Include, along with your outline:
    (1) Title of the speech
    (2) Audience for whom the speech is designed
    (3) Purpose of the speech
    (4) Outline of the speech
    (5) Bibliography of five or more sources, stated in standard reference form
        A bibliography is required to help ensure that your speech includes a variety of data and that it is based on a variety of sources in addition to your own background and knowledge. *At least two bits of data from each reference in your bibliography should be included in your outline.*

ASSIGNMENT 25: PROPOSING A CHANGE: FINAL SPEECH—SPEECH 10.

 ACTION: Present a speech appropriate for one of the situations detailed below.

OBJECTIVE:

This final speech will provide you with an opportunity to demonstrate the height of your achievement in developing your skills of public speaking.

Evaluation will be based on incorporating correctly, according to the concepts and techniques presented in this course, 80 percent or more of the criteria listed on the **Speech Evaluation Form** for the content, organization, and delivery of a speech.

ASSIGNMENT:

Deliver in your speech class an 8-to 10-minute extemporaneous speech on a *subject* appropriate for one of the following situations. In all the situations the subject involves a proposal of a change.

1. You have been asked to be on the agenda of a regular meeting of your college board of trustees, city council, county administration, or a similar official body to present your views about the enactment, repeal, or modification of a specific law or ruling on which they have authority.

2. You have been selected by an organization to which you belong to speak to a group of high school seniors who are about to vote in their first election, a county political committee, a state caucus, or a comparable group to get them to vote for your candidate or to vote your view on a specific issue.

3. You have been invited to speak before a meeting of specialists in your chosen occupation—perhaps college majors or executives in your field—to suggest changes in entrance or preparation requirements, recruitment or employment practices, or a similar subject.

4. You have been elected by your college to speak at a state or national meeting of college student leaders to recommend changes in how college courses are organized, taught, graded, etc.

5. You have been invited by a local service club, church, or community group to speak with them so they might understand and accept differences between their generation and yours.

6. You are to speak to a local group of businessmen, such as the Rotary, Kiwanis, or Lions, to present your ideas on the needs of your community and what these men should do about them.

INSTRUCTIONS:

1. You don't really need detailed instructions at this stage of your progress as a public speaker, do you? But if you have some lingering questions, please do schedule a conference with your instructor.

2. This speech will be evaluated by three of your classmates, as well as your instructor. Additional **Evaluation Forms** for your classmates to use appear in the next few pages.

FINAL SPEECH, PROPOSING A CHANGE: INSTRUCTOR'S EVALUATION FORM

Speaker: _____ Audience: _____ Date: _____

Speech purpose: _____

_____

1. CONTENT

_____ 1.1. Based on accurate analysis of speaking situation

_____ 1.2. Purpose worded correctly: from audience's viewpoint, specific, and attainable

_____ 1.3   Subject appropriate, relevant, and interesting to audience

_____ 1.4. Points, data new, significant

_____ 1.5. Includes personal and human interest stories

_____ 1.6. All material contributes to purpose

_____ 1.7. Gets to point quickly

_____ 1.8. Presents own, original ideas, structure, or interpretation

_____ 1.9. Uses audiovisual aids when appropriate

_____ 1.10. Emphasizes organization enough to help audience remember points

_____ 1.11. Includes variety of data

_____ 1.12. Data seem accurate, honest

_____ 1.13. Points valid conclusions from data

_____ 1.14. Includes examples to clarify, add interest, etc., not to prove points

_____ 1.15. Points parallel and equal

_____ 1.16. Uses smooth transitions

_____ 1.17. Includes one or more balanced lines or quotable original statement

_____ 1.18. Uses specific appeals when appropriate

_____ 1.19. Uses appropriate humor

2. ORGANIZATION

_____ 2.1. Begins with effective attention-getter

_____ 2.2. Previews subject or viewpoint

_____ 2.3. Presents 2 to 5 specific points

_____ 2.4. Arranges discussion points logically

_____ 2.5. Supports each point with data:

    _____ 2.5.1. Example

    _____ 2.5.2. Story

    _____ 2.5.3. Quotation

    _____ 2.5.4. Definition

    _____ 2.5.5. Comparison

    _____ 2.5.6. Contrast

    _____ 2.5.7. Statistic

    _____ 2.5.8. Audiovisual aid

_____ 2.6. Reviews subject, viewpoint, or discussion points

_____ 2.7. Concludes with memorable statement

_____ 2.8. Uses structure of speech, not of old-style class report or article

3. DELIVERY

_____ 3.1. Steps up to speak with confidence

_____ 3.2. Gets set before speaking

_____ 3.3. Establishes contact before speaking

_____ 3.4. Begins without referring to notes

_____ 3.5. Maintains contact with audience

_____ 3.6. Sounds extemporaneous, not read or memorized

_____ 3.7. Uses few 3 × 5 note cards

_____ 3.8. Refers to note cards only occasionally

_____ 3.9. Avoids *ah, so, ya know, well, 'kay,* etc.

_____ 3.10. Stops at end of idea; doesn't hook sentences together with *and, and ah,* etc.

_____ 3.11. Maintains good posture

_____ 3.12. Doesn't play with notes, clothes, etc.

_____ 3.13. Dresses to help, not hinder, speech

_____ 3.14. Speaks loudly enough to be heard easily

_____ 3.15. Uses aids effectively

_____ 3.16. Gestures effectively

_____ 3.17. Uses face to add interest

_____ 3.18. Moves about

_____ 3.19. Doesn't pace

_____ 3.20. Appears to enjoy speaking

_____ 3.21. Seems to care that audience listens

_____ 3.22. Speaks with enthusiasm

_____ 3.23. Appears confident and relaxed

_____ 3.24. Speaks with, not at, audience

_____ 3.25. Doesn't look at floor, etc.

_____ 3.26. Varies speaking rate—not too fast or too slow

_____ 3.27. Varies voice pitch and volume

_____ 3.28. Enunciates clearly

_____ 3.29. Pronounces correctly

_____ 3.30. Hides goofs

_____ 3.31. Doesn't pack up early

_____ 3.32. Moves out with confidence

_____ 3.33. Time: _____

Over for comments

4. COMMENTS:

Grade: _____

FINAL SPEECH, PROPOSING A CHANGE: STUDENT'S EVALUATION FORM

Speaker: _____ Audience: _____ Date: _____

Speech purpose: _____

_____

1. CONTENT

____ 1.1. Based on accurate analysis of speaking situation

____ 1.2. Purpose worded correctly: from audience's viewpoint, specific, and attainable

____ 1.3   Subject appropriate, relevant, and interesting to audience

____ 1.4. Points, data new, significant

____ 1.5. Includes personal and human interest stories

____ 1.6. All material contributes to purpose

____ 1.7. Gets to point quickly

____ 1.8. Presents own, original ideas, structure, or interpretation

____ 1.9. Uses audiovisual aids when appropriate

____ 1.10. Emphasizes organization enough to help audience remember points

____ 1.11. Includes variety of data

____ 1.12. Data seem accurate, honest

____ 1.13. Points valid conclusions from data

____ 1.14. Includes examples to clarify, add interest, etc., not to prove points

____ 1.15. Points parallel and equal

____ 1.16. Uses smooth transitions

____ 1.17. Includes one or more balanced lines or quotable original statement

____ 1.18. Uses specific appeals when appropriate

____ 1.19. Uses appropriate humor

2. ORGANIZATION

____ 2.1. Begins with effective attention-getter

____ 2.2. Previews subject or viewpoint

____ 2.3. Presents 2 to 5 specific points

____ 2.4. Arranges discussion points logically

____ 2.5. Supports each point with data:

     ____ 2.5.1. Example

     ____ 2.5.2. Story

     ____ 2.5.3. Quotation

     ____ 2.5.4. Definition

     ____ 2.5.5. Comparison

     ____ 2.5.6. Contrast

     ____ 2.5.7. Statistic

     ____ 2.5.8. Audiovisual aid

____ 2.6. Reviews subject, viewpoint, or discussion points

____ 2.7. Concludes with memorable statement

____ 2.8. Uses structure of speech, not of old-style class report or article

3. DELIVERY

____ 3.1. Steps up to speak with confidence

____ 3.2. Gets set before speaking

____ 3.3. Establishes contact before speaking

____ 3.4. Begins without referring to notes

____ 3.5. Maintains contact with audience

____ 3.6. Sounds extemporaneous, not read or memorized

____ 3.7. Uses few 3 × 5 note cards

____ 3.8. Refers to note cards only occasionally

____ 3.9. Avoids *ah, so, ya know, well, 'kay,* etc.

____ 3.10. Stops at end of idea; doesn't hook sentences together with *and, and ah,* etc.

____ 3.11. Maintains good posture

____ 3.12. Doesn't play with notes, clothes, etc.

____ 3.13. Dresses to help, not hinder, speech

____ 3.14. Speaks loudly enough to be heard easily

____ 3.15. Uses aids effectively

____ 3.16. Gestures effectively

____ 3.17. Uses face to add interest

____ 3.18. Moves about

____ 3.19. Doesn't pace

____ 3.20. Appears to enjoy speaking

____ 3.21. Seems to care that audience listens

____ 3.22. Speaks with enthusiasm

____ 3.23. Appears confident and relaxed

____ 3.24. Speaks with, not at, audience

____ 3.25. Doesn't look at floor, etc.

____ 3.26. Varies speaking rate—not too fast or too slow

____ 3.27. Varies voice pitch and volume

____ 3.28. Enunciates clearly

____ 3.29. Pronounces correctly

____ 3.30. Hides goofs

____ 3.31. Doesn't pack up early

____ 3.32. Moves out with confidence

____ 3.33. Time: _____

Over for comments

4. COMMENTS:

Student evaluator's name :_____   Grade: _____

FINAL SPEECH, PROPOSING A CHANGE: STUDENT'S EVALUATION FORM

Speaker: _____ Audience: _____ Date: _____

Speech purpose: _____

1. CONTENT
____ 1.1. Based on accurate analysis of speaking situation
____ 1.2. Purpose worded correctly: from audience's viewpoint, specific, and attainable
____ 1.3 Subject appropriate, relevant, and interesting to audience
____ 1.4. Points, data new, significant
____ 1.5. Includes personal and human interest stories
____ 1.6. All material contributes to purpose
____ 1.7. Gets to point quickly
____ 1.8. Presents own, original ideas, structure, or interpretation
____ 1.9. Uses audiovisual aids when appropriate
____ 1.10. Emphasizes organization enough to help audience remember points
____ 1.11. Includes variety of data
____ 1.12. Data seem accurate, honest
____ 1.13. Points valid conclusions from data
____ 1.14. Includes examples to clarify, add interest, etc., not to prove points
____ 1.15. Points parallel and equal
____ 1.16. Uses smooth transitions
____ 1.17. Includes one or more balanced lines or quotable original statement
____ 1.18. Uses specific appeals when appropriate
____ 1.19. Uses appropriate humor

2. ORGANIZATION
____ 2.1. Begins with effective attention-getter
____ 2.2. Previews subject or viewpoint
____ 2.3. Presents 2 to 5 specific points
____ 2.4. Arranges discussion points logically
____ 2.5. Supports each point with data:
    ____ 2.5.1. Example
    ____ 2.5.2. Story
    ____ 2.5.3. Quotation
    ____ 2.5.4. Definition
    ____ 2.5.5. Comparison
    ____ 2.5.6. Contrast
    ____ 2.5.7. Statistic
    ____ 2.5.8. Audiovisual aid

____ 2.6. Reviews subject, viewpoint, or discussion points
____ 2.7. Concludes with memorable statement
____ 2.8. Uses structure of speech, not of old-style class report or article

3. DELIVERY
____ 3.1. Steps up to speak with confidence
____ 3.2. Gets set before speaking
____ 3.3. Establishes contact before speaking
____ 3.4. Begins without referring to notes
____ 3.5. Maintains contact with audience
____ 3.6. Sounds extemporaneous, not read or memorized
____ 3.7. Uses few 3 × 5 note cards
____ 3.8. Refers to note cards only occasionally
____ 3.9. Avoids *ah, so, ya know, well, 'kay,* etc.
____ 3.10. Stops at end of idea; doesn't hook sentences together with *and, and ah,* etc.
____ 3.11. Maintains good posture
____ 3.12. Doesn't play with notes, clothes, etc.
____ 3.13. Dresses to help, not hinder, speech
____ 3.14. Speaks loudly enough to be heard easily
____ 3.15. Uses aids effectively
____ 3.16. Gestures effectively
____ 3.17. Uses face to add interest
____ 3.18. Moves about
____ 3.19. Doesn't pace
____ 3.20. Appears to enjoy speaking
____ 3.21. Seems to care that audience listens
____ 3.22. Speaks with enthusiasm
____ 3.23. Appears confident and relaxed
____ 3.24. Speaks with, not at, audience
____ 3.25. Doesn't look at floor, etc.
____ 3.26. Varies speaking rate—not too fast or too slow
____ 3.27. Varies voice pitch and volume
____ 3.28. Enunciates clearly
____ 3.29. Pronounces correctly
____ 3.30. Hides goofs
____ 3.31. Doesn't pack up early
____ 3.32. Moves out with confidence
____ 3.33. Time: _____

Over for comments

4. COMMENTS:

Student evaluator's name :_____ Grade: _____

FINAL SPEECH, PROPOSING A CHANGE: STUDENT'S EVALUATION FORM

Speaker: _____ Audience: _____ Date: _____

Speech purpose: _____
_____

1. CONTENT

_____ 1.1. Based on accurate analysis of speaking situation

_____ 1.2. Purpose worded correctly: from audience's viewpoint, specific, and attainable

_____ 1.3 Subject appropriate, relevant, and interesting to audience

_____ 1.4. Points, data new, significant

_____ 1.5. Includes personal and human interest stories

_____ 1.6. All material contributes to purpose

_____ 1.7. Gets to point quickly

_____ 1.8. Presents own, original ideas, structure, or interpretation

_____ 1.9. Uses audiovisual aids when appropriate

_____ 1.10. Emphasizes organization enough to help audience remember points

_____ 1.11. Includes variety of data

_____ 1.12. Data seem accurate, honest

_____ 1.13. Points valid conclusions from data

_____ 1.14. Includes examples to clarify, add interest, etc., not to prove points

_____ 1.15. Points parallel and equal

_____ 1.16. Uses smooth transitions

_____ 1.17. Includes one or more balanced lines or quotable original statement

_____ 1.18. Uses specific appeals when appropriate

_____ 1.19. Uses appropriate humor

2. ORGANIZATION

_____ 2.1. Begins with effective attention-getter

_____ 2.2. Previews subject or viewpoint

_____ 2.3. Presents 2 to 5 specific points

_____ 2.4. Arranges discussion points logically

_____ 2.5. Supports each point with data:

    _____ 2.5.1. Example

    _____ 2.5.2. Story

    _____ 2.5.3. Quotation

    _____ 2.5.4. Definition

    _____ 2.5.5. Comparison

    _____ 2.5.6. Contrast

    _____ 2.5.7. Statistic

    _____ 2.5.8. Audiovisual aid

_____ 2.6. Reviews subject, viewpoint, or discussion points

_____ 2.7. Concludes with memorable statement

_____ 2.8. Uses structure of speech, not of old-style class report or article

3. DELIVERY

_____ 3.1. Steps up to speak with confidence

_____ 3.2. Gets set before speaking

_____ 3.3. Establishes contact before speaking

_____ 3.4. Begins without referring to notes

_____ 3.5. Maintains contact with audience

_____ 3.6. Sounds extemporaneous, not read or memorized

_____ 3.7. Uses few 3 × 5 note cards

_____ 3.8. Refers to note cards only occasionally

_____ 3.9. Avoids *ah, so, ya know, well, 'kay,* etc.

_____ 3.10. Stops at end of idea; doesn't hook sentences together with *and, and ah,* etc.

_____ 3.11. Maintains good posture

_____ 3.12. Doesn't play with notes, clothes, etc.

_____ 3.13. Dresses to help, not hinder, speech

_____ 3.14. Speaks loudly enough to be heard easily

_____ 3.15. Uses aids effectively

_____ 3.16. Gestures effectively

_____ 3.17. Uses face to add interest

_____ 3.18. Moves about

_____ 3.19. Doesn't pace

_____ 3.20. Appears to enjoy speaking

_____ 3.21. Seems to care that audience listens

_____ 3.22. Speaks with enthusiasm

_____ 3.23. Appears confident and relaxed

_____ 3.24. Speaks with, not at, audience

_____ 3.25. Doesn't look at floor, etc.

_____ 3.26. Varies speaking rate—not too fast or too slow

_____ 3.27. Varies voice pitch and volume

_____ 3.28. Enunciates clearly

_____ 3.29. Pronounces correctly

_____ 3.30. Hides goofs

_____ 3.31. Doesn't pack up early

_____ 3.32. Moves out with confidence

_____ 3.33. Time: _____

Over for comments

4. COMMENTS:

Student evaluator's name :_____   Grade: _____

THE FUTURE

You've come to the end of this course.

Is that the end of the study of public speaking? Not according to the course offerings at many colleges and universities. Some speech departments list 30 and more different speech courses. You could go on to study—all as separate courses:

Advanced Public Speaking	Public Address
Oral Communication	Rhetoric
Argumentation	Interpretation
Persuasion	Voice
Debate	Phonetics
Forensics	Cross-Cultural Communications
Discussion	Speech Correction
Discussion Leadership	Clinical Methods
Conference Leadership	Teaching Methods
Human Message Systems	Business and Organizational Communication
Relational Communications	Internship in Speech Communication

You could move on up through the graduate courses in speech theory and research and then undertake your own study of a particular problem in speech. That's usually "under faculty supervision," as a typical university catalog words it.

Finally, the ultimate: You can enroll in the exclusive seminars in speech—"readings and papers on special problems in selected areas of speech."

If you decide to be a speech major, you can face 16 courses, 51 quarter units, in speech alone, not counting electives, according to the requirements of one typical college.

The question is, of course, do *you* need all that, or any of it?

Well, if your goal is to be able to give an effective speech in the typical speaking situations that most of us face in our careers, and if you've passed this course, you have achieved your goal.

And should anyone question that, just give them a speech.

Or show them the next page.

TESTAMUR

All Ye Who Read This: Know that the Bearer

_____

has successfully completed a course in
how to design and deliver a speech,
the course entitled

_____

as taught at

_____

Date: _____   Attested by: _____
                                                (Instructor)

I N D E X

Note: All Assignments, Check-off tip sheets, Evaluation forms, and Self-tests are indexed under those general headings, rather than under the specific type of speech.